SPENCER BRIGHT – who co-wrote the bestselling *Take It Like A Man* with Boy George – has reached to the root and heart of another extraordinary star. With a rare, deft skill and sympathetic understanding, Bright peels off Gabriel's bizarre and beautiful masks to take the reader towards a human understanding of a contemporary legend.

His new updated and revised biography of Peter Gabriel will prove, once again, to be essential reading for all those who love the music, admire the man and seek to understand both a little better.

# PETER
# GABRIEL

## AN AUTHORIZED BIOGRAPHY

## SPENCER BRIGHT

PAN BOOKS

First published 1988 by Sidgwick & Jackson

This updated and revised edition first published 1999 by Sidgwick & Jackson
This edition published 2000 by Pan Books
an imprint of Macmillan Publishers Ltd
25 Eccleston Place, London SW1W 9NF
Basingstoke and Oxford
Associated companies throughout the world
www.macmillan.co.uk

ISBN 0 330 37044 8

9 8 7 6 5 4 3 2 1

A CIP catalogue record for this book is available from
the British Library.

Typeset by SetSystems Ltd, Saffron Walden, Essex
Printed and bound in Great Britain by
Mackays of Chatham plc, Chatham, Kent

For Ian Annett, 1953–78

'Over the nakedness of truth – the diaphanous cloak of fantasy'

Eça de Queirós

# CONTENTS

# ACKNOWLEDGEMENTS

Each of the following made my task easier and the story more complete. For office assistance: Rachel Carreon, Kevin Kearney, Roger Borg, Iain Downes; Real World – Annie Parsons, Kirsty Allen, Susie Milns, Mary Lane, Mike Large, Mike Thomas; Gail Colson; Steve Hedges; Virgin Records – Paul Conroy, Jeremy Silver, Carole Burton-Fairbrother, Robert Sandall, Jon Webster; Universal Records – Ted Cummings; Geffen Records – Roy Hamm; Brilliant Media – Steve Nelson and Chris Edmondson; Witness Program – Li Li Brown, Sukanya Pillay, Erica Wolf; Reebok International and Reebok Human Rights Award – Sharon Cohen, Joanne Evans; Daniel Lanois and Melanie Ciccone; Michael Morris, Robert Lepage and Linda Beaulieu; David Eno; Mark Borkowski; Bruce Kirkland; Brett Leonard; Peter Schwartz; Chris Hughes; Julia Gaynor; Lester Middlehurst. At Sidgwick & Jackson: Susan Hill, Fiona Macleay, Gordon Wise, William Armstrong; my agent Lavinia Trevor; and Chrissy Iley for continuing love and support, and for furry comfort, Poodle and Shiksa.

The following are special mentions for helping with the first edition. My dear friend, the late Paul Vaughan Phillips for research, transcriptions and insight; Sinclair Salisbury; Lee Ellen Newman; Elly Smith; Sian Davies; Barbara Charone; Andrew Collier; Jack Barrie; Roy Burchell (*Melody Maker*); Fiona Foulgar (*NME*); Geoff and Judy Parkyn of The Genesis Information Service; BBC – Tina Ladwa, Kevin Howlett; Jenny Cathcart; Christine Gorham (MTV); Charterhouse School – Mr Peter Attenborough, Headmaster, and Dr E. H. Zillekens, Archivist.

# AUTHOR'S NOTE

In the ten years since the first edition of this book appeared Peter Gabriel has worked towards his aim of becoming an 'experience designer'. It is a term he has long used to more accurately define the broad range of his work. His core activity is still very much as a rock musician, but flaring off that creative Catherine wheel are other dazzling projects.

He has never conformed to the clichés of rock and roll, and has constantly sought new means of expression, wanting to create new worlds, whether on stage, inside a theme park or in virtual reality.

I tried to convey the fantasy that was in his mind for his theme park when I wrote the original opening chapter of this book. Although the vision has matured – and is yet to become a reality – I believe the essence of what I was trying to portray then still holds true now.

Rather than shuffle off to a rock and roll retirement home, Gabriel has plunged into even more frenetic and fertile activity, embracing technologies that were virtually in the realms of science fiction at the end of the eighties. It is Peter Gabriel's progress and achievements through these areas and his own personal development that I have charted in this new edition, giving a far more complete appraisal of one of the most original talents at work in music and multimedia today.

Spencer Bright
1999

# PREFACE

Tony Stratton Smith was concerned that he had inconvenienced me. On the morning of my arrival in Jersey to interview him for this book he started to feel very ill. A doctor had already visited and diagnosed a perforated ulcer.

I arrived at his friend Vera Bampton's large Victorian home overlooking the bay at St Helier, Jersey, just before noon. She was upset and said Tony could not see me and would have to go into hospital. I was ushered into her living room and enjoyed the view of the sea while, unknown to me, an ambulance arrived to carry Strat away.

Before being taken to Jersey's general hospital, Strat asked his financial adviser, Andrew MacHutchon, to take me to lunch. Andrew later visited Strat to report I was well fed, and drunk, and had been deposited back on the plane. I will allow Andrew his little lie about my sobriety.

Strat was cheered in those last hours with this news, and promised to bring me back out to Jersey a few weeks later so that our postponed interview could take place. From what I have learnt about Strat this was typical. Despite his own discomfort, he was still concerned for others.

I had been trying to get to him for over three months, having missed him when he had last been in London in early December 1986. He finally agreed to see me while he was visiting Vera, a friend who shared his love of racehorses. He arrived in Jersey via Lisbon and Paris from his tax exile home in Las Palmas in the Canary Islands. He had to see his legal

and financial advisers and asked Vera to book appointments
with her doctor and dentist because he did not trust the local
Las Palmas ones.

A few days before my visit I spoke to him briefly on the
telephone. He sounded happy. He was proud he had lost 22lb
in weight, although a doctor had told him to ease up because
he was dieting too quickly. He said he had an upset stomach,
but was sure he would be all right in the next few days. Both
of us were looking forward to discussing Peter Gabriel and his
long assocation with Charisma Records.

Strat died just after 2 a.m. on Thursday 19 March 1987
aged fifty-three, a few hours after surgery had revealed the full
extent of his cancer. We do not know whether he was aware
of his illness; most of his friends feel it is unlikely. They were
thankful his last days were spent not alone in exile, but
entertained and finally comforted by trusted business associates
and Vera.

In an addendum to the obituary which appeared in *The
Times* on 24 March, Peter Gabriel wrote:

Tony Stratton Smith was a rarity in the entertainment
business — a man of passion and a crusader.

He believed that rock music could, and should, be more
than teenage fashion fodder, and his love for the best of
British determined the character of the Charisma label.

The Mad Hatter's Tea Party was his choice of label logo,
and there was nowhere else you could find such diverse and
eclectic talent as John Betjeman, Vivian Stanshall, Peter
Hammill, John Arlott, the Nice, Mony Python, Genesis, Bert
Jansch, Dame Edna Everage and Lindisfarne under one roof.

Despite the competitive nature of the business, he cared
more for the quality of the work than the quantity sold,
always preferring the difficult challenge of backing outsiders.
His artists were supported as family.

His favourite occupations he listed as writing, talking
and drinking, and, in each, he could compete with the best.

Strat earned himself a unique place in the worlds of entertainment and sport, a big man with a big heart, I will miss him.

Tony Stratton Smith gave Peter Gabriel invaluable freedom to develop as an artist. He was more of a mentor and a confidant than a record company boss, never forcing Gabriel to change course despite financial and career pressures. It is doubtful whether Peter Gabriel's early career would have followed the same course without his support.

# PETER
# GABRIEL

# CHAPTER ONE

LOOKING OUT ON TO THE WILDERNESS YOU can see the sea on the near horizon. The roads leading up to this spot suddenly disappear underground. You become aware that all is not what it seems.

Carefully hidden in the trees are small buildings, little huts really. Some have stairs leading down, others mask ventilation ducts. Beneath you lies another world, the Real World.

As you descend you see what you thought was simply forest and meadows is an illusion. Stairs hug cavern walls, sunlight streams through, natural caves lead into huge underground spaces going in every direction.

Signs point to Minotaur Maze, Ride of Fears, Black Hole, Psyche Drama, Big Dipper Tripper, Hall of Digital Mirrors. It sounds like a fourth dimensional funfair.

Families with children, individuals, groups, and sightseers stroll aimlessly or purposefully. Artists, sculptors, film and video directors, avant garde and pop musicians, psychologists and visionaries have all contributed to the Real World.

You have to go underground, as in Greek mythology, to be initiated, returning to the surface and 'normality'. Those who dare enter the Ride of Fears with its twelve chambers, one for each of our most common phobias. You choose the fear intensity from one to ten. Inside, a computer detects your phobias. They become a holographic reality, crawling over and engulfing you. If you pass through the chamber without pressing the panic button you get a bravery token, if you cannot cope you eject.

*You move on, pause briefly with relief, and then gaze down a corridor. In the dim light there are muttering figures stretching into the distance. They are lifelike sculptures that gradually disappear into walls studded with countless glistening razor blades.*

*The door behind locks, it has no handle, it starts to move, pushing you forward down a corridor barely wider than a person. You must avoid getting lacerated as it gets narrower and narrower. You breathe in to try to make yourself as thin as possible, but it is no use, and you brush against a razor, your brain registering pain before the actual touch . . . only to find the blades are made out of rubber. In front is the exit.*

*You see an old fashioned crossroads signpost. You choose Hall of Digital Mirrors for comic relief. You enter a bare room with mirrors on all four walls and the ceiling. You are surrounded by images of yourself. These are not normal mirrors, but 3D video screens. You can distort your reflection, change colour, turn into an angel or monster, fly over the Grand Canyon, through Saturn's rings, or join an adventure with figures from mythology and science fiction.*

*You carry on. Throughout this wonderland, despite the sense of space and activity, there is an underlying calm. For, unlike above-the-surface theme parks and funfairs, here there are relatively few mechanical devices, the computer is in control.*

> *If you go down to Willow Farm,*
> *To look for butterflies, flutterbyes, gutterflies*
> *Open your eyes, it's full of surprise, everyone lies,*
> *Like the fox on the rocks,*
> *And the musical box.*
> *Oh, there's Mum and Dad, and good and bad,*
> *And everyone's happy to be here.*

'Willow Farm'; Gabriel, 1972

Willow Farm, a verse from 'Supper's Ready' on the 1972 Genesis *Foxtrot* album, saw the first expression of Peter Gabriel's formative ideas for the Real World theme park.

These ideas have crept into lyrics and videos throughout his career.

> *You could have a big dipper*
> *going up and down, and around the bends*
> *you could have a bumper car, bumping*
> *this amusement never ends*
>
> 'Sledgehammer'; Gabriel, 1986

The literal interpretation of this excerpt from 'Sledgehammer', even if not the connotations, is obvious enough.

Peter Gabriel called Real World 'A hybrid mix of university, holiday camp, theme park and Disneyland. A place where people can go to test themselves, to challenge themselves and entertain themselves, ideally transform certain parts of what they are.'

As yet this dream world, a place once called Gabrieland, remains hypothetical.

# CHAPTER TWO

THE LETTUCES WERE NOT BEHAVING THEM-
selves. They should have been leafy
and juicy, but persisted in bolting to
seed. The country idyll was not proving as straightforward as
Peter Gabriel had imagined.

In the first part of 1975 he had frantically performed a rock
epic to ecstatic crowds in America and Europe in his final tour
with Genesis.

Over the next year in his small cottage on the edge of the
Cotswolds, Gabriel had time to think and retreat into himself.
At first he was excited and inspired by his new solitude. But as
he started to divide his time between playing the piano
distractedly and tending to his vegetables his wife Jill began to
fear for his sanity.

'Actually, it was awful. The first little period was lovely,
for moments. But I knew that he would slowly go mad. It
seemed a very short period before I was encouraging him,
telling him, "You know you can do it, you have to do it.
Don't give it up, or you know you will go mad." ' Peter had
lost confidence in his abilities as a musician.

'I could feel this thing with the vegetables becoming quite
obsessive. He went into himself very much. He would go to
the piano and play for hours. He seemed to be going more
and more inward. I felt at that point that it was going to get
. . . it seems odd to say, it felt dangerous . . . he needed to
come outward.'

Gabriel's recollection is not so much of incipient madness as introversion, and a determination to be self-sufficient in vegetables. 'I was totally ignorant and enthusiastic, so I planted all my lettuces at the same time,' said Peter. 'I had the Week of the Thousand Lettuces! And then, after, they just went to seed. My carrots were all eaten by worms. We had some good potatoes, but any fool can grow potatoes – they just grow themselves. Runner beans we did OK.'

The preoccupation with vegetables bore out one sentence in Gabriel's farewell press statement on leaving Genesis: 'I could not expect the band to tie in their schedules with my bondage to cabbages.' But this flippancy masked a deeper dissatisfaction that had developed a year earlier when he first became a father. The group did not want to tie in their schedules to his family crises. Naïvely, he was hurt and angered that they put their careers before all else.

Jill was twenty-two and Peter twenty-four when their daughter Anna-Marie was born on 26 July 1974 at St Mary's Hospital, Paddington. Jill had been warned by her doctor that there might be complications. The doctor feared a breech birth, and advised her that the hospital and not their isolated cottage would be the best place for the birth. Until then Peter and Jill had an image of a perfect Le Boyer birth in the warmth and security of their own home. Instead Jill had to move back from Bath to stay with her parents in Kensington.

At the time Gabriel was in the middle of preparing *The Lamb Lies Down on Broadway*, destined to be his final Genesis album. The group were rehearsing in Hampshire before going off to record in Wales. Despite his work commitments he managed to be present at Anna's birth.

Doctors prevented Anna having a breech birth. But in so doing they had to turn her twice, thus wrapping the umbilical cord around her neck. For a while Anna stopped breathing, and had to be ventilated.

Peter remembered, 'Anna nearly died. She caught an

infection. I was thinking, "Get the baby on the breast, all the natural things. What came out was a green lump that was carried away in silver foil like chicken bones." Jill did not see her baby after the birth, and had to wait until the next day when she could view her in an incubator in the premature baby unit. Anna had inhaled fluid during the birth which caused complications in the lungs. Doctors also suspected that she had meningitis, and gave her spinal injections of antibiotics. Jill also suffered a subsequent infection.

'That night they came to me and told me she might not live,' said Jill. 'It took me six months to make her alive. I mentally rejected her. Peter was wonderful, but such a soppy dad. He used to say hello to her every day and talk to her through the glass of the premature baby ward.'

For Peter Gabriel the pressure was becoming intolerable. 'Those first two weeks were really traumatic and the band were incredibly unsympathetic. They were pissed off I wasn't taking the album as seriously as my child.

'Having Anna was an experience that put the rest of my life in shadow. I didn't want to be a production-line rock star any more. It was more important to me that things were right with Jill and Anna than with the record. It built up a lot of bad feeling inside the band.'

Genesis were poised for major international stardom when Peter Gabriel left in May 1975, seemingly throwing everyone's career into jeopardy. By that time Anna had fully recovered from her difficult birth. For the first time since they moved to the countryside just outside Bath in March 1974 the family had a chance to properly settle into their cottage. Jill had found the transition more difficult than Peter. She had been a town girl and felt she'd been dumped down in the middle of nowhere.

'I said I'd die leaving London. My family were there, my friends were there. People were always vital. I couldn't stand to be by myself, ever,' said Jill. But Peter, coming to terms with fatherhood earlier than he had expected to, was insistent his child should be brought up in the country. Jill was persuaded by that argument, but it took her a year to adjust. She was not helped by the suspicions of the locals.

'I wasn't accepted at first. I was this extraordinary pregnant woman walking around in a long dress in the middle of a community which was full of farming. They had heard rumours, from the previous owner of the house, that this wild multicoloured-haired pop star was coming to live there. It was as difficult for them to accept me as for me to fit in, in some ways. But in having Anna a mother who lived next door took me on, and I found a way of fitting in, via the children, and being accepted.'

In those initial months of retreat after the split with Genesis, the Gabriel family's financial future was uncertain. Peter had enough money to survive the next few years, but not enough to retire on. The cottage was bought with a £16,000 mortgage, and part of that was thanks to a loan from Peter's parents.

Gabriel's sabbatical was a period of necessary contrasts; a flight from the madness of the rock world to the isolation and beauty of the Cotswolds, according to Richard Macphail. He was a school friend from Charterhouse, Genesis' first de facto manager and roadie, then Peter Gabriel's road manager at the start of his solo career. Macphail is still one of Gabriel's closest friends. 'He let himself go in a way that he hadn't been able to do before and it was a great release. I was never worried about his mental health. It was just a complete pendulum swing in another direction. He just flopped and let it all hang out,' said Macphail.

'He just felt he had the freedom to do all the things he couldn't do while he was in the group and he just did them until he got it out of his system and the music just started coming back. He wrote "Here Comes The Flood" during that period.

'He was discovering himself as a family man. And I think

that that period really provided him with a foundation for him being able to do both now, which was what he was unable to do during Genesis. Coupled with the fact he is now in control of his own career and he's not subject to other people's decisions.

'It was a measure of his commitment to Jill and the family that he was willing to give all that up. He was willing to do something that a lot of people wouldn't do; most people let the family thing go.'

The move to the country in spring 1974 was partly prompted by Gabriel's enduring belief that society should be divided into smaller units, on a more human scale. He was initially inspired by an advertisement in a magazine which held out the prospect of an experimental community. 'I was looking for purpose and a sense of self. The idea of being self-sufficient and independent appealed to me because I felt I had become dependent on the music business, and the community seemed to be the physical embodiment of some idealism, which I had always been attracted to,' said Gabriel. Ironically the community called itself Genesis, though that was not mentioned in the advertisement.

Gabriel was impressed with the fat brochure, the manifesto and the detailed questionnaire that arrived. 'It was a mixture of psychological, spiritual, and political new thinking. It would now be described as an attractive yuppie package,' said Gabriel.

It included reports on the philosophers, writers and movements that had influenced the instigators of the proposed community. One of the most important was Henry Thoreau who, with Ralph Waldo Emerson, was a leading figure in the Transcendental Club, a romantic and reformist literary movement in New England in the mid-nineteenth century. Thoreau, author of *Walden: or Life in the Woods*, was a progenitor of the hippy ideal of returning to nature. The founders of the Genesis community were also inspired by psychologist B. F. Skinner's 1948 novel, *Walden Two*, based on life in a Utopian community and modelled on his principles of behaviourism and social engineering. They were also impressed with Werner Erhard and his Erhard Seminar Training.

Although interviewed and accepted for the experiment in community living, Gabriel never joined.

'It was being run in a very professional way, unlike most of the community things. They had auditions and they were turning people away in their hundreds. It took a long time to put together and I realized there was no way I could stay in control of my music in the community. It was full of idealism, but full of impracticalities as well. As the year went on I got back into playing music and I began to think, I don't want other people having a vote on whether I can tour, or whether I can afford to make a 24-track record or a 4-track record. I want to be in control of that.' The Genesis community never did live up to the promise of that brochure, though trial communities were set up in the United States and Ireland.

The break from the music business had allowed Gabriel to indulge his spiritual and intellectual fantasies. In the few interviews he gave during this sabbatical his ideas were muddled and his confidence low. He joked about the 'Cosmic Cadet Force', a name inspired by the Combined Cadet Force military training at public schools. 'Some people are too heavenly to be of earthly use and too earthly to be of heavenly use,' he told Chris Welch of *Melody Maker*. Perhaps having been too earthly with Genesis he was now becoming too heavenly alone.

He explored other ways of discovering himself, from trying out bio-feedback machines designed to reduce stress, to reading about the paranormal. He studied the I Ching, valuing the advice of this Chinese oracle. Though for many the I Ching became little more than a parlour game, Gabriel kept it for matters of great importance. He has taken some of his biggest decisions on the toss of a coin.

He went with Jill on a Silva Mind Control course in

London inspired by the work of the California-based Mexican Dr Jose Silva. The mind control exercises had them learning how to memorize a hundred different things and promised techniques to unlock the unconscious powers of the mind, including telepathic ways of diagnosing illnesses.

In Bath he took dance, yoga and piano lessons. 'I've never quite lived up to my Fred Astaire fantasies ... I'm not the most natural of movers, but it was something I wanted to know more about.'

He was relieved at having severed ties with Genesis. But he soon realized that he needed to reach out beyond the family and local community. 'I think I went through a strange period, I think it's similar to when people retire. Part of the way they relate to the world is through their work. When you suddenly remove that – in my case I had removed it voluntarily – it was quite unsettling.

'I didn't feel I had a base of self-respect from which to launch other projects. I didn't realize I had lanced some of myself too in cutting off from Genesis. In other words, that some of my confidence came from being an active musician who was getting a few strokes. It wasn't all bad, but there was a sense of "What the hell am I doing?" and "What purpose is there for me carrying on?" That sounds suicidal, but it wasn't. But then I did a lot of thinking. I think sabbaticals should become a part of everyone's life. People should do the opposite of what they normally do for a while, and see what happens, because you learn a lot. I think I did learn.'

Before leaving Genesis, Peter had started writing songs with Martin Hall, a poet and lyricist with a deadpan Black Country wit. It was Gabriel's first collaboration outside of the group, and he developed a close friendship with Hall. 'Peter had not only left the band, but he had left London. So he was not living in the same environment either physically, emotionally, intellectually, spiritually or any other way you could think of. It was a total change for him,' Martin Hall remembered.

'Having come out of the little cocoon that he had lived in he felt a complete change was better than still being in and around London seeing many of the same people. So he thought, let's go for broke.'

In 1974 Charisma Books, an offshoot of Tony Stratton Smith's Charisma Records, had published a book of Hall's poetry. The title poem, 'The Stan Cullis Blues', about a legendary Wolverhampton Wanderers football manager, read:

> The night Stan Cullis got the sack
> Wolverhampton wandered round in circles
> Like a disallowed goal
> Looking for a friendly linesman.

Hall and Gabriel had met in 1969, drawn by a common introversion, and artistic and mystical interests. They first thought about working together in 1973 during the recording of the Genesis album *Selling England By The Pound*. 'He came round one afternoon because he was quite troubled by his progress. I acted as a sounding board and it helped him finish the lyrics,' said Hall.

On the cover of his paperback Hall was described as a 'rock poet'. Any reader who had failed to notice his songwriting credits was promised they soon would, 'for he is currently working on, among other projects, an album with Genesis' leader, Peter Gabriel.'

Hall wishes that blurb had never appeared. His and Gabriel's idea of writing an album of songs to be recorded by other artists never materialized. They started their songwriting partnership first at the Gabriels' Notting Hill Gate flat, continuing at the cottage.

Hall and Gabriel were introduced by record producer John Anthony while he worked on *Trespass*, the first Genesis album on the Charisma label. Hall had written songs for Rare Bird, Charisma's first signing and hit act.

'John felt that we would get on and had a lot in common musically, and he was right. We became fairly close friends, but didn't actually work together for quite some time.' In October 1973 Jill and Peter were witnesses at Martin's wedding. 'Peter was my closest friend at the time,' said Martin.

'I suppose it was like a late schoolboy relationship. One of us would say, you must see this film, or must read that book. I remember Peter being very impressed by the Jodorowsky film *El Topo*, which has the flavour of a spaghetti western made by Buñuel. And I think I dragged him to see *Solaris* by Tarkovsky, hopelessly arty, but it was a general creative interchange.' Their common reading matter was the essential list for the seeker of truth at that period including *The Tibetan Book of the Dead*, Carlos Casteneda's *Journey to Ixtlan* and books on Zen Buddhism.

'He was able to investigate himself more than hitherto when he got to the cottage,' said Hall. 'He certainly didn't drink or drug. He believed in what has come to be a somewhat sneered at cliché, the natural high. He was a bit scared of losing control. He was comfortable with the environment that he was in, but he was ill at ease inside himself for a while because he was trying to find out who he was and what he was capable of, because much of his talent, ability, ideas, had, in my view, been repressed with Genesis.' The relative isolation of the cottage only encouraged Gabriel's shyness; he became nervous and hesitant in company to such an extent that it appeared he was stammering.

'He'd lived and worked in almost the same environment for a good many years. The band came out of school and on to the road, and it was almost like a divorce, I suppose. In a sense it was the first time that he had stepped out into the world. Inevitably he was nervous at times, but I never had the impression that he would go completely bananas.'

Gabriel was trying to improve as a writer. At first he did not want to perform and tried to think of new ways to stage other acts performing his songs. 'Underlying it all, of course,' said Hall, 'was a determination to prove that he could do it without Genesis.'

During 1975 Martin Hall and Peter Gabriel worked on about a dozen songs, half of which were completed. The urge to write for Peter Gabriel had been irresistible. 'I think lots of art – it seems like a grand word, but I mean painting, music, any sort of creative activity – has some therapeutic value, and it's a means of externalizing thoughts and feelings. So I was doing it regardless, and then I got into the situation that I was in at the beginning of Genesis, of being a songwriter and not wanting to become a performer, and I was having trouble interesting people in my songs. We took the songs to a few publishers.'

Gabriel and Hall could at least rely on Charisma to back them. They launched their joint songwriting career with a light-hearted number, 'You Never Know', and chose the lightweight comedian Charlie Drake to record it. Drake was a bizarre contrast to the Olympian Genesis. A buffoon on films and TV, the diminutive Drake was famous for his immortal phrase: 'Hello my darlings.'

Gabriel, inspired by his love of animation, imagined Drake as a cartoon character. 'We thought maybe we should try and get a hit record and sell it as a TV idea. We were looking at idiosyncratic comedians and Charlie Drake seemed like a good choice. I had sketches of his stick-insect type character that would have fitted in.' The character was loosely inspired by Jiminy Cricket, and Hall and Gabriel took the idea to George Dunning, the animator and creator of the Beatles' *Yellow Submarine*. He was not impressed enough to support the project.

Drake lived in a mansion block opposite Leicester Square, and Gabriel remembers him spending a lot of time looking out of his window at people walking past. 'You Never Know' was released on 21 November 1975. 'When we wrote it we were just trying to find out if we could write a song together,' recalled Hall. 'It started with me having an exceptionally mundane guitar riff and oddly enough I think Peter maybe came up with the title.

'Looking back it is not really funny. It's not a comedy song in the way you would have expected from Charlie Drake. With hindsight it is just Peter and me showing off.'

The record used an unlikely collection of some of the most respected musicians of the day; jazz fusion pianist Keith Tippett, Sandy Denny, Brian Eno and Robert Fripp, with Gabriel producing, and Steve Nye, who went on to produce Roxy Music, mixing.

The punning lyrics were typical of Hall's over-clever play on words. The bouncy up-tempo single had Charlie Drake getting as close as he could to sounding like Peter Gabriel, though he could not resist opening with 'Hello my darlings'. The first verse ran:

> You never know who the honeycombs
> You never know why the hippodromes
> You never know where the waterfalls
> You never know when the basketballs

The chorus included the lines:

> Things on wings are wonderwise, the melon sings.
> And butterflies don't want to fall!
> Pop an illusion!
> Better get the butternut, better let the lily put the lullaby.

'You Never Know'; Hall/Gabriel, 1975

A Charisma press release interpreted the line 'pop an illusion' as a send-up of pop stardom, hinting at Peter Gabriel's departure from Genesis. The lyrics were Hall's and had little significance other than in the way they sounded.

Gabriel took the Charlie Drake single seriously, said Hall. 'It was never intended as any kind of lark. Peter actually wanted to do it. It was one of his songs, albeit co-written, and he was going to produce and put the whole thing together with his choice of musicians, and he hadn't done that before.' Despite promised heavy TV and radio coverage designed to make 'You Never Know' the Christmas single of 1975, the record, as the music industry says, stiffed.

Only one of Gabriel and Hall's songs, what became the barber shop a capella 'Excuse Me', was ever recorded by Peter Gabriel. ' "Excuse Me" was one of several musical fragments he gave me on tape. I would take those bits away and come up with a title or shape a chorus into it somehow. And then we would get back together and work on it overall together where possible. "Excuse Me" was almost entirely his music and almost entirely my words. I think he changed one line of the words. It was originally called "I Want To Be Alone". It seems to be aimed at Genesis, but it wasn't,' said Hall.

When Gabriel and Hall wrote they would throw lyrical ideas at each other, praising, criticizing or suggesting improvements. 'We finished about half a dozen songs, and probably some of the unfinished bits are better than the finished bits, which is often the way. He had gone through the catharsis of that period and come out the other side as a confident solo songwriter,' said Hall.

By Christmas 1975 Gabriel's sabbatical was inexorably leading towards a new recording career. With this in mind he tried to make his songs as different as possible from Genesis'. 'A lot of my new stuff is very emotional. Genesis wasn't a platform for personal songs, you couldn't have a good dose of self-pity,' he told one interviewer. 'I'll probably record an album soon, but there won't be any heavy sell solo career and I'm not going on the road yet because that would defeat a lot of the object I left the band for.'

# CHAPTER THREE

THE RIVER BOURNE, AS IT FLOWED through Deep Pool Farm, brought out Peter Gabriel's boyhood sense of adventure. It presented a challenge that had to be confronted and surmounted.

He would gather branches, twigs, stones and mud and wade into the water. Slowly and determinedly he would construct a dam, raising the level of the water. When it was high enough he would enjoy the fruits of this labour and swim. Occasionally he would light a fire on top of the dam. 'That was a nice thing to do, because the water would eventually overflow and gradually push these smouldering embers over into the water.'

Once a year he had to face the demolition of his constructions. The Bourne is a tributary of the River Wey which flows into the Thames. Thames Conservancy workers would make their way down the river in a punt hacking down all the weeds and clearing all obstructions, including up to five Gabriel dams. 'I was obsessed with dam making and fire making, which a lot of shrinks would relate more to sex. I think if in doubt they always say sex,' said Peter.

Deep Pool Farm gave the infant Gabriel space to explore and the freedom to daydream. He would go into the farm buildings with his younger sister Anne and build dens in the hay bales connected by passages.

He was not the most gregarious of playmates, but he had

his mischievous moments, like climbing into an oak tree along the main road with a friend and flicking acorns at passing cars. When he was older he enjoyed trying to catch his and Anne's friends in the net of his imagination. One summer, during their teens, their mother held a dance for them. Peter decorated the living room with stems of maize grown for the farm cattle. He stood the maize upright in land drains left lying around by his father who was installing them on the farm. 'He constructed a tunnel made out of wood and netting which you had to crawl into to get to the dance. We greeted them at the other end in the room that was made to look like a jungle,' said Anne.

'I had this crawl-way so people coming in had to arrive in the room on all fours,' Peter remembered. 'I used to get fed up at the way people would come in to a party with an act. There was a lot of defence based on fear, but I thought it might effectively loosen things up a little, which it did. We are creatures of habit, and when the habit is broken we are much more awake and responsive; you have got to throw people off their guard before they open up.' The original inspiration came from mythology in which mazes were built for initiates to penetrate.

He was known as a pyromaniac when he toured in the early days with Genesis. Instead of stopping in transport cafés the group would buy bread and cheese and stop off in a field for a picnic, sometimes taking their guitars and harmonium. 'Even if it was only for half an hour Peter would be off with lots of soggy sticks and things to light a fire,' recalled Richard Macphail, his friend and then road manager. 'We'd all arrive at the gig stinking of wood smoke.'

Peter's boyhood sense of wonder and defiance has not left him. One of his adult constructions was a hot bath built while on holiday with friends and family. 'He got the idea he wanted to make something for the kids on the beach, so he spent all one afternoon digging a huge hole that we filled with water,' said Richard Macphail. 'Then he made a fire, collecting these great big rocks and heating them in the fire and then putting them in the water. And then, of course, he'd create this hot bath and we'd all say wonderful and we'd get in and splash around for ten minutes and then it was all over. But it's that kind of determination and single-mindedness he has to do his thing. He'd always do his best to drag everyone else into it.'

Peter Brian Gabriel was dragged into the world at Woking Hospital, Surrey, on 13 February 1950. 'As a little baby he was so happy and utterly contented,' remembered his mother Irene.

His father Ralph Gabriel was an electrical engineer working in London who employed a resident bailiff and a tractor driver to handle the day-to-day running of the family dairy farm. The 150-acre Coxhill Farm, near Chobham, in a rare unspoilt part of this over-developed and affluent county, had been in the Gabriel family since 1915.

Ralph Gabriel was brought up in Coxhill, the large country house believed to date from Elizabethan times that the farm took its name from. Its panelled walls and billiard room, formal garden and croquet lawn, inspired some of Peter's later songwriting.

Peter's grandfather died while his parents were on honeymoon, Coxhill was sold, and the proceeds divided up by the family. Ralph and Irene moved into Deep Pool, one of the farm cottages, and Ralph kept the farmland until his own retirement in 1977. The wooden beams in the more modest Deep Pool house date back to the 1620s. It had been added to through the centuries, and was extensively modernized by Ralph Gabriel.

The Gabriel name is believed to have originated in Spain. The family can be traced back to Christopher Gabriel, a plane-maker, who was born in Cornwall in 1675. He prospered and founded what became the timber merchants Gabriel, Wade and English. The family wealth derived from imported timber from Scandinavia and Russia used as sleepers for the expanding nineteenth-century railways network. Peter was not the first celebrated Gabriel; in 1866 his ancestor, Sir Thomas Gabriel, became Lord Mayor of London.

Ralph Gabriel is an inventor and DIY enthusiast. He has taken out seven or eight patents on farming and cable TV inventions. But the patents have long since run out and he has never capitalized on them. In the sixties as chief engineer for Rediffusion TV he installed the world's first public fibre optic system, Dial a Programme. He studied at the University of London, and during the war helped develop artificial direction-finding systems for use in training for the RAF. The company he worked for expanded and later built flight simulators, devices that have fascinated Peter. Ralph still works on various ideas in his sophisticated workship behind the house.

One of his biggest home improvements was the swimming pool Peter helped him construct in the garden in 1964. The Gabriels were ecologically sound even then. Ralph devised an elementary solar heating panel made from a large sheet of aluminium painted black to warm up the pool.

But Peter never shared his father's enthusiasm for the workshop or his mother's love of horses. He was first put on a horse at the age of three, but despite having a natural seat he decided horses were only for girls and by the age of five would have no more to do with them.

His mother's other passion was playing the piano, like her own mother, who sang at one of Sir Henry Wood's Promenade concerts. 'My mother played the piano very well. She could play back anything she had heard. She had perfect pitch,' said Mrs Gabriel. If her impersonation of her mother was accurate then Peter's grandmother sounded like a stern Edwardian schoolmistress booming 'C sharp in the bass, dear!'

Irene was one of five sisters, two of whom studied at the Royal Academy of Music. The family would entertain each other with musical evenings at home, a tradition carried on by

Irene Gabriel in her capacity as chair of the Chobham Music Club which holds concerts in its members' homes, including her own.

Irene's father, Colonel Edward Watts Allen, OBE, also sang, though only in an amateur fashion. He was one of eleven children, and left school at the age of eleven to help his impoverished mother when his schoolteacher father died. He started in a printer's shop, went on to help Sir Woodman Burbidge, Chairman of Harrods, set up a training school for shop assistants, and eventually became chairman and managing director of the Civil Service Stores in the Strand. Colonel Watts Allen was a keen athlete, golfer, skier, salmon fisher, bridge player and gambler. He flew with his family to Le Touquet and Monte Carlo to enjoy the casinos. 'He was a great fighter in everything. The more the odds were against him, the better he liked it and the better he did. I think Peter has perhaps inherited that,' said Mrs Gabriel.

His mother's musical tradition didn't impress Peter. 'He was bored with his piano, there was not a strong enough incentive to go on with the lessons,' said Mrs Gabriel. Peter showed no interest in music, nor was he interested in any of the other lessons his mother inflicted on him, including French and ballroom dancing, and gave everything up by the age of nine.

He would rather play with his sister Anne, twenty months his junior, with the bailiff David Wilson's children, Juliet, Jane and Jeremy, and tractor driver Bill Punter's children Pat and Sheena.

Anne did everything Peter did not. She persevered with the piano showing musical ability if not technical accomplishment, and loved horses. 'I think I was an obnoxious little girl. I liked pleasing everybody and doing what they asked me,' she remembered. 'I always learnt pieces off by heart.'

The two played together well, though Peter did take advantage of his sister's weak bladder. 'Wet at both ends, my title used to be. Peter used to sit astride me and tickle me and then say, mummy, mummy look what Anna has done.'

Anne got more attention not out of favouritism, but because she took part in more activities. Peter said, 'There were times when I would be left to my own devices. My mother and sister were both into riding and pony clubs. This didn't appeal to me, so I would find myself wandering around in a world of my own. That's probably when I started my preoccupation with fantasy.' When Peter and Anne played together she would usually follow his lead. 'I tended to look up to him for ideas. He was mainly the one who thought up what games to do.'

Peter did not always come off unscathed in his explorations. Accompanied by the other children on the farm, he once went to investigate his parents' attic. In the dark Peter inadvertently put his fingers into a live light socket. The tractor driver's daughter Pat, who was wearing gumboots, pulled him down. And a forlorn, white-faced Peter slumped down stairs.

Peter confesses to a very uninhibited sex life up to the age of ten, thanks largely to the presence of the daughters of the tractor driver and bailiff. 'That provided much open and liberated and safe sex. I think it was my first experience of sadism because there was one girl who used to love using stinging nettles in strange ways. I leave the rest to your imagination.'

'The whole lot of them used to have fun together around the farm. Peter was a bit of a loner, he wasn't the sort that wanted to have people round to play tennis,' said Mrs Gabriel.

'From my father I inherited openness, the spirit of invention, curiosity. He is more thoughtful, more reserved and shy,' said Peter. 'My mother was more musical and emotional. There were always family gatherings, five sisters all playing instruments at Christmas time and singing together.'

Though Peter and Anne was brought up in the Church of England, their parents were never regular churchgoers until their children left home. 'Prayers and bible stories were a part of our lives, but Peter and Anne didn't see it genuinely lived by us,' said Mrs Gabriel. Not enamoured of organized religion, Peter was first introduced to other spiritual traditions through his father, whose shelves were full of books on theosophy and Eastern religions. When Peter was in his teens his father took up yoga, which he thanks for his enduring health.

In most other ways the Gabriels were a conventional upper middle-class English family. They behaved formally even among themselves, with voices rarely raised. 'It seemed claustrophobic to me in some ways. There was an enormous amount of love and, latterly, an enormous amount of support, but it wasn't always as open as I wanted it to be,' said Peter.

Despite being hemmed in emotionally, Peter benefited from adventurous childhood holidays. He went deep-sea fishing in Spain and skiing in Norway. 'We went to Norway in 1960 with friends of ours. We were near the Hardanger Glacier, it was miles from anywhere, very remote, and we went for a walk. It was unwalkable in the snow so we went up the railway line and into the tunnel. There was not much room to press against the tunnel wall as a train came past. I think we flatter ourselves it was more dangerous than it was,' said Mrs Gabriel.

If he does not stumble into danger, Peter often courts it, pursuing what his mother calls his 'obstinate nonsense' against all advice, even as an adult. In the winter of 1976 he went with family and friends to the French alps. 'The local ski-professionals gave a floodlit display one evening for the tourists, including some stunts from the ski-jump,' said Mrs Gabriel. 'When it was all over, my idiot son was determined to have a go over this ski-jump. Time and time again he tried and always took a terrific purler falling backwards and cracking his head. Jill and I could hardly bear to look but the more we begged him to stop, the more determined he was to continue. He wanted to achieve one jump without falling. However, on this occasion, he couldn't manage it, but mercifully didn't break his skull.'

Peter's uncompromising nature is chronicled in his first school report in the summer of 1955 from the Cable House pre-prep school in Woking. 'Peter does his very best and would rather leave a word out than spell it incorrectly.' Even at this age he was plagued by doubt about his own ability though teachers noticed his self-confidence growing. One report said he needed to express himself more quickly and clearly. But one thing was clear when he was six, his voice: he sang 'very sweetly'.

When he was nine Peter went to St Andrew's prep school in Woking. He never liked eating meat and used to leave it at the side of the plate, causing particular problems with a master who used to try and force it down him. Nevertheless, in the Christmas term, 1959, Peter was top of the form. 'An excellent term as his place shows. But is he really as worried as he sometimes appears?' questioned headmaster W. T. C. Maynard, who obviously liked his boys to be jolly. The following year he wrote, 'Many reports condemn inattention and frivolity: in his case a little gaiety would not come amiss.' Peter must have eventually cheered up. In his final report from St Andrew's in the summer of 1963 the housemaster wrote, 'He is thoughtful, kind and unselfish and amusing.' And the headmaster wrote, 'He will be missed very much.'

'Peter was popular, he was liked, but he was a loner, in a way,' said Mrs Gabriel. 'He did quite well at school. I was surprised to see him often in the first one or two in the form. He was certainly no brilliant academic, no scholarship boy.' But, as his father remembers, he always was a conscientious worker.

In his last year at St Andrew's he became a weekday boarder to prepare him for being away from home when he went to public school the following year. That was when his idyllic and relatively isolated life ceased and when he and Anne grew apart. 'I think it was hard on him boarding at St Andrew's. He was going to be given the cane after one weekend and I can remember him crying. My parents were upset too,' said Anne.

In September 1963 Peter reluctantly continued a family tradition. His father and his father before him had been to the prestigious Charterhouse, fifteen miles away in Godalming. The school was founded in London in 1611 and moved in 1872 to its new gothic home in Surrey. Peter was put in Girdlestone House. Its inmates are known as Duckites because founder Mr Girdlestone, who had short legs, reputedly walked like a duck, and because Girdlestoneites was too much of a mouthful.

'It seemed a pleasant school, and it was near here. At that period lads did go to boarding school if you could manage it,' said Mrs Gabriel. 'It was quite impractical for Peter to live here and commute in the rush hour.

'Peter has always maintained he didn't like Charterhouse. But he never grumbled, he never complained when he was there though I got the feeling he never enjoyed it all that much. It never got to the point where we talked about it and he asked us to take him away from there.

'He grew quickly and went through a heavy stage, though he wasn't fat, and therefore wasn't able to be very quick at sports. If you were not quick at sports it was difficult to be a success. I don't think he shined anywhere.

'I think when we have talked about Charterhouse he thinks it has taught him to stand on his own two feet. I don't feel and I don't think he does think he really would have settled happily into any type of school regime. I don't think it was the school's fault.'

'With hindsight we might have chosen another school,' said his father. 'Had we known what we know now we might have chosen Dartington Hall.' Peter's upbringing dictated that he should not complain about disliking school, though clearly Irene and Ralph Gabriel later became aware of his misery.

Fifty years before Peter Gabriel, another new boy, Robert Graves, had similar sentiments later expressed in *Goodbye To All That*. 'From my first moment at Charterhouse I suffered an oppression of spirit that I hesitate to recall in its full intensity.'

The sixties saw great changes at Charterhouse, though Peter Gabriel was unfortunate to catch some of the last, worst vestiges of the old system. In common with other junior boys he had to be a senior boy's fag, making his bed, occasionally frying him an egg and getting his tuck. Older boys were also allowed to beat the younger ones. 'If someone screamed down the corridor, you ran,' remembered Philip Kingsley-Jones, a contemporary of Peter Gabriel's in Duckites, who became a comprehensive school teacher. He felt the depiction of British public schools in Lindsay Anderson's film *If . . .* accurately reflected the pent-up aggression and frustration of the brown-uniformed boys at Charterhouse who called their teachers 'beaks'.

The junior dormitories at Charterhouse consisted of cubicles six-foot square, known as cubes, designed so that each boy could have some privacy. 'Public school seemed a very hostile, aggressive and oppressive environment. I remember sitting in these cubicles and seeing the car headlights coming up Godalming Hill and the First World War anti-aircraft lights across the ceiling and the soundtrack of the boys in tears and the squeaky beds, masturbation noises. A bit of a nightmare experience for someone who had led quite a sheltered life.

'I think in a way people that flourish in public schools are either good at sport, work, the arts or gregarious, and I was none of these. So I didn't feel I fitted in,' said Peter. 'By the end of my time I felt I had carved a place for myself and was playing music and I had found something that had worked, but the first few years were pretty miserable.

'Conversation at night was very public because the dormitories were all open-topped so you heard the conversations. It was a sort of theatre. No one was allowed to talk, but those with the most physical power were the ones who would end up talking, and they would be talking wine, women and cars. Music didn't feature that well at that time.'

Peter's housemaster, John Marriott, remembers him as a model student. Part of that clearly entailed not expressing one's emotions. 'He was a very pleasnat person indeed, not the sort of person who would fling his weight around. He was a perfectionist.

'Quiet people tend to keep things to themselves. I am sure that he was under a bit of pressure to do better.

'I would not think that he was unhappy. Some boys show that they are unhappy, although I think if he had been unhappy he would not have shown it. When I was a schoolboy I would have had a bit more pride than to show I was unhappy.

'One of the most remarkable things about Charterhouse, which is not all that usual, is the friendliness of the boys in talking to teaching staff, they would always chat to you.'

Peter's school reports were undistinguished, though he could not completely disguise his dislike for the place. 'I think he is just beginning to emerge from the doldrums and there are signs that he envisages putting his spare time to better and more constructive use,' wrote Mr Marriott, in the Long Quarter (spring) report for 1966.

Like all boys at the school Peter had to join the CCF, the Combined Cadet Force. He joined the RAF section, and achieved the rank of corporal, according to Mr Marriott, though Peter does not remember winning this accolade. As a corporal his duties would have included teaching younger recruits the syllabus. 'Everyone else was keen and the RAF was a cop out. You didn't have to turn up for parade and the RAF always had the dirtiest, sloppiest uniforms,' Peter said.

'He was not the sort of chap if you ask him to play football he would say, "Yippee." He'd say, "Of course I will," remembered Mr Marriott.

'Basically one's memory was of an extremely pleasant young man. Quiet and gentle and very supportive to the community.

'He was quite able although he did under-perform in a way. When he first came to Charterhouse he did well enough in the lower forms to get promotion. The whole impression was that he was a thoughtful student,' Mr Marriott said. Peter's own recollection is that he was anonymous at school, and was never a model member of the community. He was made a monitor in his last term at Charterhouse, more as an afterthought than a sign that the school held him in great esteem.

But what rankled then as much as now was his distaste for the class system perpetuated by public schools. Charterhouse boys were told not to mix with the boys from the town. Peter bore no grudge despite getting beaten up when he was at his pre-prep school, Cable House. 'The confrontation tended to be on Horsell Common, which is where H. G. Wells had the Martians landing in *The War of the Worlds*. Once this guy Paul Wheelan and I were outnumbered twelve to two. Our caps were taken from off our heads and smudged into the mud and there was some punching and rolling around in the mud.

'We were seen as middle-class Lord Snooties, but we all came from similar homes. The choice of going to a public school was the dividing factor, as it is throughout British society. We countered the problem by riding around in a posse.'

At Charterhouse Peter got five 'O' Levels, in Elementary Maths, English, French, Latin and Chemistry. 'He took his 'A' Levels for the first time in July 1967, at a fairly youngish age of seventeen-and-a-half, and in many ways he didn't do at all badly,' said Mr Marriott.

He got a D in Mathematics, but failed Physics, and Politics and Economics. In 1968 he took two further 'A' Levels, and got an E in British Constitution and E in Economics.

'He was academically the sort of person who needed a little bit more time to master his 'A' Level subjects. I think he was a bit slow on paper and wasn't a terribly good examinee. We reckoned he was capable of achieving university level. I think his parents were fairly ambitious for him and possibly were a little worried what he might end up doing.'

He listed his interests as poetry, music, astrology, graphology, tennis and squash. According to schoolfriend Anthony Phillips he was a keen cricketer. 'We had house games in cricket which we played once a week. Everyone hated them and we used to try and fix the results so that we could get off as quickly as possible. There was always a couple of guys who would take it seriously and not want to be got out.

'Pete in one of these games was the guy who was upright and straight and refused to do the dirty just because everyone else who was in the wicket was got out. So someone had to knock his stumps over.'

Peter was a member of the natural history, debating, jazz and motor societies, and belonged to the Beerbohm (arts) Society and Beveridge (politics/economics) Society of which he was treasurer.

Mr Marriott wrote in his report for the 1964 Cricket Quarter (summer term): 'I very much enjoyed his performance on the drums in the House musical evening – it was delightfully spontaneous.' Even by his own admission Peter was a terrible drummer, and there seems to be a feeling of relief from Mr Marriott in his report for the winter of 1976: 'I am pleased to hear he is thinking of taking up playing an instrument next quarter as variety to his drumming.'

'He did enjoy all forms of music. He had a very pleasant natural singing voice, I remember it well. He also drummed and played flute,' said Mr Marriott. 'He was quiet, but when he got on stage he did lose himself.'

'I didn't want to be in the choir because I was told it would take up a lot of my free time, so I funked my choir test,' said Peter. 'I went through a fat spotty period which was an awkward entry to the arena for meetings with the opposite sex. So I decided to become a musician to impress the girls. That was not the only reason, but it was a contributory factor, it certainly helps.

'I was told I had a nice chorus voice, but when my voice broke it took a long time to acquire some confidence. I didn't like my voice very much because I could hear singers on the radio doing things that I clearly couldn't do. I think it was my ego rather than the sound of my voice that was the driving factor.

'When I was nine or ten I had a dream where I thought I could have a future as a farmer or as a singer. I dreamt of being a singer, which was strange because I wanted to be a drummer not a singer at the time. It seemed like the high road and the low road, both calling.

'The first drum I bought cost £7 from Nigel Ramage, Andrew Ramage's brother. I was incredibly proud of it. They told me it wasn't worth it at the time but I couldn't be discouraged. It was a real live drum, not a toy one. That was my first drum. My parents had given me a toy snare. Then I bought a kit for £40 from Doc Hunt's Drum Shop in Archer Street, Soho. Whenever I went to a drum shop I used to get a catalogue and I remember sending off for my first free NME from Radio Luxembourg. I was so excited at getting these symbols of another world.

'I guess I was twelve or thirteen when I wrote my first song, "Sammy the Slug". It was not exceptionally memorable. After that, I was getting into my blues and soul phase, really trying to mimic some of that writing.' Peter's schoolfriends were interested in pop and the beat groups. But true music aficionados were touched by the intensity of American black soul music.

# CHAPTER FOUR

TIGER RYAN, SILLY BILLY AND RAY FURY were waiting for Peter Gabriel and the rest of the crowd as they made their way to the second floor above Burton's tailoring store in Brixton Road. The three wrestlers were bouncers at the Ram Jam Club, a red and blue mirrored venue that put on the greatest acts of the sixties.

Even before the riots of the eighties Brixton had a reputation as a tough area, a long way in spirit from genteel Surrey. Sixteen-year-old Peter Gabriel was on a date with a girl, a million miles from Charterhouse on Sunday evening, 18 September 1966 to see Stax Records' star soul singer, Otis Redding. Such activities were frowned upon by his schoolmasters.

Redding was on his first visit to Britain with his fourteen-piece All-American Band. The Ram Jam Club was hot, steamy, sweaty and bursting at the seams. Its capacity was 800 and 2,000 people tried to cram inside. Fainting girls had to be pulled over the four rows of cinema seats in front of the stage. Peter had difficulty finding the club. 'It was very dark, I hadn't been to many clubs, and there were nearly all black faces, so it was an unusual environment for me. But the music was so warm, and he was such a big-hearted performer; you just felt the passion of this man,' remembered Peter.

Redding was vigorously punching air on stage for 'Respect', getting crushingly intense for 'I've Been Loving You Too Long', and jumping around on 'Turn Me Loose'.

The show had to be halted before The Big O could complete his set. 'We had to pull him off because it was dangerous. Backstage after the show he put his arms in a fire bucket of water up to his elbows to cool himself off because he was so hot,' remembered John Gunnell, who, with his brother Rik, promoted the Who, Cream, Nina Simone and Ike and Tina Turner at the Ram Jam. They managed Geno Washington and his Ram Jam Band, naming the club after them.

Otis Redding's first British shows did not receive a great deal of attention in the music press. But a letter from Vanessa Taylor of Heywood, Lancashire to *Melody Maker* in October 1966, after seeing Otis in Manchester, echoed Peter's feelings. 'I have just seen this incredible man and I still think he was a dream. The feeling, soul, and deep deep sincerity he put into those songs was just too perfect. I did not believe anyone could be so exciting. No one could be as good at Otis.'

In the sleeve notes on the 1965 LP, *Otis Blue*, Bob Rolontz wrote, 'The moving style of Otis Redding is a fusion of blues, pop and gospel. It comes as naturally and normally to him as crying to a baby. His sound is real. It is also personal and individual. Anyone who listens to Otis Redding understands his message. That, perhaps, is the real meaning of soul.'

When Alan Smith of the *NME* tried to interview Redding after one of his British dates he found him in a near trance state. 'Otis seemed to have worked himself to such a pitch that he found it almost impossible to concentrate on my questions,' he wrote.

The teenage Gabriel was moved by the intensity of seeing Redding. 'It is still my favourite gig of all time. It was just the way he could generate feeling and excitement, that was an up-tempo memory for me. But the strong, soulful, passionate ballads were also amazing.

'There was an energy there which I think you don't see elsewhere. Springsteen gets close at times, but it's a little more thought out. I think with Otis it was direct from the gut. He was my hero as a singer, definitely, and a lot of that music was part of what drove me to consider music for myself. I was a teenager, very impressionable and very ready to be impressed.'

Peter first heard Otis Redding at Record Corner in Godalming with Tony Banks. 'We were only allowed downtown with authorized and signed writs from the housemaster. Being caught meant a certain beating. When we were in the record shop we would listen to Otis Redding and John Mayall, the blues and the best of the early hippy things.'

Peter used to go into the billiards room, the only place where they were allowed to play records in school. 'It had this really beaten-up, old Dansette record player in a wooden cabinet. You could only play it for about an hour and a half every day,' he told Hugh Fielder of *Sounds*. 'I used to take my Otis Redding records in there and turn them up full volume and dance until I was in a frenzied sweat. This ritual gave me an immense feeling of relief.'

Tony and Peter, both shy boys, found solace in their friendship and music. Tony's experiences of Charterhouse were similar to Peter's. 'I was shy and kept to myself. I was not very happy, but it got easier towards the end. I think Peter has always been a little more outgoing than I was, but we both had that reserved element in us. It's certainly one of the things that got us to be friends.'

Tony Banks studied classical piano at prep school, but his nervousness prevented him from playing note-perfect, he was much better at playing music by ear. He gradually became entranced by the Beatles after hearing 'Love Me Do' on the radio, and worked out how to play around a hundred Beatles songs. He vied with Peter to play the dining-hall piano. 'In the end it was me on piano and Peter singing,' says Tony. 'He was always keen to sound like Nina Simone. Otis Redding was a hero, and we would do Otis Redding songs more than any others.'

The fight to get to the dining hall piano was crucial, the

combatants racing there once games were finished. As a short cut, instead of going round the passages, Peter would cut through the kitchen and slip through the serving hatch.

Peter's first group was the Milords, who he joined when he was fifteen. Formed out of Charterhouse boys all older than him they were a seven-piece semi-professional outfit playing trad jazz at twenty-first birthday parties and wedding receptions in London, Oxfordshire and Buckinghamshire during the school holidays, earning £15 an appearance.

The group took its name from 'Milord', the Edith Piaf song, which they played at hops. 'We used to play in full formal dress, top hats and tails. Peter looked pretty scruffy,' said group founder and double bass player John Wilkinson, who became a consultant dermatologist. Their repertoire included 'Sixteen Coal Black Horses' and 'House of the Rising Sun'.

'Peter was a nice enough chap. We started the jazz band and we needed a drummer. His drumming echoed round the house from the dining room where he practised so we asked him to join.'

Gabriel failed in his attempts to veer the group more towards rock. But he was given the chance to sing from behind the drums. 'He had a reasonable, quite natural voice,' said Dr Wilkinson. 'He was slightly quiet, but he was younger than the rest of us.' Tony Banks and Anthony Phillips also made isolated appearances with the group.

'It was very bad. It was funny because I was definitely right at the back. The drummer of the dance band was a very unspectacular character,' Peter said.

Peter left them in the summer of 1966 to become the drummer for the Spoken Word, a semi-professional rhythm and blues group formed at Bryanston School in Dorset. Peter was recommended by a friend of a friend. 'Peter rang me up and said he would love to do some drumming. We had no idea he had any ambitions to sing,' said Spoken Word's singer

David Thomas. Anthony Phillips was also recruited from Charterhouse. Rehearsals were held at Thomas' parents' home at South Warnborough Manor in Hampshire, and they gigged at middle-class parties around Surrey and Hampshire. They played a mixture of John Mayall influenced blues and Chuck Berry rock and roll. 'We were attracted to the music because it had a poignancy. It was classic rebellion stuff for those days. We were not aware of being middle class. It was just normal for us.'

'The only time I remember Peter singing was at a Junior Hunt Ball,' says Thomas. 'He had a go at the blues, an improvised twelve bar. It was a very hesitant start. He found it very hard to communicate at all, which is why I think everything comes out in the music, but he had the will and intention to do it. At the time we certainly didn't realize he was going to be a great and classy singer, which I certainly think he is now.'

But the group were ambitious enough to travel to London to cut an acetate of the Jimmy Witherspoon blues number, 'Evening', which marked Peter Gabriel's recording debut, albeit on drums. 'It was a simple cutting machine which did the thing on the spot from a tape,' said Thomas. 'We intended taking it around to some people to see if we could get any reaction. But I can't remember anything positive happening.'

One of Peter's dining-room practice sessions was overheard by a curious Richard Macphail. 'I was always interested in anything to do with rock music. On Saturday afternoons we used to commandeer classrooms as rehearsal rooms. You'd suddenly hear this cacophony crashing around the cloisters, and I guess one time I just walked in. I remember someone was playing a saxophone which I thought was pretty amazing. Peter was pretty fat as a teenager, in fact he was quite porky. And he was playing the drums, and I remember his drums sounded like he looked,' he said.

Macphail was singer in Anon, another Charterhouse group

formed by two younger boys, Anthony Phillips and Rivers Job, veterans of Beatles inspired prep school band The Spiders. Anon's line-up was completed by Mike Rutherford on bass and Rob Tyrell on drums, and the group played Beatles and Stones numbers. Macphail was dubbed Mick Phail for his attempted Jagger impersonations.

Peter Gabriel was disillusioned as a drummer in Spoken Word. 'I wanted to sing the songs I was writing. Then I tried writing with Tony Banks, and he could play piano better than I could. He was a real piano player and I was a thumper, still am, really, but I get by.'

During the Easter break of 1966 Richard Macphail visited Tiles Club in Oxford Street and the Marquee in Wardour Street. At Tiles he saw the Alan Price Set and a pop group called the Koobas managed by Tony Stratton Smith, who was to become the first manager of Genesis.

The following term, the Cricket Quarter of 1966, Macphail was asked to leave Charterhouse. The headmaster was dismayed at his neglect of school work in favour of pop music. Inspired by visits to London and displaying his organizational abilities, Macphail planned a school concert as his swansong. 'I wanted to try and recreate a sort of club atmosphere. It's quite an interesting thought without any women, but it caught my imagination,' he said.

Anthony Phillips asked Peter if Anon's drummer, Rob Tyrell, could borrow Peter's drum kit. 'He was very approachable, but quite fastidious, and understandably so, about his drums when he lent them to us. He insisted on coming along and watching.'

But Phillips did not suspect Gabriel's real ambition until he came across him in the house dining room. 'I remember him standing on a table singing soul songs with Tony Banks playing piano,' said Phillips. 'It was my first recollection of this other side of him, not just this straight, nice but difficult to know character.'

Music satisfied his craving for attention and recognition that lay behind Gabriel's innate shyness. He also displayed entrepreneurial abilities. He made money out of two schemes, dyeing T-shirts with bright colours, and manufacturing felt hats.

'I had this hat of my grandfather's which I used to love the shape of, it looked Cromwellian. There was this great hippy phenomenon happening in London which I wanted to become a part of. Wearing these hats I thought would be a good idea for getting me involved, so I went to various manufacturers to try to get them made up. There was an old guy in Dunn & Co. in Piccadilly who was quite amused by it and took me seriously. I wanted them in gaudy colours, pinks and purples and yellows and orange.

'Once I had a few made I took them to boutiques in Carnaby Street and King's Road. And flogged some to Emerton and Lambert in the Chelsea Antiques Market, which at the time was frequented by the Stones and the current hipsters of that period. When I came back from school one Saturday and turned on *Juke Box Jury*, there was Marianne Faithfull wearing one of my hats, and I nearly wet myself with excitement. She'd stuck a feather into it, and Keith Richards also had one. That was a real thrill, it was some tangible connection with this exciting world.

'I felt really intimidated getting on a train and going to London, going into a shop and trying to persuade these old people it was a good idea. I think it is one of the best things to teach people – to go for it.'

Gabriel did not maximize his profits because he gave some away to friends. The T-shirt dyeing business at two shillings a go also failed to make his fortune. 'This got me into a certain amount of trouble because they went into the wash with cricket whites, which then came out pink or green.'

Music seemed a safer bet, and just before Macphail's beat concert in July 1966 Peter and Tony formed the Garden Wall.

They found a drummer, Chris Stewart, and Johnny Trapman on trumpet, but had to poach some members of Anon to complete the group. Anthony Phillips, the most musicianly of them all, agreed to help on guitar, with Rivers Job on bass, as well as playing their own set in Anon with Macphail singing.

At the concert Tony Banks played piano off the stage.'No one knew I was there until the fourth song,' he said. They did Percy Sledge's 'When A Man Loves A Woman', and a soul version of Simon and Garfunkel's 'I Am A Rock'. They also did a 12-bar blues which no one could stop because Chris Stewart refused to look up from his drum kit. Peter was wearing one of his hats, a kaftan and beads and crawled around on his hands and knees.

Permission to hold the concert had been granted reluctantly by the masters at Charterhouse. One master insisted that, like a classical concert, there should be no announcement. Macphail inadvertently broke that rule and the master seized his opportunity, halting the show half-way through.

To many pupils the staff seemed fearful of the new mood in the outside world. Mike Rutherford had been prevented from playing at the beat concert because his housemaster thought rock music, in the shape of Rutherford's guitar, could ignite a revolution in Lockites House. Such paranoia was only reenforced on the last day of one term when someone painted a huge ban the bomb symbol on the armoury which housed the CCF rifles.

In November 1966 *The Carthusian*, the school magazine, gave a round-up of Charterhouse groups including the Climax, the Scarlet and Black, and the Garden Wall. It was the first time Gabriel's singing was mentioned in print. 'This group, which was formed at the beginning of last Cricket Quarter, claims to be the only true exponent of Soul Music in the school. With a distinctly earthy quality to their work, they gave some spirited performances in last quarter's Charity Beat Concert, Peter Gabriel's vocalizing being a major feature. They practise two or three times a week, but encounter difficulty when the lead and bass guitarists are occupied with Anon . . . Other features of the group are their compositions, which number two to date, and their partiality to improvisation on well-known themes. They claim to be a united group in their capacity as a part-time affair, necessitated by two of them playing with Anon, and like Anon take their music and their playing quality very seriously.'

Peter was growing out of his spotty phase and was the first of his fellow musicians to have a regular girlfriend. He met Jill Moore, a pupil at St Catherine's, sister school to Charterhouse, at a party just before Christmas 1966. Girls from St Catherine's were allowed to come to the next school hop in the hippy heyday of summer 1967 where all the regular school pop musicians played once again. Before his performance Peter together with Jill collected a bin liner full of rose petals from surrounding gardens. Peter then sprinkled them over the audience.

The first song Tony and Peter wrote together was 'She Is Beautiful', which underwent several rewrites and a change of title to 'The Serpent' before it appeared on the first Genesis album, *From Genesis to Revelation*. 'I used to stay with Peter a lot at weekends when were writing music,' said Tony. 'I got to know his family very well, they were very kind to me.

'Music was one thing we had in common. We also used to play squash and tennis, we could talk about rubbish for hours. We had lots of surface similarities and also had lots of differences. I think we complemented each other pretty well. In the early days of Genesis we wrote as a pair a lot of the time.'

Ant Phillips and Mike Rutherford took a musical career more seriously than Tony and Peter. They raised twenty guineas to record one of their rhythm and blues compositions, 'Pennsylvania Flickhouse', at a studio in Putney with the rest of Anon. Some months later they were ready to record five new songs, after a brief flirtation with blues influenced by John Mayall and the Bluesbreakers.

Over the Easter holidays of 1967 Ant and Mike hired a studio which was being built in the garage of schoolfriend Brian Roberts' home in Chiswick. Ant phoned Tony to ask him if he would like to come and play keyboards, and he in turn asked if he could bring Peter. The assembled group recorded five Phillips and Rutherford songs and the Banks/Gabriel composition 'She Is Beautiful'. 'This was the song that got the most attention, so it gave us encouragement. After that we started writing a lot of songs together. Initially we weren't interested in songwriting as much as playing other stuff and fun interpretations of things,' said Tony. Phillips wanted to sing his own songs, but he was persuaded by Tony that Peter had the better voice. What became the first Genesis line-up was now established. Macphail was out, and Gabriel, Banks, Phillips, Rutherford and drummer Chris Stewart were in.

Early that summer Jonathan King, an Old Carthusian, returned to Charterhouse for Old Boys Day. The school was proud of this international celebrity from among their ranks, and King was pleased to bathe in the glory. In 1965 King had scored a major hit while still at Trinity College, Cambridge, with 'Everyone's Gone To The Moon', and was writer, producer and publisher of 'It's Good News Week', a hit for Hedgehoppers Anonymous.

Too nervous to approach King themselves, the group's friend John Alexander did it for them. He asked King to listen to the tape and left it on the back seat of his car.

'I listened to it and I thought, "This is really good, these are nice little songs," and I thought the guy had a really nice voice. I was interested in doing more work as a producer because I wanted to become a person in the music industry instead of just another singer. So I called them up and said, "I think this is fun, let's do something." They were really amazed to hear from me, completely staggered and overexcited.'

'We were by the swimming pool,' said Mrs Gabriel. 'Tony Banks was here. Peter took a telephone call from Jonathan King and came running out saying, "We've made it." He was jumping around for joy when he said he liked their tape.'

'I would have to go down to the phone box out of school and struggle with my coins and the pip box, to try and locate this person from the pop business,' said Peter. 'At that point, everyone who was involved with the music business was regarded with suspicion, including King.' Peter became the group hustler. He had learnt to drive and bought an old London taxi for £50. He put one of his mother's dining room chairs in the front luggage section to accommodate another person.

In those early days, Banks, Gabriel and Phillips all had strong opinions on which direction the group should take. 'We were all pretty young and there was quite a bit of in-fighting,' said Banks. Mike Rutherford was more prepared to go along with their decisions.

Peter and Tony visited King in London. 'We were using the old boy network. And, I think, at that time King seemed quite happy to use the young boy network. He gave us some money to experiment with and told us to produce a demo,' said Peter.

'He seemed excited by the tape. He wanted to sign us to a five-year deal with a five-year option. We were minors and we managed to push it to a one-year, plus a one-year option. Our parents managed to sort it out,' said Tony.

'King in those days seemed quite an important man. It gave us a boost that he was interested in us the slightest bit.' The group thought they had it made and also signed a publishing contract of £40 for four songs.

The next tape of eight new songs was recorded at two studios in Denmark Street, London's old Tin Pan Alley. The songs were more complex and longer. King was not impressed, preferring the earlier ones. 'The more ambitious we were, the more he disliked it,' said Tony.

In the summer of 1967 Peter and Tony took their 'A' levels. Following Peter's moderate success in the autumn he went to a 'crammer', the prestigious Davies, Laing and Dick tutorial college in Notting Hill to study for two more 'A' levels. Peter had to move out of home for the first time and into a lodging house in Notting Hill full of other students from the crammer. 'All thickies, trying to buy their way through the exam system,' said Peter. 'My parents were very keen for me to go to university. I was not really working very hard, but going along for the ride to keep them happy. I actually found it very interesting because I had a very good politics and economics teacher there.'

Peter was offered a place at the London School of Film Technique which satisfied his parents' wishes for further education. Still unsure of his musical career, the idea of eventually becoming a film director appealed to Peter, and he seriously considered taking up the film course.

Tony Banks went to Sussex University outside Brighton where he read Chemistry, later switching to Physics and Philosophy. Ant and Mike were still at Charterhouse.

After receiving the publisher's letter expressing Johnathan King's disappointment with their new material Tony and Peter contrived to please him. 'Peter and I – it was probably the only time we have ever been calculating at all in our careers, I think – we felt we were losing King, and we felt he was the only contact we had ever had in the business, and so we sat down and thought we would write a song to please him,' said Tony. 'As he liked the Bee Gees very much we wrote a Bee Gees number, "Silent Sun", with a Robin Gibb vocal, and he loved it, so we were right back there with him.' The song is distinguished for being one of the few songs they ever wrote which included the word 'baby'. It lasted for two minutes and four seconds.

'There have been stories that say that they said to each other, "Let's write a Bee Gees song because Jonathan likes the

Bee Gees,"' said King. 'This had nothing to do with it. The whole motivation in the early days was to get them to simplify what they were trying to do. They were writing very nice songs with good lyrics and they were singing well, but their ambitions were too large. They were, after all, only sixteen- or seventeen-year-old kids and they just couldn't play any more than basic chords. So, when they tried to do an elaborate solo and things they just sounded pretentious and awful.'

They discussed a name for the group with King. 'His first suggestion, which the rest of the band have forgotten although I haven't, was Gabriel's Angels – which appealed to me. Somehow this didn't seem to register with the others,' said Peter. 'His thinking was that some of the stuff was influenced by hymns, and so this new name suggested an absurd, naïve innocence.'

But the name also represented a more personal change of direction for King. 'I thought of Genesis because I believed it was the beginning of my production career,' he says.

King produced their first single, 'Silent Sun', in December 1967 at Regent Sound in Denmark Street. He convinced them it would be a hit and to leave the promotion to him. 'We all went to Carnaby Street to buy clothes for *Top of the Pops*, which never happened,' said Peter. King arranged for a deal with his own record company, Decca, and the single was released on 22 February 1968.

Richard Macphail was working as a messenger on the Stock Exchange. 'I must have been the first person to buy the single because I bought it the day it came out and I can't believe anyone else would have done that because no one else knew it existed.' The following week Chris Welch, in the *Melody Maker*, gave Genesis their first write-up. 'I was a big fan of Chris Welch and his writing and I used to get *Melody Maker* and ring up Peter and Anthony and read things out. His review started "Dear Jonathan King, producer of Genesis, this recording, sir, is muck . . ." and then he said, "Zounds man, I am jesting, 'tis sorry sport to poke fun at one of the better sounds of the week,"' and said Gabriel's vocals were 'Peter Framptonish'.

Peter's sister Anne, at boarding school, listened out for the single on her transistor radio. 'I was very proud when "Silent Sun" came out. I remember lying awake listening to Radio Luxembourg with my friends, I thought it was wonderful.' And the Duckites were instructed to send requests to radio stations. Kenny Everett, then quite a trendy DJ, played it on Radio 1, and it got an airing on pirate station Radio Caroline. The second single, 'A Winter's Tale', was released on 10 May and sank without trace.

They sent new tapes to King, and in their 1968 school summer holidays Genesis recorded their debut album at Regent Sound. Drummer Chris Stewart was replaced by another schoolfriend, John Silver. King came up with the concept for the album *From Genesis to Revelation*, recorded in one day. 'It was supposed to be the history of the universe, altogether a very duff concept,' said Peter. The group's name had to be left off the album because a group in America claimed the same name. The name was then changed to Revelation, but someone claimed that too. The record was not released until May 1969.

The inner sleeve notes reveal an ethereal sixties mind at work. 'Sometimes, before the hard age of flitting teens, shapes are sharper, patterns clearer, ideas more simple and statements more crystal. Sometimes, indeed, wrongly so. Sometimes rightly . . .' it mused. Banks and Phillips were unhappy with King's production, particularly the string arrangements. 'I remember storming out of the session, suddenly the whole thing – this dream of a great album – had crumbled,' said Phillips, who complained their music had been butchered. But Peter did not protest as much. 'We wanted to see the record out and there's no way we would have rocked the boat,' said Phillips. 'I think after that Pete was very uncompromising, but when you're getting going you have to compromise.' The acoustic guitars, string arrangements and folky harmonies gave the album a dreamy pastoral air, all a long way from the group's soul and rhythm and blues influences. Peter's voice was restrained, and he struggled to get some high notes. He was so exhausted towards the end that he kept taking showers to keep himself awake.

Decca failed to promote the album, and record dealers were confused because it did not have an artist's name on it. According to King it got mistaken in some shops for religious music. *From Genesis to Revelation* was reviewed by Mark Williams in the underground paper *International Times*. 'The most noteworthy aspect of the group is that they are all young, from seventeen to twenty, and are therefore only in the early stages of their musical development which is an awe-inspiring thought because the ideas they express on the album are already streets ahead of so many other groups. The album sets out to recall the memories of adolescence in all their fleeting naïvety and it succeeds quite excellently. At times, however, the words border on the pretentious, but then one's teens are often pretentious anyway . . .' Peter's vocals reminded him of Roger Daltrey in *Tommy*. 'That was the best review we got. It was incredibly exciting because it was my bible at the time,' said Peter. 'I felt very much like a schoolboy trying to become a card-carrying hippy.' By the time the album came out they were gradually losing touch with King, and eventually simply drifted apart.

The group were later thankful none of their earliest recordings were hits, partly through embarrassment, and partly because early success could have stunted their future development. Having taken his 'A' levels again, Peter moved out of digs to share a flat first in Boston Place, by St Marylebone Station, and then Bramham Gardens, Earls Court with David Thomas, his old partner in Spoken Word. Tony Banks also moved in with them, and become one of Thomas' best friends.

'The flat was very important for us both. There was the sudden introduction to women and the freedom – to cook your own meal and go out and do what you wanted. It was only a few months, but it seemed like years, that period lives on in my mind,' said Tony.

The sense of freedom for Peter at Bramham Gardens was considerable. He walked through the flat with no clothes on one night in an attempt to show he had broken free. Peter later recalled the incident. 'It was flower power time. I became very angry with myself. I would get very inhibited and shy and I used to wither inwardly because I felt I couldn't articulate or express what I was feeling in any way. It would really drive me crazy that I didn't have the confidence or assurance to do that, and they would tease me about that. I thought, sod this, I'll show you.'

Gabriel shocked his flatmates, including Margaret McBain, later Tony's wife, and some other visitors. 'I walked back through the room with nothing on and was ridiculed for quite a while afterwards.' Tony Banks, despite being equally shy, joined in the acidic comments.

Though he was not seriously considering a career in acting, Peter tried for a role in the film *If . . .* He passed the first audition, went for a reading and was considered for one of the leading parts. But he told the producers he might not be able to commit himself to the film. 'They said, "Either you go for it, or you don't." And so I said, "OK, well I don't." But it was still exciting, just to get a taste of it.'

During the summer of 1969 Tony announced he was leaving to return to Sussex University, but was persuaded to stay by Peter. A week later the roles were reversed when Peter decided to quit. He then agreed to Tony's requests that he stay on condition they try to get some positive reaction to the group and play some gigs. Drummer John Silver had left to go to university and was replaced by John Mayhew, who answered the group's advertisement in *Melody Maker* for a drummer sensitive to bongos and acoustic music. With Mike also considering going back to college, Ant was the only one not to waver in his determination to succeed in music.

The summer was spent rehearsing in different parents' houses. They decided that to go professional they needed a minimum of £650-worth of equipment. 'We got £150 from each of our parents, some of whom were a lot quicker to cough up than others, I have to say,' said Peter.

Over the previous two years they had written over 300 songs between them. They would start off with chords, building them on the piano, and then develop the melody. The rhythm and lyrics would come last. Gabriel was the main lyricist, but not the only one. His words perplexed Phillips. 'He wrote some pretty eccentric things from the start,' said Phillips. 'There was one called "Masochistic Man" with a line that goes, "Carve the eglantine with bitter juices of her body." I didn't understand half the stuff he was on about.' Not all Gabriel's lyrics were that obscure. During that period he wrote the words for 'The Knife', which would become the group's first stage favourite among fans. The imagery is unusually violent for him, but it fitted in with what was becoming an established pattern of fancifulness, inspired by mythology, childhood books and poetry.

Armed with new tapes, Peter and Tony went to music publishers, record companies and agents. 'We were trying to combine electric music with vocal and acoustic influences and people felt it had to be one or the other,' said Peter. They visited John Martin and Ian Smithers at the Marquee Martin Agency. 'They very kindly took one to two hours to tell us why we should give up. I have never been so depressed as I was when we came out that day. They may have just been sadistic because they knew we were green, young and enthusiastic. Sometimes when I was feeling low I would think back on that day and say I would carry on, if only to prove those bastards wrong.' It was then that he decided to give up his fantasies of being a film director and concentrate on the band.

'I would go round with Peter a lot,' said Tony. 'He would do the talking and I would listen and assess these people. I am no good at communicating, but I was quite good at making judgements on people. You knew if you had people interested or not. To be honest, most people weren't at all interested.

'Peter doesn't mind making a nuisance of himself,' said Tony. 'It all bounced off him. I would get keyed up and get too impassioned. If I thought the song was great and these people we were playing it to didn't respond, they were such fools. Whereas Peter was more philosophical about it.'

'The more Peter progressed in music, the more every aspect of his character became streamlined into that. He seemed to lose the tubbiness. His girlfriend sharpened him up a bit,' said Ant. Peter had been the only one with a steady girlfriend. But Ant also harboured affections for Jill, according to Peter. Ant's song 'Visions of Angels', which appeared on their second album, Trespass, was said to be inspired by her. 'Every time he was trying to see her there was me in the way,' said Peter.

'Ant is definitely a gifted musician and writer, but because we are both repressed Englishmen I think we didn't shout at each other, and when he was getting pissed off at me he didn't feel able to express it. There was some sort of darkness which built up which came out in ways that I don't even think he would see or understand to this day, but in my mind that is part of the picture. I think the situation with Jill, Jill initiated, but one of my favourite quotes is "we seek the teeth to match our wounds".'

Jill also affected Peter and Tony's relationship. 'He had a girlfriend before I did,' said Tony. 'And then he was very on and off with Jill in those early days, and Jill and I used to have lots of fights. I have a slightly spiteful side to my nature, and I think I tended to attack her sometimes. When you are on top of people all the time it comes out occasionally. Peter would be more resilient to that. He's a very difficult person to really puncture, in a way, because he always remains quite aloof whereas Jill couldn't.'

Genesis played their first professional gig for £25 in September 1969 at a dance at the home of the Balme family, just across the lane from Peter's parents' home at Chobham. 'The people there were aged sixteen to eighteen and wanted the hits. We might have done some Stones numbers, but we mainly wanted to play our own material, which wasn't the best for dancing.'

Genesis doggedly kept playing their undanceable set, an attitude they maintained despite further unsuitable bookings. Richard Macphail, returning from a kibbutz in Israel, was impressed with the improvement in the band. 'I didn't really have any objective view of what Genesis were like, they were just my mates,' said Richard. 'Then I wasn't around for a while and I heard them rehearse at Anthony Phillips' house in Guildford, and it suddenly occurred to me that they were really very good, I could compare them to other groups and see they had something. From then on I became an absolute number one fan, convinced how wonderful every note was.'

He became their unofficial manager and dogsbody. Ant and Mike felt they needed a base where they could rehearse for hours on end and Richard suggested they move into a cottage owned by his parents. Isolated near woodland between Dorking and Guildford, it had been burgled that summer, and Richard's parents, who intended selling it in the spring, offered the cottage rent free.

In November 1969, they moved in and Richard's father, an executive at Rank Hovis McDougall, gave them an old bread van to help cart their equipment around. 'They figured they had nothing to lose,' said Richard. 'The pressure of their backgrounds, upbringing and education was pretty strong, and they were flying in the face of it. But music was their abiding passion and they felt there was enough of a chance of it to go somewhere.' Despite their disapproval, the parents each donated £100 to the cost of buying some basic equipment – the main item being a Hammond organ for Tony Banks.

For the next five months the band rehearsed for up to fifteen hours a day. Richard Macphail ran around for them and cooked. Each weekend they would receive Red Cross parcels from their parents. 'Mike used to come back with boxes and boxes of stuff from his mother who was convinced we were going to starve to death,' said Richard.

'Peter would be on the phone trying above the din of the others to get people to come down and see us.' Visitors included Ken Pitt, then still David Bowie's manager, and agent Pete Saunders of College Entertainments, who got them regular gigs. They were also visited by fledgling agent and manager Marcus Bicknell who in his efforts to become the group's manager found them gigs. 'The band strung Marcus along wonderfully. The guy did wonderful things for us. He had a grasp of reality, thank God, and got us leaflets and posters,' said Richard.

The band were woefully ignorant of performance for their first proper gig at Brunel University in Uxbridge soon after their move to the cottage. 'We were playing in the university bar and I remember feeling that that was the first time there was a pressure on me to deliver. I felt I was the filtering device between what we were doing and the audience. I felt that unless I could generate the electricity in the performance we were going to die there and then. That was when I realized fast the need to hold people's attention.' They argued over the position of the speakers because Peter could not hear himself if they were in their proper position out front. 'I had been given our two speakers for my birthday, so I felt that at least I had some rights in deciding where they went. I was persuaded otherwise and I had to just sing out of tune in a tradition I have carried on ever since.'

Money was a constant problem in the cottage. 'There were many heated arguments about how money should be spent,' said Peter. 'Plectrums or bread? You can't eat plectrums.' They earned the princely sum of £50 after one gig at Twickenham Technical College. But it was swiftly taken off them when Richard Macphail, who drove the van despite not having a driving licence, crashed into a car and caused exactly £50-worth of damage.

Just before Christmas 1969 they were booked in Manchester and Birmingham, regarded as 'outer space' because it was so far from their previous catchment area around London.

'Peter had really annoyed everyone by insisting he brought his double mattress along with him, packing it in the van with all the gear,' said Richard. 'In Birmingham we slept on the floor of the sports club we played in, and in the middle of the night the underground heating came on and it became too hot to touch. We were all trying to get out of this room, throwing our clothes ahead of us to make stepping stones on the floor.' After the Manchester gig they were put up in a big house in Buxton and all had to sleep in the same room to keep warm.

They received mixed receptions. Often it was negative because people wanted a group they could dance to. 'They used to do three twenty-minute sets and nobody would listen while we were cracking away in the corner expecting everyone to sit on the floor in rapt attention,' said Macphail.

The tensions in the cottage resulted in occasional outbursts from the inhabitants who tended to bottle things up and then explode. That energy was channelled into the music which became more aggressive. Though their time at the cottage was an enormously creative period, they were also removed from reality, cut off from the world in much the same way they had been at public school. The cottage helped them compose what was to become the next album. Though it bonded them as musicians it gave them a distorted view of performance. They played without time limits, and then found it hard to adapt to the needs of an audience.

Only Peter and Mike had girlfriends, but they were restricted to seeing them at weekends. 'Peter felt trapped, stuck down in the cottage and unable to influence things while his beloved was getting out in the world,' said Richard. Jill was then at the Guildhall School of Music and Drama and sharing a flat in Swiss Cottage. 'He could never come up and join my parties there or see the performances I was doing, or take part in my life up there,' said Jill. 'All I wanted to do was be down in the cottage. I was so resentful Mike's girlfriend was there.'

'I look on the cottage as the start of the professional group,' said Mike Rutherford. 'Because that is when we started to do it a hundred per cent of the time. I often think we stopped each other growing up. Normally you leave school and you go off into the world and you have experiences that make you grow up very fast. Because we were locked into this very tight unit it was very insular. We were a good, but also a very bad, influence on each other.

'The cottage was, in a way, very claustrophobic. It wasn't a specially happy time in my memory though musically it was very formative. None of us had a social life. We were actually more interested in music than sex in those days. Girlfriends were squeezed in on odd afternoons off, everything was secondary to the group.'

'It was a mistake,' said Ant. 'We were just too young to know that if you live and work together for five solid months, fifteen hours a day, seven days a week, there's bound to be friction and people are going to suffer because of it. I felt the relationships in the group deteriorated because of the ridiculously extreme conditions under which we put ourselves. The fun element, the easy geniality, was suddenly removed. It was no wonder that various people became disenchanted.'

The toil of being on the road was a strain. The group

carted all their own equipment up and down the forty steps leading to the cottage, drove to the gigs and set everything up themselves. The bread van was uncomfortable, and for Ant, claustrophobic. 'There were no windows in the van. Obviously in the front the guy next to the driver could see. But behind that was this narrow compartment in which four people had to sit. That for 300 miles would kill me.'

Tony Banks never enjoyed playing on stage because of his introverted personality. He liked the piano and found it hard to adapt to organ. 'Peter had to triumph over the quieter, more retiring side of his personality, deliberately exploit the showman,' said Ant. 'When we started to play on the road at one stage the introductions for the songs were so bad that Richard, who was always cocky and very confident, was going to come on and do the announcements because Peter didn't talk. Once he switched into this other person he was fine, but at that stage he just couldn't do it. He quickly got it sorted out, and then of course, he was magnificent.'

Ant was a perfectionist, and insisted on having his guitars properly tuned in between numbers. That delay, coupled with frequent equipment breakdowns, caused Peter to start improvising stories. 'Anthony was very meticulous about things, and he and Mike had twelve-strings. So as a diversionary tactic, because the gaps in between songs were so long, Peter started this repartee, telling ridiculous stories that he made up on the spot,' said Richard. Peter dressed on stage in a long black and white cloak he referred to as the bathrobe. He banged the tambourine, occasionally played flute, and to the increasing annoyance of the rest of the band, kicked a bass drum at the front of the stage, frequently out of time.

The group discarded the short, largely acoustic set of their first album and moved towards more epic-length aggressive rock. Though they were lumped under the category of 'progressive rock' Genesis bore little relation to bands like Led

Zeppelin, Black Sabbath and Yes, all then breaking through. They admitted *In the Court of the Crimson King*, the classic King Crimson album, was one of their favourite records during the cottage period. And they also were impressed with Family, Procol Harum and Fairport Convention. But Genesis wanted to carve out their own niche, using the 12-string guitar, the busy organ, and the dramatic vocals and frequently surreal imagery of Peter Gabriel. It was a sound that could not be categorized or compared to their contemporaries as the sixties turned into the seventies.

Marcus Bicknell booked them at an odd mixture of places around the southeast starting in February 1970. They played student unions and the Revolution Club in Mayfair, bemusing the suburban trendies who were in town for a bit of disco. They started a six-week residency at Upstairs at Ronnie Scott's in Soho in March, playing in front of literally a handful of people who were usually friends.

On the gig circuit Genesis had met a group called Rare Bird who in February 1970 got into the UK Top 30 with 'Sympathy'. The single proved a massive worldwide hit selling over one-and-a-half million copies. 'Sympathy' was the first release on a new record label, Charisma, set up by former sports journalist Tony Stratton Smith.

Rare Bird had recommended Genesis to their producer, John Anthony, who went to see them Upstairs at Ronnie Scott's. One number, 'Visions of Angels', particularly struck Anthony. 'When I first heard Genesis I always thought of William Blake,' said Anthony. 'I was quite taken with the band because I was interested in classical music, mythology, history and the general Englishness of things. I was genuinely enthralled. They were a very strong band with a commanding presence and an emotive energy.

'I spoke to Peter, which was quite difficult because he was quite shy. In a funny kind of way Jill was talking for him. I got the feeling she was the one who was checking me out as a record company weasel. I think I passed the test. I said, "I've got to have you for this record company that I work for." '

The group had drawn up a list of big and little fish in the music business who it would be worth cultivating to further their careers. Marcus Bicknell was a little fish, Tony Stratton Smith was big.

After Anthony saw Genesis at Ronnie Scott's he enthused about them to Stratton Smith. The following Tuesday he managed to drag Strat away from La Chasse, a one-roomed drinking club in Wardour Street, and got him to walk the two blocks to Frith Street. 'When he really liked something he became very, very quiet,' said Anthony. 'He soaked it up, his eyes were closed and he heard what I heard. They were signed almost immediately after that.'

Stratton Smith, then thirty-six, had struggled in the music business since 1965 as an unsuccessful publisher and pop group manager, first tasting success managing the Nice in 1967. He had been a successful cricket and football journalist, in his mid-twenties working as northern sports editor of the *Daily Sketch* before writing for the *Daily Express*. He wrote numerous sports books and narrowly missed being on the plane that killed the Manchester United football team in Munich in 1958 when he was assigned to another job. In 1964 he went to live in Brazil for a year to write a book on Pele. There he discovered the bossanova rhythm, which marked his musical awakening, and he decided to become a music publisher on returning to England.

Spurred by the demise of the Nice's label, Immediate, frustrated by his dealings with other record companies and inspired by a new group, Van Der Graaf Generator, and in particular their singer and songwriter Peter Hammill, Stratton Smith decided in 1969 to form Charisma Records. Anthony had produced Van Der Graaf for Mercury Records and Stratton Smith asked him to produce Charisma's first signing, Rare

Bird. Flushed by beginner's luck when he saw Genesis in 1970, Stratton Smith knew he had the capital to sign more acts.

'He looked on Genesis like he would later a young thoroughbred,' says Jack Barrie, Strat's best friend and managing director of the Marquee Club for twenty-five years. 'They needed nurturing and looking after. A thoroughbred doesn't come into its own until it is three years old. His groups were very much an emotional replacement for a family in the same way that horses became later.

'Strat was never motivated by money or commercialism. He was dedicated to whatever he did. He didn't rave often, but when he did it was worth listening to. He believed in what the band wanted and he would be tolerant accordingly. Without that period of development they would never have been able to achieve or to keep what they have got.'

Within two weeks the group were signed to Charisma and offered a wage of £15 a week. Such was their naïvety that drummer John Mayhew insisted they could manage on £10 a week, and their wage was dropped accordingly. As well as being their record company boss, Strat had also become their de facto manager, an unusual combination in the music business, often leading to a conflict of interests. Their wage meant the group could at least leave the cottage and find digs of their own.

The group continued gigging, becoming an established act at Friars in Aylesbury, a market town forty miles northwest of London in an area similar to their native Surrey. They were paid £10 for their first gig at Friars by promoter David Stopps. 'That's probably what they were worth at the time because they were practically unknown,' said Stopps, who upped it to £30 after that because of their good reception. Long after the demise of Friars in the late seventies, Stopps became the manager of Howard Jones.

The band were still left to organize their own gigs. Gabriel's signature is on the contract for those first Friars gigs, proving that he was still the group hustler. Friars featured joss sticks and bubble lightshows, and the audience was seated and earnest, they were not there to dance. Stopps also put on Black Sabbath, Blodwyn Pig, Keith Relf's Renaissance and Atomic Rooster at Friars.

'I suppose Genesis took more of an intellectual approach compared to the other bands,' said Stopps. 'I was very, very keen to see them succeed, that's why I put them on scores of times.' Communal life and a gruelling touring schedule strained all the friendships within the band. But Ant was suffering most because of his stage fright. 'We stopped communicating. We had seen too much of each other, so a lot of us stopped talking. I went through two months of extremely unpleasant stuff, being too frightened to talk to the others. My main memory of the gig at Ronnie Scott's was being so nervous at the start, and the relief at the end when we got through. It was like I'd got to the top of Everest,' said Ant. 'When Pete found out I had been going through bad times he made an attempt in his own slightly stuttering way to help. He would say, "You must tell them things are wrong." He seemed to bend over backwards to accommodate me.'

The group rehearsed material for their next album at the Angel pub in Godalming in early summer 1970. They had been forced to come off the road for three weeks because Ant had bronchial pneumonia. A year earlier, while doing his 'A' levels, Ant had suffered from glandular fever, and he now considered leaving the band. 'I did feel a bit guilty that I was letting them down. I thought, I did love this when I started, maybe all this stuff will pass away. But secretly I knew it wouldn't.'

He decided to carry on and after rehearsals and some more gigs went with them into Trident Studios off Wardour Street in June and July 1970 to record *Trespass*, their first Charisma album, produced by John Anthony. Two months in a studio was then regarded as an inordinately long time to spend making a record.

The most influential tracks were 'Stagnation', distinctive for its opening dreamy, soft, acoustic, 12-string feel, mainly the work of Phillips and Rutherford, becoming progressively aggressive, richly textured with organ, flute, and guitars. It set the pattern for their work for the next few years. 'The Knife', mainly the work of Banks and Gabriel, was firmly in the up-tempo progressive rock mould, the violent imagery of Gabriel's lyrics backed by a whole range of military drum beats, electric guitar and swirling organ.

The tension of making the album had affected all the relationships in the group with none of them able to openly communicate their feelings. Ant, unhappy with the album production, felt the strain most and decided to quit the band. Rather than face all of them, he chose his oldest friend, Mike, to pass the news on.

Tony Banks credits Ant as being perhaps the most dominant early member of the group responsible for the musical direction and the introduction of their then unique 12-string guitar. Banks felt the group might not survive Ant's departure. 'That was the most difficult period for me,' said Tony. 'We thought there was a kind of magic in the four of us writing, the original format. I thought once he left we wouldn't be able to do it, and I was almost surprised when we decided to carry on because the group hadn't been that successful at that point and there were other things to do, like my going back to university.

'Richard was very much a friend of Ant's at the time and Richard said there was no way we should stop just because Ant was leaving, and it made me think, here was Ant's friend saying that. Mike and Pete really wanted to carry on.

'We talked about it and I suggested we ought to get a new drummer because if we were going to have a restart we should have a fresh start in that direction as well, maybe the three of us should get together and audition guitarists and drummers.' They were all unhappy with John Mayhew's performance on the album; he had problems keeping the correct time, and instead of being the rhythmic lead tended to follow the other instruments.

In September 1970 an advertisement was placed in *Melody Maker*: 'Tony Stratton Smith requires drummer sensitive to acoustic music, and acoustic 12-string guitarist.' The advertisement was spotted by nineteen-year-old Phil Collins, drummer in the group Flaming Youth which was then disintegrating. Collins was known at the Marquee Club in Wardour Street where Strat could often be found by the bar with his friend Jack Barrie, managing director of the club. As a schoolboy Collins helped arrange seats at the Marquee so he could get in free. He asked Strat which of his groups had put in the advertisement. 'Strat said he could not get him the job, but he could get him an audition,' said Barrie.

Collins spoke to Peter Gabriel and was invited to Deep Pool for the auditions, travelling to Chobham. Collins was by his own admission at the other end of the evolutionary scale to the rest of Genesis. He was a gregarious likely lad who had been to grammar and stage school. When he played the Artful Dodger in the West End production of Lionel Bart's musical *Oliver!* he had not acted that much out of character.

'My first impression was, this is a bit of all right,' said Collins. 'They had a swimming pool and the piano was out on the patio and the drum kits were under these umbrellas. It was very different from what I had been used to, so were the people. Peter was, and he still is, an uhmmer and an aaher.'

Collins and a few other drummers were played excerpts from *Trespass*. 'For some reason what stuck in my mind was a Crosby, Stills and Nash feeling. I think it was the warmth of the music and some of the harmonies.' Collins was then invited to take a dip in the pool while the others were auditioned. He was keen to get the job. 'I just thought it was a group that was working, and I had just spent a year and a half in a group that didn't work at all hardly, apart from rehearsing an awful lot.' After the audition the customary vote was taken, with Rutherford against, and Banks and Gabriel for Collins. Peter phoned Phil that evening to offer him the job.

Collins was given his first week's wage, a £10 note, at the Charisma office and told to take a two-week holiday before playing a note as part of Genesis. They returned to rehearse and write at the Maltings, a run down oasthouse in Farnham, near Peter's parents, and were put up by Captain Rutherford, Mike's father. Phil found himself plunged into an unfamiliar, intense atmosphere with Peter and Tony having arguments and temper tantrums. 'I didn't really know what was going on,' said Phil. But Phil was approachable, cracked jokes and was not averse to putting his arms around someone. He helped bind the group together. 'I was made to feel welcome so I quickly felt at home there.'

Banks' role had become more demanding on Ant's departure. He tried to make up for the lack of guitar by playing the electric piano through a fuzzbox. They took on guitarist Mick Barnard at the suggestion of David Stopps, but he was not up to standard and left after a few months.

*Trespass* was released in October 1970, attracting some favourable press comment, but sold poorly. 'One could bring out all the adjectives for this. It is tasteful, subtle and refined, but with enough spunk in the music to prevent the album becoming an over-indulgent wallow in insipidity,' was Michael Watts' generous opinion in *Melody Maker*.

The band were still playing gigs. In their search for a guitarist Peter saw an advertisement in *Melody Maker* in December 1970. 'Guitarist/writer seeks receptive musicians determined to strive beyond existing stagnant music forms.' Peter phoned and invited Steve Hackett, who advertised regularly, to see them play at the Lyceum in Covent Garden.

They met backstage and Peter and Tony arranged to visit
Steve at his parents' council flat in Victoria. Two painfully shy
people were confronted with yet another similar character.
Steve played guitar while his brother John played flute. His
interest in songwriting, his recent purchase of a 12-string
guitar, and his attempts to play unusual chords got him the
job.

'I sensed that Pete was the prime mover in the band, he
was the driving force,' said Hackett. 'If we were at an airport
Pete would go to the nearest phone and be on the case.' But
Peter was also renowned for his lateness and tendency to go
missing in-between breaks, constantly infuriating the band and
road manager.

Steve Hackett was disturbed to find that Mike Rutherford,
then twenty, was in bed suffering from a stomach ulcer brought
on by the tensions of the group. Steve found it painful to play
in public for his first six months in Genesis. He was so nervous
at his first gig he did not realize the set had ended because he
was concentrating so hard on remembering his part.

The Lyceum date had been promoted by father and son,
John and Tony Smith. John had arranged the first Beatles
tour. Three years later Tony Smith would become Genesis'
manager. With their help, Tony Stratton Smith devised the
Charisma package tour for January and February 1971 in his
first major attempt to push Genesis, Van Der Graaf Generator
and Lindisfarne and their new albums. It became known as the
'Six Bob Tour' because all seats were 30p.

'The predominant feeling was very much of a family. But
that could include a degree of sibling rivalry,' said Peter
Hammill. They vied for the top of the bill depending on the
strength of their local following.

The first concert at the Lyceum on 24 January was
reviewed by Michael Watts in *Melody Maker*. 'It is not too far-
fetched to say that at least one of the three bands who appeared
at the Lyceum on Sunday will become a major force in the

rock world . . . Genesis emerged with the greatest honours and audience acclaim. They are harder and more incisive than the delicacy and refinement of their album would suggest, and their vocalist, Peter Gabriel, frantic in his tambourine shaking, his voice hoarse and urgent, is a focus for all the band's energy.'

Despite much toil and friction during the year the band were failing to break through to a wide public. Tony Banks described that period as one of their most difficult. 'It was a productive time,' said Banks. 'When we weren't talking about music Peter and I were as close as we had ever been. But within the music we tended to argue a lot.' In the battles between Peter and Tony, Mike could usually side with Tony, while newcomers Phil and Steve avoided taking sides.

In December 1970 Peter and Jill had become engaged and they were married on 17 March, 1971. Jill and Peter could at last live together and moved into a dingy basement flat in Wandsworth. The newlywed Mr and Mrs Gabriel found their time together was interrupted by the group's relentlessly increasing work schedule. 'In the first two years of our marriage it was him being away and coming back very late at night, and one night he didn't come back. I was actually standing and waiting at the gate until about two. And suddenly something said in my head, "He's dead! He's actually been killed!" And I actually came to terms with the idea that he had died. The doorbell rang about five and it was Mike Rutherford, and I said, "It's OK. I know what's happened." And he said, "He's in the car. He's broken his leg. He jumped off stage and broke his leg."'

Peter took his running jump in June 1971 at Friars, Aylesbury performing 'The Knife' as the finale. 'Peter got so carried away that he ran from the back of the stage to the front and leaped into the audience from a great height,' remembered David Stopps. 'I suppose it was the forerunner of his being carried around the audience.

'That first time he leaped headlong like he was going to

heaven, or something, a huge leap, and flattened about three people, and unfortunately landed very badly and broke his ankle. It was the end of the set, and I remember him being carried off in absolute agony to the dressing room. We called the ambulance. I remember thinking, "Oh my God, he really is hurt." He went to the hospital. It was very badly broken and they put a pin in it. And it's there to this day. Every now and then he gets a twinge and he says, "Oh that was the old Friars leg." He wrote a little article for our Friars magazine after that, and he said, "I shall never forget Friars. I got the best screw I ever had when I did Friars and I shall carry it with me till the day I die."'

Peter still insisted on performing odd dates in a wheelchair, using an upturned broom as a crutch. His leg was badly set by the doctors who treated him, and a few weeks later he was sent by his parents to a private specialist who had to rebreak and reset it.

The group by now had a small band of music press journalists who were championing them. Jerry Gilbert of *Sounds* was one of the first to interview them after he gave the *Trespass* album a favourable review. Genesis bore the trade-marks of British progressive rock: elongated solos, Gabriel's stabs at playing flute, tambourine and bass drum, and surreal lyrics that hinted at more depth than they contained.

'I was hooked on their music, they were experimental and different,' said Gilbert. 'Off stage Peter would stutter and stammer. You would have these great pregnant pauses. He was a very nervous person. He used to think in incredible depth when answering a question, however simplistic the question might be. There'd be these long tracks of time before the answer would come, and maybe a regal "no" at the end. He was very much the spokesman of the band. Nobody pushed themselves forward. There was no natural front man.'

For the next album, *Nursery Cryme*, they spent the summer

of 1971 at Luxford House, Crowborough in Surrey, Tony Stratton Smith's country home. They found writing difficult; Tony missed Ant's input though there were some songs dating back to before Ant had left.

Gabriel's lyrics for 'The Muscial Box' inspired the album title and the cover by Paul Whitehead with a Victorian girl staring menacingly with her croquet mallet swung over her shoulder. On the lawn are several severed heads, the Henry of the song. A manor house and some surreal images are dotted around. The croquet lawn and manor house were inspired by Coxhill, Gabriel's grandfather's house. The song encapsulated the early image of the band. Other songs are more fantastical, like 'The Return of the Giant Hogweed', about a killer weed that threatens to wipe out mankind, and 'The Fountain of Salmacis', drawn from the companion to mythology that Gabriel and Banks possessed.

The songs contained tragedy, lust, and comedy. It was all an attempt to break new lyrical as well as musical ground. Producer John Anthony and Peter experimented with different microphone techniques. It marked the start of Gabriel's never-ending search for studio innovation.

When the album was finished the group felt *Nursery Cryme* showed little creative advance. Though references to Gabriel's childhood experiences could be gleaned in 'Musical Box', the album was full of fey stories with bland observations on life that promised great depth simply because they were obscure. Released in November 1971, *Nursery Cryme*, like *Trespass*, was recorded at Trident Studios.

It was Anthony's last album for the group, to his great disappointment. But his last recording came the following summer with the single 'Happy The Man', recorded at Richard Branson's new studios at The Manor, in Oxfordshire. 'I remember Tony turning round and saying, "I really hate that," to one lyric. That was the first time I had seen that side of the band. Peter took it all very personally. He hid his light under a bushel because of peer pressure.' Anthony certainly never hid his own light. 'At that time everything I was doing was worldbeating and better than the Beatles,' he said.

Anthony, the Charisma house producer, befriended Peter and Jill more than the rest of the band. He had experimented regularly with LSD, his grandmother had been a spiritualist and he had read up on the subject. One night Anthony went with Jill and Peter to her parents' flat at the Old Barracks in Kensington Palace. They were in a cold room decorated in glaring turquoise and purple at the top of the house. 'Jill and I were having a conversation about power and strength and will,' said Anthony. 'Suddenly I was aware that the whole room's atmosphere had changed. Jill had gone into some sort of trance. Suddenly the windows blew in, followed by extreme cold, followed by this psychic phenomenon.

'Neither Peter, Jill or I were doing drugs or drinking. I realized it was a basic manifestation. I have seen it before, the room was full of cold astral smoke, psychic ether. The thing that scared me was that it started moving in the form of a tourbillion – the great wheel that projects spirits into the astrosphere. It is nothing to do with death. It is a phenomenon that can occur with people with strong psyches. If you go through one there is a good chance that if you come back you will never be the same. It is associated with high spiritual fervour, not a happy frenzy, a very disturbed state of mind.

'Peter didn't know what to do. He grabbed a couple of candlesticks and crossed them and put them over her. Then Jill went into a seizure, thrashing around, rending her clothes, that's when she started speaking in tongues and not making sense.' The noise disturbed Jill's sister Sally and her parents who came to see what the fuss was about and comfort Jill.

Anthony thought Jill's one experience with LSD was partly to blame. 'She was susceptible to a lot of metaphysical garbage.'

He also believed Peter's personality had a lot to do with the incident, something about transmitting and receiving psychic energy.

Soon after that Jill received a mysterious note full of ritualistic symbols and dates. 'She didn't know where she got it from,' said Anthony. 'Somebody was trying to frighten her. I read the note several times and I just blew it off, using a lot of knowledge I have regarding ritualized magic.' Jill and Peter thought the note might have come from an ex-girlfriend of Anthony's who had dabbled in the occult, but Anthony dismissed the possibility.

'I feel that John is very responsible,' said Jill. 'Peter and John told me the story afterwards. I have no memory of it, only of coming to and feeling ghastly and frightened. I guess it made me believe that there are other forces, or whatever, both good and evil. I think it is very stupid to dabble in it, and I never have since.'

Peter admitted he was extremely frightened. 'I saw this very old face in Jill, there was this sense that it wasn't her there. I do believe in spirit possession because I have seen it in other cultures. Whether the mind is creating it or not, something is going on which we do not understand,' says Peter.

'I tried calming her down and holding her, but nothing seemed to get through. It was very much like a clichéd horror film. The window flew open, there was this horrible coldness and we got the shivers. I think my only training for matters of that sort have come from watching Hammer horror films, so I did my best Christopher Lee. I made a cross with candlesticks, which helped, I don't know why.' The incident inspired 'Supper's Ready', the epic track that takes up the entire second side of *Foxtrot*, the subsequent Genesis album. 'I experienced a sense of evil at that point,' said Peter. 'I don't know how much of this was going on inside my head and how much was actually happening, but it was an experience I could not forget and was the starting point for a song about the struggle between good and evil.'

*Nursery Cryme* did not sell well in the UK. The group played their first foreign concert in Brussels in January 1972 in front of 200 people and soon after learnt *Nursery Cryme* was at Number 1 in the Belgian charts. In April they visited Italy for a week's tour where the album got to Number 4.

The British press was not interested in writing about the group, and the public was not too bothered about listening to them. Gabriel followed his instincts, going against his innate reserve, in an attempt to draw attention to himself and the group. He shaved the top of his head in a sort of reverse Mohican. The look was premiered on a miserable wet day in May 1971 at the Lincoln Festival where they shared the bill with the Beach Boys, the Average White Band, Monty Python and Slade. 'I was wearing an Egyptian-style heavy jewellery collar and cuffs I had spotted in Soho and quite a lot of heavy black eyeliner,' says Gabriel. The crowd of 50,000 were indifferent to Gabriel's efforts and Genesis' music.

David Stopps tried to boost the flagging interest in the band by organizing a Genesis Convention. Friars was too small, so he hired the Town Hall at Watford, Aylesbury's big neighbour, not famed for being in the vanguard of artistic innovation. 'I thought they were getting nowhere. I honestly thought they were going to split up at the time,' said Stopps. 'Watford was really too big for them, but I wanted to push them forward into some progress.'

The advertisement in *Melody Maker* was a classic. 'Home Counties Genesis Freaks Unite, Your Time Has Come To Shine,' it proclaimed, and quoted 'Visions Of Angels': 'Visions of Angels all around dance in the sky. Leaving me here forever. Goodbye.' Fans came from London and in coaches from Aylesbury. Rosettes with 'Genesis '72' emblazoned on them were given out. They looked like the type that litter gym-khanas, though the idea was to imitate a presidential campaign.

The event was also designed to attract press attention, succeeding with Chris Welch, from *Melody Maker*.

'Their music and attitude have changed, improved, and progressed, until they have reached that most exciting time for all groups, when they have not quite cracked the publicity barrier, but are enjoying the much more worthwhile and regarding acclaim of genuinely appreciative audiences...' wrote Welch. 'The feeling of excitement of a band that is happening musically, and knows it, is only rarely experienced. That feeling is happening now, with Genesis.'

Strat's first choice to produce *Foxtrot* was Bob Potter, who had worked with Bob Dylan. But after a week he decided he did not like Genesis' music and walked out. By now the group were capable of producing themselves, and needed someone mainly to help them edit. David Hitchcock met Strat in the Marquee and was offered the job. He had produced Caravan's 'In The Land Of Grey And Pink' and the experience of putting together seemingly unconnected pieces of music came in useful when Strat hired him for Genesis.

The atmosphere at Island Records' Basing Street Studios was fraught, though not overtly aggressive, according to Hitchcock. The arguments were mainly still between Tony and Peter, who tried to keep the rest of the group out of the studio while he recorded the vocals for 'Supper's Ready'. He felt self-conscious and also wanted to try out a part he knew Tony would object to because it meant editing his keyboard solo. 'Tony was outraged that I'd gone over his sacred solo,' said Peter. 'However, the rest of the band were really exicted by what I'd done and the popular vote was always the deciding factor. These were the absurd manipulating tactics which we were all guilty of – but probably me more than any other.'

'Supper's Ready' told the tale of that night at Kensington Palace, building into a universal struggle of good and evil and closing with references to the Book of Revelation. Tony Banks warned it should not be taken too seriously, a response to the endless pleas of fans desperate to know what it all meant. 'I felt it was a chronicle of some sort of adventure of the soul, this fundamental struggle between life and death and good and evil. At the end when I was singing my heart out I did feel as if I was singing for my life,' he said.

The album was generally more focused in subject matter than their earlier material. 'Get 'Em Out By Friday' saw the group's first stab at social comment, in this case a ruthless landlord. There was still an excess of florid language and imagery, particularly on the science-fiction inspired 'Watcher of the skies' by Tony Banks and Mike Rutherford.

The group were due to go off on yet another tour from late September through October 1972 to coincide with the release of *Foxtrot*. But Peter was concerned that they were not getting the attention he felt they deserved in the press. Just before the tour he cycled from his new flat in Notting Hill Gate to the Charisma office in Brewer Street, Soho, for a meeting with press officer Glen Colson and Paul Conroy who ran the Charisma Agency booking the group's dates.

'Peter was really frustrated. The group were getting reasonable money, but I don't think he thought they were going very far,' said Conroy. 'Glen said to him, "Well, look, if you're gonna want to get in the music papers, you're gonna have to do something a bit outrageous." So we dreamed up the idea of getting more theatrical.'

Artist Paul Whitehead's cover for the album depicted a woman's body in a red dress with a fox's head standing on ice floating in the sea, with numerous other surreal images including red jacketed horse riders with monstrous faces. Peter found himself a fox's head and borrowed an expensive Ossie Clark red dress from Jill that he ruined. On 28 September at the Stadium, a venue in Dublin used for boxing matches, Peter premiered his new image, going off stage during the instrumental section of 'Musical Box' and returning for the chorus in costume. It became a feature of the tour. The theatrical effects had their desired aim, and for the first time Genesis appeared on the front cover of *Melody Maker* and doubled their earnings overnight from £300 to £600 a show.

Rock theatrics were not original to Genesis. David Bowie and Alice Cooper were starting the trend towards glam rock at the same time. Gabriel said he was trying for a more humorous and surreal approach, and did not want the theatrics to dominate the music. He told the rest of the group he was going to put on the costume. Anything that meant deflecting the attention of the audience away from them suited Mike, Steve and Tony, who preferred anonymity. But it eventually backfired and was a source of resentment for them all. 'There was a tendency to put the credit for things like "Supper's Ready" at Peter's door, which was just ridiculous because it was a group-written piece,' said Tony. 'It contained a lot of stuff that I wrote in university, so I was just really pissed off. That sort of thing made you feel antagonistic towards the guy himself, which was a shame, because we still got on very well as friends.'

*Foxtrot* was favourably received by the press on its release in October 1972. It went into the album charts at Number 12, Genesis' first real UK success, helped by their new high press profile.

The stage show had now developed a unique character. Pivotal to this were the surreal stories that Peter told in between songs. Regarded by some fans as artistic pointers to the meaning of the songs, the reality was that they were developed to fill in the gaps left by constant equipment breakdowns that afflicted the first part of Genesis' career.

Their first American dates were booked for December. They warmed up in Boston before playing the Philharmonic Hall, since renamed the Avery Fisher Hall, in New York. Strat planned the New York gig as a PR exercise. Playing a prestigious, unusual venue normally used for classical concerts would, he hoped, get them valuable publicity in the States that would not come if they just started slogging around.

The concert was a technical disaster, but received a rave review in *Cashbox* magazine and a favourable response from DJs who had been flown in. Peter's stories proved lifesavers while the various electrical hitches were sorted out, though some of the American audience thought the tales were the product of a sick mind.

An abridged version of this story appeared on the cover of the *Genesis Live* album released in August 1973. After setting the scene on a busy tube train stuck in the middle of a tunnel, Gabriel went on, 'The young lady in the green trouser suit got up in the middle of the carriage and slowly started to undo the buttons on her top. Then she peeled it off and dropped it on the floor. She repeated this process with her trousers, her blouse, her little panties and her brassiere. Having taken off her shoes this left her totally naked. She then moved one hand down right in between her legs and began to fiddle about until she caught hold of a strange metal object; this was a zip.

'She then very meticulously proceeded to unzip the zip, through her body, through her breasts, right through the middle of her face and down the back of her spine. Then she lifted her fingers to the crack the zip had left, beginning to work them very slowly and carefully through the crack, separating it and then dividing her body into two neat little pieces, letting it drop on the floor, splat! However, right where she had been standing, there was now a golden shimmering rod, hovering just above the ground.

'Well, the rest of the carriage had been completely silent but this was really too much for a large middle-aged lady who was wearing a green poodle. "Stop this! It's disgusting!" she cried. The golden rod disappeared, leaving the green trouser suit on a hanger, with a cleaning ticket. On the cleaning ticket was a message. "Must fly – supper's ready." That should have been the cue for the song to start, but Peter had to improvise some more, taking pictures of the audience with his Kodak Instamatic, before they were ready to go.

In February they played the Rainbow Theatre in Finsbury Park, then London's premier rock venue, erecting a giant white gauze backdrop. The fox's head was still there for 'Musical Box'. It was later replaced by a rubber mask of an old man. More bizarre costumes followed, including batwings and a multicoloured cape for 'Watcher of the Skies'.

Peter put on a crown of thorns for 'The Guaranteed Eternal Sanctuary Man'; painted Day-Glo around his eyes to glow in ultra-violet light; wore a daisy headdress for the squeaky 'A flower?' before the start of 'Willow Farm'; and donned a red geometric box headdress and black cape – to represent the anti-christ – for 'Apocalypse in 9/8' on 'Supper's Ready'. The finale to 'Supper's Ready' saw him toss off his headdress and cape to reveal an angelic sparkly white jumpsuit. And on a few occasions he held aloft an ultra-violet tube as he sang the final line of 'Supper's Ready', 'Take them to the new Jerusalem'.

In a few months Genesis had gone from support act to headliner. Their UK tour in February 1973 was followed by a brief American tour to try to establish a firmer bridgehead on the other side of the Atlantic. They were now established as one of the top British rock attractions. Inspired by the success of their theatrics, they planned more ambitious and expensive extravaganzas. After two years of constant touring they took time off over the summer of 1973 to write and record their next album, *Selling England By The Pound*, which was released in October and reached Number 3 in the UK charts.

The group were frustrated with the time it took them to write the album, and had mixed feelings about how it turned out. They were already fragmenting as writers. Tony Banks presented a complete song with 'Firth of Fifth', including the lyrics. Despite the album's technical superiority to their past work, and a far more skilful musicianship, they felt it did not convey their spirit as well as *Foxtrot*. The album did include their first hit single, 'I Know What I Like (In Your Ward-robe)'. It was a favourite with fans for its singalong tune and Gabriel's funny walk, yokel hat and straw between his teeth, and his impersonation of a lawnmower.

Their contract with Charisma Records came up for renewal in 1973. They were approached by Chrysalis Records, the most successful of the independent labels. The group felt vulnerable handling negotiations without a manager. They were not convinced Chrysalis believed in them and stayed with Charisma on a better royalty. Strat advised them there was now too big a conflict of interest between his roles as record company boss and manager.

'Genesis approached me in late 1971 and said would I like to manage them. I said I was far too busy,' says Tony Smith, then their promotor. With his father John and partner Harvey Goldsmith he was the leading promoter in the country, mounting shows by the Rolling Stones, Led Zeppelin, the Who and Pink Floyd.

'In Glasgow on the 1973 *Selling England By The Pound* tour as promoter I had to cancel the show. The band were on stage but couldn't play because there was 400 volts of power running through everything. The organization was totally chaotic. They asked me again to manage them. By that time I decided that I wanted to get into something else, I found promoting a bit boring.

'The first thing I did as manager was sack the road crew. I fired the lot and started again. At the time I thought they were about £100,000 in the red, but it was probably closer to £250,000. At 1973 values, that was a frightening amount.' Smith officially began managing Genesis while they toured America at the end of 1973. The shows culminated at the Roxy in Los Angeles at Christmas.

Smith immediately set about putting order into their tour set-ups, and was dismayed to find their mounting debt to Charisma due to losses from touring was approaching a frightening £200,000. The chaos was the same in America to which they returned for a tour culminating in their first West Coast appearance at the Roxy in Los Angeles in December 1973 for six shows. Peter's new costumes included a black jumpsuit, a balaclava with cut out eyes and mouth, and a stick for 'The Battle of Epping Forest', and full Britannia regalia including a trident for 'Dancing with the Moonlit Knight'. The audience reception and reviews in the States were becoming ecstatic. *Selling England By The Pound* became their first album to enter the US charts. At the final Roxy dates Peter dressed as Father Christmas, despite a ninety-degree LA temperature, and took some helium to give him a Mickey Mouse voice at the end of the show to sing the sixties comic song 'They're Coming To Take Me Away Ha-Haaa!' 'I had hiccups for four or five days. It started off as very funny, but I couldn't sleep and it started to haunt me. I spent a lot of time upside down, which I think helped,' said Peter.

They returned to England for three dates at the Drury Lane Theatre in January 1974. Peter's assertion that the theatrics should not dominate the music was looking less convincing. Strapped to a harness he flew through the air for the finale of 'Supper's Ready'. It did not work so well in New York when the wire was caught around his neck. He waved his arms at the operator who was convinced this was part of the per-formance. Gabriel narrowly avoided being hanged by freeing himself a moment before the cue to raise the wire.

Later in the year they were voted Top Stage Band in the 1974 *NME* Readers' Poll above the Who and Pink Floyd. Their lives now seemed mapped out for them. Tony Smith took care of business, and the group just had to concern itself with the machinery of rock and roll. Yet another heavy touring schedule was set up for the first part of 1974 to include Europe and eleven weeks in America. But Peter was beginning to feel creatively stifled. He was tired of making music by committee, subjecting all contentious parts to the group's democratic vote.

By his own admission he had to become Machiavellian in his machinations to get his own way in the group, often facing opposition from Tony.

Impending parenthood also put pressure on Peter. In March 1974, in a brief break from touring, he and Jill moved into their cottage outside Bath. The group still found it difficult to express their personal worries to each other. Public school inhibitions lingered on and Peter did not reveal his doubts to his colleagues.

In June 1974 the group started rehearsals for their next album at Headley Grange in Surrey. Peter was interviewed by Jerry Gilbert for *Sounds*. 'I want to take more of a back seat role,' he said. 'I hope that there will be opportunities to work with other artists this year.' It was the first public indication that Peter was dissatisfied and needed another creative outlet. He had already written some songs with Martin Hall and wanted other people to record them. Later in the same interview he said, 'We are going into our new album with a strong feeling that a change is about to take place.'

Peter insisted on having a free hand to write the lyrics for the new album, but first he had to argue his case. 'I persuaded the band to go for a concept – I really had something in mind, which was *The Lamb* – but we had to go through this democratic procedure of saying, "Let's all submit ideas and let's work on the best one." I know I probably was getting difficult and obstinate as I tend to get if I'm put in a corner. We were all unfair manipulators. But Tony Banks and I were better at it than the others. Phil wouldn't come into the arguments, he tended to chicken out.'

Phil disagreed. 'It's funny how different people survey different things. I was usually on Pete's side. He would be hoping for my support because he felt Mike would be supporting Tony. Peter's a very stubborn, bloody-minded, obstinate person, and very single-minded. The more you say black the more he will say white is right.

'We would argue about anything, not just music,' said Phil. 'We used to collect Green Shield stamps when we pulled up for petrol. When you got twelve books you got a free tea-set or something. Tony was quite intense about his collecting Green Shield stamps, and there used to be almost fistfights as to who got the free Green Shield stamps. On the way to and from gigs there would be three or four fill-ups and you could actually do half a book.'

Peter had doubts about his place in the group for some time. 'Band politics are always fraught with ego struggles,' said Peter. 'So on bad days you are thinking, "Is this worth it?" and on good days, "This is wonderful." My wanting to leave was a slow process.' He thought his chance had come with the offer to work in Hollywood.

William Friedkin, who directed *The Exorcist* and *The French Connection*, was in the audience at one of the Christmas 1973 Los Angeles concerts. He thought Peter's surreal stories in between numbers showed film scriptwriting potential and invited Peter to visit him on a Hollywood film set. Six months later, soon after rehearsals had started for *The Lamb*, Friedkin sent Peter a telegram and asked if he was interested in writing a film script. Tony Banks insisted Peter should put the group first.

'I was planning to do it after *The Lamb*, but things got pretty black,' said Peter. '*The Exorcist* was an enormous film at that point, so all sorts of doors were opening for Friedkin in Hollywood. He had this idea of bringing in his own team that had never worked in Hollywood. There was a guy called Philippe Druillet who co-founded *Heavy Metal* magazine and delivered it round Paris, and Tangerine Dream. I was to be the ideas man for the script.'

When the group learnt of Peter's departure they thought about auditioning for a new singer and started drawing up a shortlist while Peter frantically tried to get Friedkin to guarantee the film project. Friedkin backed away when he realized he could be responsible for splitting the band. Jill was eight months pregnant and Peter was left insecure and out of a job with no obvious means of supporting his new family.

Just a few days after Peter left, Tony Smith told the group he thought he could get Peter back if they wanted him. They did and Peter returned. But Peter was not the only person who felt hemmed in that summer. Mike Rutherford got back together with Anthony Phillips to help him record a solo album. Both Phil Collins and Steve Hackett had already threatened to leave before, but they were talked out of it by the other members and Tony Stratton Smith.

Peter felt uncomfortable in run down Headley Grange, a house previously used by Led Zeppelin to write *Houses of the Holy*. Peter was disturbed by rumours it was haunted. There was a cold atmosphere between him and the rest of the group. 'The band were rehearsing in one room and Pete was working on the lyrics and melodies in another. There were long periods when the band didn't actually come together,' said Steve. 'I felt that the tension was really very, very strong. It was the closest I had ever come to going over the brink myself.' Steve was also going through the break-up of his first marriage.

Headley Grange was a throwback to the days of Richard Macphail's cottage. There was no telephone in the run down house and he had to cycle down the hill to the coinbox to talk to Jill.

The rest of the group went along with Peter's insistence that he should write all the lyrics, though their resentment surfaced later. 'The story had a lot of faults, but there aren't many books written by committee,' said Peter. 'I think you need leadership in a lot of artistic work because committees spend a lot of time not being bold and going for compromise solutions. You need singular vision.'

Though Peter was clear about the idea, he had few lyrics prepared, a problem that dogged the entire recording of the album. After rehearsals the group moved to Pembrokeshire where they rented a house and a cowshed converted into an ad hoc studio with softboard. Genesis wanted to get away from a normal studio atmosphere and acoustics. Soon after the group moved to Wales, Jill went into hospital in London for the traumatic birth of Anna-Marie on 26 July 1974. Peter had to commute between London and Wales, much to the displeasure of the rest of the band, concerned about the delay in his delivery of the lyrics.

The group have since regretted their unsympathetic attitude. 'The band needed a lot of commitment at that point, and he was the first to not be able to do that,' said Tony Banks. 'I can totally understand now, but at the time I couldn't, because I didn't have any children, and you don't realize what that does to you. Maybe he just matured quicker for that reason.'

In between the fraught moments Peter started experimenting to get different vocal effects. He got producer John Burns to record in a toilet and another cowshed two miles down the road. Peter was still plagued by his perennial voice problems, and could frequently be found standing on his head in the studio control room in the belief it would help. He also came equipped with herbal remedies to stop his voice from going. Peter played Burns some songs he had written on his own.

'I would say, "Couldn't we use some of these tracks?" but he said politically it wouldn't work out because they wanted to jointly write the music,' said Burns.

'*The Lamb* was intended to be like a *Pilgrim's Progress*,' said Peter, 'an adventure through which one gets a better understanding of self – the transformation theme. I was trying to give it a street slant, and that was before punk happened. I felt an energy in that direction, and it seemed that prancing around in fairyland was rapidly becoming obsolete.'

Rael, the character around which *The Lamb Lies Down On Broadway* revolves, was as far removed from fairyland as possible. He was a streetwise Puerto Rican from the ghettos of the

Bronx, and provided a transatlantic antidote to the Englishness of *Selling England By The Pound* and much of Genesis' previous work. Rael was Gabriel's made-up name. It was similar enough to the popular Spanish name Raoul to fit in with the character, but English enough to suggest both reality and fantasy.

At the time Peter was credited with the major contribution on the album. Since then all concerned have stressed their own role in what is Genesis' most controversal and for many most inspiring album.

The lyrics were mainly Peter's, but he felt he was never given enough credit for his contribution to the music as well. He regards his composition 'The Capret Crawlers' as one of his favourite melodies and the title track's chorus was also his composition with the use of the *On Broadway* theme.

Though Rael was portrayed by Gabriel on stage as a punk wearing leather jacket and jeans, the imagery of the lyrics owes more to the supernatural than subways and sidewalks. Rael's journey through his subconscious to eventual self-discovery includes a confrontation with death, 'The Supernatural Anaesthetist'; falling in love, 'The Lamia' (which are female demons in classical mythology); and sensual gratification, 'The Colony of Slippermen'. There follows a nasty castration followed by the comical theft of the dismembered organ by a bird, and his final self-realization.

The group was annoyed at Peter's delay in delivering the lyrics. But to him it was still rushed and he was not able to revise the story as much as he would have liked, which explains why some of the lyrics are so obscure. Gabriel has always been unwilling to give a precise explanation of the lyrics. Often there would be no point because much of it did not have a direct meaning other than the interplay, feel and sound of words. The understanding was largely in the feeling of the performance rather than the literal examination of the words.

The bulk of the album was recorded in Wales, but Peter's vocals were put down in Island Studios in Notting Hill, where everyone else was excluded from the studio. Just as the album was nearing completion Steve Hackett severed a tendon and nerve in his thumb when he crushed a wine glass in his hand. It was indicative of the tension that ran throughout the project. He was at a reception after seeing Alex Harvey in concert. 'I hadn't realized I'd done it,' said Steve. 'Funnily enough the same thing happened on the *Bionic Man* TV programme, and he hadn't realized why he had done it, and they had worked out that it was "an involuntary surge of adrenalin due to stress".'

Steve's accident meant the three-week tour of England billed for the autumn of 1974 promoting the new album had to be cancelled. It turned out to be a blessing because the delays in recording would have left the band under-rehearsed. Steve had completed all his overdubs, so the album was not delayed further.

*The Lamb Lies Down On Broadway* took five months to complete, turning into a double album because of the surfeit of material, and was released in November 1974. It was called a 'concept' album when the term concept had already become passé.

*The Lamb Lies Down On Broadway* tour started in America in December 1974. Gabriel spent most of the show wearing the for him uncustomary uniform of leather jacket and trousers. The plot was visualized on three backdrop screens showing 1,000 slides.

Gabriel did not put on his first costume until 'The Lamia', three-quarters of the way through the set. He was covered in a cone-like object bathed in ultra-violet light that was meant to signify the tourbillion, the wheel that catapults beings into the mystical world. 'The Colony of Slippermen' followed, represented on stage by Gabriel in a monstrous, bulbous costume with outsized inflatable genitals. Earlier in the set a dummy of Gabriel had a light shone on it. The prop created the illusion of two Gabriels. However, the roadies played tricks. On one gig the dummy had a banana stuck out of its flies, and on the very last show of the tour the dummy was replaced by a stark naked roadie.

For Jill this was the first time that Peter had exposed his sexuality so strongly on stage. 'He was angry, and it was a very powerful performance. He totally opened himself and put himself on the line to the world, but he wasn't in his relationship with me. I would say to him, "Why can't you be like that for me?" I remember sitting in the audience and feeling completely turned on by this guy who I was married to. But he was not able to be that person outside the stage. And that is what has slowly broken down over the years, being able to take that part of himself into his everyday life.'

Soon after *The Lamb Lies Down On Broadway* tour started Gabriel made his final decision to leave the group, breaking the news to Tony Smith in Cleveland, Ohio.

'I argued the case that maybe it wasn't the right time,' recalls Tony Smith. 'I wasn't angry with him, I argued that he could do what he wanted to do on a solo basis within the band. I was very worried about what would happen to the band and what would happen to Peter.'

*The Lamb Lies Down On Broadway* shows had accentuated the rift and resentments in the band, projecting Gabriel as the star while the rest of the group were static. Gabriel knew he would not be allowed to exert as much creative control on any subsequent album. And he was finding it hard to cope with the added pressures and responsibilities of fatherhood. He wanted to leave almost immediately.

'The rest of the band were told a few days later in Canada. Their position was that we had worked eight years to get this far, and now, finally, we were about to make it and I was pulling the carpet out from underneath it all,' Gabriel told Hugh Fielder of *Sounds*.

'I felt terrible, but I knew that I'd made up my mind, and

I can be really obstinate. I wanted a career where I had the opportunity to take on other projects but the band had this army-like attitude. There was no room to be flexible – if you were in the band you were in it a hundred per cent, or you were out.

'I had no idea of what I wanted to do, but I knew I was sick of rock, the business, and everything about it. I just wanted to get out.' The pressure for Peter to stay from the rest of the group became intense. Tony Stratton Smith even tried to intervene, offering Gabriel extra cash which was refused, but when word of that got around everyone wanted a share.

Eventually Gabriel was persuaded that if he completed the tour of Europe, due to take them through six months to May 1975, there was a good chance the band could pay off their huge debts. He agreed, though when he left the debt was still around £160,000.

'I spent a long time trying to persuade him at various times to reconsider,' said Tony Banks. 'Not so much during that tour as afterwards. I didn't want him to leave, I still thought we were a good creative unit. I knew in my mind that there was going to be a problem when he left with the public and the press. I was wrong about that. There was a degree of unfairness, I thought, that we had built up a thing together and he was the only one who was going to walk away with the chance of a career, I thought the band would fail. It seemed such a big thing at the time, but now I think everyone has to have the freedom to come and go in a band. At that point, at the back of my mind, I did think about leaving myself and doing a solo record.'

Steve Hackett started planning a solo career that led to his *Voyage of the Acolyte* album before leaving Genesis, and Phil Collins considered forsaking Genesis for his jazz-rock band Brand X. But Tony Stratton Smith showed great faith in the ability of the rest of the band to continue without Gabriel. In the end they agreed to work on a new album and try to hold back from announcing Gabriel's departure publicly until as late as possible.

Gabriel played his last gig with Genesis at St Etienne in France in May 1975. He was cheated of an emotional fanfare because St Etienne was meant to be the penultimate date of the tour, but after that appearance the final date was cancelled.

'I had a big lump in my throat when we did the last gigs in France. A big chapter in my life was coming to an end, and I couldn't tell anyone. We had a policy of doing no interviews throughout that tour.

'I felt a real sham, I couldn't tell people what was going on. But I'd made an agreement, because I felt so guilty, that I would keep quiet about it until the band had time to sort themselves out.'

News of Gabriel's departure eventually leaked out in the *NME* in July 1975, seven months after Gabriel had made his decision. The rumours were at first denied by Charisma Records. By then Gabriel had retreated to Bath, and Genesis were writing their next album, *A Trick of the Tail*, destined to be more successful than their previous records with Gabriel. They searched for a new singer to replace Gabriel, but when no one suitable was found thought they might as well try Phil Collins and get a drummer to replace him.

Six weeks after the rumour first appeared in print, Genesis finally admitted Gabriel had left. The following week Gabriel drafted his own statement to the press which he requested should either be published in full or not at all. All the music papers complied and printed it word for word.

I had a dream, eye's dream. Then I had another dream with the body and soul of a rock star. When it didn't feel good I packed it in. Looking back for the musical and non-musical reasons, this is what I came up with:

OUT, ANGELS OUT – an investigation.

The vehicle we had built as a co-op to serve our songwriting became our master and had cooped us up inside the success we had wanted. It affected the attitudes and the spirit of the whole band. The music had not dried up and I still respect the other musicians, but our roles had set in hard. To get an idea through 'Genesis the Big' meant shifting a lot more concrete than before. For any band, transferring the heart from idealistic enthusiasm to professionalism is a difficult operation.

I believe the use of sound and visual images can be developed to do much more than we have done. But on a large scale it needs one clear and coherent direction, which our pseudo-democratic committee system could not provide.

As an artist, I need to absorb a wide variety of experiences. It is difficult to respond to intuition and impulse within the long-term planning that the band needed. I felt I should look at/learn about/develop myself, my creative bits and pieces and pick up a lot of work going on outside music. Even the hidden delights of vegetable growing and community living are beginning to reveal their secrets. I could not expect the band to tie in their schedules with my bondage to cabbages. The increase in money and power, if I had stayed, would have anchored me to the spotlights. It was important to me to give space to my family, which I wanted to hold together, and to liberate the daddy in me.

Although I have seen and learnt a great deal in the last seven years, I found I had begun to look at things as the famous Gabriel, despite hiding my occupation whenever possible, hitching lifts, etc. I had begun to think in business terms; very useful for an often bitten once shy musician, but treating records and audiences as money was taking me away from them. When performing, there were less shivers up and down the spine.

I believe the world has soon to go through a difficult

period of change. I'm excited by some of the areas coming through to the surface which seem to have been hidden away in people's minds. I want to explore and be prepared to be open and flexible enough to respond, not tied in to the old hierarchy.

Much of my psyche's ambitions as 'Gabriel archetypal rock star' have been fulfilled – a lot of the ego-gratification and the need to attract young ladies, perhaps the result of frequent rejection as 'Gabriel acne-struck public school boy'. However, I can still get off playing the star game once in a while.

My future within music, if it exists, will be in as many situations as possible. It's good to see a growing number of artists breaking down the pigeonholes. This is the difference between the profitable, compartmentalized, battery chicken and the free-range. Why did the chicken cross the road anyway?

There is no animosity between myself and the band or management. The decision had been made some time ago and we have talked about our new direction. The reason why my leaving was not announced earlier was because I had been asked to delay until they had found a replacement to plug up the hole. It is not impossible that some of them might work with me on other projects.

The following guesswork has little in common with truth: Gabriel left Genesis.

1) To work in theatre.
2) To make more money as a solo artist.
3) To do a 'Bowie'.
4) To do a 'Ferry'.
5) To do a 'Furry Boa round my neck and hang myself with it'.
6) To go see an institution.
7) To go senile in the sticks.

I do not express myself adequately in interviews and I felt I owed it to the people who have put a lot of love and energy supporting the band to give an accurate picture of my reasons.

The statement fudges the reasons why Gabriel did not announce his decision to leave earlier, for the sake of harmony with his ex-colleagues. In spite of its mystical introduction, the statement manages to convey Gabriel's feelings, and his doubts in 1975 about wishing to continue in the music business.

# CHAPTER FIVE

THE DEPUTY HIGH COMMISSIONER IN SINgapore entertained the Rolling Stones in February 1965 despite their most recent outrage, being arrested for urinating against a service station wall. These were the days of headlines like, 'Would You Let Your Daughter Go Out With A Rolling Stone?'

The group were on a tour of the Far East and Australia and with their manager Andrew Oldham accepted the invitation to lunch with Mr Philip Moore. Mr Moore's two daughters, Sally, then fifteen, and Jill, thirteen, were proud their father was not stuffy like other diplomats, though the family's tolerance ended at Brian Jones asking Sally to go out with him.

The Moores were soon to come to the end of their sevenyear stay in Singapore and return to West Byfleet, Surrey. 'Singapore seems like my childhood and my home. Those years are very strong for me, I feel emotionally involved with them,' remembered Jill.

'The most important thing to me was that we lived with Chinese, Malay and Indian people. The English – the local men were forces English – aren't an exciting memory. The memory is that those three nationalities, races, were incredibly different. As a child it stood out very much to me to have such extremes, and I think that has been the reason I have always been fascinated with people.'

Jill, as the second daughter, was the dreamed of boy who would play rugby for England. Her father was an Oxford Blue in rugby and hockey, and had played rugby for England, and cricket for Oxfordshire.

Since rugby was naturally out of the question, Jill's chosen sport was swimming. She took it seriously from her arrival in Singapore aged six through to the age of eleven. 'I was a sports fanatic. They were training me for the Olympics. Actually I wished to get sick and get out of it. When I saw the backstroke record being threatened I couldn't face the idea of my dad running up and screaming at me. I managed to get a fascinating illness. They never discovered what it was.' Her faked sickness and defeat marked the end of her swimming career.

Jill's parents kept their daughters with them, unlike many diplomatic families who sent their children to boarding school in England. 'They were very anti the idea of us being spoilt kids and colonial kids. My parents were very unusual in that they were very close friends with all the servants. We would get into real trouble if we dared to be rude to the amah who looked after us.'

Jill was self-conscious when their driver took them to school in the official limousine, and begged to be dropped before the school gates. This was during Singapore's transition from British colony to independent state and its breakaway from the Malaysian Federation. 'We would drive in the riots. We had to come out of the gates of our driveway to drive to school, and stones were thrown. That was exciting, it was wonderful.'

The family returned to Surrey in August 1965. Mr Moore became head of public relations at the Ministry of Defence. Instead of a residence with servants the girls were back living in a row of houses with their mother cooking for them.

While they were in Singapore, Jill had not been aware of her father's prestigious public position. But life in the stockbroker belt never got the chance to be too ordinary. Just over a year after their return Philip Moore, at forty-five, was chosen as the Queen's assistant private secretary.

Jill had failed to get into the local grammar school and both Moore girls ended up at St Catherine's girls' public school, near Guildford, sister school to Charterhouse. 'I hated that school because it was single sex and I felt very odd, terrible. I was really uncomfortable, the girls were crazy. They'd look out of the window for boys.'

At the end of her first term, Jill was invited by friends to a Christmas party near Chobham. She was spotted by a Charterhouse boy dressed in a yellow satin shirt, a black velvet 'hippy' waistcoat speckled with gold, and black satin trousers. 'I was standing in a group of girls and he came up and asked me to dance. He seemed incredibly full of himself. I didn't have any understanding of people. I thought, "Well, he's good looking, so I'll dance with him, but I'm not sure I like this character." I still say to this day that he actually smelled of beer, but he promises me he couldn't possibly because he never drank.' Jill Moore had just turned fifteen and her new hippy-looking friend Peter Gabriel was sixteen.

'I must have given my telephone number because the next day he rang me up and we agreed to meet in a Wimpy Bar in Woking.' Both were on Christmas holidays. 'My mother was extremely worried about this, as she dropped me off. She was quite worried because I was a terrible flirt from the age of ten. Of course Peter does not eat meat, so it was a most extraordinary thing for him to arrange to meet in a Wimpy Bar. I couldn't understand it at all.

'There was something fascinating about him, although the main reason I went out with him from then on, for a long time, was that he was good looking.

'I remember going to a dance which he was singing at and it was flower power time, and it was wonderful to go along and be his girlfriend because he was the singer. And he started leading us around in a circle in this dance, we had to follow him.'

Jill felt stupid following him around this circle. She realized that her first impression of him being aggressive was way off the mark. It was hard enough to get him to talk. 'The fascination sank in for me, the life-long thing for me, which I enjoy most . . . people. He was the target for the rest of my life. I only know that in retrospect, but it was a matter of getting him to open up. I felt that we were both lost people. I loved the fact that he was different. And even then he had ambitions as a pop singer. To me that was wonderful. The analysis that I would marry a famous person, like my father, came a lot later.'

Jill had experienced a traumatic transition from the near idyll of Singapore to the isolation and confusion of adolescence in an English girls' school. Her close and loving family was unaware of her sense of loss, and could have done little to alter it.

Philip Moore wanted his daughters to emulate his intellectual and physical prowess, giving Sally the mantle of brain and Jill the brawn. 'I was this "boy" sports player. It was uncomfortable to meet Peter when I'd just played in a hockey match, a lacrosse match, a netball match, and been captain. I'd change out of uniform when we met, I would pretend and do anything to avoid that image. So I was half trying to please my dad and half trying to please Peter. And I remember deliberately deciding to let go of the sports side. I would be a rebel, and pop music became stronger. I couldn't make it on the academic side, and so I hated those years.' Jill got five 'O' Levels, like Peter, but this was regarded as a disaster.

Peter and Jill used to sneak out of school and meet at a lamp-post in the middle of Guildford. They did not date enough for Jill's liking, but it was hard for Peter to escape. 'He was a quiet rebel. The way he could exist in school was to be like that. I don't think he wanted to stir up trouble for himself. It was so painful he just wanted to withdraw. There was this excitement about meeting me, but he wasn't going to go too far and really blow it.' Unfortunately for Peter he was spotted on one of his forays and was summoned by his housemaster, Mr Marriott. Peter had to drop his drawers so that the cane could be administered. 'We had to shake hands afterwards, typical public school,' he remembered.

Peter's picture of himself as a fat and spotty adolescent is a great exaggeration, according to Jill. 'He said that by the time I met him he had fought that, but I don't think he was ever as bad as he imagined.'

While Peter found his first taste of freedom when he went to London to cram for his 'A' Levels from autumn 1967 to summer 1968, Jill was stuck at home, and felt threatened by his independence when he later moved into Bramham Gardens, Earls Court, with friends David Thomas and Tony Banks.

'It was a very frustrating time for him, we were very close, we were like sister and brother, in a sense. But he wanted to be free . . . I think at that point he could already feel the grasping of me and knowing that he still wanted to be with me, but he didn't want me clinging, like a mother still there. When he was in the flat in London I would always write and he would even write letters back. I'm painting it as if he wanted to run away, but he wasn't, he just didn't want it to be so tight, and we were still so young. But I'd sort of blown my future, so my pressure was very heavy, "how are we going to be together?" We were meeting at our parents' houses and I couldn't stand that.' Jill was allowed to visit Peter in London for the day, but she was never allowed to stay the night.

In the winter of 1969 Genesis went into retreat in the isolated Macphail cottage near Dorking. During that period Jill left home for London to attend the Guildhall School of Music and Drama, moving into a flat in Swiss Cottage. Having failed to fulfil her father's dreams in sport, Jill tried to fulfil her mother's dreams – she had been an actress in rep in Oxford when she met her husband.

Jill gave up her 'A' Level studies and was admitted to Guildhall when she was seventeen, a year younger than the usual entrance age. Her intention was to eventually teach drama, though her mother hoped she would act.

Now it was Jill's turn to be free, fulfilling all her parents' fears. 'I was completely the opposite to Peter, and still am, in that I am a chain smoker. I would try absolutely anything if I was given the chance. It was wonderful for me to be with Peter because he kept a rein on me in many ways in those years. Actually at college I tried smoking dope, which also Peter hadn't done, but he wouldn't approve. I had also heard of all these people and their acid trips, and I had in my head this image that they were all putting it on, making it up, it couldn't really be like these people was saying. I was always curious . . . terrible. And so I got this chap and said I wanted some. He gave me enough for seven people. I remember him saying, 'This is enough for seven people!' And me in my naïvety thought, rubbish! I don't believe this. So I took it. And I was actually going into a class at college.

'The next thing I knew was I found myself in this class – having missed out a whole section, I had no memory of it – and the panic came on. A friend there told the tutor and he said, "Well, take her home."

'I then found myself desperate to get to Peter. I had gone back to this girl's flat and I had to somehow find Peter, I was going mad. I saw creatures on the wall and everything. And I went on the tube. I said to this girl, I'll be fine! I'm going to get to Peter who was only just out of London for a concert at Brunel University in Uxbridge. So I caught the tube train with the doors slamming and shutting. I was absolutely determined to get there. When I got to this concert I thought, I'll be saved, I'm going to live! And when I told him he just went, "I've got a concert, I'm too busy . . . !" It was like, Oh, God, this nightmare isn't actually going to end! I'm never going to come out of it. It took three days really to come out of it. It was the first and last. I'm so glad that did happen because it stopped me from ever taking anything again.'

Jill believes it was Peter's turn to feel threatened by her living in an independent environment. But she soon left the college, disillusioned and upset with the unwanted attention of a tutor. By that time her parents had moved from West Byfleet into the Old Barracks at Kensington Palace, a grace and favour home provided by the Queen. Jill moved in with them before deciding on her future.

The Moore girls kept their contact with the Royal Family to a minimum, in keeping with their rebellious hippy self-image. But they did have to go to Balmoral every summer. On one occasion Jill was able to take Peter with her. They both attended the Queen's Gillies' Ball for the gamekeepers and sportsmen. 'Peter had to dance with Princess Anne and I danced with Prince Charles. I don't remember it at all except that I thought it was funny.'

While she lived at Kensington Palace, Jill took a shorthand and typing course but got thrown out because her tutors could not read her shorthand, then she worked in a stationery shop. Jill and Peter wanted to live together, but their parents were set against it. Her mother persuaded her to join her sister Sally, who was taking her finals at Trinity College, Dublin. 'It was a wonderful period. I worked as a waitress at nights. I really had deliberately gone away from Peter to think, "What the hell are we going to do?" And just by going away I think it got him to think, "Oh well, I'm not prepared to lose this." And he actually came over and visited me.'

Jill's sister shared her flat with fellow student Chris Davison, himself later to become a pop singer under the name Chris de Burgh. 'I loved that time. It was somewhere where I could enjoy life. There was this side of me that thought this would be much better for me, this laughter, and total lack of intensity.'

Jill stayed for six months and came back to find herself under the same pressure. 'My parents were worried by Peter, although they have always been very fond of him. They were very concerned, my mother thought at one point he was schizophrenic.' They were also worried about his pop career.

For Jill there was only one solution. 'I remember very clearly we were walking in Hyde Park, and me saying to him, "We get married or it's over." And he said, this is our romantic proposal, "Well, I haven't got much choice then, have I?" And when he actually told Dad, my dad, who is a really good-natured character, completely freaked, and disappeared out of the house. I was absolutely astounded, and we went round Kensington Gardens in opposite directions, I was trying to find him. His fear was: "How will you manage financially? Peter's getting £10 a week! What will you do?" He was very fond of Peter, and I think a genuine panic came over him. It was his first experience of a daughter saying she was going to marry. He calmed down very quickly and came round to the idea.'

Jill had felt compelled to force the situation. 'I couldn't think of another escape. We really should have lived together. My parents weren't incredibly strict, but you just didn't live together then. I just really think I wanted to spend all my time with him. My need for him was strong, excessively so.' If Peter's need for Jill was not as strong, it was because his work was also a consuming passion.

Peter gave Jill an engagement ring on her nineteenth birthday. Jill's father could claim a perk of the job, seeing his daughter married in a royal chapel, and got his way despite Peter and Jill's opposition. 'Peter and I were very unhappy about it. When I look back we were so naïve. He desperately didn't want to get married there. I didn't want to very much. Both Peter and I were anti-class and rebellious.'

The wedding took place on 17 March, St Patrick's Day, 1971, at St James's Chapel and the reception at St James's Palace. 'The wedding is a very vague memory. Just that it was incredibly flash and posh and there were these wonderful characters coming to the wedding from Charisma Records. My parents were wonderful in retrospect. My father was very tolerant. There was Tony Stratton Smith with his hair down to here, and all of them with their hair down to here, and these extraordinary clothes. And then my parents' generation in their top hats and tails. I'm very fond of my parents for that. It never seemed difficult for them.'

Their honeymoon in Tunisia, a wedding gift from Jill's parents, was disastrous. 'Peter got violent food poisoning and had to be injected. And it rained all the time.' It did not fulfil the promise of their wedding night. Peter had booked a room with a four-poster bed in an historic hotel before their flight from Gatwick. 'Driving out to that is my strongest memory because we got away from all these people,' said Jill.

Back from their honeymoon they were faced with their marital home, a dingy basement in the then unsalubrious fading Victorian hinterland of the London Borough of Wandsworth. The first six months' rent of just over £7 a week was paid by Peter's parents as their wedding gift, clearly useful on Peter's £10 weekly wage from Charisma.

Jill had a frustrating choice: to travel around with the group and suffer the discomfort of the backs of vans, the boredom and the indignity of being an appendage, or to try and get a job with the likelihood she would not see much of Peter because of clashing hours. Her efforts to join the band on their first trip to America in December 1972 were thwarted through lack of cash, though she did go with them on tours of England.

A year after moving into Wandsworth Jill and Peter found a new flat in Campden Hill Road, Notting Hill Gate. The combination of a new, cosmopolitan, lively area and a lighter flat prompted Jill into action. 'Everything seemed to take off from there. Peter was trucking up and down to the North in vans, there was the feeling he was beginning to go somewhere.'

She thought she would try going with him as much as possible. 'I began to turn into something that wasn't for me,' she told Frankie Mcgowan in a 1978 interview with *Over 21* magazine. 'I spent a great deal of time trying to look nice, which isn't how I normally behave, and constantly fighting something inside me which said, "God, this is pathetic." But it's what most wives do on tour. They start off trying to look good for every concert, which becomes impossible and exhausting after a while.'

She took a job with a Notting Hill florist delivering roses in a van, which she enjoyed. Then, despite her lack of qualifications, she got a job at the Barbara Speake Stage School in East Acton teaching eleven-year-olds. It was the same school that Phil Collins had been to as a child actor.

'I loved that teaching. I got £16 a week and felt so rich and excited about earning money. It was very frustrating because although I really enjoyed it I was hardly seeing him. We would pass in the night. I would be getting up conscientiously to be at the school at eight o'clock, and he would be coming home from the North at five.' Jill negated self-fulfilment at work for the sake of her husband's career. 'I made my constrictions for myself. Peter would have loved it had I developed.'

Being a relative failure at school, college and work was easier than matching the exacting standards set by her parents. But there was one role where she was sure she could win parental approval. 'I remember distinctly my father saying to me, "But you'll be a good mother and housewife." That seemed to me the next thing to bash on with. It didn't occur to me that I could be anything else.

'I said to Peter, "We should have our own kids." And he didn't want that, either. He was quite right, again. But I was determined if I couldn't teach at school I would want my own kids. I was finding a role for myself.'

Jill was pregnant before her twenty-second birthday in

1973. She had been touring with Genesis in Britain and joined them on their tour of America where they were promoting their latest album *Selling England By The Pound*.

'That tour was good. I was healthily pregnant, and it was really great to be there with him. It's just that it was a very difficult tour. He had very little time for me. It was a terrific strain because he couldn't be feeding me and my insecurities and doing his work. He tried his best but there were a lot of demands.'

Jill found the emotional pressure of being in the background intense. Before she ever toured she remembers someone from the group management warning, 'Never take wives on tour because the one thing they will do is go off with someone.'

'But I went because Peter wanted me to, and eventually I did have an affair,' she told Frankie Mcgowan. Instead of bringing Peter and Jill closer together her pregnancy only highlighted the emotional gap that had grown between them. It must have been extreme for her to have the affair with road manager Regis Boff at such a sensitive period.

'I desperately wanted to be famous, too. I used to dream about it right from when I was at school. But neither Sally, my sister, or I ever seemed to be able to succeed at anything. And we tried so hard.

'And there was Peter up on stage, glamorous, fêted, fawned over and not particularly liking it either. I was so jealous of him. So envious. The affair was my pathetic little bid for attention.'

Jill was lonely sitting around hotels while Peter had inter-views or talks with the management. Once she was picked up by the police while walking around the wrong area of Chicago and escorted back to the hotel. 'Things that cheered me up were someone exciting coming out to join us or a good reception. But often Peter would be tired and he hated receptions anyway. Occasionally I went, not often, without him, but he didn't like it very much. Mostly I felt it was my duty to stay with him so I didn't go in the end either.

'I found it very hard to cope with him being the star. Most wives pretend to be very supportive but if they were really honest they would say that most of the time they were really jealous. Jealous of the person who is chauffeured everywhere, fêted, clamoured over by women, and you? You're just an appendage who gets things done for you because you happen to be with the star, never for yourself.

'I got very twisted about it all,' she continued in her interview with Frankie Mcgowan. 'Very bitter and then I had an affair. It was at the beginning of my first pregnancy, I was feeling really down like you do at the beginning. Every night I would go to the concert and there were always these beautiful girls hanging around.

'It was such an intense tour and Peter couldn't give me what I needed at the time, constant reassurance. It's not as though he went off with anyone else, it's just that I needed to know I was needed.

'My affair caused all sorts of problems. He was a good friend of Peter's and it caused a rift, obviously, between them. I think in Peter's heart he knew what was going on; that's why he was so patient. No one solved it except for me and Peter. It was terrible while it lasted.

'We both knew it had been caused by the pressure of a hard tour and the fact that I couldn't come to terms with this extraordinary fantasy that it should be me who was the star, the actress, the singer, whatever, up there.

'Watching Peter night after night, resenting the fact that he wasn't very struck with it, and then me dreaming all night that I could get up there too. Ridiculous. In a childish way I suppose I was trying to pay him back.'

The affair and its conclusion proved one of the most trying times for Peter and Jill. It brought to a head conflicts that had been present in their relationship almost since the beginning. He could never devote enough time to Genesis and Jill for both sides to be happy. She needed someone who would listen and give her attention. Jill carried on touring until May 1974, when she was seven months pregnant, and was then faced with living on her own at the Gabriels' new home in the country-side outside Bath.

Early in the summer of 1974 Peter felt torn by his commit-ments to Jill and the group. Leaving briefly in the hope of writing a screenplay with William Friedkin was an act of desperation and frustration. Matters did not improve after he rejoined the band to write *The Lamb Lies Down On Broadway* at Headley Grange in Hampshire and record it in Wales.

The day before Anna was due Peter and Jill went for a walk up Glastonbury Tor. 'Peter wanted Leo children, and he's got two, only just. We walked up Glastonbury for the sunrise on the day it was coming into Leo. Two things happened. One was that we walked up to the very top and I was standing on my own, and there was this terrible screeching, sounding like hounds, and just as they stopped the sun came round. At that point I had this terrible fear that something was awfully wrong.

'We hadn't thought of a name, and he said, "I shall ask the first person that walks by." And I was saying, "Oh, you can't do that, please don't, how embarrassing!" But he did, and it happened to be these nuns, a teaching nun and a student nun. The student nun said Bartholomew and the older nun said, "If it's a girl, Anna-Marie".'

Anna was three months old when Peter insisted on taking her to Miami with Genesis on *The Lamb Lies Down On Broadway* tour. He felt it was better for her to see him under trying circumstances than not at all. Jill's anxiety over her baby combined with Peter's embarrassment at having to stop cars for nappy changes and feeds created a lot of friction. 'I know touring definitely affected Anna. For a long while after a tour she wouldn't go near any men because quite often she would wake up, if I took her backstage at a concert, and find all these strange faces looming over her.'

Nine months after Anna was born Jill decided she needed time on her own for the first time in her life, and left Anna with Peter, who had just played his last show with Genesis and was now free of the group. 'The affair couldn't be, and yet it wasn't working with us. I went off for two weeks to Corfu, and I actually called myself different names. For me it was really like a breakdown point, not really knowing where the hell I was going.'

Jill longed for independence, and the couple planned to separate. But Jill realized she could not be happy without Peter and Anna. 'I came back and we had a pillow fight on the cottage roof. That was the only way Peter could let out his anger. Somehow that seems very relevant to me. I made a strong decision that I would make it work.'

Jill chose a bizarre method of expressing her need for independence. 'I went into the bathroom and shaved my hair off,' she told Frankie Mcgowan. 'When I came out thank God Peter just laughed. My mother cried and cried. I'd played this game of dressing up and being so cool for so long that I couldn't remember who I was. I was simply playing a role. I had waistlength hair that I used to hide behind, not confident enough ever to be without it.

'I thought, "If I want to start again the hair has got to go too." So it did. Peter in the end shaved his to keep me company. No one seemed to notice, which illustrates what I mean about wives. The best thing they can do is to fade away, pretend they don't exist.'

Now she views it slightly differently. 'I think it was very much an exorcism. In retrospect it was probably self-punishment, but at the time I wasn't aware of that.'

Peter's sabbatical marked a period of peace for the couple and by Christmas 1975 Jill was pregnant again. Melanie was born on 23 August 1976, in St Mary's Hospital, Paddington, like her sister, though this time in the private wing. Jill and Peter were pleased they had another Leo daughter, though they were born at either end of the sign. 'We had really committed ourselves to making it work again and so everything worked very well for Mel,' said Jill. 'Despite the problems we had when Anna was induced the doctor insisted on Mel being induced too.' Peter was writing material for his first solo album and planning its recording at the time of Melanie's birth. He was able to avoid work pressures and devote time to his expanding family.

# CHAPTER SIX

L ARRY FAST, WHO WAS TO HAVE A LONG musical association with Gabriel, first met him in 1973 when he was a law student. Fast also worked at his college radio station in Pennsylvania, and got the chance to sit in on an interivew with Genesis.

Three years later Gabriel and Fast met for the second time. They had brunch together in New York to talk about working on Gabriel's forthcoming solo album. Gabriel was interested in Fast's skills at the synthesizer.

In those intervening years Fast had postponed a planned career in law to pursue music. He had played with rock band Nektar, and in May 1975, aged twenty-three, released his first solo album as Synergy, with the weighty title *Electronic Realization for Rock Orchestra*.

The Synergy album was released on small independent label Jem, parent company of Passport Records, then American importers of Genesis records. Fast knew Tony Smith through their mutual connections with the company. And through them word got back to Gabriel about Fast's skills.

'We found we had a lot in common, and a few months later when Peter was about to record the album I got a call saying can you be there with your equipment.' Fast, Robert Fripp, and pianist Josef Chirowski, chosen after Bruce Springsteen's keyboards man Roy Bittan was prevented from participating by his management, were the only musicians selected for the album by Gabriel. He left the rest to producer Bob Ezrin.

Gabriel said, 'I think I was very lucky. I had a lot of doubts about quite what to go for, and I made a decision to separate the style from anything I had been associated with before in Genesis, so I went to try and get a different rhythm feel using more American players, who were partly chosen by me and partly chosen by Bob Ezrin. And that was, in fact, when I met Tony Levin who I have been working with ever since. There were some really fine musicians there.'

The debut Peter Gabriel solo album was mainly recorded at Nimbus Studios in Toronto in autumn 1976. Ezrin's mighty ego, his 24-carat gold necklace dollar sign, and, worst of all, his whistle very early on started to annoy some of the band.

'It reminded me of going back to school when you know you haven't done your homework,' says Fast. 'Ezrin had a postman's whistle. He would walk up to anyone who was doing something he didn't like and blow the whistle at them. You lived in terror of him. Peter was terrified of exposing himself to all these hotshot musicians who had never heard of Genesis.

'It was very intense and tense at the same time. We broke into two distinct camps. Ezrin's boys went off to dinner and had $200 bottles of wine, which Peter would be paying for. Peter, Robert and I would go to a vegetarian restaurant for our little intellectual discussions and talk about how the album was going. Peter was going for a very different sort of album from what he had worked on before and this was part of the price for breaking the mould. I didn't hear him complain about it, but Peter doesn't like anyone else to waste money so I am sure he resented it.

'I was very flattered to work with Peter. I didn't realize it was going to be anything as long-term as it was going to be.' Fast was a member of Peter's band for nine years up to the beginnings of work on *So*.

Before Gabriel, Bob Ezrin had produced every Alice Cooper album, Lou Reed's *Berlin* and *Destroyer* by Kiss. He had no
time for Genesis-style agonizing, though he did appreciate
meekness in others.

'If there's anything that made me want to work with Peter
Gabriel in the first place it was his natural sense of humility.
Humility in the Christian sense of the word in that he is a
humble guy. I was impressed that a person that brilliant could
also hold himself on such a realistic level of esteem. Then I
knew it would be a most fruitful match,' Ezrin effused to
*Sounds* writer Barbara Charone.

'He's so damned inventive! He's not a linear thinker.
Because of that his inventiveness goes off in a thousand
different directions. Consequently he needs someone to hold
him down to the very best of his good ideas. All I do is edit
him, cut out the bits that aren't necessary and reduce the thing
down to the bare essentials. That way it's all great stuff.

'People criticize me for my attitude and say it's sterile
'cause I say I'm in it for the bucks. But this is a job, a
profession.'

Ezrin's stance could hardly have been more opposed to
Gabriel's. Yet Gabriel found the no-nonsense Ezrin refreshing
and stimulating after the posturings within Genesis. He also
needed Ezrin because he lacked the confidence to direct such
seasoned musicians. Never before or since has Peter Gabriel
surrendered so much artistic control. Ezrin gave the album a
live feel lacking in Gabriel's piecemeal and what Fast called
'pointillistic' later method of working.

'Bob is very bright and has an instinctive reaction to
production. He felt it important to be the big producer in
charge. He had strong personal tastes which did not always
coincide with my own. There was a guitar solo that I got
Robert Fripp to do on "Here Comes the Flood", which
apparently disappeared, erased by accident, something which

made my blood boil. I think Bob only got away with it because I was pretty naïve.'

Gabriel preferred the version of 'Here Comes the Flood' that appeared on Fripp's album *Exposure*. 'It was much closer to the original demo we had recorded together than the version on the record, which I think was a little overblown.

'I wanted an American rhythm feel with a European style of songwriting, which would include some acoustic elements, such as on "Solsbury Hill".'

Soon after recording started, Gabriel began to prove his worth to the wary musicians whom he viewed with awe. 'I felt inadequate in some ways in that I was not able to write or read music well, like some Limey that had managed to get himself a record contract and buy these mercenaries. As it turned out, they were very encouraging and really liked the material. So, it was a battle won for me.' He found the abuse hurled at everyone in the studio a refreshing contrast to the muted atmosphere of Genesis recordings.

Barbara Charone had seen him before he left London, and noted that his initial insecurities and self-doubt seemed to have since disappeared. 'While clearly enunciated sentences articulately replaced garbled half-phrases, several character traits remained. Slightly awkward, he still constantly changed position on the couch, shifted his legs often and restlessly put his hands behind his head throughout the interview.'

The songs were more personal than the Genesis material. 'More dependent on feel and emotion than sound,' Gabriel said. 'I particularly wanted to get away from my past. It would have been very easy for me to come up with another European keyboard-orientated rock band. But that wouldn't have been right for me, that wouldn't have broken any new ground.

'I now want to qualify my success. Success no longer holds the key to happiness for me. I wanted it badly once but it's an experience I had. Now I can get on with being a human being among other things. I won't throw myself into it quite the same way I did before,' he said during recording.

'I've got complete control now. The rock biz is a strange hybrid of hypocrisy. You get to the point where you're not really being yourself. You're selling something. You get the feeling that the rock star is really some sort of teenage creation realized for the most part by people who are no longer teenagers.

'All that tends to devalue things. It makes people eat out their souls because they begin separating what they are from what they're selling, yet still trying to sell themselves as an entity.

'I could see myself becoming that. I just didn't want to go on being a member of a rock group, growing old like the rest of them. Although there was a lot in Genesis that I'm proud of, there was always some sort of time clause on it for me for freshness and vitality.'

The album took three weeks to record in September and October 1976, with extra sessions in London and New York, and was released in February 1977. 'I am not sure he was making the album he was truly shooting for,' said Fast. That, he believes, did not come until the third album. But for Richard Macphail, this album was crucial. He saw Gabriel maturing into artistic adulthood through it, and believes that tracks like, 'Solsbury Hill', 'Moribund the Burgermeister' and 'Humdrum' are among his best. 'I think people were a little surprised when they heard the songs. But pleasantly so.' Some of the ideas for songs had germinated during the end of Gabriel's time with Genesis, though by the time they were put on the record they had gone through the extensive Gabriel filter.

Genesis had never been a singles band. The only hit while Gabriel was in the group was 'I Know What I Like (In Your Wardrobe)' from the *Selling England By The Pound* album which got to Number 21 in April 1974. His first solo single,

'Solsbury Hill', was released in March 1977, one month after the album, and got to Number 13.

'I was surprised with "Solsbury Hill", because it's in 7/4 for a start, which is a bit unlikely for a hit. But I was very pleased when it was a hit. I think it was important that it did happen but it wasn't designed to be, "This track's the single, let's radio it up a bit".' Gabriel lived near Solsbury Hill, one of the ancient mounds that dot the West Country, and used it as a beacon of hope for his new life away from Genesis.

> So I went from day to day
> Tho' my life was in a rut
> 'Till I thought of what I'd say
> Which connection I should cut
> I was feeling part of the scenery
> I walked right out of the machinery

'Solsbury Hill'; Gabriel, 1976

'By letting go, you create the space for something new to happen. It's a personal struggle to learn to jump off the diving board.'

Apocalyptic imagery is scattered throughout the album, usually as a metaphor for personal change, as in 'Here Comes The Flood':

> Lord, here comes the flood
> We'll say goodbye to flesh and blood
> If again the seas are silent
> In any still alive
> It'll be those who gave their island to survive
> Drink up, dreamers, you're running dry.

'Here Comes The Flood'; Gabriel, 1976

'I was quite obsessed by short-wave radio at that point and I was fascinated that when the sun goes down suddenly the radio just springs to life. I think night time is more of an internal landscape because you have more sensory information, so that started me off. I felt the barriers between people really work only if you do not know what the other person is thinking. I had this sense that people have instinctive psychic abilities which we don't really understand, that there might be a breakthrough of evolution in our species that will make us realize more of these abilities and some people would swim and some would sink.

'I went up to the hill just above the cottage where we lived for a walk, and I got this sense of energy coming out of the plants. There were these descriptions in Castenada, that I had been reading at the time, of people responding to special places and plants and the spirit world in general. So I think I was predisposed to find it, and did.

'I was running along the hill with my eyes closed and trying to feel things. "Here Comes the Flood" was a case of a lyric coming out effortlessly, which is very rare in my case. I felt I had plugged into something. I dashed back to the cottage and turned it into gold.'

He did not think it inconceivable that such a psychological breakthrough, or evolutionary leap, would one day be possible. 'I had this vision of telepathic advance in the sense that people do have the ability to pick up what other people are thinking and feeling, much more than is acknowledged. If it is developed at one point within the species, which is how I pictured it, then those people who are used to being straightforward and expressing what they were thinking and feeling would be much better able to handle it than those people used to secrecy.

'This might sound too far-fetched, but I've seen it as Armageddon images. And this seemed to me to be something that might happen, whether it be the result of radiation or whatever.'

Gabriel anticipated considerable emotional and social

upheavals for the rest of the seventies and beyond. 'I am interested in changes of consciousness and the forces that bring about these changes,' he told Allan Jones of *Melody Maker* just before the release of the album in 1977. 'There are a lot of things happening in religion, in the fringe sciences – new ideas, new concepts, that are beginning to change the way we live.

'You have to face the fact that there's a lot that's savage and terrible in the world, and you have to confront it and reflect it. It's obviously important to project something positive sometimes, but you can't delude yourself. You risk becoming bland and shutting yourself off from reality. I'm concerned to achieve some kind of balance . . . I don't want to present something that's irredeemably bleak. There has to be some kind of humour or irony to make it tolerable.'

That was most evident in the dry, tongue-in-cheek jazz and blues of 'Waiting For The Big One', a tribute to the style and wit of Randy Newman.

> *The wine's all drunk and so am I*
> *Here with the hoi-poloi, don't ask me why . . .*
>
> *Once I was a credit to my credit card*
> *Spent what I hadn't got, it wasn't hard . . .*
>
> *Waiting for the big one*
>
> 'Waiting For The Big One'; Gabriel, 1976

Despite his efforts, he was not entirely successful in shrugging off Genesis-like imagery and melodies. The opening track 'Moribund the Burgermeister', about St Vitus' Dance, has a typically Genesis fantastical title and grandiose melodic passages. 'Solsbury Hill' and 'Here Comes The Flood' in its over-arranged form could also have comfortably fitted on to a Genesis album.

Peter Gabriel's first eponymous solo album was released exactly a year after *A Trick of the Tail*, the first Genesis album without him. By now Genesis' success had confounded the commentators who had said the group were doomed without Gabriel. 'The popular misconception when I was with the band was that I wrote everything, did everything. Then when I left and the band produced apparently just the same things without me, the popular misconception then was that I did nothing. And the reality lies somewhere in between.' *A Trick of the Tail* was not a creative advance for Genesis, rather a statement of competence, proving the creative musicianship of the group did not rest solely with Peter Gabriel.

A twenty-date North American tour, Gabriel's first as a solo artist, was set up to promote the album for March 1977.

Bass player, Tony Levin, who had worked with Paul Simon, asked Gabriel if he could tour with him a few days after the sessions and is the only musician from the first album still with him. The rest of the session group from the album joined him, but, except for Larry Fast, they were replaced after the first tour.

Gabriel played New York's Palladium at the end of the month stripped of all the theatricality seen on his previous visits with Genesis. He was more restrained, projecting himself more as a musician, and surprising everybody by playing the piano. The elaborate costumes and masks of Genesis had given way to a simple grey tracksuit.

'Peter stands on the brink of massive success in America, if the reaction to his New York debut is any guide,' wrote Chris Welch in *Melody Maker*. 'Songs like "Solsbury Hill" are reaching a new audience in the vast American market who perhaps have barely heard of him before.' 'Moribund the Burgermeister' was a throwback to Genesis, Marvin Gaye's 'Ain't That Peculiar' hinted at a greater soul influence yet to come, and for the encore he kept faith with sections of the audience by playing 'Back In New York City' from *The Lamb Lies Down On Broadway*, dressed in Rael's leather jacket.

Supporting him in New York were critically acclaimed

New Wavers, Television, who were booed by old wave elements in the audience. The music scene in Britain, and to a lesser extent America, was convulsing from the onslaught of punk. Genesis were members of the rock aristocracy that punk set out to depose. Gabriel largely managed to escape the stigma of being over twenty-five and an ex-member of Genesis. His album and the single 'Solsbury Hill' were both hits in the UK, it looked like he had cracked it. But the records did not do so well in the USA despite well attended concerts.

Gabriel embraced punk more readily than his peers. He went to see the Sex Pistols in London before their infamy. 'I didn't go for the music much, but I enjoyed Rotten. I was interested at that point because other people who I was with hated them with a venom I hadn't seen for a long time. I thought anyone who can produce that reaction must be interesting.' And he enjoyed the music of the Jam and XTC.

In the autumn he played his first solo UK tour following a few initial dates in the spring. Looking forward to those concerts, stripped of costumes, masks and make-up, Gabriel said, 'I'll live or die naked and exposed.' According to Allan Jones of *Melody Maker*, he appeared uncertain of himself and was reluctant to confront the audience directly. 'There was a detachment that frustrated the spectator and Gabriel's apparent informality seemed too choreographed to be genuine,' he wrote.

But by September, at the start of the tour in Glasgow, all that had changed, according to Jones. '. . . such criticisms as I've directed at the London concert can now be declared redundant . . . His obvious relish at being faced with such an appreciative and demonstrably affectionate audience liberated him completely from his previously distanced stage persona . . . It's really rather curious this ability Gabriel has to commu-nicate occasionally complex (and sometimes rather confused) emotions and ideas: he is essentially an awkward and clumsy performer – his attempts at dancing extend no further than a cumbersome goose-step and he has little of, say, Bowie's omnipotent presence. Neither has he the sexual drive of Jagger nor the camp flash of a Rod Stewart. Yet he had a convincing charm and a sincerity that demands the attentive concentration of his audience.'

Gabriel's charm and sincerity was not immediately obvious to the vigilant Swiss police during the last leg of the European tour in October 1977. They pointed loaded guns at him and the rest of the group who they suspected of being terrorists in the Red Army Faction believed to be based in the Swiss–German–French border region around Basle.

They were halted while travelling in two dirty Mercedes on their way to Besançon in France for that evening's gig. They stopped off in St Gallen, Swizterland, at a phone box close to a bank because Gabriel wanted to phone his office in London. Gabriel looked suspicious with his face half-covered by his black scarf to keep his throat warm for singing. Some locals who saw him, bald-headed Tony Levin, and the two Mercedes with their engines running thought they were bank robbers and called the police. When the police nabbed them they dismissed the bank robbery idea, and thought instead they might be the terrorists responsible for the killing of the West German industrialist Dr Hanns-Martin Schleyer the day before.

'When we said, we are musicians, they said, where are your instruments,' said Richard Macphail, then Peter's tour manager. The instruments had been transported separately. Police suspicions were not abated when they found Macphail's briefcase full of money in four currencies.

They were detained for three hours while the police checked their story. In a further attempt to prove they were musicians Gabriel and the rest of the group sang the apt a capella song 'Excuse Me' to the police. 'There was a slight quaver in the voices,' said Gabriel. 'But otherwise the performance was intact.'

'A week or two before we had played in Berne and I still

had a copy in my briefcase of the local permit which the promoter had to organize,' said Macphail. 'It was a very official-looking document with the names of the musicians on it.' They were finally released after three hours' detention when their Swiss promoter verified their story, and they managed to reach that night's gig within minutes of its starting time.

After the first hit album and single, and a successful audience response on the tour – despite a phenomenal financial loss of $200,000 – Peter Gabriel looked set to fulfil expectations that he would soon be a major rock figure to rank alongside David Bowie and Bryan Ferry. But though he enjoyed his commercial success, Gabriel was not happy with all of Ezrin's work.

Robert Fripp's minimalist approach was the opposite of Ezrin's, as was his attitude to the music business; being commercial was his last concern. Gabriel had admired Fripp's work since the King Crimson album *In the Court of the Crimson King*, which the fledgling Genesis listened to incessantly stuck in their cottage near Dorking.

Fripp reluctantly played on Gabriel's first album out of friendship. Ezrin was not enamoured with him, and kept trying to make him play rock guitar, a style Fripp could not stomach.

'I liked a lot of the material on that album, but I have severe reservations about the way it was recorded and the kind of pressures Peter worked under. Basically, it was the producer's album, with Peter as an excuse for the producer to make his solo album. That was how I read it. Peter maintains that choosing Bob was the right decision, that it was what he needed at the time. Bob gave him a lot of confidence, push, and support. But I have other considerations. I wasn't really allowed to be myself on that album and, if I'd had the courage of my convictions, I would have left on the second day. In fact, when I agreed to do the album, I said I reserved the right to leave if it didn't work out. But, in fact, when you turn up, and you're booked there for two or three weeks, and you're doing a friend's album, you don't actually turn around and leave.

'I originally agreed to play on the album pseudonymously – and that was a number in itself. I had a lot of pressure put on me to have my name on the album – which I was unhappy about, because I didn't feel that Robert Fripp played on the album.' Fripp also toured with Gabriel under the alias Dusty Road. He insisted on playing at the side of the stage, hidden by the speakers, because he did not want to be associated with the guitar parts.

Despite this, Fripp agreed, albeit with serious reservations, to produce Gabriel's second album in Holland and New York in late spring 1978. He wanted to capture the essence of Gabriel, but found giving Peter Gabriel all the freedom he needed also had its drawbacks. 'I would describe Peter as being a person who knows exactly what he wants but is unable to make up his mind. If you think that sounds paradoxical, you're right. He writes beautiful songs but he's not spontaneous; he is more compositional. He has a conception of how a piece should sound and he's not happy until he hears on tape what is in his head. I wouldn't call that being a perfectionist, either; I would call it being a fiddler or pussyfooter. Recently I wrote this little blurb for Charisma Records as a publicity thing, explaining what it was like to produce Peter; the title was "Peter Gabriel: Pussyfooter or Creative Giant?" I concluded that Peter is a pussyfooter,' said Fripp, soon after the album's release. He felt Gabriel was trying to become too sophisticated which would remove all his gaucheness, a quality he felt endeared him to audiences.

Gabriel saw himself and Fripp as 'passive aggressives', a tag given to them by a friend. 'I can see something in that because I can float along quite happily, but when I get moved to do something then I can get quite . . . obstinate.'

Gabriel finally got Bruce Springsteen's keyboard player,

Roy Bittan, to play on the album, overcoming the managerial problems encountered before the first album. 'He plays exactly what I would play if I could play the piano as well as he could,' Gabriel said. Tony Levin and Larry Fast were still there. By now drummer Jerry Marotta had joined the band, which also included guitarist Sid McGinnis, who had played with Leonard Cohen and Barry Manilow, and saxophone player Timmy Cappello, later to find fame pumping iron and playing in Tina Turner's band.

Most songs contain a variety of frequently complex themes. 'Animal Magic' with its 'Join the Professionals' chorus is, according to Gabriel, about virility and the politics of the battlefield and bedroom.

The album marked the first recorded songwriting collaboration between Peter and Jill, on 'Mother of Violence'. They had worked on a song to be used as a kids' Christmas carol in their village church. Peter liked the melody so much he adapted it and used it on the album. Instead of the innocence of a carol he twisted the meaning on itself, leaving it with a sense of foreboding; 'Fear is the mother of violence.'

'D.I.Y' was a plea both for personal independence and for people not to be intimidated by society.

> Don't tell me what I will do, 'cos I won't
> Don't tell me to believe in you, 'cos I don't
>
> 'D.I.Y'; Gabriel, 1978

'Rather than just change your attitude, change what you do. In other words, one has responsibility for a lot more than most people are prepared to accept. I believe in small groups of people having a lot more control over themselves than they do at the present,' he said.

Gabriel was unhappy with the production on various tracks, like 'D.I.Y', where he felt the vocals were not as light as he intended. 'Robert was very keen to get everything fresh.

We kept a lot of early takes and kept the production very dry. The second album is more spontaneous. There are some rough edges and some mistakes but leaving them in makes it more alive.'

Despite his reservations he said he thought it was a better album than the first, not a view taken by Atlantic Records in the United States. Their fears that Fripp would produce a less commercial record were confirmed. They were after another album filled with 'Solsbury Hill's, and 'Modern Love's. They were assuaged by an idea of Gabriel's for a singles project. 'It's not a concession to the record company. I do what I want on albums, but I'll see if I can give them something they can go out and sell to all those people they are sure won't buy my album.'

The second album bore no title, something else that rankled with the marketing men, though it was informally known as *Scratch*. 'Other acts on each album very much try and present a brand new face, a bit like marketing soap powders; new added ingredients, WM7 and sparkling blue bits and all the rest. So I thought much more interesting for me would be just to keep exactly the same title, the same typeface, the same position, so the only way of telling the difference from the outside was by the difference in the picture, so it looks a bit like a songwriter's magazine that comes out once a year.'

The cover picture was as stark as the mood of the album with Gabriel's clawed hands ripping giant white scratch-marks out of the black cover. On the reverse side a bleak figure scurries along a slushy desolate New York street. And on the inner sleeve an unidentifiable Gabriel is hunched and looks like he is under secret surveillance.

A hit album would have been very useful. His bank balance was still reliant on royalties from Genesis. 'If I consider my current financial situation realistically, I would say that I'd be able to survive in this cottage with my wife and two children living fairly decently for five years. No more than that, and that's being generous, and therefore I am concerned about compromising, that's all . . .' he told Nick Kent of the *NME* in June 1978. He wanted to be a commercial success.

On the melancholy track 'Indigo' he was inspired by Paul Robeson's song 'Old Man River' which was played on tour while people were leaving the auditorium.

> *I was good at the art of survival*
> *I've always tried*
> *To keep my troubles deep inside*
> *Where I can hide them*
> *Now I'm wide open . . .*
>
> *I got nothing to fear from the showdown*
> *I'll go down quiet.*

'Indigo'; Gabriel, 1978

In writing the song he had in mind the father of a small family who as he approached death had a change of attitude, 'a new rush of sentimental and romantic feelings'. Gabriel stressed that his songs have a universal application, there is a danger of reading too much into them. Even so, the lyrics to 'Indigo' were prophetic of Gabriel's later voyages of self-discovery.

# CHAPTER SEVEN

SHAVING HIS HEAD NEVER MADE PETER Gabriel look very pretty. Not that it was done for aesthetic reasons. 'People react to a shaved head differntly to how they do to a soft hairy one,' he said. 'There were experiments in stations in London to test people's reactions to the same subject with different outfits and hairstyles, and there is no question that you are seen as more aggressive with a shaved head, whether you are or not.'

In the summer of 1978, he aired the style in public for the first time. It was 'not to get attention' but for what he termed spiritual and practical self-improvement.

The second album had just been released, and proved only a moderate success; his solo career was not taking off. This was all thrown into sharp relief by his erstwhile colleagues who were getting their first taste of megastardom.

By September 1978 when Gabriel gave two open-air concert appearances he looked like a skinhead with a 'Number One' crop. Gabriel shared the billing both times with a big furry punk panda toy, with a chain around its neck, accompanying him on the humorous 'Me And My Teddy Bear', a song from his childhood, for which he adapted the words.

First he supported Frank Zappa and the Tubes at Knebworth where earlier that summer the increasingly successful Genesis headlined a triumphant concert before 100,000 people. He was then special guest star with the Stranglers at Battersea

Park. This appearance left the *Melody Maker* reviewer, presumably a punk fan, confused. 'Peter Gabriel (motto: "A festival a week keeps the blues away") was the first of the day to get the audience off its collective ass, but his recent surge to credibility is perplexing: to me, he is as anonymous today as he ever was with Genesis. But the rest of the audience enthusiastically endorsed Gabriel's oddly arranged music and went quite wild over his punk parody of "Whiter Shade of Pale", which I found both unfunny and unspectacular.'

After Genesis' concert at Knebworth in June, Gail Colson, managing director of Charisma Records, quit her job. She had rowed with Strat over his A&R policy. When she left after working with him for ten years he forced her to sign a piece of paper stating she would not poach any of his artists for rival record deals.

'I had no idea what I was going to do,' said Gail. She had considered leaving for some time, and had hinted as much to Peter before he re-signed his recording contract with Charisma Records. 'I was trying to tell him that I would not be there forever.'

Tony Smith had carried on managing Peter after his departure from Genesis. The group were getting increasingly unhappy with Smith dividing his time between them and Peter. They wanted his full attention, but Smith resisted their pressure and pledged his loyalty to Peter. However, the workload for Genesis and Peter Gabriel was increasing and Tony was forced to delegate the handling of Peter's affairs to his office staff.

After a holiday following her departure from Charisma, Gail returned to London for a meeting with Tony Smith who offered her the job of managing director of Hit and Run Music, the management company for Genesis and Peter Gabriel. 'Genesis were a different band without Peter. Within two months of working there I realized that was not what I wanted to do and that Peter needed separate management.'

Peter was aware he needed personal attention and asked

Gail to manage him. She came to an agreement with Tony Smith and together they set up Gailforce Management. Colson still shares the same Knightsbridge offices with Genesis and Phil Collins. Tony Smith retained his share in Peter Gabriel's management through Gailforce.

In the autumn of 1978 Peter Gabriel went on a tour of America and Europe under Gail's guidance for the first time. His next London appearance was in the week before Christmas, playing five dates at Hammersmith Odeon. Promoter Harvey Goldsmith had inadvertently double-booked Christmas Eve for Peter Gabriel and Tom Robinson. A gentleman's compromise was suggested by Goldsmith: Gabriel and Robinson should do a joint show for charity.

On the last song of the last show on the last date of his tour, the day before the charity show at Hammersmith, Gabriel got more excited than usual and inadvertently drew blood from Tony Levin's shaved head.

'I turned my back on Peter as I did a lot, I used to face Jerry. I thought a rock hit me from the audience, a very heavy rock,' said Levin. 'I started to bleed and left the stage before the song had ended. Every night during that show Peter used to pick up his mike stand and smash it into the footlights. On the last night he was holding a swivel mike stand by mistake which swung round and hit me.' Levin did not turn his back on Gabriel for more than ten years, and still has the Fender Precision bass with the blood stains.

Tom Robinson's first public encounter with Gabriel was through the pages of the *NME*. In the spring of 1977 he was guest singles reviewer, and the releases for that week included 'Solsbury Hill'. This was six months before Robinson had his first hit with '2-4-6-8 Motorway'. He remembered, 'The first sentence of the review read, "I never listened to Gabriel's Genesis, because I didn't like them," like the Guinness ads that said, "I never tried it because I don't like it." I'm pleased to say that I gave it a rave review.'

Gabriel and Robinson agreed to meet to see if there was any common ground for a joint concert. Robinson took the train to Bath. 'This very shy individual met me at the station in his car and drove me through the streets of Bath, off to the little cottage where he lived at the time. I was very struck by a children's swing which was in the garden, which was stuck together by gaffa tape. Gaffa is used by roadies to stick everything together on stage, it was nice to see it extended to the children's swing as well.'

Their friendship soon developed once they found they were the same age, and shared common schoolboy influences like the Spencer Davis Group and Manfred Mann. Any fears about musical incompatibility were soon overcome, and they decided to turn the show, still two months away, into a party. It was billed as 'Rob and Gab Xmas 78'. Each chose a worthwhile charity to donate the proceeds to and approved the other's choice. Gabriel's was One Parent Families and Robinson's the Northern Ireland Gay Rights Association.

They collaborated on two new songs for the show. 'Merrily Up On High', on Robinson's next album *North by Northwest* had Robinson's lyrics with Gabriel adding the music. 'Bully For You', the next Tom Robinson Band single, had Gabriel's music inspiring Robinson's lyrics.

Instead of separate sets they decided to appear together, playing each other's numbers interspersed with rock and roll standards. The illustrious backing band included Elton John on piano, Andy MacKay from Roxy Music on saxophone, Phil Collins on drums and Paul Jones, their old Manfred Mann hero, on harmonica.

The show was memorable more as an occasion than for the quality of music. 'I massacred "Solsbury Hill", for my sins, and he sang "Hold Out",' remembered Robinson. He recalled one reviewer complaining, 'One sings, the other doesn't.'

Chris Welch in the *Melody Maker* was kinder. 'It was an unlikely, unexpected pairing, and yet it seemed to work. Tom, the brotherly fifth-form prefect, took Peter, the Owl of the Remove, under his wing, and between them they presented a bold front to the school bullies in the audience.' The rowdy crowd did not take kindly to magician Simon Drake's opening act, and used the paper hats, balloons and whistles to disrupt the evening, quietening only on the arrival of Rob and Gab.

Welch continued, 'Take the piano player, for example, an oik from the senior school called Elton John who gave his keyboard a severe thrashing, his percussive power adding to an already impressive rhythm team under the tutelage of the old master, Phil Collins. The whole evening was just full of surprises . . .

'The music was not just aimless jamming. They had rehearsed well, and on rock standards they sounded like hardbitten pub rockers. On a more artistic level, it was intriguing to hear Rob and Gab (as they were billed) swap songs, although Tom had a struggle singing Peter's tricky "Solsbury Hill". They were at their best singing together on the co-written "Merrily Up On High".

'Their slightly neurotic voices twinned surprisingly well, but the best vocal performance of the night came from Peter with the moving "Here Comes The Flood", the maestro accompanying himself on piano with saxophone prompting from Andy MacKay.'

In the new year Gabriel started to look for musicians he could rehearse and form a band with for his third album. He mentioned he was on the lookout to a friend, artist Graham Dean, who still admits to little knowledge of the rock world. But Dean did recommend rock band Random Hold, who he had seen play in Oxford where the group members were at college. David Rhodes was the group's singer, songwriter and aspiring guitarist. 'Technically I could barely play, but I used to make some nice noises,' said Rhodes.

Gabriel, Gail Colson and Tony Stratton Smith went to see Random Hold at the Rock Garden in Covent Garden. Gabriel was impressed and wanted Gail to manage them and Strat to sign them to Charisma. In the end they did neither, though Peter Hammill later produced the Random Hold album *The View From Here* after they signed to Polydor. The album failed commercially but the group still hung together.

Gabriel asked Random Hold to go to Bath to rehearse with him. 'It was pouring with rain when we got to the house and we couldn't find him anywhere. Then we heard some people making noises around the side of the barn, and there were three people covered with mud. The barn had been flooded and Peter had been helping with a few of the road crew to dig a channel to divert the water. He was wearing a pullover and wellingtons and an old school cap,' said Rhodes. They eventually got down to work by the fireside in the barn on the reeking damp carpet.

It became clear that Gabriel was mainly interested in Rhodes who later went down on his own for three weeks of rehearsals. Though Rhodes did play on the forthcoming album, he was still committed to Random Hold who toured with Gabriel the following year, though the group fell apart soon after that.

Gabriel had leased Ashcombe House, down the hill from the Mill Cottage where he then lived, for £12,500 in 1978. He needed somewhere he could write, play and record without the restrictions of time and money imposed by commercial studios. The rambling farm house had a croquet lawn and a long low barn at the bottom of the garden that Peter first converted into a primitive studio using egg boxes. By the time Rhodes came down to join rehearsals it was still a fairly basic eight-track studio. They rehearsed new songs including 'Biko', 'Not One Of Us' and 'Milgram's 37', a song that had to wait six more years before it got on vinyl.

Gabriel considered using guitarist Anthony More, from the quirky Slap Happy, to produce the next album. He was impressed with their albums. More and Gabriel rehearsed several times at Ashcombe. 'He is a colourful person, a bon viveur. He was positive and gave me confidence with some of my new approaches,' said Gabriel.

Gabriel's writing was changing, developing rhythms first instead of chords and melodies. It was a crucial change that helped shape his future success, and was spurred on by a breakthrough in technology. Larry Fast got him the first programmable drum machine, a little rhythm box called a PAIA, made by friends of his in Oklahoma City. There had been drum machines before, but they were the home organ variety that could give you a tango or bossanova beat from preset buttons. The PAIA dispensed with that giving the user the ability to tap in his own rhythms and store them for later recall, a facility now common to many home electronic keyboards.

'On the first two albums Peter wasn't working to get a rhythm, he was writing more in a traditional "sit down at the keyboard and play your chord pattern" mode of songwriting. When he got this box it was working the music through the rhythms. It became the fundamental part inspiring what was going to happen,' said Fast.

'I felt I wanted to write music for the eighties and that the place to begin was with a rhythm track. Rhythm being the spine of music, if you change the spine, the shape of the body changes as a matter of course,' said Gabriel.

The first song written with the help of the rhythm machine was 'I Don't Remember'. 'I wrote much more simply on top of that. Whereas if the rhythm isn't there I'll normally try and keep my own interest alive by making things a bit more complicated in terms of chords and melody.'

He needed a producer willing to experiment in a similar way. Gabriel was impressed by the feel of Siouxsie and the Banshees' records. They were produced by 24-year-old Steve

Lillywhite whose hit productions included 'The Sound of the Suburbs' for the Members, 'Hong Kong Garden' for Siouxsie and 'Making Plans For Nigel' by XTC.

When Lillywhite got a call from Gail Colson to arrange a meeting with Gabriel he thought it was one of his mates phoning up as a joke, although working with Gabriel was not totally unacceptable to a post-punk producer. Unlike Genesis, Gabriel had leapt over the credibility gap on the arrival of punk.

'He had heard my XTC work, but my feeling was, "Peter, you could use anyone, you know, why do you want to use this kid who came from a completely different school?"' said Lillywhite. His engineer on the XTC albums was Hugh Padgham, just three weeks Lillywhite's senior. 'I remember we were doing a project one day and Steve said, "You'll never guess what! Peter Gabriel's rung up. I can't believe it. I'll go down and have an interview." But we were still fresh-faced in those days and we didn't think we'd have a chance of doing something like Peter Gabriel. He was a big act,' remembered Padgham. His bigness at that time was more reputation than sales. When Lillywhite was offered 'the gig' he asked Padgham to join him.

The one rule they established when they got together was that if something sounded normal, it should not be used. 'That was the basic thing we reminded ourselves of all through the LP, which really helped open me up,' said Lillywhite. 'It was great for me because I was experimenting with a lot of different dimensions of sound.'

During their first meetings Lillywhite asked Gabriel to play him some songs. What he got instead were musical ideas without lyrics. 'Lyrics are the most difficult things for him to put together, and without any lyrics you don't really have a song, so you were always slightly in the dark. It wasn't as if he would say, OK this is the song and this is how we are going to present it. It was always, well, I've got this riff and I'll do this, and it sort of evolved.'

Since the split with Genesis, Gabriel had maintained sporadic contact with the group, mainly through sharing the same offices. He was friendliest with Phil Collins, whose first marriage broke up in 1979. Collins, always a workaholic, had even more time to play on other people's sessions. 'Pete wanted to rehearse some songs for his new album, and I heard from Gail that he didn't have a band because he could not afford to keep them on a constant pay cheque,' said Collins. 'I said, "Look, if he wants a drummer I will be there any time he wants." He rang up and said, "That would be great, come down to Bath."' Gabriel was booked to play at Reading Festival on August bank holiday and at the old Genesis haunt Friars of Aylesbury. Collins played at both, playing Gabriel's new material and duetting on *The Lamb Lies Down On Broadway*.

Recording for the album started in summer 1979 using a mobile at Ashcombe House. And then mixing and overdubbing was done at Virgin Records' Townhouse studios in Shepherd's Bush where Padgham was a house engineer. Studio Two, where Gabriel was to record, had stone walls that made the sound 'splashy'. The studio exaggerated the resonance of the cymbals. Padgham and Lillywhite had countered this before by distancing the microphones away from the drums, a technique Gabriel also used in his own studio.

Collins was booked to record with Gabriel for the first time since *The Lamb Lies Down On Broadway* more than five years earlier. The components were now in place to create what was to become one of the most distinctive and influential sounds of the eighties.

'Peter suddenly announced that he didn't like cymbals and hi-hat because they were too normal. We said this is great news because now we can get a really big ambient sound by putting the mikes further away,' said Padgham.

Phil Collins became very disorientated. His cymbals and hi-hats were taken away leaving him to thrash out where instinct told him they should be into thin air. 'It was so strange for him that he couldn't stop himself from going up as if to smash the cymbals. So we hung two or three drums off big mike stands where a cymbal should be and that cured the problem. He'd do a roll where normally a drummer would hit a cymbal, and he hit a big drum.' Collins was fooling around on his kit trying to develop a drum pattern for 'Marguerita', a song destined never to be released. As Collins was playing away he became aware of the effect he was creating via a cheap microphone relaying the sound back through his headphones. The sound he heard went through a gate compressor unit, the first of its kind fitted to the studio's new Solid State Logic desk. The gate compressor unit both shut off the sound and squashed it. Lillywhite and Padgham were experimenting with these devices.

'For some reason I had this thing in and Phil was playing,' said Padgham. 'It was suddenly boom-boom tshh . . . And then he started playing to the sound, in other words the way the noise kept shutting off. Pete was in the control room and he suddenly heard it and he said, "Fucking hell, listen to that!" And we said, "Yes, that's amazing!" and Phil said, "Yes, that's amazing." It was something we had never heard before, nor had anybody else. It was an enormous sound because we were compressing the death out of this microphone, and it wasn't what it was supposed to be used for.

'So Pete said to Phil, "Play along for five minutes," so Phil just sat there and played boom-boom tshh . . . boom-boom tshh . . . for five or ten minutes. And Pete said, "Thank you very much. I'll go home and write a song to that."' Gabriel decided to use the drum sound not for 'Marguerita', but instead for another track. That drum sound opens Gabriel's third album on 'Intruder'.

The technique became known as the 'gated reverb'. The

'reverb' came from the reverberation in the studio, a sound that can be imitated electronically, and the 'gate' from the cut-off device on the control desk. Phil Collins was inspired by the sound he helped develop on 'Intruder', and used the gated reverb extensively on his own album *Face Value*, recorded in the same studio with Hugh Padgham as co-producer and engineer. It featured on the song 'In The Air Tonight', his first major solo hit. Collins ultimately got more recognition for creating that sound than Gabriel. 'It's silly really. At the time I was pissed off because Phil's album was an enormous seller, and then people would say to me, "Oh, you are copying the Phil Collins sound,"' said Gabriel.

Collins saw all this slightly differently. 'That was one of the best examples of Pete's bloodymindedness. He didn't want any metal on the album, so I said, "Why? Some sounds would sound great like that, but others would be great with metal." He said, "No, I don't want any metal." So I said, "What do you want me to do?" And he said, "Instead of hitting a cymbal you hit the drum."

'I started playing this drum sound and Pete straight away put his hand on the intercom and said, "Listen, that sounds great. Play that for ten minutes." At the end of it I said to Pete, "If you are not going to use that I would like that," because as far as I was concerned I had written this drum part and I said I would like to use it. So I took a tape away with me that night. I took it to mean, "OK, you can use it if I don't."

'Now that opens up a whole can of worms. When I used it was I ripping Pete off by using my sound? To me I was using my sound and I would defend that to my dying day. It was my brain it was me that played the part with the sound that Hugh created. I am not saying that I created the sound at all, but I didn't think it was particularly Pete's thing. You can see how tricky it was.

'I heard he had this song called "Intruder" and he rearranged it to fit with what he had on the drums. When I heard about this I said to Gail, "Can you ask Pete if he could give me credit on the album for writing the part," because I felt it was very me. So he wrote: "'Intruder' – written by Peter Gabriel, drum part by Phil Collins" – which was fine by me.

'Of course when my album *Face Value* came out everyone said it was very Gabrielesque and I didn't think any of it was apart from the drum sound which I had used on Pete's album. If you listen to "Intruder" and "In The Air Tonight" and all the other drum parts I have done they are all very different.'

'Phil was not nicking that idea,' said Padgham, who as well as co-producing *Face Value* also went on to produce Genesis. 'He was just impressed with an engineer's ability to create new sounds, his enthusiasm and everything else. Phil had never heard his drums sound like that before.'

'I really think the third album was the first where a Gabriel style crystallized,' said Gabriel. 'We have pioneered a few things. I felt bold enough to say to the drummers "No cymbals!" and made a few rules like that which I think gave it character.

'I stopped the session we were working on and said, "This sound is going to revolutionize drum sounds." I didn't create it, but I saw some of the possibilities and used it. Hugh and Steve had done something with XTC using the gated reverb, so it was not the first record it was on. But it was the first record where it was really allowed to happen in the sense that it was the dominating sound.

'I remember talking to Nile Rodgers afterwards and he said as soon as he heard that he said, "I've got to have this!" and spent a bit of time creating it for himself. When you get those moments and there are few in the studio, and you think "here's something we've come across and struck gold" which is a really exciting feeling, something that is really going to excite musicians all round the place and you feel their sense of discovery, it's a great moment.'

'I think a lot of people have quoted Peter's third album as being a new departure in sound. It's been used so much now I've gone off it a little bit,' said Steve Lillywhite.

He had a unique perspective on Collins and Gabriel working together. 'They are complete opposites. Phil will say, "Right, let's do it." Whereas Peter will say, "Right, let's do it. What are we going to do?" Or, "How do I do it?" Or "How can I do it differently?" For Phil there's no questions, for Peter it's a hundred questions leading to another hundred questions.'

After the initial sessions at the Townhouse the Gabriel party moved down to Ashcombe House with the Manor mobile studio parked outside. Larry Fast took charge of the electronic production as well as keyboards, with the now regular team of Tony Levin, Jerry Marotta taking over on drums, and David Rhodes, plus visiting musicians.

'I see Peter as a really important artist,' said Lillywhite. 'He's extremely talented, but he has to push himself. He has to work hard. It doesn't come easy, unlike Phil. Things probably come easier to Phil than to anyone I've ever met. And things come more difficult to Peter than to anyone I've ever met. He will put off making a decision until the last possible moment, but that's only because he doesn't con himself into thinking he knows what he's doing.'

The new rhythmic approach prompted Gabriel to explore an idea that had been with him since September 1977. That was when he heard the news of black South African political activist Steve Biko's death on the radio over breakfast. It prompted Gabriel to acquaint himself more with the situation in South Africa, though the lyrics were the last part of the song to be written. Biko's death generated what was to later become Gabriel's commitment to the cause of human rights throughout the world.

The music for 'Biko' was inspired by music heard on the radio at breakfast on another occasion. Gabriel had been fiddling around with his short-wave dial and picked up a

Dutch station playing tribal rhythms from the soundtrack to
*Dingaka*, a South African film that starred Stanley Baker. That
sound formed the rhythmic core of the song. ' "Biko" and
"Normal Life" are probably the farthest away from my old
style of writing. "Biko" is much simpler musically than anything I had written previously, it only has three chords. This is
an approach I would not have used before if I hadn't begun
with the rhythm first,' Gabriel said. 'Normal Life' was a
variation on a Bo Diddley melody.

While 'Biko' was being recorded Gabriel came across the
soundtrack of a news documentary on Biko's funeral. Some of
the singing from this tape was used at the beginning and end
of the track. 'The remarkable thing to European ears is that
the music is really hopeful – happy is perhaps the wrong word
– and positive. Western funeral music is always very down and
sombre and serious,' said Gabriel.

As well as the 'gated reverb' on 'Intruder', and the African
rhythms of 'Biko', Gabriel also pioneered the use in rock music
of the marimbas, an African and South American instrument
similar to the xylophone, on 'No Self Control'. Avant-garde
'systems' composer Steve Reich's album *Music for 18 Musicians*
was the inspiration for the marimbas, played by percussionist
Morris Pert. 'No Self Control' also saw the first collaboration
between Gabriel and Kate Bush.

But Gabriel also broke new technological ground as the
first person to use the Fairlight CMI (Computerized Musical
Instrument) synthesizer in a British recording studio.

Sid McGinnis, who had been with Gabriel on his second
American tour, was playing on a session with Carly Simon at
the Power Station in New York when Peter Vogel, the
Australian co-inventor of the Fairlight, came by to show his
wares. The Fairlight was named after a hydrofoil that crossed
Sydney harbour.

McGinnis knew this new gizmo would interest Gabriel and
Larry Fast and telephoned them both. 'Larry wasn't that

convinced by the instrument,' remembered Gabriel. 'He comes from a different background where part of his craft is synthesizing sounds, which he is brilliant at. Whereas the sampler seems like a cheating device to him in some ways because it is taking wonderful textures that exist already and manipulating them. So it is collage rather than creation. For me that was a dream come true because I had pictured in my head something that would just allow you to go round with a microphone and grab anything and start manipulating it and being able to use it in your palette.'

Fast's memory varies from Gabriel's. 'I thought it was amazing and I said to Vogel, I am going to be working with Peter Gabriel, this is where I will be, when I get to England phone me, I am sure you can be picked up. Peter is always pushing the boundaries, from high-tech with the Fairlight and very low-tech, using cheap horrible amps and abusing equipment, but using it always creatively. That's where Peter's mind is brilliant, he can use either way.'

Vogel did contact Gabriel when he got to England with the Fairlight a few weeks after meeting Fast and took it to Ashcombe House where he stayed for a week. Gabriel put the Fairlight to immediate use smashing milk bottles and banging bricks, and then playing melodies using the sampled sound. Though it did not change the album drastically it did give it additional colour. It can be heard in the fade out to 'I Don't Remember', a pulsating drone drowning out the incomprehensible whisper of the amnesiac's memory.

Also invited to the studio when Vogel arrived was Gabriel's cousin Stephen Paine, then trying to mark out a career as a synthesizer session player. Paine was well versed in synthesizers through selling them at the London Synthesizer Centre.

Paine shares his cousin's fascination with technology and was inspired to get in on the act and propose to Vogel that he represent him in this country and start importing the Fairlight.

That was the impetus to set up Gabriel's company Syco

Systems, in 1980, which had the exclusive rights to import Fairlights and Synclaviers. The initial European distribution of these Rolls Royces of keyboards was conducted from the ramshackle and rat infested Ashcombe House.

'Although the commercial oppotunity was fairly easy to see, it was not the main stimulus,' said Paine. 'Syco deals with high end, state-of-the-art technology. Peter's interest was in establishing a company that was involved in music production technology so that it could allow him quick access to the latest and the best technology as it became available.' Paine uses terms like techno-artist and techno-flow. He believes Gabriel is one of the former and in the latter.

'Now we take that technology for granted. What the Fairlight was doing was incredibly basic. It was able to record a sound and play it back on the keyboard at any pitch, polyphonically and as chords. Up to then something similar only existed on the Mellotron. On that each note on a keyboard has a continually rotating tape loop. When you press a key it places a replay tape on the head. It is incredibly laborious and expensive.'

Steve Lillywhite and Hugh Padgham were not the only representatives of the New Wave on the third album. Paul Weller of the Jam was recording in another studio at the Townhouse when they returned there to complete the record. He accepted an invitation to play guitar on 'And Through The Wire'. 'There was one track which we couldn't get the right guitar feel on at the time and Paul was able to go straight to it,' said Gabriel. 'We were looking for a certain rhythm that Paul was very good for. The way he plays that rhythm stuff is amazing; he's got this sort of liquid energy in him and in the way he plays.'

'Peter was always interested in punk, and was always fascinated with what kids are doing at any point. You have to have the right attitude working with Peter rather than technical ability,' said Lillywhite.

All this breaking of artistic sound barriers was the last thing Gabriel's American record company Atlantic wanted if it meant being uncommercial. During the recording the musicians had to put up with the visits of Atlantic's head of A&R, bearded Californian John Kolodner. After the Townhouse sessions the bulk of the album was recorded at Ashcombe House using the Manor mobile studio. It was the first recording Gabriel had made on home territory. Kolodner went to hear what was going on.

'His big thing in music is "fuck art". The best record in the world is the one that sells the most. End of story. And he used to come over occasionally during the album and hum and ha,' said Lillywhite.

'We were very childish in a way. And when we knew Kolodner was coming over we'd make sure the control room in the studio was really cold because we knew he liked it warm. And we used to have table tennis tournaments during the recording of the album.

'We would think we had something really good going, and he would come in and put a damper on it. Everyone was nice to him, there was never any animosity.'

Kolodner's most memorable remark came while he was listening to 'And Through The Wire'. 'I was in the studio when Kolodner said, if you do this, this, and this it will sound like the Doobie Brothers. I had enough, I walked out of the studio,' remembered Gail Colson. Paul Weller's guitar was used as a suitable antidote.

When the album was finally completed in February 1980 Gail went to New York with the tapes. 'I made the mistake of making them sit down and listen to it,' said Gail. In the room were Kolodner, managing director Jerry Greenberg and the president and founder of Atlantic Records, Ahmet Ertegun. Gail attempted to explain every song as they went along, but was met with hostility. 'Ertegun said there was no point in writing a song about Biko because no one in America was aware what was happening in South Africa. He thought "Family Snapshot" was too controversial (the song is based on the thoughts of an assassin stalking his prey). And when he heard "Lead A Normal Life" (about conformity) he asked if Peter had any mental problems.

'The meeting went downhill,' remembered Gail. 'I think they had decided they were going to drop him. Kolodner didn't want Lillywhite, he had wanted an American whizz kid.'

They broke up for lunch, and Gail met them again in the afternoon. 'They said, we have an idea,' said Gail. 'When Peter comes to his senses we will have the next album. And I said that's not on, you either have him or you don't, so they passed.'

Kolodner concluded the album would be 'commercial suicide', believing it would not sell above their minimum requirement of 100,000. Atlantic was forced to pay Charisma Records £75,000 for passing on the option. The album would have been Gabriel's last for Atlantic anyway as his contract was due for renewal.

Gabriel called Atlantic's decision 'an example of the short-sighted, bigoted attitude commonly found in the hierarchy of the American record industry. It will be ironic if this album turns out to be more successful.' It was, and Gabriel derived great satisfaction when 'Games Without Frontiers' became his first UK Top 10 single, reaching Number 4 in April 1980 and boosting sales of the album. But Gabriel could not take credit for the release of 'Games Without Frontiers' as a single; he and Lillywhite disputed Colson's belief that it should be the first single from the album.

Gabriel enjoyed the idea of being out of contract in America for the first time, believing he now had a free hand to find a company sympathetic to his work. What he did not realize was that Tony Stratton Smith still held the option for his American releases, and Strat placed the album with Polygram's American label, Mercury Records.

Gabriel and Colson had their doubts about Mercury, an arm of the giant Polygram group who were strong in Europe but lacked marketing muscle in the United States. It was known as 'The Graveyard of the Record Industry' and someone referred to the company as 'Mercury Poisoning'. Their fears were unfounded; the third album sold a healthy 250,000 copies in the United States, outselling the second album by 100,000 copies. Sales were helped by extensive play of 'Games Without Frontiers' on US Top 40 radio, though the song was not a hit in the States. Atlantic Records apart, the third album is regarded as the one that established Peter Gabriel as an important artist, and paved the way for future success. Within two years of dropping Gabriel, Atlantic were offering to buy him back for an advance of $750,000.

In the UK the album, again just known as *Peter Gabriel*, went straight to Number 3 after its release on 31 May 1980. The following week it became Gabriel's first Number 1 record.

The album's themes are frequently disturbing, even if the music is more accessible than his previous work. On 'Intruder' the menacing whistling and scratching guitar echoes the lyric; 'The sense of isolation inspires.'

'I liked the idea of the intruder and intrusion of different sorts. Implied within that there's obviously the cat burglar, just the house-breaker, but there's also the implication of sexual intrusion as well which I tried to leave fairly open and I think I was trying with some of it to exaggerate the moment of fear.

'I think there are various physical states that we get in when our adrenalin is pumping hard which leave much bigger mental imprints than information which goes in under normal circumstances. So it was trying to cultivate a sense of urgency.

'I have a belief that in some ways a victim is guilty as well as the assailant,' explained Gabriel to Bruce Elder of *Melody Maker*. 'We are excellent casting directors and writers of our own psychological dramas, and we choose to surround ourselves with people who will perhaps produce a certain set of reactions that something within us needs.' That message reflects EST and Zen teachings.

But it is a belief Gabriel takes to its extreme, agreeing with an American study that in certain cases people might psychologically invite a mugging and other crimes.

'I think that rape being such an explosive subject it's very hard for anyone to logically accept that a victim has any responsibility, but where it maybe is easier for a rational mind to see some sort of pattern is in wife-beating, where some wives will go from one man to another man to perhaps a third, all of whom would be violent men. And in a sado-masochistic tie-up that sort of pattern and relationship is present, and in a lot of other things that consciously or logically we can't accept, nor could our legal system.'

The terror is continued on 'Family Snapshot', this time it is the assassin and his victim. The song is based on *An Assassin's Diary*, the notes and scribbles of Arthur Bremmer, who shot and crippled Governor George Wallace of Alabama in 1972. When Gabriel introduced the song live he related how the discarded diary was found under a bridge in Washington DC by a passer-by before finally reaching the hands of a publisher. 'It was a really nasty book, but you do get a sense of the person who is writing it,' said Gabriel. 'Bremmer was obsessed with the idea of fame. He was aware of the news broadcasts all over the world and was trying to time the assassination to hit the early evening news in the States and late night in Europe to get maximum coverage.' Bremmer originally went after Nixon, which explains the references to the presidential cavalcade in the song. Gabriel dropped his stage references to Kennedy's assassination having been convinced a solitary assassin was not responsible for that murder.

*I don't really hate you*
*– I don't care what you do*
*We were made for each other*
*Me and you*
*I want to be somebody*
*You were like that too*
*If you don't get given you learn to take*
*And I will take you*

'Family Snapshot'; Gabriel, 1980

The song is viewed from inside the assassin's head. Gabriel believes that criminals are not the alien beasts caricatured in the popular press, but merely act out what is for the rest of us an imaginary part of our existence. The assassin and victim both had an impending sense of their fate. 'As though they're each preparing, getting dressed up for this occasion,' Gabriel said.

When it is over the killer flashes back to his unloved boyhood. 'Some clichés are true – patterns of behaviour begun in childhood do carry through. I see that in my own life.'

There is not much more cheer throughout the rest of the album. 'Games Without Frontiers' suggests war is as simple as child's play, while satirizing the slapstick and frequently inane TV contest *Jeux Sans Froniteres*. 'Not One Of Us' and 'And Through The Wire' deal with alienation and isolation, while 'Lead A Normal Life' proffers the banality of what is on offer to those of us who conform. Gabriel agreed that anguish is a common theme on the album, but it was not by design. One track that never made the record because the lyrics were unfinished was the frivolous 'I Go Swimming', later to appear on his live album.

'I see some parallels between this new album and blues music in a way, although not obvious at all. People ask me why is it always so depressing and dark, this new music, and I think that blues music can be very depressing and dark and quite often self-pitying, but at the same time it does provide people, when they listen to it, with an opportunity to release those feelings within themselves and perhaps come out of it more optimistic, more positive, but only by having been through or experienced that sort of negativity and pessimism,' he told Bruce Elder of *Melody Maker*.

Again the album had no title and the cover was stark, this time one half of Gabriel's face was distorted, a process achieved by rubbing the emulsion on a Polaroid picture before it was dry, inspiring its informal title of *Melt*. It is literal self-effacement. He was still holding to his belief that all the albums should look like magazines.

The critics were mixed in their views, he was anything from a genius to a middle of the roader. Dave Marsh got carried away down an intellectual black hole in *Rolling Stone* in September 1980. 'Lucid and driven, Peter Gabriel's third solo album sticks in the mind like the haunted heroes of the best *films noir*. With the obsessiveness of *The Big Sleep* (or, more aptly, Jean-Luc Godard's *Breathless*, since Gabriel is nothing if not self-conscious about his sources), the new LP's exhilaration derives from paranoia, yet its theme isn't fear so much as overwhelming guilt. If rock and roll is capable of comprehending original sin, then Peter Gabriel might be the man for the job.

'Gabriel's methods are similar to those of Graham Greene, Raymond Chandler and Eric Ambler. The singer establishes an "innocent" character of society from a distance until he finds himself being pulled inexorably towards the centre of events. Finally, he's uncertain where observation ends and complicity begins. This is the essence of modern-day moral geometry – even the passive man must act – but that doesn't make it any less scary . . .' And so he continued for a few hundred more words, concluding, 'Peter Gabriel has seen a hellish future, and there's no exit.'

Nick Kent in the *NME* wrote: 'Although I've only possessed the record for some three days, the sheer ferocious power of conceit, vision and performance that blazes out of virtually every bar of music on this, Peter Gabriel's third solo album, is so obvious and so courageously implemented that this reviewer is currently in a state of virtual awe at the achievement.'

Kent concluded, 'It is destined, I'm already convinced, to become one of the eighties' seminal works. On the one hand it is the sound of a man breaking stride and grasping for his moment, on the other it is the sound of an artist fully coming to terms with himself and his sense of values. The result is a courageous tour de force that anyone who even cares slightly about the current state of rock should take heed of.'

The following week, Kent's *NME* colleague Paul Morley was less charitable, calling Gabriel 'the thinking person's David Essex'. He went on: 'A suitable package of puzzlement, pessimism, abstraction and paranoia, acted out professionally and containing enough philosophical and political flavour to soothe the rumbling guilt of the passive rock consumer . . .' Morley called Gabriel's 'honesty admirable; the art shallow'.

Gabriel was stung by Morley's gratuitous insults, and has gradually grown to distrust the music press, rarely granting them interviews. 'I think for any artist to pretend that he isn't hurt by bad reviews would be dishonest. They hurt and they're discouraging,' he said of reviews for another record, though the same holds true for all his work.

The *NME*, apart from Nick Kent, were particularly scurrilous in their attacks, provoking intolerance in return from Gabriel, who instructed that no concert tickets, press information and records should be sent to the *NME*. In 1987 hostilities abated and the paper, under a new regime, made attempts to repair the fractured relationship.

# CHAPTER EIGHT

GABRIEL DID NOT RELISH BARING HIS soul to a room full of strangers. He found it hard enough to open up on an individual basis. So he was not over-keen when Richard Macphail urged him and Jill to take part in an Erhard Seminar Training session in 1978.

He shelved responsibility and said he would abide by Jill's decision, feeling sure she would say no. 'I thought I was quite safe there, because she's sceptical about all these things. But she said, "OK, I'll do it." So I was thrown.' Actually, it was not that Jill was seeking enlightenment so much as jumping at the chance of getting away from the kids for two weekends.

Richard Macphail was so enthused by EST he encouraged all his friends to follow suit; most did not want to hear about it.

Together with Macphail and his girlfriend, Peter and Jill did the EST training at a London hotel in July 1978, one month after the release of the second solo album. They paid around £170 each for two intensive weekend sessions.

EST was portrayed by the media as cranky and a rip-off. This was not surprising considering founder Werner Erhard's background. Originally a car salesman named Jack Rosenberg from Philadelphia, he left his family to seek a new life. His new name was inspired by West German Chancellor Dr Ludwig Erhard, who transformed post-war Germany's economy, and the rocket scientist Dr Wernher von Braun.

Werner Erhard went to California where he became a successful businessman selling educational aids for an organization called Parents. He became involved in the burgeoning 'human potential movement' of the late fifties and sixties, and devised the training from his own experiences at the Esalen Institute in Big Sur, California, the centre of the growth movement in the sixties, as well as involvement with Zen Buddhism and Silva Mind Control. He was later reunited with his family.

The EST training aimed to force participants into confronting their deepest emotions, motives and relationships, in the hope this would unlock their hidden potential. Part of that process of self-confrontation included the discomfort of sitting for hours and hours on end, baring your soul if you chose, or listening to others bare theirs. People frequently screamed in anger and burst into tears. All this public heartrending was a revelation to Gabriel and Macphail, who were brought up to not show their emotions.

'My parents never rowed openly, it just wasn't done, so I just learned never to express anger,' said Macphail. 'Anger was unacceptable. It's something I've relearned to do to overcome that sort of conditioning. And I think Peter's done the same. I think it's a great mark of our relationship that we allow ourselves to be angry with each other.'

Gabriel also never heard his parents row, and their voices were hardly ever raised against him. As a child he expressed his frustration obliquely. 'I remember quite often when I was angry with my parents slamming the door and going down to the piano and playing particularly discordant things which I knew would bug the hell out of them, particularly my mum. Totally senseless,' said Gabriel.

'Expressing anger is something I had to try and come to terms with and I'm still working on it. It's difficult because it is a sort of wild impulsive thing that I've been taught to buckle up. And it's absurd, really, because people know when you are angry, it's just that you can't make it honest. And if you can't get angry with other people then they can't get angry with you and all this hidden resentment builds up, so it's really unhealthy.'

Gabriel had already read about EST in Californian underground magazines. 'It was a real sort of threatening experience, in a way, which I think is partly why I didn't do it up until the time Richard decided to go for it.

'It's a hotch-potch of ideas culled from all sorts of places. I view it now mainly as a vehicle, something you can use to get from point A to point B. People were very critical about Erhard and about money and the philosophy. When I buy a car I don't ask for psychological backgrounds of the people that built it. If it's going to get me from one place to another then I'm happy to use it,' said Gabriel.

'I think for some people it's a useful training, so I have recommended it to a few people, one of whom actually committed suicide, I don't think as a consequence of that, but he got very involved with EST. He was unstable, I think, before then. But it's strong stuff, and the most important single idea, I think, is that it says, "You are responsible for what happens to you. You are not a victim." And that, I think, has enabled me to do a lot of things that perhaps I wouldn't have done before.

'It was part of a process of a much more honest communication between Jill and I, and between other people, key friends and relationships. For instance, one of those jobs that you don't want to do, like firing someone, maybe in the old days I would have asked someone else to do it. Now I would do that myself. I have a lot of difficulty doing it, but I feel better for having done it.'

'It was a very dramatic event. Trainers were purposely very, very straight with people in a way that is quite unusual. I sat bolt upright in my chair and it terrified me and fascinated me at the same time. It was such an enormous relief for me,' said Macphail.

'There is something about it being in a large group that stops people being damaged. It's hard to explain it any more than that. In terms of emotions I experienced everything there was to experience during that course. You agree not to hit anyone else or intrude on anyone else's experience. You are in the chair for those hours and hours and hours. People are sharing and interacting with the trainer, and it just sparks off stuff because you begin to empathize and realize you've felt like that, you go through that, so you don't have to get up and say anything, just by being there it rubs off on you.

'It had an enormous impact on all of us, and immediately afterwards we went and spent a whole week down at their cottage together, just the four of us, and continued the process. In a sense it started a process that has never changed. It drove our relationship down, much deeper, we just opened up to each other in a way that is quite extraordinary, unprecedented, because that is what it is about. It is the basis of a very close bond between us. It shifts your attitude to things in a way that, if you choose, will never leave you.

'It had a very powerful effect on Peter and I would say that I can still see the effect. For instance, the whole character of his lyrics changed after the training. He may not put it down to this but instead of being all this wishy-washy gnomes and goblins stuff that characterized Genesis, you know, pretty unspecific and heavily symbolic, it became much more straightforward and he just started to write what he was feeling in a way that wasn't tricky to understand. So he discovered a sort of directness of approach. It was a very important turning point in my life and in my relationship with Peter, and I would say his life too,' said Macphail.

'Peter did change dramatically, he was able to talk openly to people in a very different fashion. So there was much more of an extreme change in him than me,' said Jill. 'Richard would like to be stronger about the EST influence than I think Peter or I would, partly because he was so involved. I don't think EST changed my life, though it did have a positive influence. I think it did change Peter's lyrics, but I still have the feeling Peter would have got there anyhow, it was just accelerated growth.'

Macphail reviewed the training in 1981, he supervised courses and organized weekends, though despite earlier aspirations decided not to become a trainer. The original EST training has now been softened and moderated. EST, according to Macphail, had a lot to do with helping Peter and Jill through later crises in their marriage.

EST was an effective tool helping Gabriel confront his own conditioning. Though it was capable of having deep psychological effects there was nothing mystical or necessarily spiritual about the experience. When he wanted to probe further into his psyche he preferred esoteric teachings to formalized religion. He shunned the short-cut to Nirvana chosen by so many of his contempories through drugs, notably LSD. But he was willing to experiment with technological devices that appeared to have similar effects to meditation.

'Acid was the only drug I was interested in, but I was too frightened ever to do it. I used to have a pretty powerful dream life and I think I was afraid of losing control. Maybe I'm less afraid of losing control now, but I'm not so interested in it any more. Sometimes I have been pretty scared when my head gets going into overdrive, and I didn't want to unleash it.'

Part of his resistance to trying drugs was his loathing of peer pressure from schooldays, whether it was being one of the sports set, in the art group or smoking cigarettes and drinking. 'I was pretty much of a dud growing up, so I thought, don't go into competition you might not do well in.'

He had two experiences with hashish. The first time he

giggled a lot and then threw up. The second was more scientific; he ate some hash cakes provided by a roadie at Ashcombe House and sat down at his desk with a notebook and tape recorder. Nothing happened, so he ate a lot more. He then leaned over the desk and felt 'these two bolts of metal shoot up the back of my neck, like mercury in a thermometer. They came crashing round the front of my head, and I thought, "Uh-oh." And panic began to set in deep.'

Convinced he was going to die he headed for home. 'I decided I would try and get home in time to say my last words to my wife and kids. It was about half a mile across fields to where I was living, and I was still talking to the tape recorder, so there's this very funny tape of me thinking that I was going to die. I was getting revelations, as I approached my death, about the meaning of life. I was certain that life was actually organized into five videotapes, which were all running slightly out of sync. And very soon after I came upon this profound piece of wisdom, you hear me collapse into a ditch.'

Eventually he found his way home, where he had milk with sugar and went to bed. 'Jill thought I looked very pale and thought I must have been in a traffic accident. I looked shocked, was her assessment, but my kids didn't notice any difference.'

A failure as a drug user, Gabriel prefers the intellectual and psychic to the chemical search for enlightenment. He was to try what appear cranky methods to help induce dream-like states. 'I feel I have had experiences that are a little out of the ordinary. Just being at some remote place and getting a very quiet meditation. Maybe there's a clear sky and a full moon and my mind starts zapping. I think we keep our other lives incredibly contained.

'Dreams are important. We spend a third of our lives asleep, and probably a third of that time dreaming. And I think it's part of the process through which the brain organizes what has been going on in the conscious and the unconscious, and not to take notice of it is, I think, foolish. I do jot them down when it's strong, but it's not a daily event, maybe once a month. It is all influential stuff going on in our head and it is not often acknowledged. I think it is quite a powerful and a motivating force.'

He has extensively read the works of Carl Jung, and like him jotted down dream experiences. Jung wrote in his auto-biography, *Memories, Dreams, Reflections*: 'I wrote down the fantasies as well as I could, and made an earnest effort to analyse the psychic conditions under which they had arisen . . .

'In order to grasp the fantasies which were stirring in me "underground", I knew that I had to let myself plummet down into them, as it were. I felt not only violent resistance to this, but a distinct fear. For I was afraid of losing command of myself and becoming a prey to the fantasies . . .'

Jung continued: 'It was clear to me from the start that I could find contact with the outer world and with people only if I succeeded in showing – and this would demand the most intensive effort – that the contents of psychic experience are real, and real not only as my own personal experiences, but as collective experiences which others also have.'

Dreams have served a dual purpose for Gabriel, as well as helping him delve into his psyche they were an inspiration for songs. He paid homage to Jung in 'Rhythm of the Heat' on the fourth album. It was originally titled 'Jung In Africa', but he abandoned that because it sounded pretentious.

*Smash the radio*
*No outside voices here*
*Smash the watch*
*Cannot tear the day to shreds*
*Smash the camera*
*Cannot steal away the spirits*
*The rhythm is around me*

*The rhythm has control*
*The rhythm is inside me*
*The rhythm has my soul.*

'Rhythm of the Heat'; Gabriel 1982

This final verse is similar to a description of Jung's while in Africa in 1925: 'Thousands of miles lay between me and Europe, mother of all demons. The demons would not reach me here – there were no telegrams, no telephone calls, no letters, no visitors. My liberated psychic forces poured blissfully back to the primeval expanses . . .'

'Rhythm of the Heat' has a pulsating, primeval drum sound that builds into an all-encompassing crescendo. It is one of Gabriel's most direct expressions of rhythmic power.

Gabriel described 'Rhythm of the Heat' as 'the adventures of Carl Jung in the Sudan – Great White Thinker – inventor of the concept of the shadow, frightened by his own shadow emerging as a result of rhythm'.

The song refers to an incident when Jung, trekking across Africa, became terrified of the very thing he was searching for, the continent's mystical power. Though no humour is apparent in the song, Gabriel was amused at Jung's comical attempts to shut off the magic. A tribal dance was put on for the visiting psychologist, but he was alarmed to see the participants possessed like a wild horde as the rhythm of the dance and drumming intensified. Cracking his rhinoceros whip, swearing at them in Swiss German and passing around cigarettes Jung managed to scatter them into the night.

The promise of more dream-like states encouraged Gabriel, in early 1981, to buy a Samadhi flotation tank. Not quite the fiendish sensory deprivation tank depicted in Ken Russell's film *Altered States*, the tank is a calm, immensely relaxing environment. The Samadhi, resembling a fat wedged coffin, has about eight inches of water and Epsom salts, kept at skin temperature to give the sensation of gravity loss.

Gabriel has not cited any musical inspiration that has come to him in his tank. 'I've daydreamed a lot. You know, in that state in which ideas do come.' It would be a useful escape over the traumatic next few years. The songs on *Peter Gabriel* four, recorded in the year after he got the tank, do show more of a mystical leaning – 'Rhythm of the Heat', 'Lay Your Hands On Me' and 'San Jacinto' – but the songs are also the result of many other influences dating back several years.

He was inspired to get the tank after reading *Centre of the Cyclone* by American psychoanalyst John Lilly who designed and experimented with tanks to attain 'psychological free fall'. His findings were the opposite of those of CIA researchers who first developed tanks in the fifties to explore sensory deprivation which they believed could induce madness.

Lilly's book is full of flowery out-of-the-body experiences which became even weirder when he started experimenting with LSD. It was these experiences which inspired Paddy Chayefsky to write the fictional *Altered States* on which Russell based his film.

'I moved into universes containing beings much larger than myself, so that I was a mote in their sunbeam, a small ant in their universe, a single thought in a huge mind, or a small programme in a cosmic computer . . . Waves of the equivalent of light, of sound, of motion, waves of intense emotion, were carried in dimensions beyond my understanding.' Lilly concluded: 'All and everything that one can imagine exists.'

The isolation tank highlights one of the paradoxes of Gabriel's character. He never indulges in drugs because he fears losing control. The isolation tank promised altered states. He was willing to gamble on losing control in the tank, although in the end there was little risk.

Whatever mystical possibilities first enticed Gabriel to buy a tank, he has used it to help enhance creative thinking. The scientific explanation for this is the tank's stimulation of the brain's theta waves. Beta waves are generated when we are awake, alpha when we are relaxed and calm, delta when we are deeply asleep. But theta waves occur in fleeting instants when we drift in and out of sleep.

According to Michael Hutchison in *The Book of Floating*: 'The theta state is accompanied by unexpected, unpredictable, dreamlike, but very vivid mental images, accompanied by intense memories, particularly childhood memories – theta offers access to unconscious control, reverie, free association, sudden insight, creative inspiration. It is a mysterious, elusive state, potentially highly productive and enlightening.'

Gabriel lent his copy of *The Centre of the Cyclone* to Richard Macphail. 'He wrote in the front, "Peter Gabriel's – feel guilty if not returned." I actually gave it back to him about five years later, and stopped feeling guilty,' said Macphail.

Advocates of floating point to more practical benefits like weight loss, reductions in smoking and drinking, and counteracting drug withdrawal symptoms. Floating is said to stimulate the brain to secrete endorphins, the pain-killing euphoria-creating substances described as the body's natural opiates.

Gabriel's interest in machines that could induce mood changes or detect them dated back to his days in Genesis when he first investigated bio-feedback machines. He saw in them a potential for increased self-awareness. Bio-feedback machines with electrodes attached to the body monitor involuntary bodily movement like brain waves and heartbeat. Seeing the level of these normally unconscious movements on a dial or oscilloscope can supposedly help the individual gain conscious control of them.

In the early seventies Gabriel visited companies in the United States that made the devices. He planned to attach the machines to the group on stage to alter the light and sound according to the moods the machines monitored, for *The Lamb Lies Down On Broadway*. The band were doubtful it was technically or financially feasible and the plan was eventually abandoned.

During his sabbatical period in 1975 Gabriel learnt a yoga

technique called Breath of Fire, which induces a form of hyperventilation. Gabriel demonstrated with some fast breathing, then took a deep breath and held it. 'You can mess yourself up if you don't do it right. But you sort of flush the system. It's quite strong medicine. That, too, gets my head floating.'

In 1982 during the recording of the fourth album he was introduced to gravity boots by Jerry Marotta. The boots were strapped to the legs and had large metal hooks protruding from them which could support someone hanging upside down from a gravity bar. Gabriel then had prolonged struggles with a children's climbing rope to find a satisfactory way of hanging upside down. The theory is that the spine and back benefit greatly from stretches and exercises performed the wrong way up, more blood is pumped to the brain and the endocrine system is stimulated.

By now Gabriel had got rid of the aversion to most sports he developed at school, and became a keen jogger. During various sessions at Ashcombe House, particularly with David Rhodes, he would go for a run up to Solsbury Hill, and still jogs sporadically.

Physical exercise and the expansion of the psyche were part of his continuous quest for self-improvement. Despite being open to many esoteric influences, he had a natural aversion to organized religion. 'I'm not a practising religious person, in the sense of belonging to a faith or a church. I've been very interested in Zen Buddhism and Taosim, those two I think fit my way of looking at the world better than anything else, and yet in moments of crisis I still pray hard because that is instinctively built in from childhood. So I think there is a mixture there, but I think religion is one of those things that once you have created the hole in the psyche for religion, it always has to be filled with something even if it is anti-religion.'

Jill retains stronger church links through her father Lord Moore, ennobled on his retirement as Private Secretary to the Queen in 1986, who became vice-president of the Society for

Promoting Christian Knowledge. Jill has been an active member of her village Anglican congregation, once putting on a play which sent roller-skating children through the church to the consternation of some older members. 'Peter believes in God, and he believes in Christ, but I don't think he believes in the church, and I can see that, and I have great battles myself.'

Anna and Melanie were both confirmed and christened at the Self-Realization Fellowship in Los Angeles. 'It was lovely, actually, a mill in the middle of this wonderful lake, and they were christened in six different religions,' said Jill.

Gabriel made no apologies for continuing on an inner search when he spoke about these things in the eighties. 'My formative years were in the sixties. I was born in 1950, so I was seventeen years old in 1967 and I think seventeen is a critical age for a lot of people because they are just getting a sense of how they fit into the world. You are trying to think things through an awful lot during that period. There was an openness then that made a big impact on me. My father has always had this inquiring mind, there were always books around. And it seems to me that a lot of those ideas which went underground in the seventies are beginning to resurface again in the eighties, except that they are a lot less naïve, partly because a lot of the people who are still working with them are now in their thirties, rather than in their teens or their twenties, so that's exciting me.' He saw these attitudes seeping into our lives, from healthier food and exercise through to the global awareness generated by Band Aid.

Gabriel is a long-time fan of the *Whole Earth Catalogue*, which has promoted alternative technology and campaigned on environmental issues since its inception in the sixties. Through an introduction to one of the people closely involved with the Californian community around which the catalogue is based, Gabriel was offered the chance of the most extraordinary journey he, or anyone else, was ever likely to make.

Gabriel had been corresponding with Tom Mandell, a fan who worked as a futurist at Stanford Research Institute in Palo Alto, just south of San Francisco. Mandell, an engaging letter writer, informed Gabriel that Peter Schwartz, his boss at the institute, was visiting London, and suggested a meeting. Schwartz was familiar with Gabriel's music and was sure he was the musician he needed for the first documenatry feature made in space.

Peter Schwartz, a brilliant thinker with a child-like enthusiasm for the ideas that captivated him, was a good friend of Stewart Brand, founder of the *Whole Earth Catalogue*. Brand, a former army photographer, campaigned to get the first picture of the earth from space published, naming the catalogue after it. 'The picture was significant because it showed the unity of the whole planet,' said Schwartz. The catalogue is one of the few successful surviving remnants of hippy idealism.

Schwartz, a self-confessed old Californian hippy, wanted Gabriel to join his mission to make a film on the Space Shuttle after their meeting in 1978.

'"Why me?" he said. Peter is a modest man. He thought, "It couldn't possibly be me." On the other hand he loved the idea, and he was tickled and fascinated by it,' said Schwartz. 'Like anybody in his situation you are approached with lots of harebrained schemes. And this, in fact, was one of the harebrainer he had encountered. He took it seriously because I presented it seriously and I came from a relatively serious organization. I had come recommended by someone he knew, so he didn't think I was a nutcase.'

Schwartz wanted Gabriel to compose the film soundtrack inspired by what he would experience in space. The project would also include writer Peter Mathiessen, a traveller and 'spiritual explorer' who would write the narration; Schwartz would go as producer, with a yet-to-be-chosen cameraman shooting in 70mm. Schwartz had also interested Tom Wolfe, then working on *The Right Stuff*, in writing about the project.

It is easy to see how Gabriel became captivated with Schwartz's scheme. Schwartz has an incisive mind and talks with conviction. Both Schwartz and Gabriel, who have become close friends, share similar 'spiritual' ideals. That idealism inevitably makes them appear naïve and cranky, but that is the risk any innovator takes. It has not stopped Schwartz's high-powered career which has involved working on identifying 'future critical problem areas' for the White House, and steering a large team as acting head of strategic planning at the London Stock Exchange.

Schwartz had been fascinated with space travel since boyhood, and nurtured dreams of becoming an astronaut into his adult life. In 1968, as a student of aeronautical engineering, he spent his vacation working as a junior engineer on the Apollo mission for the National Aeronautics and Space Administration in Philadelphia. Then, in 1974, at the Stanford Research Institute he worked for NASA again, in mission planning for the Space Shuttle programme.

Schwartz was convinced Gabriel was perfect to write the space film soundrack. 'Firstly; I liked the aesthetics of his music. It is just very good entertaining music. Secondly, it was clear that he was prepared to push the frontiers of music, and this was going to be an innovative enterprise. And third he has brought together – and this is, I think, remarkable – a kind of broad cultural diversity, global in character, and a depth of spirit, which is quite unique. And that is what I wanted the movie to represent, all of those together. And no one represented that better in music than Peter.

'There are not many people who can integrate across the kind of profound gulfs you find between the arts and sciences. There are people who are comfortable in the world of science and people who are comfortable in the world of arts. But there are very few who can meaningfully bridge across that.

'Peter has the discipline to master the tools, and it takes a lot of discipline. It's really quite remarkable to watch him work in the studio. Getting something down right will take him not hours, but days, weeks, sometimes months.'

Schwartz was dismayed that the American pioneering spirit had all but disappeared from the Space Shuttle programme. 'Somehow or other we had to communicate the real sense of adventure, the profound phenomenon of man going off into the universe.' The men from NASA were unsure how to respond when they received Schwartz's request in 1978. Their idea of commercial spin-offs from the space programme was creating new products like Teflon.

One of the film project's advisers was Rusty Schweickart, an astronaut on the 1969 Apollo 9 mission. Schweickart had undergone what amounted to a mystical conversion during a forty-minute space walk. He later formed the Association of Space Explorers dedicated to the peaceful, non-nuclear use of space, which he co-chaired with Alexei Leonov, the first Russian to walk in space.

Gabriel was told that if the space film did go ahead he would have to undertake the same rigorous training all aspiring astronauts undergo. All the participants would have to go into wilderness areas to see how well they functioned as a team and train on gravity machines.

The loss of Schwartz's financial backers combined with NASA's procrastination and delays in the Shuttle programme forced Schwartz to abandon his dream at the end of 1978. 'The whole thing caught my imagination for a while. It looked like it might happen,' said Gabriel. Schwartz is still convinced he will one day travel in space.

At the time the space film was starting to look shaky, Schwartz was approached by two Hollywood scriptwriters who wanted to model a film called *The Genius* on him as a child. Schwartz does not blanch from confirming he was a child genius.

Schwartz recommended a more interesting plot, partially based on his own experiences as a youth when he became one of the first computer hackers, breaking into two Department of Defense computers, one controlling the trajectory of missiles. The film became *War Games*, which grossed $100 million at the box office.

On the basis that it takes one to know one, Schwartz is sure he can recognize the qualities of genius in others. 'Peter is a great genius. Genius is not simply a function of the blinding insight. That happens from time to time, sure. It has to do in part with having very open eyes to be able to see clearly. And I think Peter forces himself to look hard at the world.

'He travels a great deal, he visits people, he doesn't really sit in his little studio in England and say, "Well, I'll read some things and listen to the tapes people send me." He's out there! "What's happening there in the world? What do I feel when I take a trip to Senegal and Brazil, or Nicaragua?" I took him to the high technology places in California, and he, like a good trained observer, sees things that others don't see. So he has very open eyes, I think that is terribly important.

'I think another part of genius is the ability to bridge. That is, to make connections that others don't make. What is beautiful about Peter's connections is that they cut across so many curves; the cultural, i.e. he really is able to tap the rhythms of many cultures – they are still very much in his own idiom of rock and roll of the West, because he's intimate in that idiom. There is a kind of political–spiritual dimension; he wants to make the world a better place. It isn't simply "I like to make nice sounds", it is "I have a deeper purpose in life". And that affects both him as a person and his thinking, it moves him, inspires him. I don't think he has an innate love of hardware technology; he loves the tools and what they can do for him. He has to discipline and really force himself to master it and not be satisfied until he has got it. I think very few artists have that.'

# CHAPTER NINE

THE CONFLICT OVER THE CREATIVE INPUT and ownership of *The Lamb Lies Down On Broadway* lingered long after Gabriel left Genesis. More than any of his other group projects, Gabriel felt most possessive towards *The Lamb*.

Having got the group to originally agree to give him complete artistic freedom in devising the story and lyrics, Gabriel decided he deserved to own them as well, and without consulting the rest of Genesis, copyrighted it.

That action in itself, in a group that had prided itself on its democratic ownership of all material, caused a rift. But then Gabriel compounded the sin in 1979 by writing a screenplay and then asking his former colleagues to return to the studio to re-record the soundtrack. He had no choice but to ask them to help as the Genesis line-up of 1974 still jointly owned the music.

'The band were a little reluctant to re-work old material, and also old material in which I had figured so prominently. So there was a certain amount of resistance. It occurred to me that up until the time of my leaving Genesis everything had been co-owned. I should have, through writing melodies and lyrics and quite a few things, done quite well. But I had been possessive enough to copyright the story of *The Lamb*, which caused a certain amount of friction at the time. I thought that as it had been my story I should have the right to do other things with it as I wanted to, and was able to. The music, of course, is co-owned.'

When it became clear the band weren't prepared to re-record, Gabriel thought about writing some new material for *The Lamb*. 'I think I could have legally recorded my own version of *The Lamb*. But that would have been a somewhat dumb thing to do.'

Gabriel felt deeply about Rael and *The Lamb* not only because he believed in its visual potential, but also because of the resemblance Rael bore to himself. Superficially Rael, the Puerto Rican punk from the Bronx, created over a year before the real punks hit the music scene, was far removed from Gabriel, the polite product of middle-class Surrey. But as if to confirm how much of himself was in Rael, Gabriel planned to put himself in the lead role of the film.

In the early seventies Gabriel had been greatly impressed with the film *El Topo* directed by Alejandro Jodorowsky. 'There are scenes in *El Topo* which will stay with me forever,' Gabriel said. The film appears to defy description. Gabriel's attempts to locate Jodorowsky, the Chilean-born son of Russian Jewish parents, were thwarted several times, but he eventually tracked him down to his Paris home and met him in early 1979.

'I had an original story, it wasn't very long, about twelve pages or something. Alejandro then did his own version of that. I don't think my thing was very strong in the first place, I certainly didn't like it, where it had gone, so I sort of killed it off.'

*The Lamb Lies Down On Broadway* was to be a twentieth-century *Pilgrim's Progress*. Rael, the young Puerto Rican convict from the Bronx, was carving out a career in New York City. But the street punk and graffiti artist was forced to make an unexpected detour into his own psyche. Rael was thrust into a fourth-dimensional world inhabited by mythical creatures and bizarre characters. It was a surreal tale of sex, violence and death. Gabriel, who had mounted a highly theatrical live show when performing with Genesis, planned to make extensive use of cinematic special effects.

'We spent about four to six weeks working together, developing a script. It was great, a very exciting time.' After a break Gabriel and Jodorowsky continued their work during the summer of 1979 in Bath at Ashcombe House. 'He's an incredible character, and has been a breath of fresh air in helping me re-evaluate my own career,' Gabriel said at the time. 'We've been talking about getting a producer, and it's very exciting for me because he's the master and I am the apprentice.' They modified the story considerably. Jodorowsky persuaded Gabriel to abandon plans to play Rael and stay behind the scenes and co-author.

'At the time I only knew his songs, I had never seen him on stage,' said Jodorowsky. 'I said he should not play Rael, but now I would say yes because I know how he performs.'

The proposed feature film was entrusted to Charisma Films who looked to raise a relatively modest £5 million. But when Gabriel was dropped by Atlantic in 1980 there were immediate delays in getting the necessary American backers. Charisma were told financiers wanted to see Gabriel selling records in America first before they would commit themselves. Despite the third album's ultimate success, they were still not convinced.

After working with Jodorowsky, Gabriel hoped filming could begin in the summer of 1981. He hung on tenaciously to the idea for a few years after that. 'It just died, it wasn't ever resolved with the band,' he said. Conflict was avoided by default.

Gabriel was captivated by Jodorowsky's 'cosmic enlightenment'. Soon after working with Gabriel he made a children's film about elephants called *Tusk*. But his Russian and Latin temperament and surreal vision were too much for film financiers who doubted his commercial appeal. Jodorowsky survived by giving Tarot readings.

'I think Peter has a marvellous unconscience [sic]. In some ways he understands me, but in an enormous way I understand him. In order to understand Peter you need to close your ears and look at how he walks. There you can start to understand him,' Jodorowsky attempted to explain.

Jodorowsky's career never took off, despite being the first to hold the film rights to Frank Herbert's science-fiction epic *Dune*. He wrote a script for the movie and put togther the design and special effects team only to have the project taken off him and given to director David Lynch.

Film was not an infatuation for Gabriel in the way it becomes for most successful rock stars who believe they can carry their talents over to celluloid. He gave up the chance of a course at the London School of Film Technique at the age of nineteen to stay with Genesis in 1969. It was ironic that film, through William Friedkin's invitation in 1974 to write a screenplay, was instrumental in spurring his departure from the group.

Gabriel's visual sense had always been strong. Jill remembered a painting he did at school depicting the skeletons of dinosaurs all in a line in a cavern with a man walking over the bones into the cavern. The psychological explanation is open to debate.

When Gabriel was offered the chance to go to film school he wrote a screenplay based on his feelings having run over and killed a bird in a car.

'He was so intensely moved by that. That's why I loved him. I mean, that was partly what attracted me to him, he felt it really deeply, and he wrote the most amazing film script because of that, and was accepted,' said Jill.

Little more than a year after Rael was conceived, Gabriel invented the 'mercurial stranger' Mozo. 'He was partly based on Moses, but he was a fictional character who came from nowhere, disrupting people's lives and causing changes and then disappearing,' said Gabriel. Mozo was part of a 'master plan' dreamed up during his sabbatical in 1975–6 which he alternately wanted staged or filmed.

Mozo was inspired by *Aurora Consurgens*, a medieval alchemical treatise based on The Song of Solomon. It was brought to light by Carl Jung who thought it the work of St Thomas Aquinas. The text is full of alchemical and religious symbolism and apocalyptic imagery.

Jung saw alchemy and psychology as having the common aim of self-transformation. Gabriel was captivated by Jung's alchemical writings. 'I have always been interested in transformation of one sort or another,' said Gabriel. 'When Mozo came in he upset the status quo and the story is about the struggles after his appearance.' Mozo was a catalyst for spiritual change. This was true alchemy of which changing base metal to gold was a mere analogy.

Mozo was at the core of what Gabriel tries to express in music. Perhaps he sees himself as that mercurial stranger able to transform and uplift people.

Gabriel wanted to scatter songs about Mozo over several albums, though they would make a complete story when put together. The songs were 'Here Comes The Flood' – an apocalyptic vison; 'Down The Dolce Vita' – a ship leaving harbour on an intrepid journey; 'On The Air' – Mozo and his fantasy world; 'Exposure' – the struggle for salvation; 'Red Rain' – denying one's inner feelings; and 'That Voice Again' – judgement.

'Mozo is set in this fishing village, which is very upmarket, not quite Mediterranean, but something of that ilk,' explained Gabriel in 1987. 'There is this volcanic sand which gives the sea a red colour. Everything is focused on the sea, which is very rough, and the great macho feat is to cross the water, which no one has done.

'Mozo is discovered in a tip, in a house built out of rubbish, on the edge of the city. And initially kids and passers-by are just very curious to look inside this little shed, and they see in it what they are most afraid of. They project their fears on to him because he is different.

'I remember in Horsell Common near Chobham, where my parents live, there was this beaten up old caravan, with newspapers in the windows. I used to think there was a witch inside there. And I think it probably fuelled this setting for Mozo.

'Eventually the people who have discovered Mozo in this hut on a tip get disturbed. They are getting upset by what they are seeing, by what they are projecting on to him and they try and kick him out. He escapes, and he proves later on that he has crossed the sea. So he goes from being the tramp underneath society to the hero on top of it.

'And then having been placed above other people he is challenged by the people who put him up there. They then have him as a target to push down to the bottom again.'

'On The Air', on the second album, introduces Mozo, who lives in a fantasy world created by what he picks up and transmits on his short-wave. 'Through short-wave radio he becomes whoever he wants, but in real life, on the street, he's totally ignored,' explained Gabriel.

> I got power, I'm proud to be loud; my signal goes out clear
> I want everybody to know that Mozo is here
> On the air . . .

> 'On The Air'; Gabriel, 1978

'Down The Dolce Vita', from the first album, introduces characters setting out on the intrepid journey across the sea. Aeron and Gorham, like Mozo, have corrupted biblical names.

'Here Comes The Flood' was written at the height of Gabriel's fascination with short-wave radio. If radio signals got stronger at night, he reasoned, maybe psychic and telepathic awareness could be similarly increased and made to flood the mass consciousness. Those who were honest and straight-forward could take on board their new insights, while those who hid their thoughts and feelings would be lost.

> When the flood calls
> You have no home, you have no walls
> In a thunder crash
> You're a thousand minds, within a flash
> Don't be afraid to cry at what you see
> The actor's gone, there's only you and me
> And if we break before the dawn, they'll use up what we used to be

'Here Comes The Flood'; Gabriel, 1976

'Exposure', from the second album, is stark and minimal. The music was co-written by Gabriel and Robert Fripp, who named his 1979 album after the track. The version sung by Gabriel on Fripp's album is introduced by a recording of English sage J. G. Bennett uttering, 'It is impossible to achieve the aim without suffering.'

The final Mozo-linked songs to appear on record were 'Red Rain' and 'That Voice Again' from the So album. 'Red Rain' is about repressed feelings and pain that become expressed by the elements.

'That Voice Again', Gabriel explained, was about 'judge-mental attitudes being a barrier between people. The voice is the voice of judgement. A haunting internal voice that instead of accepting experience is always analysing, moralizing and evaluating it.' The song was originally called 'First Stone', but Gabriel abandoned the biblical allusions. He went through three sets of lyrics before David Rhodes came to the rescue and co-wrote them with him.

Gabriel first sought backing to perform Mozo in early 1976, soon after the Genesis album A Trick of the Tail became their biggest success to date. It was an unfortunate time to make an approach. Genesis' good fortune overshadowed Gabriel's. There was little enthusiasm from publishers and record companies for what promised to be an expensive exercise and Gabriel was forced to wait until he had commercial success as a solo artist.

He had discussed his ideas with Bob Ezrin, the producer of his first solo album. Ezrin told him about the Czech theatre Laterna Magica and the pioneering Josef Svoboda. Gabriel visited him twice in Prague in the late seventies. He was interested in Svoboda's 'perforated screen' combining cinema with theatre. In it a film was complemented by live action using a device that made actors appear to go in and out of the screen.

Gabriel was later introduced to Czech animator Raduz Cincera who developed his 'Kineautomat'. Cincera was working on opera sets for the London Coliseum when he met Gabriel. 'The Kineautomat has cinema seats with yes/no buttons,' said Gabriel. 'There were about a dozen decision points, the plot chosen by vote. So, for example, an actor would come out of the screen and say to the audience, "Should I stay with my wife, or go with this woman?" And the cinema would become as lively as a football match.'

Eventually the Mozo idea lost impetus, though in autumn 1985 Gabriel was still considering working on developing the story into an hour-long video. 'Maybe I should look at it again some day, there's still stuff in it I like. It's always the thing, the new is more attractive than the old,' Gabriel said in 1987.

Teaming up with Jodorowsky, Friedkin or Hall before him, was indicative of Gabriel's belief in cultural cross-pollination, developing ideas from those he admired in all the arts. Graham Dean, who he met in 1978, gave him several books including Leni Riefenstahl's photographic essays *The Last of the Nuba*, and *The People of Kau*.

'The first time we met was at a private viewing theatre in

Soho where he invited me to see a film by Jodorowsky opening in London. We went to shake hands and missed. People who know Peter would say, "Yes, I understand." Things are slightly off with him,' said Dean.

'Peter and I have been battering ideas over the years. As you get to know him you see he is an ideas person, he goes off on many tangents. He is one of the most creative people I know. The trick is to discipline the creativity, he would admit that himself. Everyone can come up with ideas.'

Dean has never been in favour with the art establishment or critics. 'Leo and Mona', his 1974 visual joke, showed the master and subject in bed together. The following year he exhibited 'Memories', originally titled 'Refugee From England'. It shows an exiled Queen Elizabeth looking through a scrapbook at her days of former glory. His earlier work in acrylics had a photographic clarity, metamorphosing more emotional and abstract giant smudged watercolours.

In 1981 Dean asked Gabriel to do the soundtrack of *Undercurrents*, a fifteen-minute film. The title was a pun on images of water blended with the sinister undercurrents of Dean's disturbing paintings of skin disorders.

They booked a recording studio for an afternoon to make the soundtrack, and went on for three days and three nights. Dean repaid Gabriel with a painting called 'Tropicans 7', an unsettling image of a young negro with a multi-coloured skin disease. A six-minute extract from *Undercurrents*, with its atmospheric music, was shown on the BBC2 arts magazine programme *Riverside*. It was a useful test bed for Gabriel's later feature film soundtracks.

Dean travelled around London with Gabriel, frequently using public transport. 'He is the least likely looking pop star you will meet. I can't remember a single instance where he has been recognized because he doesn't act the pop star.' But that was before the success of *So*, which robbed Gabriel of the luxury of virtual anonymity.

Gabriel now has a keener sartorial sense. But Dean remembers when it was otherwise. 'On one occasion a few years ago I was having an exhibition in Paris. He had a dark grey roll-up plastic mac like the ones your parents used to make you wear. He suddenly unrolled one of these and put it on and we walked through the streets of Paris to the show at the Olympia.

'International art fairs are mega European style conventions, the rich of Europe parade themselves, and there was Gabriel walking around wearing his mac. I kept giving him hints, saying are you sure you aren't warm inside that. They looked at this funny person in this peculiar looking mac. Once I said Peter's name people recognized him. The funny thing is he is so visually oriented, yet the way he put himself together was the opposite.'

Dean introduced Gabriel to sculptor Malcolm Poynter in early 1980, then working in a studio in Butler's Wharf, opposite the Tower of London. Gabriel was impressed by Poynter's sculptures: 'white, bald, naked figures that stood around in little sets'. Poynter talks about wanting to 'gobsmack' people. 'Throw the images straight into people's eyes, jar them, shatter them. I like disturbance levels. All these things are perception raisers or lowerers. We are basically myopic in the way we see things, we are cotton wool surrounded, we never experience much nowadays, we are becoming visually blasé because there is so much visual imagery everywhere. I am just using ordinary images, but you can really disturb people by the context you use them in.'

Gabriel and Poynter enjoy collaboration. It is not just a matter of using other artists as source material, but, for Gabriel, also having enough courage and belief in what one is doing to make it happen. 'If you have people who inspire you with their work, very often, if you are determined enough, you can get to them, and it's like touching Jesus' cloak. It is possible if the willpower is there,' said Gabriel.

'And when people send tapes to me, which they do all the

time, I think it's very rarely the music that is going to make the difference with whether they make it or not, it's their psyche: a) whether they need it badly enough, and b) whether they have the willpower to go for it. I think, different to most people, that a lot of talent is acquired and not God-given or hereditary.'

Gabriel found Malcolm Poynter, a bluff South Londoner, refreshing. 'I think Peter is very unused to being challenged personally because of his manner and who he is. I love people like that because I know underneath them they're really waiting to get out.

'Peter has the ability to draw people out, but because of his attitude most people give in to him. The only way to counter-act or contradict him is actually not to take any notice of that but to confront him as the individual that he is and not to worry. I have felt like shaking the shit out of him sometimes.'

Gabriel and Poynter discovered a mutual interest in the work of Professor Stanley Milgram. 'It was a revelation that both of us knew and had an understanding about his work. It made it easier for us to become friends.' Milgram's book *Obedience To Authority* is based on his psychological exper-iments at Yale University in the late fifties and his disturbing findings about the cruelty people are capable of inflicting when ordered to do so by a figure of authority, in this case a white-coated scientist in his imposing laboratory.

'Two people come to a psychology laboratory to take part in a study of memory and learning,' wrote Milgram. 'One of them is designated as a "teacher" and the other a "learner". The experimenter explains that the study is concerned with the effects of punishment on learning. The learner is conducted into a room, seated in a chair, his arms strapped to prevent excessive movement, and an electrode attached to his wrist. He is told that he is to learn a list of word pairs; whenever he makes an error, he will receive electric shocks of increasing intensity.'

But the real focus of the experiment is the teacher, the learner is merely an actor feigning pain. 'At what point will the subject refuse to obey the experimenter?'

Gabriel grew up hemmed in by the authority of an English public school. He was obedient despite his alienation from the system, joining the Combined Cadet Force, and in his last weeks at Charterhouse even becoming a monitor. Much of his adult life has been spent peeling away the protective layers culture and convention imposed on him through authority figures. He identified with Milgram's experiments, though they were prompted by a hell far removed from the playing fields of Charterhouse: the Nazi concentration camps.

'Facts of recent history and observation in daily life suggest that for many people obedience may be a deeply ingrained behaviour tendency, indeed, a prepotent impulse overriding training in ethics, sympathy, and moral conduct,' wrote Milgram.

Gabriel first started performing his song 'Milgram's 37' in 1979. It referred to one experiment highlighting the easiest form of cruelty – getting someone else to do the dirty work, in this instance to administer the shock. 'In this situation thirty-seven out of forty adults . . . continued to the highest shock level on the generator. Predictably, subjects excused their behaviour by saying that the responsibility belonged to the man who pulled the switch. This illustrates a dangerously typical situation in complex society: it is psychologically easy to ignore responsibility when one is only an intermediate link in a chain of evil action but is far from the final consequences of the action.'

Gabriel first intended recording 'Milgram's 37' for the third solo album, released in 1980, but the track never made it. The live version of the song at the time had just one line: 'We do what we're told, told to do.'

It was repeated in a moronic virtual monotone, with a steady hypnotic beat. On this occasion when the audience sang the words it was not an expression of unity, more an uncomfortable reminder of how crowds encourage obedience and conformity.

By the time 'Milgram's 37' reached the *So* album seven years after it was first conceived the song had changed into 'We Do What We're Told' with the subtitle 'Milgram's 37'. The song gently builds up into an eerie chant against a pulsating rhythmic backdrop. After the repeat of the lyric 'we do what we're told' the song's chorus is:

> *One doubt*
> *One voice*
> *One war*
> *One truth*
> *One dream*
>
> 'We Do What We're Told'; Gabriel, 1986

For Peter Hammill, it is Gabriel's least satisfying work. 'I thought it was pretty half-baked. I just thought, it won't do. As a comment or a song about the Milgram experiments, I don't think that the lyric as it stands is acceptable. "We do what we are told" is not the point of the Milgram experiment.

'For somebody who doesn't know anything about Milgram it just presents another Kafka-esque vision. The whole point is much deeper than that. It's the stuff of what we are inside. It is my belief that if you are going to do something about an area like Milgram's that it becomes a very complex thing, you want people who don't know anything about it to become interested to find out something about it, you want people who do know something about it to have their perceptions changed in some way, or at least to present them with an alternative view.

'I think if it was to be reduced simply down to one line, more accurate would be "we aim to please". In reality, in terms of writing something like this, I would obviously write a different song. But if I had been doing it in Peter's psyche, writing it in terms of various phrases like that, I would probably want to combine "we aim to please", "we do what we are told", "we suffer the suffering". Something like that so one would end up with a bit more of a spread of the psychic disturbances involved.

'The only reason I bring this up is I do think he gets elements of that into other quests. "Biko", obviously, is an epic stand precisely because it flips from the mundane to the absolutely global, and that is what "Milgram's 37" doesn't.'

Gabriel spent a long time tracking down Professor Milgram on the telephone to ask his permission to use film excerpts of the experiment for possible use in videos or on stage.

'I was interested in the film because they seemed very ordinary American people, the type who would quite happily shop next to you in Safeways. Yet they were capable of performing horrific things on their fellow human beings. It was quite an eye opener. At the time it was quite controversial and Milgram got into a lot of trouble because it was seen as potentially harmful for the volunteers in the experiment.' When Gabriel finally got through to Milgram on the telephone he found him cordial. He believed Milgram was well-disposed towards him after checking him out before their conversation and finding some of his students were fans. But Milgram's attitude changed on the second call.

'I think he was cautious of another spate of sensational publicity, as he saw it. His quote in the end to me was, "Academic research and entertainment aren't happy bedfellows". He came up with this quote after he talked to his colleagues, so I think it was peer group pressure.' Milgram died in 1984, two years before 'We Do What We're Told (Milgram's 37)' was finally released on the So album.

Gabriel and Malcolm Poynter first teamed up in 1980 to make an experimental video at the offices of Syco Systems in

Paddington. Poynter took along some of his sculpted heads, and film editor David Gardener borrowed a VHS camera. Poynter got Gabriel to crawl around the floor, while Gardener shot Gabriel's reflection in a giant flexible mirror with elongated shots of his head.

Gabriel wanted to experiment with reversing the conventional 'write a song and then make the video' process. He wanted to create a video scenario and then write a song that worked with it.

Nothing came out of that evening at Syco until two years later when Gabriel was stuck for a cover design for his fourth album. He contacted Gardener and Poynter and they met up at a Soho editing suite to try and get some stills from the video.

They played around with a vision mixer adding special effects to the original video and swapping colours. They found a video camera in the next door studio and started making another film, using a piece of blue plastic tubing that was lying around which Gabriel put between his teeth. Poynter took slide shots of the images on screen, and Gabriel used them on the inside cover of his fourth album, released in 1982.

The collaboration with Poynter and Gardener was the result of Gabriel's lifelong fascination with film and later video. His first flirtation in Hollywood in 1974 via William Freidkin had been thwarted. But in 1983 he was delighted to be approached by Martin Scorsese to compose the soundtrack to *The Last Temptation of Christ*. Though it was to take another five years before the movie was filmed and ready for Gabriel's input.

In between came a more straightforward commission from director Alan Parker for *Birdy*, which became Gabriel's first major movie score. Chastened by his first experiences with the world of rock and roll working with Roger Waters and Pink Floyd on *The Wall*, Parker was hesitant about approaching another rock musician. But as a fan of Peter Gabriel's music he suspected he might be dealing with a different temperament. 'Peter's not of that world. He's a very exceptional person. He doesn't have any of the hang-ups or the unpleasantness of that particular business. We got on so well, he's such a sweet man, it was such a refreshing change from working with megalo-maniacs like Roger Waters.'

Parker, director of *Midnight Express*, *Bugsy Malone*, *Fame* and later *Evita*, and his producer Alan Marshall met Gabriel in September 1984 at Pinewood Studios. Gabriel was shown the two thirds of the film that had been shot. Already behind preparing his next album, Gabriel agreed to halt that project to work on the *Birdy* soundtrack; he enjoyed the discipline.

Parker had made a tape of excerpts from Gabriel's music that he liked, including 'Rhythm of the Heat' from the fourth album to give Gabriel an idea of what he wanted. Parker had already put some Gabriel segments on to a rough mix of the film soundtrack.

Gabriel needed some assistance in the studio and approached Daniel Lanois on the recommendation of David Rhodes, impressed with his production of composer Harold Budd's album *The Pearl*, which features the multiple sounds of pianos. A Canadian, from Hamilton, Ontario, Lanois had also produced more mainstream acts Martha and the Muffins, and co-produced the U2 album *Unforgettable Fire* with Brian Eno. Gabriel contacted his old friend and occasional collaborator Eno who assured him Lanois could handle the project. Lanois was able to join Gabriel and Alan Parker at short notice.

'We went back to the original 24-track masters to a great deal of the things that I love, I couldn't believe the richness of them – things that weren't even on the album,' said Parker.

'Peter's record company were very difficult to begin with, and so I phoned them to ask if they'd mind if Peter took off a little time to do this, and they said as long as it didn't take more than a couple of months because Peter was already a year late, or something.'

For once Gabriel found the strict deadline invigorating. During October he worked a fourteen to sixteen hour day trying to meet the Christmas deadline. The film opened in New York in December 1984, without Gabriel's soundtrack, to make that year's Oscar nominations. It was premiered in London in February 1985 with the soundtrack. He may have had to speed up, but Gabriel still made sure he had the final say in what he did. 'He had strong views and I would never be able to persuade him to do something he didn't feel comfortable with, but we didn't have any confrontation as such,' said Parker.

Gabriel's music had inspired Parker, but he was also attracted by similarities between Gabriel's nature and the two main characters in the film. Birdy himself is naïve, unworldly and obsessive, but with an inner strength. He is not affected by the scorn of his peers, pursuing his passion, paying little attention to the condemnation of others. In contrast his friend Al is worldly and good with the girls. Al and Birdy are conscripted to Vietnam where they are both injured. In hospital Birdy withdraws into a catatonic state, sucking strength from Al, who disintegrates so that his friend can come back to life.

'It is a film with a number of layers. It is a bit dodgy just zooming in on one thing,' said Parker. 'The reason I wanted to make the film was that it was about friendship, but it was also about the way in which war in general takes away young lives. And also it's about the dreams that we have to explain the world that we are in. We all take flight one way or the other, through music or film or whatever.'

Gabriel was sparse in his use of music to aid the narrative. 'When you have wall to wall music in the classic Hollywood movie scores the music ceases to have any effect because there is no light and shade. It's the same as an album mix, really. If you just have head on stuff right the way through it ceases to be powerful. It is the quieter moments that make the louder stuff work,' said Parker.

'The rhythmic percussion on the flying scenes was the most original use of his music in the film. It was not the normal way to do that kind of scene. It was a much harsher sound than goes with the fluidity of flight. Normally it would be very lyrical, but it's not, which makes it very powerful.'

Concerned that his fans might feel ripped off by the repetition of music that had been released elsewhere Gabriel put the equivalent of a Government health warning on the album cover.

When I was asked to do this soundtrack, the intention was to build it out of elements of existing tracks. Some of these Alan Parker had already chosen.

We worked for a couple of weeks with unorthodox explorations of some of the sounds, rhythms and themes of existing tracks. This provided many moods, but I felt some new material was needed as well. So, what you have here is a combination of both.

For those people who know my records, I have included (in brackets) the titles which have been obviously raided. I do not wish anyone to be deceived by the sleeve. However, I am not revealing all my sources. I leave that for your detection.

Three of these tracks did not make it to the last round – the film. But the music on this record was chosen to make a compatible collection of moods . . .

*Birdy* sold far fewer copies than Gabriel's previous albums, just 25,000 copies in the United States, though worldwide it reached 150,000, a respectable number for a soundtrack.

Gabriel enjoyed the idea of making diehard fans work out his musical sources. His own sources are drawn from a wide range of stimuli, not least a prodigious reading list. He has occasionally acceded to requests from fans wanting to know his influences. In autumn 1982 he gave a list of his favourite things: '*The White Hotel* by D. M. Thomas – book of the month; *Sergeant Bilko* – TV programme of the month; Spike Milligan – favourite comic; Talking Heads – favourite group; Nusrat Fateh Ali Khan – singer of the month; *M* by Fritz Lang – favourite film; *Sunday Times* – favourite newspaper; Ian Pollock – favourite illustrator; Crest – favourite toothpaste; Redcurrant and Peach – favourite yogurt flavour; New York – favourite City; Italian – favourite language; 'Old Man River' [no category, presumably favourite song] – Paul Robeson; Nicol Williamson – favourite actor.'

He repeated the exercise in similar fashion in spring 1984: 'Books: *The Dream and the Underworld* by James Hillman; *The Complete Poems of Anne Sexton*; *The Life and Death of Yukio Mishima* by Henry Scott-Stokes; *An Anthology of Modern Day Japanese Haiku* by Makoto Ueda; *Hotel* – various authors and photographers; *My Last Sigh*, autobiography of Louis Buñuel; *The Tree* by John Fowles and Frank Horvat. Magazines: *New Scientist*; *Coevolution Quarterly*; *Zoom*. Favourite illustrators: Ian Pollock, Matt Mahurin, Janet Long, Russell Mills, Grizelda Holderness, Glen Baxter, Peter Till, Duncan Robert-Wilson, George Hardie.'

Before working on *Birdy* in autumn 1984, Gabriel had already tasted involvement in Hollywood. He contributed a track to *Gremlins*, the furry fantasy from the Steven Spielberg factory, directed by Jo Dante. Because of Spielberg's insistence on strict secrecy Gabriel was only given a copy of the scene he was to write for. He came up with 'Out Out', featured in a bar where the mischievous gremlins create havoc.

The music was an indication of the funkier direction Gabriel's next album was to take. 'Out Out' was recorded with Nile Rodgers, the producer who funked up David Bowie at New York's Power Station. But Gabriel was also attracted to Rodgers' less known more playful sound, heard on Carly Simon's song 'Why'.

Gabriel took up the offer to work with Rodgers some time after receiving a telex from him when he became successful

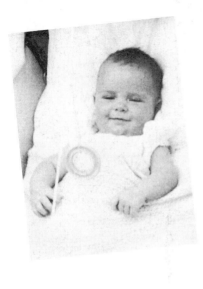

CLOCKWISE:

The utterly contented angel Gabriel, aged nine months.

His mother calls this his 'dirty grin'. On holiday in Bognor Regis at the age of two.

Peter in a fetching Red Indian cardigan holding forth while his sister Anne listens with rapt attention.

ABOVE: Peter and his sister Anne pulling a boat to shore on a river bank. Water, boats, mud and the natural world have all been recurring themes in Gabriel's artistic life.

BELOW: Continuing the boating theme, some thirty years later he rows a rubbery vessel, inspired by the artist Yayoi Kusama, during filming of the video of 'Lovetown'. (Stephen Lovell-Davis)

RIGHT: His early enthusiasm for dressing up was rewarded with first prize for this matador outfit at the age of eight on holiday in Wengen, Switzerland.

BELOW: Peter, aged fourteen, with his first modest drum kit, getting help from a schoolmaster at Charterhouse.

ABOVE: Peter and an attentive Phil Collins at Genesis' first foreign gig in Belgium, 1972.

LEFT: A fetching flared glitter suit worn at Drury Lane Theatre, London, in January 1974 during the *Selling England by the Pound* tour was one of his more sober costumes. Note the shaved forehead, here reaching the end of its two-year lifespan.

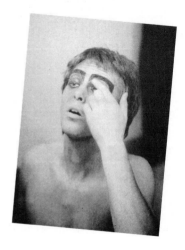

RIGHT: His hippy locks having recently been lopped off, Gabriel applies make-up for his punk character Rael, a precursor of the punks about to emerge on the music scene, featured in *The Lamb Lies Down on Broadway* tour in March 1975. (Robert Ellis)

ABOVE: Tony Banks is troubled with more than Gabriel's self-defiling haircut during the fraught writing and rehearsing for *The Lamb Lies Down on Broadway* at Headley Grange, Hampshire, in June 1974.

BELOW: The dreaded parental wedding line-up. Left to right: Ralph and Irene Gabriel, Peter and Jill, Lord Philip and Lady Joanna Moore.

ABOVE: The long-haired contingent at Jill and Peter's wedding outside St James's Palace on 17 March 1971. Left to right: Tony Stratton Smith; Richard Macphail; Steve Hackett; Gail Colson; Genesis producer John Anthony.

LEFT: The young father with Anna, left, and Melanie wearing his Genesis masks at home near Bath in 1977.

ABOVE: Kate Bush and Gabriel during her vocal sessions for 'Games Without Frontiers' and 'No Self Control' in October 1979 at the Townhouse Studios, London. (Larry Fast)

BELOW: David Rhodes and Gabriel recording the third album outside Ashcombe House, near Bath, in early autumn 1979. They developed a close friendship and Rhodes became Gabriel's fifth and final permanent guitarist. (Larry Fast)

ABOVE: A powerful performance at the first WOMAD festival in July 1982 was given added tension by the looming financial crisis. (Robert Draper)

BELOW: Newly shorn in Central Park, New York City, in July 1980.

asking if they could work together. 'I thought maybe this is a good chance to try it out,' said Gabriel. 'The trouble is I am used to working at such a slow pace and experimenting, and I hadn't actually got the song ready when I went over there. So it cost a fortune in American studio bills and really wasn't a very good song. There were sections in it I liked, but it didn't work a hundred per cent.' He was not too impressed with the way the song was put over in the film. 'It's a bit of a disappointment when you think, "This is it! Films! Hollywood!" And then you get smothered by some gremlin throwing up!'

Gabriel could not resist delivering the finished track personally to get a peep at Warner Bros' studio in Hollywood. He received 'medium VIP' treatment on the set and met Jo Dante, though Spielberg was nowhere to be seen.

Also in 1984 Gabriel recorded and produced the song 'Walk Through the Fire' for use in the romantic adventure *Against All Odds*. The film was directed by Taylor Hackford, who made *An Officer and a Gentleman*, and starred Rachel Ward and Jeff Bridges. Gabriel's optimistic rhythmic congatinged music was used as background in a tense bar-room scene where Bridges seeks information that will help save his life. 'Walk Through the Fire' was released as a single in May 1984 but only got to Number 69 in the charts. 'It could have been a good song. The ingredients are there but it's not quite right,' Gabriel said. The song had originally been intended for the third album before getting reworked for *Against All Odds*.

He was invited to contribute to the soundtrack by Tony Smith, the film's music producer along with Genesis, Mike Rutherford and Phil Collins obliged. Just over a month before Gabriel's single was released Collins got to Number 2 with his title track 'Against All Odds (Take A Look At Me Now)'.

Gabriel used *Gremlins* and *Against All Odds* to gain experience in the film world, as well as earning some pocket money during lulls in his own recording. In 1985 he was reluctantly drawn into another film, *Lorca and the Outlaws*, again through

Tony Smith, its executive music producer. Smith, who also had Tony Banks writing for the film, pressed Gabriel to appear on screen as a favour. Gabriel was filmed at Shepperton Studios peforming 'San Jacinto' from his fourth album and can be seen performing the song as a supposed holographic image brought up on a twenty-first century jukebox. The film, a weak science-fiction thriller, was only released on video in the UK.

Gabriel has not ruled out acting, though his enthusiasm appears to have waned. 'As a rock musician and writer you get to act out the characters you created, so theoretically the job should be less hard. An actor is really hollowing himself out and fusing someone else's character with the residue. It is a very skilled profession and it's very presumptuous for musicians to think they can do it, or for actors to assume they will make good musicians.'

# CHAPTER TEN

FIRST IT WAS GOING TO BE CALLED MUSIC From The Edges of the World, but that implied that Britain was at its centre. Then it was going to be Rhythm '82, but that was abandoned because it sounded too much like a BBC jazz programme. The only way to encapsulate everything memorably was to find an acronym.

At that point, in early spring 1982, a choice had to be made. A World of Music, Arts and Dance certainly summed it up. But some wag suggested WOMAD might be mistaken for a drug to combat menstrual pain. There were later inquiries for more information on this supposed women's festival. WOMAD's suffix seems apposite given the débâcle that followed.

WOMAD developed from an idea Peter Gabriel had in late 1980. 'I was getting very excited by some of the things I was coming across. So I thought, if they are so exciting to me, I'm sure they will be interesting to a lot of other people too. So I was sitting on a train one evening and I thought, wouldn't it be great to have an event which could bring in a large audience with a few rock and roll groups, and have that audience exposed to a lot of this stuff.'

He had started gathering tapes of music from around the world, including Africa, Bali and Australian aborigines. 'I feel that an important influence on music over the next few years will be ethnic in origin and I can hear it being combined with electronics and more expressive, emotive use of the synthesizer,' he presciently said at the time. 'Also I have been listening to and enjoying some of the recent material by Talking Heads who seem to be in that area and the tape made by David Byrne and Brian Eno. What I am actually trying to do with some of this stuff is to sift out rhythms which have a clarity and simpleness to them. I think that much of the Afro-rock and Afro-influenced music of the past had tended to use the more complex rhythms which I find less interesting.'

Producer David Lord, who owns Crescent Studios in Bath, introduced Gabriel to Thomas Brooman, known as Thos. Thos was one of a group of Oxford graduates living on the dole in Bristol who had developed the *Bristol Recorder Talking Book*, a combined magazine and LP. The mix of community arts and politics in the *Recorder* appealed to Gabriel, and he agreed to an interview as an almost local musician. Gabriel also donated three tracks from his 'live cassette box': 'Not One Of Us', 'Humdrum' and 'Ain't That Peculiar'.

The *Recorder* people, Thos Brooman, Martin Elbourne, Stephe Pritchard, and Jonathan Arthur, with their eclectic tastes, seemed ideally suited to help organize his planned concert since no commercial promoter was likely to take it on.

'We felt quite flattered to have been asked. We'd just been listening to Gamelan music (from Java and Bali in Indonesia) and a bit of Pakistani music, and were getting fairly bored with local pop groups,' said Thos. 'Peter said he had been listening to some sounds and he just thought it would be a good idea.'

'We had meetings in Ashcombe House and started getting up plans, it was a very exciting time,' said Gabriel. He was also encouraged by a positive response from Talking Heads, and Bath neighbour Steve Winwood.

The event was originally planned for spring or summer 1981. 'We started talking to people and the whole process of finding the music was like a detective trail. It was a very potent idea and the further we went into it the more it became clear that if we were going to the trouble of assembling people from elsewhere it would be a good idea to do it with more than just African groups. And that in terms of logistics and costs it would have to be more than an indoor venue because it became quickly clear that finance and backing was not readily available.'

In April 1981 Thos went to the eighth Rennes Rhythm '81, part of the French Festival of International Arts. In particular he wanted to see the Sabri Brothers from Pakistan, masters of qawwali, the musical and ceremonial expression of Sufism, the mystical branch of Islam. He also came across the Master Drummers of Burundi, peasant farmers from the hills of this tiny impoverished nation, and was spellbound. Thos wanted both acts to come to what was to become WOMAD.

The Burundis were already known in the West through a somewhat obscure sixties album of their music. Since then there had been some borrowing, notably by Joni Mitchell on *The Hissing of Summer Lawns* in 1975, and later by Adam Ant and Bow Wow Wow, offshoots of the Malcolm McLaren image factory.

'The Burundis were very angry about all this because it was done with a lack of understanding of what it was being borrowed from. They were called warrior drummers, which they are not, never have been and never will be,' said Thos.

On his return it became clear that the summer 1981 deadline would be impossible to meet and WOMAD was put back a year.

It grew from a single concert to a planned six-day festival that was to include everything from traditional music from a wide range of cultures to high-tech Western music.

The WOMAD workers set about trying to raise finance from the Arts Council, public bodies and private sponsors, including Coca-Cola, but without success. Gabriel used his influence to contact people in the music business on both sides of the Atlantic. Apparent salvation came from Charles Levison, then chairman of WEA Records UK, who agreed to a $150,000 advance on a double album to be released prior to the festival. Pete Townshend, David Byrne, Gabriel, Peter Hammill, the Beat, the Burundi Drummers and several of the Third World acts contributed tracks.

Another apparent breakthrough came when the BBC agreed to film the festival for their prestigious *Arena* arts documentary slot.

The date was finally set for the weekend of 16 to 18 July 1982 at the Royal Bath and West showground near Shepton Mallet, Somerset: six days had become three. As well as the promised extensive TV coverage of the 300 performers from twenty-one countries there were cultural exhibitions, lectures, films, workshops, and arts, crafts and food from around the world. There were four stages with concerts running concurrently.

The idealism that shaped the festival was also to contribute to its downfall, best exemplified by the festival poster. All musicians, regardless of fame or prestige, were given equal and alphabetical billing. The alternative, which was rejected, would have put the British like Gabriel, Echo and the Bunnymen and Simple Minds above artists like Tian Jin from China, Les Musiciens du Nil from Egypt and Sasono Mulyo from Indonesia. 'It was just not a commercial poster, it reflects a mistaken sense of idealism,' said Thos. Using big names to draw in crowds did not have to be negative if it turned them on to different traditions.

'A fundamental principle of what we have always done, which was directly as a result of Peter's influence, was that all the artists were to be respected as artists and that their billing is part of the respect that the festival has for them. His sense of principle and his ideas completely shaped what we did.'

They had to rely on financial dribs and drabs and a tolerant bank manager. The *Bristol Recorder* staff put in the few thousand pounds' profit they had made, and Martin Elbourne from the

*Recorder* cashed £4,000-worth of shares, Gabriel gave £3,000 and fundraising events amassed a few thousand more. It was hopelessly underfinanced, but benefited from a lot of gifts and goodwill – for example, the colour programme's only real cost was the paper.

Any real chance of making back the investment was scuppered by the showground authorities insisting that rock acts like Gabriel and the Bunnymen performed inside the Showering Pavilion, restricted to an audience of 4,000. They were the biggest crowd-pullers so the authorities perversely limited how many people could see them, fearful of a repetition of the crowd problems at the heavily over-attended Bath rock festival of 1969.

'We were over-ambitious and inexperienced, but a cardinal error we made was to be dictated to by the site. They demanded we put all the pop acts indoors and we very foolishly agreed,' said Thos. Tickets for Gabriel and the Bunnymen were sold out three weeks in advance.

Projected costs were approaching £250,000. This included £90,000 in air fares for the fourteen Burundis and two Government officials, plus a further twelve musicians from around the globe.

The deal with the BBC was a co-production allowing the BBC to film, 'above the line' costs were to be paid by WOMAD. American backers promised to secure WOMAD world TV rights. 'That was the cornerstone of our finance. We were being asked to come up with £50,000 in front of the project. But our co-producers in the States in the end would not come up with the money because they did not trust that it was all above board,' said Thos.

The BBC unexpectedly announced they were pulling out two weeks before the event. The news was received just as the Burundi Drummers were in the air. 'To say it was a bodyblow would be an understatement. It started to feel like we were building a hotel on quicksand. We had got to the point where

we had spent around £40,000 in a gamble that might recuper-
ate £200,000. The question then is, do you say goodbye to
£40,000 or carry on to the end of the road to risk getting all
that £40,000 back or lose still more? In any promotion, big or
small, there is always a deciding point like that. We passed that
point fifteen days before.'

The WOMAD sampler double album, which included
many of the acts appearing at the festival, should have provided
much-needed publicity as well as vital revenue. But the album,
planned the previous summer, was delayed. It finally took
eleven months to complete and was not released until two
weeks before the festival, allowing the final instalment on the
advance from WEA to be forwarded to WOMAD. 'When the
advance finally came through it completely cleared the over-
draft and we carried on spending, which sounds in retrospect
like it was almost calculatingly foolhardy. But it was simply
what had to happen because the machinery was in process
then, it was running and it couldn't stop.'

The financial débâcle obscured what was a mammoth
cultural achievement for Gabriel and the WOMAD team.
They provided a British audience with a glimpse of a wide
range of different musical styles whose influence on Western
music is still being felt.

Gabriel was keen to stress the input of children at WOMAD.
With 7,000 schoolchildren attending the first day's event he
could justifiably regard that as a success. But it was also obvious
on that first day that the adult audience was badly lacking.

'It wasn't until the Friday had actually been that it was
quite clear that the audience was not coming on the day,' said
Thos.

By now Gail Colson, who had advised Gabriel the idea
was a folly from its inception and refused to have anything to
do with it, could no longer bear to see it go so badly wrong.
She brought an accountant from Hit and Run to Bath to try
and sort out the mess.

'By Saturday morning the accountant had been working all night, finding out the liabilities, and we realized we were potentially anything up to a quarter of a million quid adrift.

'Then the decision was, "What do we do now?" And on the advice of people much more experienced than ourselves we decided to go through the weekend on the analogy, say, of a Laker aeroplane that has already taken off from Heathrow to go to New York. What do you do? Turn round and take it back to Heathrow or carry on to New York and then say the company's bust? So we just carried on, feeling like the end of the world had come.'

The question of the glaring gap between revenue and costs was raised with Gabriel by *NME* writer Vivien Goldman a few days before the festival. 'Yes, that discrepancy might lead us to interesting places . . . like the bankruptcy court,' he said.

Goldman also asked him where cultural exchange stops and ripping-off begins. 'Gabriel seems to love debate and dialogue; a warm smile shows he's thought the subject through many times. "I'm not sure of the value of that argument. All art steals from other art. The important thing is deciding what to steal and doing it with respect. If through WOMAD, rock people acknowledge their sources, the sources are also much more likely to sell."'

Goldman bumped into Gabriel towards the end of the third day. 'As far as I can see, Peter Gabriel deserves a slap on the back and some red roses. But the man did not look happy, despite his brightly-coloured festival waistcoat that probably doubled as a pair of hiking boots.' This was a reference to the festival's popular consumer buy, clothes that changed into other clothes, hats into bags, trousers into shirts.

'I knew instantly. Artistically, the festival had been an unqualified success, a three-day musical orgasm, in fact. It could only be the bucks that brought a frown.

'"Have you had enough people here to cover costs?"'

'"In a word . . . no,"' said Peter, bravely trying to force a smile. I recalled his crack the week before about there being interesting places like the bankruptcy court.'

Throughout the eighteen months while the festival was being planned, Gabriel had been writing and recording his fourth album. He finished it less than a fortnight after WOMAD, and first performed some of the songs from the album at the festival. His band were dressed in black track-suits, but presumably they were not in mourning. They played 'I Have The Touch', and 'Rhythm of the Heat' with the group Ekome. It was filmed by London Weekend Television for a *South Bank Show* documentary. Gabriel gave an impassioned performance of 'Rhythm of the Heat', falling to his knees, his body vibrating and swivelling, looking like he was making love and performing the limbo at the same time.

He also premiered 'Across The River', his contribution to the WOMAD Music and Rhythm album, which also later appeared on a compact disc single with 'Big Time' in 1987, with L. Shankar on the violin and Stewart Copeland of the Police on drums. The song is one of Gabriel's most haunting. The surrounding trauma no doubt helped add authenticity to the venting of his tortured soul.

'Peter was panicked. I think all of us were,' said Thos. 'There was still this complete conflict of things. On the one hand, well, it's a great event. And on the other, God, haven't we fucked up. Just an absolute turmoil of contradictory things.'

'We started to realize things were collapsing during the event,' remembered Gabriel. 'There were concerns before then, but we were confident we were going to get a much bigger audience than we had. We had the rail strike against us, and we had appalling publicity, which was a pity because I thought it was ideal colour supplement material.

'Because I wasn't working on it full time I didn't want to tell the WOMAD people how to do it. Some of the pros in the business were very sceptical and cynical about the whole thing, Gail particularly, saying, "This isn't going to work and blah blah, blah." We were saying, "Oh yes it is. People will like this idea." We were very confident and naïve. But I didn't want to come in the big rock star; "You've got to do it this way. This is the way things are done." I think I was a bit stupid in that way. I should have been more aggressive. I had no idea I was going to be seen as the only one worth chasing as things went down.'

Gail and the accountant salvaged what they could. 'She worked almost the whole weekend at the festival itself, helping where she could and advising with a very limited amount of cash on who should get paid the cash on the weekend,' remembered Thos. 'And as a result of her advice all the visiting artists were paid cash first. I think there was a sense of really active involvement by then, and almost a sense of energy generated by it. There were several creditors who came personally for us, they felt so angry. Afterwards nobody could understand how the festival had happened with the minimal investment that it had received.

'But it was limited and we were protected by the law. At the same time I think the pressure on Peter was so much worse because the companies we owed money to realized that he was the only one of us who might have any, and so he was under real personal pressure.'

The final debt was £189,000. Gabriel was the main target, and had irate debtors at the door. 'I was the only fat cat. Jill actually got a death threat aimed at me, an anonymous caller saying, "I'm going to kill you afterwards," and all that stuff, very nasty. Not the sort of thing I want to live through again.'

Help came from an unexpected quarter. Tony Smith, still 50 per cent owner of Gabriel's management company, discussed the débâcle with Genesis. 'We said, "Listen, this is ridiculous, why don't we help him out?" said Phil Collins. 'We can't have Pete go bankrupt, though it didn't turn out to be that serious. We offered to give him some money towards it or play a benefit, or lend him the money until he could pay us back.'

The offer of money never got as far as Gabriel's ears because everyone knew he was bound to refuse. 'We decided maybe the money was not such a good idea, so why not do a concert,' said Collins. That autumn Genesis were on a tour of the UK, so it was not difficult to slot in an extra date for a WOMAD benefit.

'Peter has a tendency to get involved in this sort of thing, which is great as it's part of his personality,' said Tony Banks. 'Originally it was not going to be with Peter, although doing it with Peter seemed like a good idea. In rock music it is very easy to raise a large sum of money. And this particular thing was to help a friend, so it seemed to be a damned good thing to do. And it also got rid of this terrible thing of everyone wanting a reunion, so we killed two birds with one stone.'

'At that point I was so freaked out I would have done anything,' said Gabriel. 'I was very touched that they were prepared to do it, to bail me out. Because although I didn't feel personally liable, I had been part of a team that was naïve. A lot of the decisions which were partly responsible for the problems I didn't feel I had created. Except that I had instigated a thing and left it to the WOMADers. I felt responsible in neglecting to take a heavy-handed financial role. I think I would have made some attempts afterwards to pay off what could have been paid. But I wouldn't have been able to get that sort of audience.'

He agreed to the suggested reunion immediately, despite artistic reservations. 'I had been trying for years to get out of these associations, and here I was jumping back into it.'

Five weeks after the WOMAD festival the Genesis reunion was announced in the London *Evening Standard*, which called the event the year's major rock event after the Rolling Stones. It was set for the open-air Milton Keynes Bowl early in

October with everyone gambling on the clemency of the autumn weather.

Rehearsals took place at the Hammersmith Odeon just before the shows. Gabriel listened to new tapes and studied lyric sheets to refresh his memory. 'We felt a bit strange. We had to decide what songs to do, and obviously the idea was if we were going to do a reunion we should do the classics like "The Musical Box" and "The Knife",' said Phil Collins. 'Pete has always had difficulty remembering words. It was under-standable then, he had not sung them for years and his head was full of other things.

'I thought some of the songs I had been singing for years didn't sound that much better with Pete singing them, take that as you like. But when we sat in Milton Keynes and did it, it was the overall thing.'

On Saturday 2 October it rained all day, turning the Milton Keynes Bowl into a mud lake. Despite that 47,000 people came, some flying in from Japan and the USA, and many bravely watching the support acts throughout the afternoon.

'Genesis drifted onto a blue-lit stage. The lights broadened and four pallbearers brought on a white coffin which opened up to reveal Gabriel in make-up. It was his old Rael disguise, and it became obvious that Gabriel was prepared not just to sing old Genesis numbers, but to perform them with his old costumes (brown cloak and mask/the sunflower etc.) brought out of the mothballs,' wrote Paul Strange in *Melody Maker*. 'Rael's anthem "Back in New York City" opened up the historic set, the sound initially dodgy and variable, with Gabriel valiantly coping with a naff mike.'

This was not viewed so charitably from the stage. 'What was extraordinary was having seen Peter quite a few times since he left the band, I noted how his mike technique had improved so much and his pitching was great. They were all the things he had trouble with in the group,' said Tony Banks.

'But then at the reunion he was right back to where he was before. It just shows, because he was singing other people's melodies, the complexity of them made it much more difficult for him to do. Whereas with his own stuff he had no problem because he could sing exactly as he wanted.'

'His mike technique was as bad as it used to be. Which must be why he wears one of those radio mikes, he can't muck that up,' said Collins. 'There were some wild moments, but we carried it off because people were so pleased to see us together again.'

The group included the newer Genesis recruits Chester Thompson on drums and Daryl Stuermer on bass. The set included some post-Gabriel material, including 'Turn It On Again' where Gabriel and Collins embraced each other while passing on stage as Collins went to the front to sing while Gabriel took over the drums. The fans were then surprised by the appearance of Steve Hackett for 'I Know What I Like (In Your Wardrobe)', finishing off with 'The Knife'. 'A reunion that is unlikely to ever happen again. The rock event of the year,' the *Melody Maker* concluded.

'It was just like returning to some sort of family reunion,' said Gabriel. 'It felt really warm, though it was terrible weather. Musically it wasn't very good, but emotionally it was very strong. I was given at Strat's funeral his notebook in which he wrote some notes around that concert, and he was obviously touched.'

# CHAPTER ELEVEN

THE BIDS TO WIN PETER GABRIEL'S RECORD-ing contract for the United States peaked at one million dollars in 1980. The major American record companies, including his former label Atlantic Records, were after him, following the success of the third album.

The year was to be taken up with touring, so Gabriel had time to carefully consider the offers since he had no plans to start on his next album until the following year.

One of the companies most interested in Gabriel was Geffen Records. It had only just been set up that year by David Geffen, respected for his work with Asylum Records which he ran in the sixties with acts like Joni Mitchell, Neil Young and Jackson Browne. Geffen was known for his per-suasive powers. His latest achievement had been to tempt John Lennon back into the recording studio.

Both Peter Gabriel's and Phil Collins' contracts for America were available in 1980. Geffen Records considered both artists. At the time, before *Face Value* helped make Collins the most successful British artist in America in the eighties, Gabriel looked a safer proposition. After all, his last single, 'Games Without Frontiers', was his first to get airplay on US Top 40 radio. It is a moot point whether Collins would have signed to Geffen if they had made an offer, considering his close relation-ship with Ahmet Ertegun at Atlantic Records.

David Geffen and company president Ed Rosenblatt did

not see Gabriel in concert while he was touring North America in June and July 1980. But they had clearly made a decision to get him if they could by the time they flew to Portugal to see him perform and discuss a deal. Geffen and Rosenblatt arrived in Lisbon in October 1980 and went to the coastal resort of Cascais to meet up with Gail Colson and Gabriel.

'Peter Gabriel is someone we were both familiar with from his Genesis days,' said Rosenblatt. 'We knew his first couple of albums and then all of a sudden the third album was out on Mercury and we were unaware why.' They soon found out when John Kolodner, ironically, joined their company from Atlantic as A&R director.

Geffen and Rosenblatt met Gabriel and Gail Colson in the lobby of their hotel in Cascais. They all drove up the coast for an early dinner before Gabriel's concert that night. Gail and Peter were wary, they were not happy about Kolodner joining Geffen. They were also meeting opposition back home from Tony Stratton Smith, who wanted a new deal allowing Charisma to license them in America. Rosenblatt believed a rival company was spreading rumours that he and Geffen knew nothing about Gabriel's music.

'I'll never forget this,' said Rosenblatt. 'After saying, "Hello, hello, how was your trip" and things like that David immediately went into the John Kolodner situation and answered the remarks that this person from another company had told Gail. I believe David completely disarmed Gail and Peter.

'These are things you normally get in the pursuit of an artist: "I'm the greatest, you're the greatest, we're the greatest!" And you leave any kind of negativity under the rug some place. But the reality of life was that a 3,000-pound rhinoceros was sitting with us on the dinner table while everybody was looking around pretending it's not there. We got that out of the way within the first five minutes of the dinner.

'Peter was quite hurt over this Kolodner situation. But

John feels very badly about it to this day. He didn't feel at that time that Peter was being as commercial as he could have been. He certainly knew that Peter was a great artist. I don't think he ever believed Ahmet Ertegun would ever allow Peter to leave the label. He was just giving his opinion as an A&R person. It's not John Kolodner who should be blamed, but Ahmet Ertegun.'

Geffen's offer was not only below the biggest advance of one million dollars from a company Gail Colson refuses to name, but also below Atlantic's $750,000. Gabriel's prime consideration was not to get a huge advance, deductable anyway from royalties. He needed complete creative independence from an artistically sympathetic company with a sharp business sense. He took David Geffen at his word and agreed to the deal.

After their dinner in Cascais, Rosenblatt and Geffen stayed an extra day, travelling on the tour coach to Oporto in the north of Portugal. The tour was nearing its end having started back in February 1980 in Britain.

Perversely, Gabriel had called it The Tour of China 1984. It was his little dig at groups getting competitive about being the first to play Russia or China and then producing expensive merchandise to commemorate the event. Since Gabriel was twisting the truth he made it the 1984 tour for its Orwellian overtones. He thought he would take a short-cut and not bother to go east, while still issuing the merchandise.

Gabriel explained, 'I thought it would be a lot more interesting than The 1980 Tour of England.' The tour programme was a little red book made up of cut-out graphics from Chinese newspaper advertisements, political posters, comic books and the odd exotic girlie shot dug up by Gabriel on a visit to Soho's Chinatown. His head, usually with a contorted expression, was stuck on other people's shoulders, including a muscle man's, and used as part of a political propaganda poster.

Gabriel wanted someone with studio experience to be sound engineer on the 1980 tour and asked David Lord, who ran the local Crescent Studios in Bath, if he wanted the job. For Lord, a softly spoken classically trained composer, it was an enticing idea, though he could not predict how much of a culture shock life on the road would be.

Gabriel had met Lord in 1977 and the following year asked for his help in transcribing some of the music from the second album for the band to perform live. Crescent Studios was growing in popularity thanks to a healthy local punk music scene.

Lord found life on the road somewhat disconcerting. In Las Vegas, in empathy with Tony Levin, Gabriel decided to once again shave his head. 'He likes upsetting plans very much,' said Lord. 'If a tour has been carefully worked out by the tour manager he likes looking for the unusual. It is very difficult organizing a tour, but at the last minute he'll want to change it.

'He loves cutting things fine, he doesn't like being in good time for things. He is always a madman catching planes and things. I think there have been many times when they have had to virtually reopen the doors.

'I remember us getting on to a train very early. The tour manager had given us the wrong time to make sure we would be there early, and we sat on this train for twenty minutes and everyone was relieved because Peter was there, it was the last train, and about two minutes before we were due to go he said, 'I'm just going to get a paper,' and dashed off to the paper stall a few platforms away and the panic started. It was like that all the time.'

In June 1980 Gabriel and the band spent a week rehearsing for their American tour at a Los Angeles warehouse belonging to Supertramp. They wanted to play a warm-up gig and found a small club in Santa Ana, Los Angeles. 'We were playing some quite big venues, so we were attracted to the idea of playing a 200-seater club,' David Lord remembered. 'The word got around that he was going to play there. People hitchhiked down from Canada and tickets were being sold for vast sums. We started the show and it was absolutely packed until the doors were bursting.'

The fire marshalls who had been monitoring the club for possible offences decided to stop the show. Police helicopters were called in with spotlights shining down. 'The police raided the place, they drove all their cars up against the doors so nobody could get out. They came in and photographed everybody so they had proof the fire regulations were being broken. It was touch and go as to whether the audience would riot because they were so annoyed at the show being stopped.

'Peter was trying to persuade the police to let us carry on, saying it would be less dangerous, but they wouldn't listen to him.' The club owner, who had broken the hire agreement by advertising the show, was prosecuted for the fire offences.

The American leg, which ended in New York three and a half weeks later, was buoyed by the success of the third album. It moved into the US Top 40 while the tour was on, proving to be Gabriel's best seller yet. It gave Gabriel the satisfaction he wanted in proving Atlantic Records wrong in dropping him.

Later that summer David Lord worked on his first major recording project with Gabriel, mixing the German album which had translated lyrics at Crescent Studios before setting off on the final European leg of the 1980 tour finishing in October 1980.

The following year Lord engineered Gabriel's first attempt to produce another artist since the Charlie Drake episode. This time it was someone equally unexpected; Jimmy Pursey, leader of the then defunct Sham '69, the yobbo punk group whose success proved too much for its eccentric leader, sending him into premature retirement.

'I think Peter took pity on him,' was Lord's assessment.

'They started off writing songs together. It was pretty hard going, he was a bit over the top, but Peter was very clever with him.' In March 1981 Lord engineered the single 'Animals Have More Fun' at Crescent Studios, matching Pursey's lyrics to Gabriel's music. The B-side, 'Sus', was also co-written.

Gabriel, who was impressed with Pursey's energy, had first met him in 1978, when he invited Sham '69 to open for him at a concert in Belgium. Three years later it was Pursey who contacted Gabriel when he was looking for a producer for a single. 'I was despondent about me as a producer,' said Pursey. 'The only person I could think of who could do the job was Peter Gabriel. I gave him a buzz, he liked the idea of the song, and about two days later he came to see me on my farm in Guildford.

'We talked about all the ideas I had. We walked around the farm and chatted. He thought I had some great ideas, he wanted to carry them a bit further. I told him about this line I had, about "Animals Have More Fun"; he said that's a great starting point.'

About a week later Pursey went to Bath to rehearse at Ashcombe House. 'I spent one night out in the garden. I refused to sleep in his barn because it was full up with his heads and masks. It was very, very eerie to say the least. There were ethnic masks and also ones he'd used on stage, surrounding the whole room, just piled on top of each other. It all looked like something out of a Ken Russell movie. My imagination was running too far ahead of itself. I wasn't even on marijuana, I was straight as a die.

'In the kitchen I saw a rat run across the floor. I didn't think I was going to get any peace and quiet that night. I pulled one of the settees out, stuck it in the middle of the garden and sat in the garden all the time contemplating the next day and trying to forget about these masks and heads that had been staring at me in the next room.

'The day after that we continued to work. He was very

amused by the story. He made me breakfast and we chatted about what had gone on. In the studio he would be in control of the music side of what was going on, while I was coming up with the lyrics to the song.'

'Animals Have More Fun' was released in June 1981, three months after it was recorded. Pursey disputed the press comment that his pairing with Gabriel was a strange one. He believed they were compatible as musicians and people. Pursey's lyrics went:

> Piggy banks, Russian tanks,
> Animals have more fun.
> The human race, are we lost in space,
> Animals have more fun . . .

Pursey explained: 'As we sit around and think of certain things, there are other things that don't think, they are just living. Whereas we spend most of our time analysing and making judgements, and these are the judgements and analysations [sic] that are not necessary in life.' The B-side, 'Sus', originally titled 'The Shining', was about extra-sensory perception and telepathy, a subject also of interest to Gabriel. 'He was very, very patient with me. I can be an arrogant and self-opinionated sod. Peter Gabriel was the perfect producer,' Pursey said.

The single was greeted by Radio 1 DJ Simon Bates as a future Number 1. That, in Pursey's opinion, ruined its chances because it was a record that was meant to grow on people. The record received unfavourable criticism in the music press. 'Co-written with fellow self-styled tortured artist Peter Gabriel, this shows Jim the Baptist trying to drop us in the same hole that he's in. The puerile lyrical theme is offset by a grinding 'n' grandiose backing track,' commented Record Mirror's reviewer. 'Animals Have More Fun' failed to make the Top 75.

Early in 1981, in preparation for Gabriel's fourth album,

David Lord helped Gabriel upgrade the Ashcombe House studio. They redesigned the control room and Lord rented Gabriel a console. Various technical problems conspired to delay recording.

Gabriel already had a clear idea of the direction he wanted to go in, even if the material had not yet been conceived. He told Ray Coleman of *Melody Maker* in February 1981, 'I can hear in my head now a sort of music which involves a lot of percussion, very little of the regular drum kit, and a lot of electronics. In other words pulling out and virtually removing the emphasis which has always been there from guitar, organ and piano and leaving it more naked.

'This is my ultimate direction. I don't expect to have much on the next album that will sound like that, but that's the direction that's consuming me at the moment and that I'm involved in getting down.'

In spring 1981 London Weekend Television started filming a documentary on Gabriel for the *South Bank Show*, narrated by Melvyn Bragg. They wanted to chart the progress of an album from start to finish. They expected to stop filming that autumn, but were hopelessly optimistic, having to wait until October 1982 when the fourth album was released and they could transmit their show.

Gabriel showed them a case full of cassettes with recordings of different rhythms from around the world taken from the radio, *The World About Us* TV programme, and records. He was being helped in his research into different musical cultures by the people at the *Bristol Recorder*, then starting to plan what became the WOMAD Festival in July 1982.

'I'm certain the Third World can have an increasing influence on our culture and in music a very vigorous hybrid will be produced which is based on this non-European influence and the new technology which is going to get very cheap and this facility will open up a new age of electronic skiffle,' he told the *South Bank Show*.

'Initially when you first walk into the studio it's like walking into another world of masses of knobs and buttons which are totally foreign. Then, as you spend more and more time in the studio, you learn what they all do and how to manipulate things . . . At this point in the process much the most important tool for me is the drum machine and the rhythm box. This allows me, with the sound of real drums, to store in computer memory any drum pattern I can conceive of or steal and use this as the basis for my songwriting. When I have the rhythm set up I can start adding patterns in there. When I've got my rhythms locked into the drum machine I can begin improvising and finding which synth sound then forms around the rhythm.

'In the process where you start to develop these rhythms there's probably over one hundred starting-points. I then begin developing the best of these ideas.' Gabriel already had his demos of 'Jung In Africa', later to become 'Rhythm of the Heat'. Lord described it as having 'just a raw voice and backing, there's no words'. The embryonic song showed that Gabriel was continuing with his technique, started on the third album, of building songs around rhythms rather than chords and melodies. On 'Rhythm of the Heat' most of the music had already been composed, for other songs they would have to work on musical ideas in the studio.

'At this point I've only got outlines for lyrics, so I use odd sounds. I'm trying to enlarge what I do with my voice not through technique but by the sound. We all make noises, particularly when we get emotional about something. The tones of those noises change, they are all representative. There are guttural noises that are built into the rhythms and into the atmosphere as a whole, the tension and the excitement of it.

'In opera you have this very abstracted form of singing – a brilliant technique, but to me it doesn't have the emotional impact that I get when I listen to great soul or blues rhythms. I think in rock as a whole there's been many great songs which

have had really appalling lyrics and others which have had
great lyrics and appalling music. You might as well make the
music as appropriate as you can and try and communicate
something.'

Having amassed a selection of rhythmic ideas and rough
recordings, Gabriel was ready for the musicians booked for the
new album to start recording with him. Drummer Jerry
Marotta was the first to arrive to work on the rhythms. Marotta
resisted Gabriel's increasing reliance on the drum box. 'A
machine is a machine and you can't programme emotion at all
into a machine,' Marotta told the TV interviewers. 'In this
case it's important for me to feel this emotion. It's basically
what music is all about, the emotion inside you. The machine
and I split the work fifty-fifty, it's very hard.'

The other musicians arrived to put down the backing
tracks, laying down each instrument individually so that
Gabriel could later manipulate the sound as much as he liked.
'I like to leave my options open and always think tomorrow
I'll find a way in which it will work perfectly,' said Gabriel.
The nucleus of musicians on the album was still the same as
for the third album, with Tony Levin on bass, Larry Fast on
keyboards and synthesizers, and David Rhodes now installed
on guitar.

Having left Random Hold the previous year, David
Rhodes was signing on the dole and had sunk into a
depression. In his misery he too shaved his head. 'I stayed in
my bedroom for six months and wrote some not very good
songs,' said Rhodes, who sent Gabriel copies of his songs.
Gabriel wanted to use him. Gail Colson was instructed to send
a keyboard to Rhodes with demos for the forthcoming album.
'I would get called in to do bits. I was given a nickname while
we were working on "Wallflower", they called me "Dial-a-
weirdie",' said Rhodes. 'There were loads of people better
than me technically. It's the rhythmic feel, the grooves that
Peter liked. No fancy finger work.'

David Lord was still finding his confidence as a producer. 'I hope very much to interpret his ideas because I don't think he needs very many of mine,' Lord said at the time. 'People tend to think they need producers, but I think it's more a liaison between what he wants to get and overcoming technical problems.'

With hindsight of several years, Lord thought he should have been more assertive. 'I think we are both very similar characters in the way that we are never quite sure that we are right. It was the first big production that I had done, I was probably too much in awe. If I had a strong idea I should probably have stuck with it much more. He could probably have done with someone a bit sterner, his manager always hoped there would be somebody who'd make him bring in a record on time, an eternal desire that never happened,' Lord said.

After several weeks' work at Ashcombe House, Gabriel was left with twenty-seven sixteen-minute tapes, over seven hours of material comprising eighteen possible songs, seven of which were running over ten minutes. For the next three months Gabriel, Lord and Fast used the latest technology to develop the material. According to Melvyn Bragg's TV narration they 'began a search for an entirely new sound'.

'We try treating sounds to put them in perspective in this picture we're building up. For instance, you could have a keyboard sound which you think is occupying too much space and has too much weight. Then I may stick it through something to make it thin and wavy so its personality changes. Everything will at some time go through the electronics and be blended in with newer sonic textures.

'It worries me sometimes that I'm taking so long over these things, then at the end I think it doesn't really matter anyway if the end product works. There are mountains of reels, of try-outs and overdubs. Very often, when you get down to the final mix, very little of it is used. But that's a sort of compositional process, really. Some people would go through it before they go into the studio, most of Peter's work in that aspect is done in the studio.'

Both Fast and Marotta had arguments with Gabriel over musical direction. Resentment was also building in Fast for what he saw as a lack of recognition for his contribution to Gabriel's records. Recognized as a world expert on the synthesizer, Fast had felt he deserved a co-production credit on the third album, and thought after three months' work he deserved the same credit for the fourth album. 'There are things that he absolutely wants to hear and he will pipe up about it and get it. It is his career, so for the most part there is no fighting about that,' said Fast.

After Fast finished in the studio, Gabriel and Lord continued for several more months to refine the sound. When the final selection of songs was edited down, Gabriel added his vocals, remixing, rewriting and revising many times before reaching the final version. Lord's views of working with Gabriel echo those of Fast. 'I like the way he really perseveres and struggles through things that you might not think would work. I could be sure he wouldn't get a song out of this idea, sure that he was going round in circles and not getting anywhere – he always knew at the end of it he would, he always had to prove that he was right. He doesn't like being proved wrong, though he is not dogmatic.

'Most of the people I think are interesting musically would regard Peter as being influential, though I don't know how much effect he has had on the mainstream hit parade stuff.' Lord and Gabriel developed an easy working relationship.

In contrast to the previous album and the intrusions of John Kolodner, Gabriel was now being visited by Geffen executives, who supported what he was attempting, despite the delays. 'We established a relationship with Peter,' said Ed Rosenblatt. 'And when Peter went into the studio to make the album I said, "Look, I know how you feel. But if you want another ear to listen to this record while you are in a formative stage, we have somebody who is a great fan here, Gary Gersh, our A&R director, and you can either listen to what he says, or don't listen to what he says, put out whatever you want to put out." So I'm sure Peter had a certain sense of confidence that we were going to put out whatever he gave us, regardless.'

Geffen kept to their word and did not interfere creatively. But there was disagreement over Gabriel's continued insistence that his albums should have no title other than his name. Gabriel finally agreed Geffen could put a sticker on the American cover and call the album *Security*. 'I think he was thinking that it would make the record company feel secure,' said Rosenblatt.

The fourth album was not as well received or as commercially successful as the previous album. It went straight into the UK charts at Number 6, but quickly slipped out again. The third album had benefited from the success of the single 'Games Without Frontiers'. But there was hardly anything that was commercially accessible on the fourth album. The single 'Shock the Monkey' made it to Number 58, while 'I Have The Touch' did not even make the Top 75.

The album suffered from an over-long gestation period, and the mood was one of unrelenting intensity. Yet it contains some of Gabriel's strongest and most popular live songs. 'Rhythm of the Heat' is Gabriel's most powerful expression of rhythmic power and explores his obsession with spiritual transformation, through Jung's experiences in Africa. 'Wallflower' is an inspiring gentle hymn of hope.

'Shock the Monkey' is as close as he gets on the album to being playful, a satire on sexuality and jealousy and how it makes monkeys of us all. Musically it was a signpost to his future direction as he tried to capture the sound of early Tamla Motown. By the time the song was finished not much of that influence was evident, though there would soon be further explorations of sixties soul and rhythm and blues.

The song alluded to sex more obviously than he had previously done in lyrics. Influenced by the use of innuendo growing up on a farm, he drew on one agricultural term for sexual coupling – cover me.

> Cover me, when I sleep
> Cover me, when I breathe
> You throw your pearls before the swine
> Make the monkey blind
> Cover me, darling please . . .
>
> 'Shock the Monkey'; Gabriel, 1982

'Lay Your Hands On Me', like 'I Have The Touch', reveals aspects of Gabriel's own personality, and in particular upbringing, where touch was taboo. 'Lay Your Hands' explores the emotional extremes of alienation and belonging and the need for trust.

> Sat in the corner of the Garden Grill, with the plastic
> Flowers on the window sill
> No more miracles, loaves and fishes, been so busy with the
>     Washing of the dishes . . .
>
> But still the warmth flows through me
> And I sense you know me well . . .
>
> I am willing – lay your hands on me . . .
>
> 'Lay Your Hands On Me'; Gabriel, 1982

'I Have The Touch' takes the need for physical contact to a pathological extreme. The character is outwardly a complete opposite to Gabriel.

> Any social occasion, it's hello, how do you do
> All those introductions, I never miss my cue . . .

But inwardly he is not so different to Gabriel, or any of us, in our more manic moments.

> *Pull my chin, stroke my hair, scratch my nose, hug my knees*
> *Try drink, food, cigarette, tension will not ease*
> *I tap my fingers, fold my arms, breathe in deep, cross my legs*
> *Shrug my shoulders, stretch my back – but nothing seems to please*
>
> *I need contact . . .*
>
> 'I Have The Touch'; Gabriel, 1982

Gabriel explained, 'I think I'm pulled in both directions, wanting to put a distance between myself and some things or people, and then wanting to break through and make contact. When I'm writing lyrics I'm not conscious of that, I'm just really following subjects that interest me.'

That included books on body language, on how brain stimulation is dependent on touch, and on how race determines how frequently we touch. 'There was this experiment carried out in restaurants in different capital cities around the world. In Puerto Rico they noted one table with about 250 body contacts within an hour and in Paris it was down to about thirty while in London it was down to two – the hello and goodbye – so I think this is pertinent for an English person.

'"I Have The Touch" is made almost humorous with this alien English person who is really getting off on any skin contact because he's so deprived of it. So in formal situations where he's shaking hands it's an amazing turn-on for him. Whereas the other person thinks he can retain his distance and formality and hold the status quo.'

'The Family and the Fishing Net' is lyrically one of the most extraordinary songs that Gabriel has written. It is an impressionistic view of the ritual of marriage. 'I was looking at the undercurrent of symbolism within a normal everyday

Western wedding in a church. The territorial battles between fathers' daughters and mothers' sons, the ring, all sorts of sexual undertones.'

Gabriel said it was written 'under the influence of Dylan Thomas'. Like Dylan Thomas, Gabriel has an interest in often surreal images, unexpected rhythms and rhymes, and tightly compressed imagery which sometimes seems, superficially at least, confusing. Dylan Thomas urged his readers not to 'understand' his poetry, and in so doing gave a clue to what Gabriel aspires to. 'I can give you a rough idea of the "plot",' Thomas wrote. 'But of course it's bound to be most superficial and a perhaps misleading idea, because the "plot" is told in images, and images are what they say, not what they stand for.'

'The Family and the Fishing Net' has many images in common with Thomas' poetry and prose: images of the sea and shores and the people who live off them, and much Christian symbolism. Rarely are Gabriel's images more potent than in this song.

> Silence falls the guillotine
> All the doors are shut
> Nervous hands grip tight the knife
> In the darkness, till the cake is cut
> Passed around, in little pieces
> The body and the flesh
> The family and the fishing net
> Another in the mesh
>
> The body and the flesh.

'The Family and the Fishing Net'; Gabriel, 1982

Because the recording of the fourth album coincided exactly with the organizing of the WOMAD festival, Gabriel was constantly getting fed new sounds from around the world. Ethiopian pipes formed the harmonies around which 'The Family and the Fishing Net' was written. The surdo drum and

Brazilian rhythms inspired 'Kiss Of Life'. Gabriel said the song was about 'a large Brazilian woman with abundant lifeforce raising a man from the dead'. The surdo is also used on 'Rhythm of the Heat', along with Ghanaian drums banged by the Ekome Dance Company, an Afro-Caribbean performance group from Bristol.

'San Jacinto' expressed his long-standing fascination with American Indians. He described it as a 'mixture of American Indian culture and Palm Springs – Sinatra golf and pool images.' San Jacinto is a mountain in California, overlooking Palm Springs and some Indian reservations.

The song evolved out of an encounter between Gabriel and an Apache brave who worked as a porter in a Cleveland hotel. Returning from a gig, Gabriel spotted the Indian looking agitated and wandering around looking for a taxi. 'He'd heard that his flat was burning down and he was trying to get in from this fairly remote hotel to where his flat was, so I gave him a lift back that night and got talking to him afterwards, for most of the night, and he was describing how he was initiated to becoming a brave.

'He was taken up into the mountains with this sort of shaman character, a medicine man, and he was carrying a rattlesnake in his bag, and the medicine man took it out and held it to the boy's arm and the snake bit him. And if he came down again from the mountain after fourteen days he was a brave, and if he didn't he was dead. Apparently nearly all of them got through it, and he was describing the way they hallucinate really strongly for that period. I think there are hallucinatory materials in the poison of the snake.'

Gabriel received some scathing reviews. The single 'Shock the Monkey', released at the same time as the album, was too much for Dave McCullough in *Sounds*, who equated Gabriel's innovations with Genesis' traditional melodic approach. For McCullough Gabriel epitomized wealth, greed and shallow sentiment. 'Forget heavy metal, punk, the Rolling Stones, forget the most horrendous musical niche you can think of – because the most horrendous of the lot is the Comfortably Middle Aged Set at which Genesis and associates sit at the head of the (leather-bound) table.

'Genesis, Roxy Music, Gabriel – all comfortably well-off, middle-aged and classed, cheapies who are characterized by a smugness, a fascismo organization around them as big as a multi-national, and a music as predictably fascismo-bland to match. These are the people we really ought to go for, in a sense there is so much ill-used wealth here that the multi-national tag is really apposite . . .

' "Shock the Monkey" is so middling in every respect, middling white harmless reggae trash – geared for the charts with a slide rule and a snide smile . . . In a context where Genesis can cruise comfortably, the more arseholes, guttersnipes, piss artists and madmen around to match the extremes of contradiction that are inherent in music, the very much the better.'

Gavin Martin's album review in the *NME* was equally unforgiving. 'Gabriel is a far more influential character (more's the pity) than he's been given credit for. Hardly a day goes past without another sweatshop independent outfit sending me a single that bears a sizeable trace of Gabriel's theoretical overwrought hollow sorrow. The image that this LP throws up is that of an alienated artist trapped in Bath (Bath!) struggling with the contradictions of civilization, the soul, our very existence . . . Gabriel seems entrenched in white liberal guilt, working from the premise that for truly great art to be created torment and suffering must be encountered at every turn. It's also echoed in the music, an endless barrage of stilted electronic devices, feebly constructed dire attempts to produce dynamics and atmospherics . . .'

More vitriol follows including 'half-assed posturing and nebulous conceits', 'stagnating in dank, painful introspection', 'the incredibly selfish notion that we must look to tribal civilizations to understand ourselves (as if they'd been created specifically for the purpose)', 'bland wet condescension' and 'what are we going to do with these arthouse bores?'

Chris May in *Black Music and Jazz Review* did not agree, harking back to his own review of *Music and Rhythm*, the WOMAD album. 'I observed that Gabriel brought a guileless honesty and wit to his music which kept it entirely in character with his source material. The same is true of his latest release. Sadly, the honkie poseurs of the rock press don't agree, so Gabriel has been crucified in their weeklies for "cultural imperialism". Which mainly serves to illustrate the double irrelevance of half-understood Spartist concepts once they're applied to an area as intangible and human as music.'

Not all the music press were dismissive. 'Gabriel walks a fine line between brilliance and churning out a load of old cobblers,' was the *Record Mirror* verdict. And in the end of year album roundup in *Melody Maker*, Simon Scott wrote, 'With this album, Peter Gabriel continues to extend the barriers of rock music, and furthers the realization of his ideas totally unhampered by traditional restrictions. His preoccupation with primitive rhythms is explored with stunning results, and although this is not an easy album, the patience needed to enjoy it is well rewarded. Gabriel's skill in pursuit of his visions make this one of the most innovative albums of the year, and sets a standard that other rock artists have only hinted at.'

Gabriel gave his views on the criticism to the *South Bank Show*. 'Part of it is straight reaction to the music and I'm not dodging that, but I think a lot of it has to do with fashion. One of the real satisfactions with me with this record is that I'm played on black stations in America, and even though in the white press I had some fair slagging this time, I had some very good reviews in black magazines. Even though I don't think my music has much in common with black music, for me it's great to feel that the rhythm is strong enough to get through to black people. There are definitely elements of this album which are a progression for me. I want to continue exploring this hybrid between electronic non-European influences. I think a lot more musicians are now working in this area and there will be a style of music to emerge in the eighties which I think will be very important and influential.'

Early in 1981 at the same time as Peter Gabriel started work on the fourth album, the family left the cottage, their first home in the Bath area. Peter had fallen in love with a large Victorian house overlooking Solsbury Hill. But Jill found it 'monstrous'.

'We knew we had to move because the cottage was too small. But I was totally unhappy at the new house. It was vast, we had hardly any furniture in it, and we couldn't afford to do anything with it. Peter was hardly there at all, he was writing and then recording the album at Ashcombe.'

After six months at the house Jill could take no more. The studio cook at Ashcombe was leaving and she suggested Jill take over. 'She knew that the pressure on our relationship was really bad at that point, we just weren't seeing each other. But she cooked three-course Cordon Bleu meals, it was unbelievable and she had to cook extra courses because of the vegetarians.

'Something inside me said, "You really have to go for this." Because I was really unhappy up there and wasn't seeing him it seemed a logical move. So I moved with the kids to Ashcombe and left the other house deserted. I told Peter he had to sell it, which he didn't want to do at all. In retrospect it was crazy, it was a good property and cost a lot of money, but I was totally emotional, I just hated it!

'All four of us slept in the same room above the kitchen because we had the whole band housed there, and I took on the cooking. When I started it had a tremendous value. I took it very seriously and learnt how to cook the way she did, she gave me the odd hint.

'I took it on to run the house, do their washing, keep it

clean, and do the cooking. It was a full-time job and I was still trying to look after the kids. It was a means of getting closer to him. In fact that was the joke because of course you don't get closer at all. It was a nightmare because I was closer to him and even further away. We couldn't relate, and it would end up at two in the morning, he would come to bed and I was wrecked anyhow.

'I think that was the picture of how our lives weren't working. It intensified, it couldn't possibly work.

'The kids were definitely suffering at that point, because they couldn't get through to either of us then. I was always working, always cooking something, there were all the people around us, always somebody talking, Peter was working. So it was a very difficult time for them.'

In June 1982 the album was at last nearing completion. Peter and David Lord working through a couple of nights to finish the mixing before Peter went to New York to personally deliver the master tapes to Geffen. He had to catch a 7 a.m. flight and just after dawn in the sunshine outside Crescent Studios he was seen off by the small group of people who had worked so intensively on the project. Among them were Jill and David Lord.

'I think everyone felt very lost and shattered – it had been so intense, and it was all over,' Jill remembered. 'We all stood there and there was a very empty feeling that it was all over. The feeling of loss for me was just enormous.'

Jill felt isolated, having no one to go to who could understand her feeling of desolation. 'It sounds so corny, but it is like having a baby. It was as if it were taken away and we were all just left there.' Jill mentioned to David that they should all meet up. 'It was an incredibly empty day, and as I drove away I thought, "I could go and see David." Not that we were that close, because we weren't. We hardly communicated, really. But I did think I could relate to him. There was another person I could have gone to but I made a decision to go and see David partly because I thought he was extremely safe, funny really. I drove over that evening, and we talked for ages, and we did end up sleeping together, which was very strange, but I came back to the kids.

'I probably regret nothing more in my life than that. Peter often said, "Well, you couldn't have found a better way to hurt me." I wasn't consciously thinking, "This is the way to hurt Peter." Our relationship was very bad at that point. I was asking for attention he couldn't give, his work was so intense. Peter has always said, "I will always go one better than you." And he always has, he is always capable of that. So I managed to punish him. He managed to punish me better.'

'We met at fourteen and sixteen years old, you are very different people at that age, so it's been a very bumpy ride,' said Peter. 'We've swapped over roles. Initially I was the good guy, she was the bad guy, and then maybe four or five years ago the roles reversed and she became the really solid one, working hard to keep the relationship going, and I was the one mucking around.

'It was partly neglect on my side, because when work becomes obsessive, as it does for me, you don't give enough time and energy to the relationship. And relationships, I have discovered, don't run on neutral, you're either working on them or they're getting worse. So I think she just felt totally ignored by me during that period and so ended up getting involved and then I got badly hurt. I think we've both been pretty hurtful to each other. I think what happens is that when things go bad you desensitize yourself, and you actually cut off from the hurt that you are causing.'

Jill and David's affair continued, at that point unknown to Peter, throughout the WOMAD débâcle. Just before WOMAD, in July 1982, Lord helped produce the German language version of the fourth album while keeping up the pretence that nothing was going on. In the end it was too much to bear, and the day before the WOMAD festival Lord feigned illness and let the studio engineer take over his job.

In September Peter went to the continent to promote the new album. On his return he confessed an infidelity to Jill. 'That showed up the state of our relationship because Peter is tremendously loyal, but there must have been a great distance in many ways, and I must have been giving him nothing.' Peter's admission prompted Jill to confess her relationship with David, which he had not suspected.

Peter felt betrayed and arrived at David's doorstep in the middle of the night. Both men are calmly spoken and slow to anger, so a lot of quiet anger was expressed.

The situation was getting too intense for Jill, and she decided to take drastic action. She saw a newspaper advertisement for a cottage to rent in the Lake District, packed the Range Rover with her own and the children's belongings, confronting Peter with the news just before making off. 'That was my bid to go away and sort out my life.' Though her relationship with David had started off almost casually, she was now trying to decide which man she wanted to be with.

'I knew I must be on my own with the children because they had been having a shitty time. Cumbria was wonderful because I solidified my relationship with my children, and found myself in many ways. Stupid things like being cut off without a telephone and teaching the kids every day were very important to me. We had a routine and lived on a very small amount of money.'

Though desperately upset at Jill's flight with Anna and Melanie, Peter was powerless to do anything about it. Soon after he was off on a six week American tour and went up to Cumbria to say goodbye. The family kept in touch by post. Jill sent him letters and he sent cards to the girls. 'Despite all the rubbish, one thing we did was that we never said a bad word against each other in front of the children. The kids knew everything, he talked to them, and then I talked to them.'

Jill struggled with the elements as winter came on, for the first time in her life she was faced with having to fend for herself. 'She actually did very well, she'd always had a sheltered life. And the kids liked it because they had undivided attention,' said Peter. David visited on Jill's thirty-first birthday, 2 December, and she had pre-arranged with Peter for him to call her at a given time at the local callbox.

'In that phone call I said to him, "Have you had other relationships?" and he said, "Yes, five." That was devastating.' Unknown to Jill at the time, one was a serious relationship with actress Rosanna Arquette, due to find fame in 1985 starring with Madonna in *Desperately Seeking Susan*.

Jill decided to return to Bath for Christmas. Peter was also back having finished touring. They were living together at Ashcombe House, but Jill was looking for a house for her and the girls.

Peter thought Jill could not have found a better person to hurt him with than David. Likewise she thought he could not have found a better person to hurt her with than a young, beautiful successful actress. 'In many ways Peter holds the cards in our relationship and I actually love that about him. I am a very fiery person and I give him a hard time emotionally, but in the end he is actually more powerful. And that was the ironical thing about that time, he held me in a sense with Rosanna. It was strange, but it turned everything around and it was a good punishment for everything I had ever done from our whole past.'

Jill made a befuddled attempt at suicide. She resolved to drive to nearby Solsbury Hill, made famous by Peter's song, and take an overdose.

'One of the things that I suffered from was unbelievable guilt,' said Jill. 'I felt incredibly bad about being unfaithful. We had just reached a pitch one night and I said to him that he should look after the children and I should just go away, and he reacted with "Fine" and went to bed, which kind of gave me permission. It felt like he was saying, "I agree with you".

'I had a lot to drink, I planned to make it quite comfortable. I took with me a blanket and lots of pills and more drink. I was driving in a complete daze.' Jill attempted to drive on to Solsbury Hill only to find her path blocked by an eight foot high mound of clay. It had been put there by the National Trust fearing a hippy peace festival. She felt it was an ironic omen for which Peter was responsible by drawing public attention to the hill in the first place.

'It sounds pathetic now,' said Jill. 'It felt like God was saying "Fuck you". I had come to my senses in a way when I saw the mound. I drove back, it was very frightening because I felt scared of God. It was my first and last thought of suicide.'

Jill eventually rented a cottage in a village several miles away and moved in with the children, while Peter stayed in residence at Ashcombe House. 'I was mixing the live album and a furniture van came. I knew about it, but it was still pretty traumatic,' remembered Peter.

Throughout this time Jill continued seeing David. 'I think I was incidental to the whole thing. I was just one chapter in the story of their relationship,' said David Lord. 'I wasn't trying to split them up. Jill and I had a genuine relationship. It was actually very strong and quite rewarding, without the complications of a three-way relationship. It came to the point where I just had to leave her on her own to make up her own mind.'

'I decided to go to Senegal and to Brazil,' said Peter. 'I thought "It's silly to sit around, moping. Do something positive!".' His relationship with Rosanna Arquette carried on, as much as hopping across the Atlantic would permit.

Peter and Jill's contact revolved around his visits to the children. 'We would meet up to take the kids out and we would talk, and sometimes there were quite good, positive sessions. I think what has sustained our marriage has basically been a great friendship, a great sense of companionship. So though we often have periods when we don't talk, when we do get into deep talk it's great.'

In the spring of 1983 Peter and Jill were recommended a visit to Robin and Prue Skynner's Institute of Family Therapy in London. Robin Skynner and comedian John Cleese, a former client, wrote the bestselling *Families and How To Survive Them*, which illustrates some unnerving characteristics of all relationships. Perhaps the most remarkable being 'that people unconsciously choose each other because of similarities in the way their families functioned'. The book gives plausible proof of this hypothesis.

Skynner is particularly illuminating on how we all screen off emotions that make us feel bad. The act of screening-off is an approximation of repression, while the screen itself is the unconscious. Skynner explains: 'Although we all want to be loved by our families and not display feelings that upset them, we also have a keen hunger to be whole, to be complete. When we sense, and are drawn to, the denied parts behind the screen in our partner, we're really hoping, deep down, to get back the missing parts of ourselves again . . . The extraordinary paradox is that your partner is exactly the one you can best grow with . . . but also the one you can get most stuck with. Even . . . the one you can end up hating most of all.'

Peter was sceptical. 'I thought "Shrinks! Who needs it?" It struck me as a lot of Californian nonsense that I'd never been attracted to.' But his opinion soon changed. 'The Skynners are wonderful people. They would do it together so you have the male and female sides presented. They wouldn't really take sides, but they both had their independent opinions. There would be three or four other couples, many of whom were breaking up. It wasn't an attempt to get couples to stay together, it was an attempt to get people to communicate well, and to handle whatever was going on.

'Doors began to open in the relationship and some of the

hurt slowly healed. I had a real sense of emptiness without them. I think it is a sense of self you get through the family unit, having had it and being so really proud of my kids. I love both of my kids, I loved that part of the family life, even though I didn't give it enough time. It was very important to me, so there was a real sense of mourning and loss, and I think once we had got through several layers of pain, both Jill and I, we began to feel there was still a really strong bond.'

Peter was unable to commit himself to regular marital therapy sessions because of his work schedule. 'I actually finished us going to the thing. Sometimes I think that is a pity because we could have done with longer.'

In May 1983 Peter combined a trip to Brazil with a visit to Disney's Epcot Center in Florida and a holiday with Rosanna in Antigua. Peter spent the autumn of 1983 touring Europe, and for much of 1984 became involved in writing music for films. He stayed in close contact with Jill and the children, but neither Jill or Peter could contemplate divorce.

No one was happy with the unsettled situation. 'It had gone on so long, we were all fed up thinking about it to any degree,' said David Lord. 'I felt I should leave them to it. And if she decided she was going to split up with him then whether I did anything with her was another question. But I don't think it was a situation where she might leave him for me. They were two different things.'

In August 1984 Jill went with the girls to join her parents at Balmoral. Peter went to see Rosanna in New York to resolve the situation. 'When I got back he came over and I asked if he had decided, and he said, "I have, I have decided I will stay with you." And then we attempted to start up again.'

Peter's love for Anna and Melanie was a major factor in his reuniting with Jill. 'He's terribly in love with his daughters, and they with him,' said Jill.

His daughters still had to put up with their father's through work. Despite a strong affectionate bond he tried to absence make their lives less sheltered than his own upbringing. 'I believe in discipline, in giving a strong wall for kids to bounce off,' said Gabriel in 1987. 'I was a sixties liberal, but now I'm more realistic. We still have the teenage years ahead, but I think you do children a greater service by being yourself and giving them something to push against. They want a battle, that's what they need.'

Eighteen months after Jill moved into her own cottage Peter reunited with the family. They stayed there until they bought a new house nearer Bath in 1985.

Peter felt it was important that the conflicting people in his life should meet to try and dissolve any enmity that might remain and allow him to stay friends with Rosanna. Jill agreed and went with him to New York for two days. 'I thought I would survive. You know, the age, the extra years, I thought I would be able to hold my own and feel better for what I did. She was very young and bouncy and full of energy.' Jill was intimidated and did not feel the encounter was a success.

The situation appeared to be resolved when Rosanna visited London in early 1987 with a new boyfriend, former keyboard player in Elton John's band and film score composer James Newton Howard, later to become her husband. Peter asked Jill to accompany him to lunch with the couple. 'The two meetings with Rosanna are an intensely hysterical memory for me.' Jill was again intimidated, this time by the way Rosanna's charisma captivated not only her luncheon companions, but also the other men in the restaurant. 'I can see the value if I had been a strong enough person, if I had more belief in myself like I have now. At the time I didn't feel I had anything compared to what she had to offer.'

David Lord has had no contact with Jill since she and Peter got back together in 1984 and has only exchanged pleasantries with Peter when they have bumped into each other.

The separation was a major catalyst for change in Jill's life. She became more assertive and began looking for a career, feeling her experience was well suited to counselling. Her first attempt was helping the Samaritans, but that was halted when she went to Cumbria. Before her divorce she explained, 'I stopped doing anything with my life because I thought I was too stupid to. But I have ambition for the first time. It has taken me so long because I lived through Peter initially. It was my way of avoiding taking hold of myself.' Jill finally realized her ambition of becoming a marriage guidance counsellor a few years later, after the divorce was finalized.

# CHAPTER TWELVE

I N 1980 MIAMI STEVE VAN ZANDT, STILL guitarist in The E Street Band, was in Los Angeles mixing Bruce Springsteen's album *The River*. While taking time off he came across an art-house theatre showing old movies. Waiting for the film to start, he was struck by the interval music.

'The projectionist put this tape in, and it was this most extraordinary thing. I had no idea who it was or what he was singing about, but it was very, very moving. I went upstairs and said to the projectionist, "What was that?" It turned out to be Peter Gabriel singing "Biko" and I went out and got it. I got such an emotion from that song I had to find out what it was all about. That's the ultimate musical accomplishment, I guess, to move you to do something. And then I began to look at US foreign policy in general. It had always been in the back of my mind to find out more about South Africa.'

In the summer of 1984 Little Steven, as he liked to be known after leaving Springsteen's band, visited South Africa twice, including the Sun City resort in the tribal 'homeland' of Bophuthatswana. Initially he set out to do research on his next album. But he put that on hold, deciding instead to organize what was to become the Sun City Project.

Gabriel heard of Biko's death the day it was announced in September 1977. 'I made a note of it in my diary. When I started getting into African rhythms on the album it seemed appropriate and I began buying books about him and researching as much as I could.'

Stephen Biko, a Bantu medical student, was founder of the South African Students Organization and was a leading figure in the South African Black Consciousness Movement. He became a banned person in 1973, and was put under house arrest at his home in the Eastern Cape. He had been detained several times before his final arrest at a roadblock. A month later he sustained brain damage after a 'scuffle' with his police interrogators. He was then transported naked 600 miles in the back of a police van from Port Elizabeth to the prison hospital in Pretoria. He died aged thirty on 12 September 1977 on a mat in the corner of a cell.

> *You can blow out a candle*
> *But you can't blow out a fire*
> *Once the flame begins to catch*
> *The wind will blow it higher*
> *Oh Biko, Biko, because Biko . . .*

'Biko'; Gabriel, 1979

Biko's friend Donald Woods, editor of the *East London Daily Dispatch* at the time of his death, wrote, 'Steve Biko represented, in my opinion, the last hope for a peaceful accommodation to resolve the growing South African race crisis.' Woods was himself detained when his articles condemning the South African Government became too controversial. He secretly wrote his biography of Biko in jail, eventually escaping disguised as a priest.

Gabriel met Woods in July 1983 when he performed at a concert in aid of the Lincoln Trust, founded by Woods to counteract censorship and South African Government propaganda throughout the world. Gabriel topped the bill in front of 20,000 people at Crystal Palace Football Club's ground in south London, helped by Phil Collins on drums, who had been brought in to help Gabriel's regular drummer, Jerry Marotta, who was suffering from back pains.

'I think Biko was a key youth leader, and had he lived, he would have emerged as a world figure for young people, rather than as just a black South African leader,' said Gabriel. 'If one reads any of his writing he seems in many ways a well-reasoned and sensitive leader.'

The song appeared on record three years after Biko's death. 'Biko' became one of the most moving moments in Gabriel's shows. It is Gabriel's most effective 'message' song, and has become a virtual anthem for Amnesty International. But Gabriel was disappointed when 'Biko' failed to reach the Top 30 on its release as a single in August 1980.

Even so, it earned over £50,000 in royalties. Gabriel sought to donate the royalties from the song to the Black Consciousness Movement of Azania, which Biko founded. The movement embraced the Black Peoples' Convention, set up in London just before Biko's death to co-ordinate the activities of South African exiles in the UK, which received all the proceeds from the record. The money was used partly to find better premises for the movement in Gower Street, Bloomsbury, and kept it running for three years. The rest of the money was apparently sent to help refugees in Botswana, Lesotho and Swaziland, to the Black Consciousness Movement within South Africa, and used for medical equipment at the Impelweni Clinic in the Eastern Cape, founded by Biko under the Black Community Programme. The Black Peoples' Convention closed its London office in 1983 through a lack of funds and its activities have been absorbed by the refugee committee of the Pan African Congress.

In October 1987 Gabriel got the chance to re-release a live version of 'Biko' as a single to promote Cry Freedom, Sir Richard Attenborough's biopic on Biko. Though the song was not a part of the movie soundtrack, its accompanying video included clips from the film as well as live footage of Gabriel performing the song. The royalties again were to be donated to the anti-apartheid cause.

The new democratic multiracial South Africa has been able to allow Stephen Biko to rest in peace. Gabriel was personally thanked for his tribute by President Nelson Mandela on 12 September 1997, exactly twenty years after Stephen Biko's death. They joined Donald Woods, Richard Attenborough, Denzel Washington, Kevin Kline, Richard Branson and Biko's widow Ntsiki at the ceremony to unveil a statue of him in East London, South Africa. Mandela said Gabriel's song had 'helped to keep the flame alive'.

Gabriel was taken unawares when asked to sing at the ceremony. He acquitted himself helped by a CD copy of 'Biko' used as a backing track over the PA, a choir and the crowd of 25,000. For Gabriel the experience was 'very emotional. After living with the words of the song for so long, it gave me a sense of completion to be here.'

At the same time as the ceremony the policemen who murdered Biko were brought before the South African Courts of Truth and Reconciliation. They were immune from prosecution under the terms of the commission and under South African law which prohibits prosecutions for murder after twenty years have elapsed.

In September 1985, five years after first hearing 'Biko', Van Zandt recorded the *Sun City* single and album, raising over $500,000 for the Anti-Apartheid Movement, a school, and the families of political prisoners. 'We had this list of people we were trying to find to record with. Peter's name was on the top of the list because of "Biko" with Gil Scott-Heron because of his song "Johannesburg".'

By coincidence, Gabriel was at the Power Station studios in New York at the time recording for the *So* album. Van Zandt and producer Arthur Baker visited Gabriel and recorded a vocal segment for the 'Sun City' single. He can just about be heard in the chorus of the title track, and can

be seen momentarily in the video singing 'I' in the studio
in between shots of Bruce Springsteen's 'I' for the chorus 'I
ain't gonna play Sun City'. What started out for Van Zandt
as a single ended up as an album because of the wealth of
material he was left with once everybody from Bob Dylan and
Jackson Browne to Bob Geldof and Run DMC had made
their contributions.

'Peter just began to improvise. In the end I am listening to
this thing, I love it so much, I thought, "My God, I can't use
five seconds of this in a single, this thing is a total song." I
brought in some musicians and put some more chords into it,
and wrote some lyrics around it, and that became "No More
Apartheid",' said Little Steven.

At the session Gabriel explained, 'Our music is based on a
black heritage. That has now become absorbed, and generated
a huge income for white people. So it's about time some of us
paid some homage to our sources.'

On the album Van Zandt wrote, 'I would like to especially
thank Peter Gabriel for the profound inspiration of his song
"Biko" which is where my journey to Africa began.'

Van Zandt is forthright in his praise of Gabriel. 'I think
Peter's one of the most important artists of our time and I
don't say that lightly. I would have said that even before he
became a good friend of mine because he communicates so
well and so purely. It seems to come right from his soul to
yours, soul to soul, rather than the other things that get
between.

'Everybody knows he is wonderfully innovative, but it's
the emotional side that really gets to me more than the
technical side. He is just a great, great singer, which sometimes
is forgotten. I love the way he combines different kinds of
music. I do the same thing, so I can appreciate how good he is
at it. I think he is the best at that, combining things in a very
natural way.'

Apart from the righteous condemnation of the British

music press, Gabriel only gained in credibility through 'Biko'. He was then in a unique position to view the criticism thrown at Paul Simon over the recording of the *Graceland* album in South Africa.

Both men got a chance to discuss the issue in San Francisco in February 1987 on the first leg of Simon's *Graceland* tour of America. They met backstage after the show and Simon went back with Gabriel to his friend Peter Schwartz's home in Berkeley. Several other people were present, including Jon Mcintire, manager of the Grateful Dead, a close friend of Schwartz. They all stayed up engrossed in conversation until 4.30 a.m.

'I liked the *Graceland* album but felt that he had handled it wrong, and had maybe been a little naïve,' said Gabriel. 'He was arguing and said, "Did anyone think I was for apartheid?" and he said, "Have you tried to get approval from the ANC?" The musicians he wanted to work with weren't being allowed to leave the country. So the only way he could work with those musicians was to go in there. At that time he asked about the UN ban. He was advised the ban meant live performances as opposed to studio performances. So I think he was quite shaken by the uproar that emerged.

'He was then advised, when he had finished the recordings, that the ban did apply to studio work. I think he was genuinely innocent of that, but I think he could have had a little more foresight of the possible consequences, and also made a strong declaration earlier on. If you worked with a group of, say, Jewish musicians in Germany just before the Second World War you were bound to know something was going on. And not to make reference to it is, I think, strange. I don't think you can take the role, "Oh, we are just musicians, I don't want to get involved."'

Simon's riposte to that comparison later appeared in *Rolling Stone* magazine. 'To go over and play Sun City would be like going over to do a concert in Nazi Germany at the height of the Holocaust. But what I did was to go over essentially and play to the Jews. That distinction was never made.'

'I think *Graceland* has done an enormous amount for South African music,' said Gabriel. 'What really pisses me off about the bans are that I support the prevention of rich white musicians, or Westerners, going to South Africa and taking a lot of money out and supporting the government in that way. However, there are many black artists, writers, painters, musicians, that need to get heard, and that are really talking about their experience in that country at this time. The Musicians Union ban and the Equity ban can forbid their voice being heard. And that must be counterproductive.'

The charge of cultural imperialism has frequently been thrown at Gabriel, and it is one he readily refutes. 'I think there is a lot of bullshit talked about it. Show me an artist who is pure and doesn't feed off other people. Show me a musician who is pure and particularly show me a rock musician who doesn't feed off other people and other styles and other traditions.

'I think what Paul Simon does is healthy, he has a tradition of doing this. He was the first white musician with any measure of success to take reggae music seriously. Reggae wasn't hip at the time he was working with it. He helped get an interest in South American music and folk music, and that definitely helped musicians trying to get work in Europe and America. And he has definitely increased the stature of South African music with this album.

'The problem occurs when all the money goes in one direction. "Soweto", the Malcolm McLaren track, is one of my favourite records of 1983. And I gather that was pretty much intact before McLaren stuck his name on top of someone else's song.' McLaren and producer Trevor Horn visited the Soweto township in South Africa as part of a trip around the world. The single 'Soweto' reached the UK Top 40. For Gabriel, McLaren was a plunderer because he blatantly passed off other people's tunes as his own. Paul Simon was the opposite, painstakingly acknowledging his sources.

'I think I can hear Paul Simon's digestive system, if you like, the music going in and coming out, it's not just imitative,' said Gabriel. 'Personally I would probably try to remove it a little further from the source music. I feel more comfortable doing that, but I don't think what he did was wrong. And if you go to Africa you hear the influence of the West is just as strong there as the influence of Africa is in the West. It's always been that way.'

Gabriel first made contact with Amnesty when he visited their London offices to get some books and brochures for his research into 'Biko'. His first personal involvement came around 1981 through a friend who suggested he join the Amnesty scheme whereby individuals adopt certain political prisoners and write on their behalf to the presidents, prime ministers and gaolers who are holding them.

'I think it has practical and achievable goals and the prisoners are continuously being released and got out of torture as a result of Amnesty's efforts. And I think quite often now, when I sit down with my benefit priority list, which numbers many hundreds, it has to be related to how I respond emotionally to the subject, and also to how practical and effective the work is.'

He maintained a low profile allowing his name to be used on leaflets handed out by Amnesty. Then in June 1986, when Amnesty celebrated its twenty-fifth anniversary, Gabriel became one of their major public supporters. He cancelled a planned promotional tour of Spain, Portugal and Japan to join the Conspiracy of Hope tour across the United States after an invitation from Bono of U2.

The bill included U2, Sting and the Police, Lou Reed, and Bryan Adams and along the way Bob Dylan, Tom Petty, Jackson Browne, Joan Baez, Joni Mitchell, Little Steven and Miles Davis. At first Gabriel met resistance from Geffen. The

*So* album was just about to be released and they wanted him to tour soon after not before. In the end he placated them by doing his own tour of the States in November and December 1986. Gabriel took a new band out with him, as well as Tony Levin and David Rhodes he now had Frenchman Manu Katche on drums, with Larry Klein, Joni Mitchell's husband, on bass, and Ian Stanley of Tears For Fears on keyboards. During their half hour set they played two songs off the *So* album for the first time in public, 'Red Rain' and 'Sledgehammer'.

The tour was conceived by Jack Healey, executive director of Amnesty USA. 'In many ways Peter was the heart of the Conspiracy of Hope tour,' said Healey. 'I remember the first night we were out in San Francisco and I was very worried about how it would go. As soon as we heard Peter we knew we were OK. We were in the hands of a master and we were cooking. It was the first time he had played "Sledgehammer". His set was overpowering.'

Gabriel was not the headline act, going on before the Police and U2. 'They were all different things to the tour. I don't want to sound silly, but Sting's music is more intellectual, U2 are the explosive part of the tour, they were the power, and Peter was the heart of it.

'The tour was bigger, better and more powerful than anything we thought it could be. We were hoping to get six prisoners out, we got two out, one in the Soviet Union and one in South Africa. We said we would like to raise between two and three million dollars, we raised $2.6 million. We wanted 25,000 new members and got 40,000. We wanted to leave the music industry happy and we have. Everyone on the tour ended up selling more records. We played to a total of 150,000 people.

'Artistically all the equipment worked perfectly. We had eleven hours on MTV live from Giants Stadium, East Rutherford, across the river from New York City, and it came within ten seconds of schedule. There was a three hour Amnesty radio show. For the bands themselves they all liked one another and they all got to be friends. It was a gigantic success, it's becoming legendary, bigger than it actually was.

'What Amnesty had to worry about was the interfacing with human rights. And that's where Peter was the keystone because "Biko" held it all together in a human rights manner. You could feel it in every one of those six shows.

'There were about forty prisoners of conscience at the Giants Stadium. They were all personally touched by Peter and wanted to meet him and shake his hand. "Biko" blows them all away because they feel he is singing about them. Biko was killed the day I arrived in South Africa as a peace worker on my way to Lesotho. Having been an observer, knowing the agony of South Africa, remembering Steve Biko and his approach to non-violence, the beauty of that song was over-powering, I was deeply touched by that song.

'I grabbed one of the prisoners of conscience who had been imprisoned on Robben Island in South Africa and went backstage with him. The song gave him hope of one day overcoming apartheid. We thanked Peter, there were tears on our faces, we all cried like big babies, it was wonderful.'

Gabriel mentioned two incidents from the shows. 'After the show in San Francisco, a South African who had been imprisoned with Stephen Biko came backstage with tears in his eyes. "I didn't know there were people who cared."

'In New York, there was a brave Chilean woman that we met. She was talking to the press conference about the torture she had received. Three days later her son was mudered.'

'I don't know how to tell you how much respect I have for Peter as a professional singer and as a person, knowing Jill and his kids,' said Healey. 'I have the deepest respect for him in every way. I think he is one of the forces in the world able to communicate to people what human rights means. He is somehow bigger than life that way.

'He is a very rare and exceptional, dedicated person to our cause. He is very rare because he is deeply interested in issues of human rights. He wants to meet prisoners of conscience. There is a driving force behind him which is admirable and at the same time very serious. He is just a damn good person, there are not many. He is always available as a friend and adviser. I think to a great extent Amnesty represents his own intellect and his own mind. He is basically shy, very bright and very determined to get things done in a reasonable way. I think Peter has his own shyness about being famous and powerful. Peter is better at causes than he is at his own material, it frees him up working for a cause than for himself. He is very shy singing for himself.'

On the Amnesty leaflets given out at his shows, Gabriel states:

> The work that I have done with Amnesty is very important to me. I was very moved to meet some of the people that had been rescued from torture and unjust imprisonment, for whom Amnesty had been the only line of hope.
>
> Although there is still so much that needs changing, there is no doubt that Amnesty, in its twenty-five years, has changed the attitudes of governments on human rights all around the world. Through the simple tools of letter writing and the embarrassment of publicity, Amnesty has been surprisingly effective.
>
> It is part of a process that is making ordinary people aware of the power and responsibility they have in improving our world.
>
> I ask you to get involved.

Gabriel says it is only in Britain that his middle-class background is constantly used against him, along with being ex-public school and ex-Genesis. Being a white liberal is another common, if not strictly accurate, term of abuse. In

1982 'Wallflower', on the fourth album, a song that has become closely identified with Amnesty, came in for criticism because of its theme.

> Hold on, you have gambled with your own life,
> And you face the night alone
> While the builders of the cages
> Sleep with bullets, bars and stone
> They do not see your road to freedom
> That you build with flesh and bone
>
> Though you may disappear, you're not forgotten here
> And I will say to you, I will do what I can do

'Wallflower'; Gabriel, 1982

Gabriel aired his doubts to Tom Robinson after recording 'Biko'. 'He said it didn't matter if you were exploiting this position for entirely the wrong reasons,' Gabriel told Adam Sweeting in *Melody Maker*. 'If what is achieved is that attention and money get directed in the right direction, you can be as much of a hypocrite as you like, it doesn't matter. So that helped quieten any doubts.'

'I think that has to be the criterion for anything that happens in the pop world or anywhere else. By their fruits shall ye know them,' Tom Robinson said. 'Motives are so questionable, particularly in the pop business, that you'd go bonkers trying to work out what the true motives were for anything and whether or not they were valid. It's really the results, and the massive classic example that's come up since then, of course, is Live Aid, where you can say so what if Bob was trying to save a desperately sinking career, who gives a shit, it was Adolf Hitler in reverse. And by the same token, if "Biko" raised consciousness about the South African problem, even for totally wrong reasons, what the hell? Peter was saying to me, "I don't know whether I wrote that for the right reasons, whether it was actually my concern or whether I just wanted to establish some credibility, I'm not sure, sometimes I lie awake and worry about it."'

Robinson continued, 'The conversation came up because he was asking me, "How do you get over it, you must get accused of it and you must wonder yourself." And I said, "Well, of course I do, I will never know whether 'Glad to be Gay' helped the gay movement or whether the gay movement helped my career."

'Peter is certainly given to racking himself with questions. But it may be that he needs to question it that much in order to be Peter Gabriel. That if he didn't go into things in that fine, nitpicking toothcombing detail, then the quality of his work would not be such as it is.'

Ready to support the causes of human rights and world peace, Gabriel pointedly steered clear of supporting any political parties in the eighties. His sentiments are left of centre, but his beliefs cross party barriers, he believes in enterprise and competitiveness running hand in hand with co-ownership. He argued that the enormous social change created by the information revolution would necessitate a new ideology.

'Marxism/socialism was a response to physical exploitation. It assumes work is available to all people. If you start going at it from another point of view, that there isn't work for all people because machines and computers can do most jobs better than we can, then how do you sort out income and employment, and what do people do with their time?

'I think there needs to be some sort of restructuring that means people's rights are established without reference to work. I don't know how it will come, but it will have to come because there has to be somewhere a response to the selfishness of the Thatcherites and yet I don't see that coming out of British or Labour thinking.' He was to change his views with the election in May 1997 of Prime Minister Tony Blair and a revamped New Labour Party, for the first time openly backing a political party. His name was in the published list of supporters donating £5,000 or more.

He had faith in the ability of information technology to decentralize power allowing even the remotest of villages around the world to tap into computer information systems. 'I think it has enormous consequences because information is going to be quite hard to contain, as the Russians are beginning to understand with both satellite broadcasting and personal computers.

'I don't say that it will make it a safer or happier world, but it will give people more power. How they choose to use it is another question.'

These views, pre-dating the advent of the internet and the collapse of the Soviet empire, became recurrent themes in his thinking as the information revolution insidiously engulfed every aspect of modern life.

His Conspiracy of Hope appearances were the latest in a line of benefits he had played since he started performing as a solo artist. In August 1977 he performed for the International Youth Festival of Hope for Mankind in Ockenden near Haslemere, Surrey, organized by the Ockenden Venture. He was impressed with the work of Joyce Pearce who set up the venture after the war to help refugees settling in the UK, and continued it rescuing refugees from war zones around the world, notably Vietnamese boat people. He described her as 'an English Mother Teresa'.

Gabriel kept in touch with Joyce Pearce over the years. 'She rang me up one day and said there was a group of people who were campaigning hard to prevent war or minimize the outbreaks, and was I prepared to help. It seemed a fairly ambitious task, so I asked her a little more about it and agreed to meet up with some of the people because I had enormous respect for her. She was not someone I would say no to.'

The meeting eventually led to a trip with the family to

Costa Rica in August 1986 to investigate first hand the activities of the University for Peace. The university was the brainchild of Rodrigo Carazo, president of Costa Rica from 1978–82, a nation that disbanded its army in 1948. The university's charter was adopted by the General Assembly of the United Nations in 1980. It operates as a post-graduate university offering a plethora of peace studies from mediation in international disputes to foreign debt and refugees.

Gabriel was enlisted to help in the Music for Peace programme formed to raise funds for the university's Global Computer Network. 'As more and more power goes into the hands of the military, the people who are working to improve this planet need to start a database information network linking the various peace groups,' he declared. 'The idea is that the system will halt the aggressive competition that exists between the East and West over information – the "I-know-something-you-don't-know syndrome".'

He agreed to help with a compilation album. Various artists were approached, including Paul McCartney who made a demo of a song originally titled 'The Politics of Love' with Gabriel. The two visited each other's homes for rehearsals. Gabriel was helped by Hiroshi Kato, a London based representative of Japanese record and creative companies and adviser to the President of the Council of the University for Peace.

On 16 September 1986, designated the International Day of Peace during the International Year of Peace, Gabriel performed four numbers on the North Lawn outside the UN building in New York. His band included Steven Van Zandt and Youssou N'Dour. Gabriel got hold of N'Dour at short notice. He was so keen to have him he flew him from Senegal to Paris and then on by Concorde to New York where N'Dour arrived an hour and a half before the performance, flying back the next day.

On the day of the concert Gabriel met Hiroshi Kato, Van Zandt and officials from the University for Peace to discuss a proposal from the UN Secretariat. They wanted, rather belat-edly, to hold a concert to round off the Year of Peace. 'I suggested Japan because they are the leading economic power, they have too much money and they do not contribute enough to other societies,' said Kato.

The money raised would go towards the Global Computer Network. Kato believed it would not be too cold to hold the concert outdoors. The plan for a compilation record was postponed.

The Hurricane Irene concerts were held in Japan on 20 and 21 December 1986. With Gabriel and his band the line-up again included Van Zandt and Youssou N'Dour, as well as Howard Jones, Lou Reed, Jackson Browne and Nona Hend-ryx, all of whom had appeared on the Conspiracy of Hope tour, plus musicians from Japan and the USSR.

The concerts, held during the afternoon at the 30,000-capacity Jingu baseball stadium in Tokyo, were well below capacity, with a combined attendance for both nights of 32,000. The temperature was mild, but a cold wind forced the audience to wrap up. The promoters obligingly provided everyone with instant chemical heat pads. Despite such set-backs, the University for Peace raised approximately $300,000 from the event and sales of a concert video.

Gabriel returned to Central America in May 1987, osten-sibly to discuss a film project with director Alex Cox. He was as admirer of Cox's film *Repo Man*. Cox was in Nicaragua on his biggest project to date, filming *Walker*, a historical drama about American adventurer William Walker, who became president of Nicaragua from 1856–7.

While in Nicaragua Gabriel had an unscheduled hour-and-a-half meeting with Sandinista President Daniel Ortega. He travelled with Matt Mahurin, an illustrator and video director, and Marina Kaufman from the University for Peace. Gabriel's visit was arranged by Bary Roberts, executive assistant to the President of the University for Peace. Though a Costa Rican and cousin to former President Carazo, Roberts ironically was a key figure in the overthrow of Nicaraguan President Somoza.

During the revolution Roberts commandeered crop spraying planes to form the Sandinista Air Force. 'They would tie themselves with rope to the side of the plane and take the doors off the hinges and have home-made bombs which the guy with the rope tied round him would then drop out of the aeroplane,' said Gabriel. Roberts was one of those who tied himself to the plane.

Through his exploits Roberts had become a personal friend of Ortega's and he was able to introduce Gabriel to him. By chance they also met Tomas Borge, the Minister of the Interior, in a hotel lobby.

'He's a national hero, a small Napoleonic character, quite jocular, but a little scary. He was curious to find out who we were. Bary introduced us, and said we were going down to the Alex Cox film set. Borge hadn't heard about the film and wanted to go down and see it.

'He spent fourteen years in gaol under Somoza and one year of that he was wearing a bag over his head, a method of torture, so he has reason to be a little bitter, and he is bitter. Unfortunately there are now some human rights abuses committed under the Sandinistas, under his jurisdiction.

'He was making eyes at this English girl, who was nick-named by one of our party the "Purple Peril" because she looked like an extra from a James Bond film. She spoke many languages, was very bright and not backward in coming forward. She was in the hotel lobby, and El Commandante's eyes remained glued to her. She somewhat brazenly came up and started chatting to him, and within two minutes had given him her phone number. El Commandante invited her to come and visit the film and then I think he had qualms of conscience and decided he should be going with his wife, so he rang up his wife, who arrived in a Jeep-type vehicle loaded with guns in the back. There were two army Jeeps at the front and the back, each with four guards with machine guns, with the wife plumped in the middle.

'He invited me to travel with him rather than in the bus the Sandinistas had made available for us. And you don't refuse your Commandante. So I got in there and I was a little surprised to see the Purple Peril approaching us, walking through the guards, and come up to the window. She picked up that I was a rock singer and started beaming at me as well as El Commandante, and then quick as a flash the Commandante, sitting in the driver's seat with his wife next door to him, turned round to me and said with a wink, "You are doing all right tonight, Peter," and invited her in the back of the car.

'Each time the car stopped or turned round all the guards with machine guns would jump out to the four points around the car. We went right through red traffic lights. It was scary.'

Gabriel was sceptical at first when Bary Roberts told him he could arrange a meeting with Ortega. 'Cox had told us he had been trying to arrange it since he was down there to meet up with some of the ministers, let alone the president. And there were lots of journalists we met in the Inter-Continental who couldn't get an interview with him. So I was a little dubious it would come off.

'We were told, "OK, it's going to happen today sometime," but we were never told when. Then suddenty we were driving along in the bus and were told, "OK, we are here." We were at the Nicaraguan equivalent of the Pentagon. It is a pretty small building with a six-foot concrete wall outside and four guards on the way in.'

Gabriel, Roberts, Kaufman, and Mahurin faced Ortega and two ministers. Ortega, not surprisingly, was not familiar with Gabriel's records. No doubt he was briefed he was important enough to meet. 'Apparently they used me a little bit. The front page of their daily newspaper wrote of the "short three-day visit of international singer Peter Gabriel, here to see all the US atrocities". I guess it's wartime.' Gabriel was moved by his visit, and despite reservations on the Sandinista human rights record, supported the regime.

'It's really the first government to reach power mainly from the Beatles generation, so there is an open-mindedness that goes with sixties children reaching political power. And the other aspect is the Christian side which I discussed with Ortega in some depth. It is a Christian country first and a communist country second, and you don't normally hear about that, particularly in America where it's reds under the bed.

'Ortega told some stories about religion and how the Catholics were trying to use the faith of the people against the government. There had been this old man who had had a vision of Christ in the mountains, and Christ had said that communism was bringing evil into the church and they should burn all the Sandinista books.

'And then Ortega said the church realized this wasn't having enough effect. So they called up the old man and asked him to have another vision on the first hill outside Managua, which he duly did. Only this time he saw the baby Christ with his mother Mary, and the baby had these two tooth marks in his backside. These were symbolic of the influence of the Sandinistas on the purity of the Church.

'The second half of the vision was to say that people of Managua could also be privileged to see the vision if they stared at electric light bulbs. And most of the population, including Ortega's mother, were then spending the next couple of weeks staring at electric light bulbs. This was not long before I went there.

'And he was trying to tell her, "Mum, this is crazy! This is just propaganda on behalf of the Church." And she was slapping him and telling him not to be so disrespectful. And sure enough she saw something in the light bulb, as did many others.

'Ortega was full of good-humoured anecdotes and at other

times his face would be close to tears as he was talking about the war and the killing. I was quite moved. I think he has a lot of personal charm and charisma, and a gentle strength.'

Gabriel also met Cardinal Miguel Obando y Bravo, Archbishop of Managua, who was pro-American and anti-Sandinista, in an attempt to get a balanced view.

Gabriel's meeting with Cox seemed secondary after that. He talked to Cox about filming the last leg of the 1987 European tour in the autumn.

Though Cox left the chance of working on the film open when Gabriel left, he subsequently ran out of time and was too involved in the *Walker* project to direct Gabriel in concert.

THIRTEEN

L EAPING HELTER-SKELTER INTO THE AUDI-
ence had proved a disaster when Peter
Gabriel first tried it in 1971, and broke
his leg. Such a violent outcome had, of course, not been
planned, but it left him wary of similar exploits as a member
of Genesis, preferring to vent his dramatic urges on stage in a
theatrical setting.

When Gabriel returned to performance as a solo artist in
1977, after two years off the stage, his simpler show was a
deliberate attempt to distance himself from Genesis and its
associations. He did not dispense with all theatricality. Stark
pool room lights dangled over the stage, and the grey tracksuit
he wore was more of an anti-costume.

Forever idealistic, Gabriel was looking for a new form of
direct contact with the audience that was dramatic but also
personal. His initial faltering steps were made on his first solo
tour which started in the USA and Canada in the spring of
1977, helped by the new innovation of the radio microphone.
As the introduction started for 'Waiting For The Big One'
Gabriel would disappear off the stage, and accompanied by the
tour manager make for the back of the hall or any other
vantage point. A spotlight operator would wait for a flash from
the tour manager's torch to pinpoint where Gabriel had got
to. The song has a long bluesy introduction, and he would
then start singing in the darkness. The audience would assume

he was on stage only to realize they had been fooled when the spotlight turned on him in the auditorium.

'It was always a nice feeling because people seated furthest away from the stage are always feeling a bit miffed; if you then shift the performance to where they are it's a good moment.'

Chris Welch described Gabriel's voyage into the audience at the Palladium in New York in 1977. 'Suddenly he disappeared, only to reappear lying like a Cheshire cat on one of the theatre's balconies, singing through a radio microphone.

'Then he pranced into the audience, hotly pursued by fearful security guards, still singing and occasionally disappearing under a sea of clutching hands.'

During that first tour Gabriel played to one of his biggest crowds at the 12,000-seater Montreal Forum. Gabriel and the road crew, then headed by road manager Norman Perry, decided to vary the theme, and came up with the idea of lifting Gabriel on a sheet of plywood about three feet wide and six feet long.

'The road crew looked like they were four pall-bearers and carried him out into the crowd. Peter was very agile and managed to hold on very well. It was the first version of what eventually became throwing himself into the crowd and having the crowd pass him around. It was very spontaneous and the crowd went wild,' remembered Perry, who became one of Gabriel's Canadian promoters.

'Those first concerts were brilliant. I think Peter has always been an excellent performer and what he was doing was stepping out of the preconceived anticipation of the audience. It was very stark and the emphasis was on Peter as a performer as opposed to the props and slides and theatricals that people associated with Peter and Genesis.'

But it was not always straightforward. 'It was funny the first night I went running out into the audience,' he told Chris Welch. 'Our roadie, Chip, was sent out to look after me and make sure I got back on to the stage, and one of the house security men saw this guy following me and thought he was trouble.

'They bopped him. There was our security man, being beaten up by the house security man, while I was poncing away, totally unaware of what was going on. A few nights I didn't think I'd get back on stage, and I've doubled my life insurance. At some places the audiences have been very polite, stayed in their seats and shook my hand. At other places they mobbed me. But I think if you stay on stage and seem to be above the audience, that invites much more aggressive tendencies. But if you walk around being vulnerable, then people are very friendly. I'm not putting over any big superstar thing so there's nothing to hit out at. At least that's what I tell myself as I go in wearing my bullet-proof vest!'

The next tour in 1978 was labelled the 'Fluorescent Tour' by the band because Gabriel made everyone wear uncomfortable bright plastic orange vests as worn by traffic wardens or police on traffic duty. Members of the band would rebel and take them off soon after the performance started, complaining the plastic made them perspire. But as they went along on the tour they picked up anything fluorescent they could find including hats and collars which would then be worn on stage. Gabriel wanted the look more unified to make it look more like a band than a collection of session musicians as it had originally been on the first tour.

During 1978, touring Europe and America from August to December, Gabriel carried on his experiment of going into the audience, varying it between 'Solsbury Hill', 'On The Air' and 'I Go Swimming'.

He was inspired to try something even riskier after reading the book *New Games* which he had found through the *Whole Earth Catalogue*. 'The book was a guide to new psychological group activities,' says Gabriel. 'A group of people fall backwards to the point where if they didn't catch you you'd do yourself some harm. You had to learn to rely on trusting them sufficiently to catch you. Some people had trouble with that exercise.' It was one thing trusting people alongside you to not let you fall on the floor and at worst bruise yourself, and quite another to trust an audience many feet below to cushion you from real harm.

The Dive, as it became known, started on the next tour, the anachronistically named 1984 Tour of China, which started in February 1980. For the encore he would perform 'On The Air' from his Mozo repertoire. Larry Fast remembered having to improvise on the synthesizer. 'When Peter got stuck in the audience we had to keep the song going for a long time, it was something that could be extended or contracted.' Gabriel experimented using different numbers for the Dive, including, again, 'Solsbury Hill' and the apt 'I Go Swimming' where he would mimic an Edwardian bather on stage and then fall face down onto the awaiting outstretched arms.

The three-and-a-half-week US leg ended in New York where the band played two medium-sized open air concerts in Central Park. Gabriel arranged an extra date for New York fans to experience the full effect of the show's elaborate lighting as the Central Park shows had been in daylight. The gig was at the Diplomat Hotel, a club venue. It was the final date of the tour and Gabriel thought the rest of the band deserved to experience the exhilaration of the Dive. With some trepidation they all lined up on the edge of the stage. Jerry Marotta, the most strapping member of the band, was also the most apprehensive about falling off the stage. 'The crowd opened up in front of him,' said Larry Fast. 'He had a big beard and looked like a mountain, it was like watching the waters part. I was standing next to Jerry and he did hit the floor. He was not hurt, they just lowered him to the floor. If you see someone like me coming it's not going to be any problem.

'We had seen Peter doing it for God knows how many shows and he had come back and said, "It feels great! It's like a big moving mattress that holds you above." It sounded kind of interesting. Normally there wouldn't have been an opportunity for the rest of us to do it. I felt good about it, so we all dived in. I had a great time, it was almost like defying gravity. There was a little bit of movement, it was like waves on the ocean that don't really carry you out, but don't carry you back in.

'The problem was that normally the front rows are made up of, say, smaller girls who are a little shorter and they don't block the views of the slightly taller people behind them, and that is who you are falling on, although Peter will sometimes take a dive and end up a few rows back.'

Towards the end of the 1978 European tour one crowd was far too hostile to even contemplate the Dive. Gabriel was booed off stage, an experience he had always dreaded, supporting Frank Zappa in Berlin. The audience were older and more impatient than usual. 'I think they thought who is this arrogant little shit getting up and doing these stunts? But I made myself vulnerable, too, to see if there was any possibility that it would allow a change of mood. It didn't work,' he told Timothy White of *Spin* magazine.

'People were throwing stuff at me, wanted to punch me. There was a guy yelling, "English Pig, Go Home!" I crawled back up on stage and started to do "Here Comes The Flood", which was literally the quietest number I had at that point, and that didn't work either. I walked off.

'It was my worst night ever as a performer. Up until then I'd always been afraid of it happening. Now it had happened. Once the hurt and the shock wore off, I began to adopt a different frame of mind. After a day's break, the next show was in Bremen with Zappa, and even though it wasn't going over again, I felt relaxed, intact. I began laughing and feeling at home, and the crowd responded. In the end, we did much better – it still wasn't fantastic – but I'd overcome my fear of being challenged, of being rejected by an audience.'

The following tour, of North America, ran from October

to December 1982, coinciding with the release of his fourth album dubbed *Security*, which included 'Lay Your Hands On Me'.

Gabriel attempted to shift audience complacency right from the start. The band were dressed in black Japanese martial arts type outfits with white knee pads. They entered from the back of the auditorium pounding out the beat of 'Rhythm of the Heat' on big marching drums while powerful hand-held torch beams combed the auditorium. 'It was great because people didn't expect it, they thought it was police or security guys coming in,' said Gabriel.

Later in the set he would alternate between walking back into the audience, scurrying over their seats clutching their hands, gripping their heads with his hands, or diving in for the aptly titled 'Lay Your Hands On Me'.

> *I walk away from light and sound, down stairways*
> *Leading underground*
>
> *But still the warmth flows through me*
> *And I sense you know me well*
> *It's only common sense*
> *There are no accidents around here*
>
> *I am willing – lay your hands on me*
> *I am ready – lay your hands on me*
> *I believe – lay your hands on me, over me*

'Lay Yours Hands On Me'; Gabriel, 1981

'The song was about trust, about healing and sacrifice. It's been misconstrued, with reviews saying that I'm acting like Jesus Christ, and that's not what I'm trying to do with that at all. I feel I am trying to gradually involve the audience emotionally with what we are doing with the music. I feel it's an offering of trust to the audience. Clearly it is a dramatic moment which is contrived, in a way; I am not denying that.

But I think the effect is strong because really what an artist is trying to do is engage the viewer, the audience, the listener in what they are doing and get them to feel and become part of the experience and not separated from it. I think it really works like that, it does help bring people in. Because most concerts are a part of long tours, people think, well, this is going to be the same if I see it in ten days' time or two months' time. And as soon as you involve the audience you introduce the unpredictable. You cannot know for certain when I am going to get back to the stage, what's going to happen to me down there, and so I think it keeps things interesting.'

On his first dives into the audience Gabriel went forwards, face down, but he would frequently be turned over. Then he began falling backwards, so he could not see immediately where he was going. 'Falling backwards is a real show of faith,' he said.

Gabriel, not alone in the rock firmament, can inspire quasi-religious fervour. He probably takes more time and care in replying to fans than most stars and in one instance met a woman to break her out of her obsession for him, hoping she would realize he was a fairly regular guy; it apparently worked. Some fans like to call themselves Gabriel's Angels. In 1977 one shouted to him on stage in Hollywood, 'You are God!' 'No, we are just good friends,' came the reply.

A review of Gabriel's USA tour of 1982 in *The Northern Star of Illinois* newspaper did not please Mr Mark Kinsella. He wrote to the editor, 'In the Dec. 7 *Star*, Sharyl Holtzman's "Peter Gabriel: Command Performance," deeply saddened me. After reading about Gabriel climbing a "tower-like stand", demonstrating his incredible hold over a crowd, being "clapped and chanted to" and finally being "swept up by the crowd and passed overhead", I have to ask Miss Holtzman to come out of her Gabriel fervor and remind her Mr Gabriel is only a man. I don't see a man who should be worshipped, chanted to or clapped to. I see a man who may gain the whole world but lose his soul. I see a man who hasn't realized that the humble will be exalted and the exalted humbled.' Mr Kinsella gave his address as 'Northern Lights, College Ministry of Glad Tidings, Assembly of God.'

Gabriel made various efforts to improve his movement on stage. In 1982 he spent three or four days with choreographer Laura Dean to enlarge what he called his vocabulary of movements. Gabriel, Rhodes and Levin would stretch and warm up before the gig, and incorporated some of Dean's ideas on 'Shock the Monkey' where Gabriel bounded across stage bent like an ape with dangling arms and jumped up and down crazily with Rhodes. Gabriel has subsequently used other choreographers to help iron out awkward movements, notably Charles Molton, who helped him in 1986 with the silly walk on 'Big Time', and on 'No Self Control'.

Much of Gabriel's movement is taken from the rituals of other cultures. Michael Argyle's book *Bodily Communication* was a source of inspiration. One gesture, the outstretched hand with the palm facing out used while performing 'In Your Eyes' from the *So* album looks deceptively like Gabriel is giving a blessing.

'I watch some of the Indian and Pakistani singers and they have this gestural language too, and there is definitely a sense there of energy exchange, which sounds like a post-sixties term. But for me there is a real joy with 'In Your Eyes', and I think some of that comes through to the audience. If you really want to beam in anyone, who they are or what they are, you can do so through their eyes, and so that is acknowledging that. But I am not trying to put myself over as the preacher.'

Gabriel has an unnerving gaze off as well as on the stage, his eyes relentlessly stare directly into your own almost as if there is a contest as to who can stare the longest. 'I never used to do that but I know I can look into people if I want to now.

It's something that happens if you start allowing yourself to be looked into. You get what you give. I used to do some sort of eye meditation. A Japanese meditation which you do with a mirror, where you look at your own image until it disappears. You try and put your consciousness into the mirror image, rather than where you are. What happened for me was that I would get a flash, I would lose myself, effectively.

'I think if you want to talk to someone and get close to them you can just look into each other's eyes, as lovers do, and find out a lot about what's happening – the old thing about mirror of the soul.

'I feel that at times I should be of use to people. What I like in other people's work is things that make me think about what I am doing – gives me an awareness of something I didn't know about before, activates my conscience, my imagination, or my spirit, and I think when what I do is working well and is pure, then other people can use it in that way. So partly that is what I am trying to do with 'Lay Your Hands'. I really do try and get a picture before I go into the audience of the circle around all the people. So there are images going through my head at that point, some of which I feel happy to talk about, others I don't. I am not trying to dominate that moment, I am trying to serve it.

'I think partly what is interesting for people that are into what I do, is that they see me going through the struggles, and representing their own struggle. I feel all right about it when I feel there is some strength in it and some commitment in it. But when I feel I'm floundering, as I do occasionally, then I don't like it.'

Gabriel is notorious for forgetting the lines of even his most well-known songs when he is on stage. It was more understandable with Genesis who specialized in contorted lyrics. More recently, an over-long introduction and Gabriel shuffling over to Tony Levin on stage are signs that he has forgotten his lines.

In his earlier solo shows the lack of lyrics was occasionally intentional. At Stony Brook, Long Island in New York State in October 1978, Gabriel introduced a song called 'The New New One'. He told the audience, 'When you sit down there and you watch some shows you get the feeling that you are watching a very rehearsed band who know exactly what they are doing. Well, our policy is to provide the opposite of that. And to that effect there are a few new numbers which as yet have no words and no melody and a few loose ends and we are playing these in slowly. This is one of those and it may give you an opportunity to watch us mess up. I hope you enjoy it.'

The words appeared to be the stream of consciousness variety with little meaning, most of them could well have been gibberish. 'The New New One' was a bouncy up-tempo rock tune. There were other songs that were played a few times on stage, but never appeared on record, including 'Why Don't We' and 'John Has A Headache'.

The lyrics always come last for Gabriel, but that has not stopped him trying out unfinished songs on audiences. At the Reading Festival in August 1979 he had written the music for 'Biko', but was still forming the lyrics. The only identifiable word at that performance was Biko. The improvised sounds he makes are referred to by his fans as 'Gabrielese'.

Ever since he has performed as a solo artist, Gabriel has wanted to incorporate different multimedia elements into his shows. But his ambition ran ahead of available time and finance.

In the Playtime 1988 programme for the 1982/3 tour there is a mock-up picture of Gabriel in a space suit, another of him at what could be a space mission control and a picture of an airship. The copy reads:

Peter has been toying with a number of playful and inventive ideas for future stage shows. Perhaps the most ambitious of these is to suspend a full stage set from a helium-filled airship and to sail the thing slowly around the world. This idea is reported to be popular with overworked roadies, but so far lack of necessary cash – not to mention airship – has relegated the notion to pipe-dream status.

This comes after a 1980 attempt to convert a train into a mobile stage.

Also on the drawing board, and far more feasible, is a project being researched in America to create a multimedia show using the latest development in video and 3D, some of which can be seen at the Epcot Center in Florida and the New York Institute of Technology.

It was self-mocking, but not entirely fanciful. Multimedia would become pivotal to his future activities.

Gabriel saw the value of video long before pop promos became essential marketing tools for record companies. When he signed his new solo contract with Tony Stratton Smith in 1978 he insisted his video work should be excluded. 'In other words, by selling or contracting my records, I do not accept I have contracted my video performances, or video work. And at the time no one would argue that case at all. I remember Strat thinking I was just off my rocker. But it turned out to be extremely useful.'

His first solo single, 'Solsbury Hill', released in March 1977, had an accompanying video directed by Peter Campus, a video artist with the prestigious Leo Castelli Gallery in New York. 'It was a little conceptual, dealing mainly with close-ups of my shoulder. And it was not greeted with enthusiasm by the record company first of all.' The video was made in a small town north of Boston using personnel from the pioneering Boston TV station WGBH.

Three months later 'Modern Love' was released. Gabriel was photographed spreadeagled in the nude intending the picture to be put on the record label. But Charisma Records thought it improper. 'The idea was when you put the record on the turntable the little thing in the centre sort of gave me generous endowments. I was quite pleased with the idea at the time but it didn't go down very well. I think it joined the long list of misses from my single releases, of which there have been many.'

For the video Gabriel dressed up in an American football outfit and wore a fencing mask. He was filmed on the escalators at the Shepherd's Bush Green Shopping Centre surrounded by model girls. The modest video was made by Peter Medak who directed the 1971 film *The Ruling Class*.

The upholders of public decency at the BBC deemed the next video, 'Games Without Frontiers', to be unsuitable for transmission on *Top of the Pops*. Filmed in February 1980 it was directed by David Mallet, who made David Bowie's 'Ashes to Ashes' video later that year. In the video children dressed as adults are seated round a banqueting table, mimicking their self-important seniors. Gabriel, with short hair, is seen in various guises in front of blown-up images of bald naked dolls, and crawls around invisible to the arguing children peering at them. A segment with a newsreel film of a girl saluting Hitler at the 1936 Olympic Games was taken out and replaced with custard pie throwing before it even went to the BBC for approval.

'The idea of the song was countries behaving like playground kids,' said Gabriel. 'It's against nationalism, but they had seen me moving around the table with the kids and thought that I was leering at them like a dirty old man. At the end there was a whole series of children's toys, and they thought that the Jack in the Box was an obvious reference to masturbation. So it says a lot more about the minds of the people who ran *Top of the Pops* than it did about my video.'

Gabriel sought out the latest video innovations and experimental artists in the USA during his 1982 tour with a view to using video effects in a future outing. In Washington DC he visited a video festival run by the American Film Institute. He investigated the video synthesizer and a company attempting to make 3D TVs.

In Los Angeles he saw videos by Laurie Anderson and The Residents. In Hollywood he met a special effects designer on *Star Wars* and *Close Encounters of the Third Kind* who was pioneering work on holograms. And in New York he met the curator of the Video Section of the Museum of Modern Art, who introduced him to experimental video-makers. He was most amused by the work of William Wegman, one of whose pieces featured him crawling on the floor spitting a mouthful of milk into a thin white line. His dog then went in the opposite direction licking up the line of milk that his master has spat on the floor. As well as the planned stage uses of video, Gabriel wanted to fulfil a long held ambition to make a long form video.

Gabriel's first big production video came in September 1982 for 'Shock the Monkey', directed by Brian Grant, part of probably the first big video promo company, MGMM – Millaney Grant Mallett Mulcahy.

Gabriel was depicted alternately as a businessman in a dark suit, and then a shaman with elaborate face paint and a shaved head in a white suit. The exterior normality was contrasted with the primitive man inside, the monkey hurt by jealousy. It did not make easy viewing with scenes of Gabriel running in the forest as if he were being hunted, imprisoned in a cell, and then being captured by dwarves.

The next video, for the live version of 'I Don't Remember' was even more disturbing. Gabriel was surrounded by the nearly naked white painted bodies of the Rational Theatre Company. Inspired by Malcolm Poynter's uncompromising sculptures, it was directed in July 1983 by Marcello Anciano, and looked like it was filmed in Bedlam.

It was a journey through the unconscious, exploring an

amnesiac's memory. It opens with Gabriel's death mask lying on a rubbish-strewn floor, outside the window all is red, inside there is dripping water. Gabriel metamorpheses into an old man with a hideous grin, then he is back to normal, he lies down, then wakes up in a sweat. Eventually appearing to overcome his memory loss, he walks across the room to find a framed picture on the floor. He picks it up and wipes the dust off to show a picture of Gabriel as a young boy with his parents gazing at his baby sister Anne in her mother's arms. He then goes to lie down on a couch with a beautiful woman, and they both turn into screaming, agonized, ghost-like figures and then back to normal. The journey continues with the caressing woman, gangsters with poisonous blow darts, and South American Indians. He appears to escape from the cell, only to find himself locked up again. Not surprisingly, regardless of artistic merit, it did not receive much TV airtime.

Gabriel planned to make a 3D video that autumn, but the project never came off. He was impressed with some of the 3D images he had seen. 'Some of the most haunting images in 3D for me are not those using gimmicks or with things jumping out of the screen, but landscapes, full of texture and detail which really provide one with the experience of being in another situation and not merely observing it. It's like being in a dream,' he said.

Gabriel discussed a video collaboration with Laurie Anderson after being impressed with her show 'United States' in London in spring 1983. He wanted to produce as well as appear in a thirty minute programme with different artists.

That idea never came off, but in December 1983 he and Anderson were invited by Vietnamese director Nam June Paik, a veteran of the sixties American multimedia scene, to appear in *Good Morning Mr Orwell* broadcast by the Public Service Broadcasting network on 1 January 1984. Gabriel and Anderson performed 'Excellent Birds', a song they composed together over twenty-four hours in New York. They were filmed seated looking at animated storm clouds rushing by; animated birds, and snow and computer images are also incorporated in the video. Gabriel and Anderson are finally depicted suspended, treading the air.

'Excellent Birds' appeared on Anderson's 1984 album *Mister Heartbreak*. Gabriel's more dance-oriented version 'This Is The Picture', subtitled 'Excellent Birds', appeared on the *So* cassette and CD, though not on the album. There was a gap of nearly three years from his last solo video 'I Don't Remember' until the next video, 'Sledgehammer', in April 1986.

# CHAPTER FOURTEEN

THE BIG TIME BECKONED IN 1986. GABRIEL was now ready to embrace the success he had forsaken eleven years earlier.

'I'm on my way, I'm making it,' he predicted on 'Big Time' for the *So* album released in May 1986. Within three months his singles and albums had topped the charts on both sides of the Atlantic.

A few die-hard fans argued he had lost some of his spirit; for them *So* stood for sell-out. But Gabriel was never more spirited, self-confident and playful. He even looked different with a trendy new haircut from Knightsbridge and a wardrobe of fashionable clothes from New York.

'Big Time' is as much a piece of self-mockery as a comment on the success ethic. 'It is a satirical story about a basic human urge. A small man from a small town achieves all his ambitions, with all parts of his life, personality and anatomy growing larger than life, and consequently very heavy.

'In America, which is still a vigorous and enthusiastic nation, success has reached religious significance. This drive for success is a basic part of human nature and my nature.'

Gabriel shunned stardom in 1975, leaving Genesis for his family, his sanity and creative freedom. The situation was inverted in 1983 when his family left him through neglect caused by work. Freed from the constraints of family life Gabriel underwent a personal transformation, similar to the transformations referred to in his own songs. It helped clear away some doubts.

'At the time of coming back he had tremendous determination,' said Jill. 'He said, "I do want to make it! I do want to succeed!" The album came out of it. Instead of going along with the idea he is different, special, unique, precious, behind a wall, this last album was about him saying, "Fuck that! I am going to come through, I'm going to allow myself to succeed". This period has been a big change for him, it puts him on the line far more. He could go along with being a respected artist and not going for big success, but the challenge is breaking through.'

'He loves success,' said David Rhodes. 'After working for a long time, to get recognition is good. He enjoys it and it has made him more confident in trying to achieve all the other things he wanted to do. The success he's had with this record has given him much better opportunities of contacting people, speaking to people, he's not just treated as a reasonably well-known English artist who used to be in Genesis.'

Success is a theme that Tony Banks pursued. 'He would probably disagree with this, but I think he has always wanted to be famous. I think with this last record he compromised just enough to get it. To take the most obvious example, the cover has his face. Obviously he's good-looking and he has never really let that come through before by shaving his head and appearing on all those covers with squiggly lines through them. Finally he has a cover with a title even, marvellous, and a good-looking portrait of the guy. The songs are shorter, more direct and simpler lyrics.' If this is a contrivance of Gabriel's then Genesis clearly learnt the lesson a lot earlier and better.

'Compromise is a bad word,' continued Banks, 'because it implies that it's a very conscious thing. I think it came naturally, but there's no doubt it's an easier album. I think it's a very good album, but I personally like the ones that came before it because I prefer the more difficult albums.'

For the first time Gabriel allowed himself to get caught up

in the awards circus. He was the only artist to receive two awards from the British Record Industry in February 1987, as Best British Male Artist and for Best British Music Promo Video. On receiving his second statuette at the Grosvenor House in London in front of an estimated TV audience of 400 million, Gabriel noted, 'Now I have two of these, I'll investigate the mating potential.'

He was nominated for four American Grammy Awards, and attended the ceremony in Los Angeles in April 1987, but came away with nothing. He was willing to be identified with wanting success. 'It's a very painful process, but he had to put himself on the line to actually be there,' said Jill.

Gabriel was nominated for eleven MTV Awards and on 11 September 1987 the 'Sledgehammer' video won an unprecedented nine out of the sixteen categories. The headline in *Variety* declared 'Gabriel Pulverizes Field . . .' In addition Gabriel was inducted into MTV's *Video Vanguard*, a video hall of fame. It was ironic that this time Gabriel was unable to attend. Instead he sent a video message of thanks from Stockholm where he was appearing on the night of the awards.

The 'Sledgehammer' video won a clutch of other awards and Gabriel won a host of polls in music papers, becoming the first artist to win three sections in the *Rolling Stone* magazine poll.

The *So* album elevated Gabriel into the bottom of the first division of superstars. If Live Aid had been held in 1987 instead of 1985 it would have been unthinkable not to include Gabriel in the line-up.

The personal turmoil in Peter Gabriel's life had peaked and appeared to be on its way to a resolution as the musical and lyrical direction for the *So* album started to gel during late 1984. One song on *So*, 'Don't Give Up', has strong associations for Jill Gabriel. To such an extent that she finds it hard to watch Kate Bush held in Peter's arms on the video. 'Don't

Give Up' was inspired by a TV programme on the effects of unemployment on relationships and home life, and by a photograph by Dorothea Lange – 'In This Proud Land' – showing dust-bowl conditions in America during the Great Depression. But it was the parallel with his own family life that so moved Jill.

> *No fight left or so it seems*
> *I am a man whose dreams have all deserted*
> *I've changed my face, I've changed my name*
> *But no one wants you when you lose*
>
> 'Don't Give Up'; Peter Gabriel, 1986

Doubt is replaced by hope based on self-respect in Gabriel's lyrics. The pain can be soothed by the succour of loved ones. One-liners in the lyric could almost be aide-mémoires from Peter Gabriel to himself: 'you worry too much', 'you're not the only one', 'you still have us', 'you know it's never been easy', all interspersed by 'don't give up'.

'When he gets into very deep depressions, I am always saying don't give up,' said Jill. 'I think that song is very much about us.'

The separation gave Peter the chance to live out his stud fantasies. Though he had expressed sexuality on stage throughout his career, he had never openly celebrated sex through music as much as he was to on *So*.

Having resolved not to sit around and mope during the separation, he paid two visits each to Brazil and Senegal in 1983 and 1984, which brought in fresh rhythmic and melodic influences. He had for a long time harboured ambitions to make a rhythm and blues album, and also at one time had wanted to put out an album of cover versions of his favourite soul music. Unlikely ever to find the time to indulge in these projects, he decided to incorporate all those influences on the new album.

He started preparing the rhythm tracks for the *So* album early in 1984 after a three-week holiday over Christmas and New Year with the family in Australia and Singapore.

Peter made slow progress in 1984 on the new album, sidetracked by writing 'Walk Through The Fire' for *Against All Odds*, 'Out Out' for *Gremlins* and, in autumn 1984, the soundtrack to *Birdy*. But he did make one crucial move forward. His search for a new co-producer was over having found Daniel Lanois, co-producer of *Birdy*. Work on *So* started in earnest in February 1985 at Ashcombe House.

Gabriel wanted to get back to more traditional forms of songwriting after the instrumental atmospheric moods of *Birdy*. He was aiming for more intimacy with his listener. 'I wanted to be more playful, a bit more open, less mystery . . .' he said. The moods were less sinister, the music more accessible and his spirit stronger. It was ironic that the music was more 'up' considering the emotional pain that preceded the album's composition. 'It was a dark period for me and one in which I had to become a little more open to the world,' said Gabriel.

'One of the contributing factors to the album was that Peter was not into darkness like he once might have been,' said Lanois. 'I like the darker side, but I wouildn't say I gravitate towards heaviness, certainly not on *So*. I think Peter was heading that way already and he saw that in me and thought this is going to work. As a personality I tend to be of the soulful category, meaning that I am not the sort who would lean on technology, I would lean on feelings, emotions and mood. I knew that Peter was interested in being more focused and having a song record.'

'Six months of the record was pre-production preparation,' Lanois continued. 'Most of the ideas were formed to a certain degree.' He was only booked for six months, but was forced to postpone subsequent commitments to complete the album. 'We had to screen the many ideas that Peter had, which were maybe twenty foundations for songs, and narrow that down to twelve of our favourites. Having done that we had to come up with arrangements.'

Larry Fast, for the first time in Gabriel's solo career, did not appear on any of the final recordings. He is credited on the album sleeve with 'thanks for additional work' having helped with treatments on completed tracks, but Gabriel himself took over most of the keyboard work.

Jerry Marrota's influence on the drums was also starting to wane. None of Gabriel's backing band ever gets formal contracts, their loyalty has always been enough to guarantee commitment. They all fix their other considerable session or production schedules so as not to conflict with Gabriel's plans. But that is not helped by Gabriel being prone to delays.

Marotta, who joined Gabriel on his first tour in 1977, was an antidote in those days to the likes of Genesis and Robert Fripp. 'They would butt heads with one another in what I think is a very English way, as opposed to the way I would butt heads with Peter, which is to start yelling at him, and somehow force some sort of reaction out of him.

'I was working with Hall and Oates after I did the first tour. After that Peter called me up and said "I'm going to be doing another album and I don't have any money, I can't afford to pay a lot of money." I said, "Don't even talk to me about money, I'm just going to do it. If you want me to do it I'll be there, and whatever you can pay me, pay me." That was always my feeling with Peter. For the first few years of working with him, there wasn't a single person from the road crew that wouldn't have gone out on tour for no money at all, just to be involved with this guy and his calibre of music and professionalism.'

Marotta was convinced Gabriel was displeased with him for missing one session on So because he was drumming for Paul McCartney's album. Stewart Copeland, who had worked with Gabriel on the fourth album and played with him at the first WOMAD in 1982, filled in. Eventually Marotta did a seven-day week taking time away from McCartney to play with Gabriel. But Marotta's harder rock approach was increasingly at odds with Gabriel's sparser, more direct approach. One track on *So* Marotta was convinced would be put out with his drumming was 'Big Time', but Copeland's session was used instead.

'It was one of the best things I have ever participated in,' said Marotta. 'We had cut this very powerful, traditional sort of Gabriel track. I literally had goosebumps. I said, "Peter, look they don't go away, I can't get rid of them." I had them for days. And what ended up on the record was this kind of funky, pop version of the powerhouse we had cut. It was more conventional, more commercial sounding than our original idea.'

Marotta's favourite Gabriel album was the first. 'I get the feeling that back then he wasn't concerned with being successful. Nowadays, I get the feeling that that's more of a concern with him – being successful and selling records.'

In early 1986, before the release of *So*, Gabriel selected his new touring band, and the line-up did not include Fast and Marotta. 'He picked me up at a coffee shop in Notting Hill Gate,' said Marotta. 'I was hitching a ride to Bath with him and he could hardly talk, he was so flustered. I'm sure he felt terrible. I spent most of the time calming him down, telling him it's OK. It's all right, you know, no problem.

'But I'd like to be working with Peter. I don't know what to say, it's one of those things. I guess if Peter had asked me to do the tour I probably would have done it. We're still friends, but our friendship was based on working together.

'He said we're trying to go for a different vibe, a different feel. The drums were a very prominent part of the shows I did. Everyone was just blown away by the power coming from the drums. Maybe he wanted to back off from that a bit and focus on some other aspect.

'My only funny feeling about that is working with somebody for nine years, I would have thought he could have sat down with me and said, "I want to move into this, can you do it?" It's hard to say anything nasty about Peter, we all like one another. There's no real reason for what happened except for me to say it's his perogative, he's the boss, and he just decided he wanted some new people.

'It's really funny because one weekend when I was in Bath working on the album with Peter he made a big point of saying, "I want you to know that you are definitely doing the tour," and I'm learning at my age that you really start worrying when people start reassuring you.'

Larry Fast had a similar experience. 'He gets very shy and awkward and makes an awkward face and mumbles an awful lot. There wasn't a tour, but he thought it best to let me know he was thinking of trying other musicians. I felt crestfallen, but then that is natural when you have put over a decade into it. But it isn't as though it is the only thing that I do. It's just the way this business works, there are no guarantees. It is inherent in what Peter does that things are going to change.

'With Peter you know that nothing is permanent, things change, it isn't a democracy. That doesn't change my respect for him musically and liking what he does. As to whether the changes were successful, you would have to ask someone else.' That Gabriel had difficulty breaking this news was confirmed by his old friend Richard Macphail: 'He agonized over it for a long time.'

By the summer of 1985 most of the rhythm tracks for the album had been completed, though the lyrics were more behind than usual. Recording was originally scheduled to finish on 31 July 1985, but it was a hopelessly optimistic date.

In early September, Gabriel and Daniel Lanois spent five days at the Power Station in New York, recording with a horn section that included Wayne Jackson of the Memphis Horns, the original trumpet player for Otis Redding, for the funkiest numbers on the record, 'Sledgehammer' and 'Big Time'. Backing vocals were laid down for 'In Your Eyes' with Jim

Kerr of Simple Minds and Michael Been of unknown band the Call. It was during those sessions that Gabriel was tracked down by Steve Van Zandt to sing on the 'Sun City' single.

Another voice was added to the backing vocals for 'In Your Eyes' when Gabriel invited Senegalese singer Youssou N'Dour to Ashcombe House in June 1985. Gabriel had first seen N'Dour exactly a year before, performing during his first visit to England at the now defunct Venue in London. Ten days later Gabriel was in Paris and went to see N'Dour again. Gabriel went backstage and introduced himself. The twenty-four-year-old N'Dour had never heard of him. They agreed to meet later that night at Phil One, an African club, but missed each other. A month later Gabriel, accompanied by George Acogny, a Senegalese who lives in Bath, and later producer of Donny Osmond, the last person to record at Ashcombe House, turned up unannounced at N'Dour's home in Dakar, Senegal.

Anyone in town who wanted to see N'Dour, a Bob Marley figure in his homeland, had little choice but to go to his home since he had no telephone. Gabriel and Acogny were invited to see N'Dour perform that night at his own club, the Sahel. N'Dour's lyrics, as a devout Moslem and member of the Mouride sect, are coloured by religious sentiments and social comment.

N'Dour's background is explained in the Peter Gabriel tour programme. 'His mother was a Gawlo who sang in the tradition of praise singers and story-tellers bringing the history and myths of ancient empires and ancestors right down to our own times Youssou. stepped into that line as if to a vocation and he first came to the attention of the Senegalese public at the age of fourteen, with his homage to a great Senegalese saxophonist – MBA. His voice quickly captured the mood of a nation anxious to re-find its national and cultural identity after years of colonialism. He knew how to use the traditional dance rhythms and percussion of his country and match them with more modern flexible instruments to create a new popular music which he calls Mbalax.'

N'Dour's appearance on 'In Your Eyes' was unscheduled. He was playing with his band The Super Etoile De Dakar at the Town and Country Club in London. His friend Jenny Cathcart, a researcher at the BBC who had met him while working on the TV series *The Africans*, phoned Gabriel to invite him to the concert. Gabriel was unable to attend, but invited N'Dour to lunch in Bath that weekend. The 'In Your Eyes' session followed that afternoon.

'It was one of the most incredible days I can ever remember,' said Cathcart who accompanied and translated for Youssou. 'He said to Youssou I want you to listen to this. He attempted to get him to sing in English, but Youssou translated 'In your eyes, the light the heat, in your eyes, I am complete' into Wolof, and stood up and sang to this track, improvising all the way like the Gawlo that he is. Peter joined in and everybody was incredibly uplifted. Youssou didn't even know he was going to do this, it was as if it was meant to be.'

'It was really the beginning of my awakening to Peter's music and to modern music in general,' said N'Dour. 'To me Peter is like a true Moslem brother.'

N'Dour returned for more concerts in England in July 1986, playing again at the Town and Country Club, and a few days later at the WOMAD festival in Clevedon, near Bristol. Gabriel agreed to appear on BBC TV *Breakfast Time* with N'Dour on condition that he only talked about N'Dour and the WOMAD festival. Gabriel then invited N'Dour back into the studio to add more vocals to a remix of the American released single of 'In Your Eyes' released in October 1986, and also put on the B-side of the UK single 'Don't Give Up' released in November 1986. The result was one of the most enchanting moments on any Peter Gabriel record.

In September 1986 N'Dour joined Gabriel ouside the United Nations building in New York for the International

Day of Peace concert. By November he had joined the Peter Gabriel world tour, accompanying him over eleven months.

'What was really touching was that Peter came out on stage and said, "I want you to listen to these marvellous musicians, they make the best music coming out of Africa", which was very humble of him, he didn't need to do it,' said N'Dour.

'People said what's this, but when we finished our thirty minutes I felt they were thinking, let's see some more of this. By the time we got back on for "In Your Eyes" there was a very strong feeling.' Gabriel also brought African dancers on stage for the joyous 'In Your Eyes' and danced with N'Dour, who stayed for the 'Biko' finale.

'I thought about Peter producing my next record, but Peter said no, he was not a producer. He said he would sing on it if I wanted him to, that would make him very happy as he felt very close.' N'Dour's association with Gabriel led to him singing on the Paul Simon hit 'Diamonds On the Soles Of Her Shoes' from the *Graceland* album. He became a star in the West in his own right duetting with Neneh Cherry on the uplifting 1994 hit 'Seven Seconds'.

Another completion date was set for the *So* album, 14 December 1985. But, like the 31 July date, that passed with still more work to do. The major delay was now caused by Gabriel's lack of lyrics. Daniel Lanois was so frustrated he resorted to drastic, supposedly playful, action. He locked Peter Gabriel in a back room in the studio, nailing up a sliding door, and said he would not be let out until some lyrics had been completed. 'It was meant to be a joke, but he didn't take it as a joke. He did a few hours later,' said Lanois.

'I think it is the most upset I've seen him at the studio,' said David Rhodes. 'One of the technicians let him out after about twenty minutes.' Throughout the recording of the album, Gabriel would frequently interrupt the sessions in the evening to maintain his tradition of "kissing time", leaving the studio to wish Melanie and Anna goodnight, before carrying on recording. He would also aim to drive the girls to school in the mornings.

'I always think that the way Peter works makes the studio very much a natural part of his life,' said David Rhodes. 'If he's not in a great mood then that sometimes spills over. I think albums three and four are darker, but that was him not letting his more playful spirits out. I don't know whether he would agree with that.'

The final touches were made to the album in January 1986. On Saturday, 8 February, Ed Rosenblatt and Gary Gersh from Geffen Records arrived with Gail Colson to hear the album. The following Tuesday, 11 February, pressing of the *So* album started. It was exactly a year and £200,000 after the first sessions.

Ten days later the album artwork was finished. Gabriel had decided on an unadulterated picture of himself for the cover for the first time and went with pictures by Trevor Key.

An ordinary, quite flattering, moody picture would not be noteworthy for most other artists. But for Gabriel it was a departure not to deface himself. His precious excuse had been that he did it to annoy his mother. The *So* photograph represented the final casting off of his mask, it betrayed a greater self-confidence and pride. It was also a good move commercially, as Phil Collins had found with *Face Value*. He succumbed to record company pressure and gave the album a proper title. But *So* is about as close as one could get to not having a title. 'It has a nice shape but very little meaning,' said Gabriel.

The single 'Sledgehammer' was released on 24 April 1986, one month before the album's release. It was a new and unexpected departure for Gabriel. Upbeat, up mood, and rude. Gabriel thought up the funky groove and the title long before the rest of the lyrics followed.

In notes about the album, Gabriel wrote: 'This is an attempt to recreate some of the spirit and style of the music that most excited me as a teenager – sixties soul. The lyrics of many of these songs were full of playful, sexual innuendo and this is my contribution to that songwriting tradition.' He told one interviewer: 'Part of what I was trying to say was that sometimes sex can break through barriers when other forms of communication are not working too well.' The sledgehammer was the physical means of breaking through. 'There is a phrase by Nietzsche about what constitutes a good book, which he said should be "Like an axe in a frozen sea". That triggered me off to think of tools, not to put too fine a point on the word. Obviously there was a lot of sexual metaphor there. I was trying to write in the old blues' tradition, much of which is preoccupied with mating activities. The idea was the sledge-hammer would bring about a mini-harvest festival.'

Gabriel had been sent a showreel of fledgling American video director Stephen R. Johnson, by Tessa Watts, then Director of Video at Virgin Records. She had met Johnson through top video director Steve Barron who recruited John-son to his Limelight Productions company.

Watts was intrigued by Johnson's technique of pixellation on a showreel he showed her which included a college film called *Homebody*. This was first spotted by David Byrne of Talking Heads who used Johnson's technique on the award winning video 'Road to Nowhere'. Pixellation is a technique of shooting movement frame by frame to give the illusion of human animation. Johnson had perfected the technique through a method of synchronizing the mouth with the soundtrack.

As Watts expected, Gabriel was intrigued by Johnson's showreel. 'He called me up out of the blue,' said Johnson. 'I was fearful of doing something with Peter Gabriel because I had such a high respect for his past work like "Shock the Monkey". I enjoyed his stuff, I didn't want to do something with such high stakes.' But Gabriel persisted and suggested a meeting. They met in London, Johnson then went to visit

Gabriel in Bath where they spent three days talking about the meaning of life over the occasional glass of wine. 'He endeared himself to me,' said Johnson who tried to convince him he should do a simple performance video, but Gabriel wanted animation.

Once the direction the video should take was settled, Johnson and Gabriel worked on the storyboard. They brought in Aardman Animations of Bristol, known first for their TV-animated plasti-man Morph and Scotch Videotape advertisement skeleton and later for their Oscar winning films, *Creature Comforts* and *The Wrong Trousers* starring Wallace and Gromit. Stephen Johnson was impressed with the special-effects work of Stephen and Tim Quay, known as the Brothers Quay, who animated the fruit, fish, fowl and model-train effects on the video. 'The first idea that I had for the video before I involved The Brothers Quay was the fruit theme, which set the style for the rest of it. I took it as a purely sexual metaphor,' said Johnson.

The day before shooting began on 7 April, 1986, Johnson had last-minute doubts about the effects working. 'Steve was saying, "We will never do it, I think we should cancel it", because everything was so wild and undecided,' said Gail Colson. But everyone held their nerve. It took 100 hours of shooting over eight days at the Aardman Studio and Bristol University's Glynne Wickham studio theatre. Gabriel posed twenty-five times for every second of final film, once for each frame.

He had to suffer for his art. 'At some points I was in agony,' Gabriel said. 'For the train sequence, which lasts ten seconds, I had to be in the same position for six hours – the track had to be built up a little bit each time and the smoke had to be moved round as the train moved along. The fruit smelt all right after a few hours under the studio lights, but the fish stank.'

The video starts with a constellation changing into a field

of plasticine sperm, which appears at various points later on. A series of surreal scenes follow including the model steam-train going round his head, to match the opening line of 'Sledge-hammer', 'You could have a steam train'. Then comes a paper plane and clouds cover his made-up face. It took six hours of shooting to get the effect of the sky covering Gabriel's face suspended in the clouds, which was used only for a few seconds in the final edit.

Countless images make up the video, the visuals are as densely packed as some of his lyrics. The big dipper and bumper cars, the fish around his head, the fruit-cage and the face made up of fruit, the plasticine model head of Gabriel that metamorphoses into sledgehammers, limbs and naked figures, and the head which finally disintegrates. Almost imperceptible are the quail and pheasant used to give the illusion of growth after hatching from the dancing egg, all before the headless plucked cabaret chickens, bought from Sainsbury's, start to strut.

Gabriel dances with animated wallpaper as a backdrop with black soul sisters in formation behind him. He sits on a stool and then makes way for momentary cameos from his daughters Anna and Melanie, followed by some schoolfriends who dance around their father.

The final sequence is of a constellation of stars, in reality Christmas-tree lights, against a black backdrop. Starman Gabriel is swathed in lights and walks off into the universe, ending as he began. The final scene, a last-minute addition after filming had finished and already gone over budget, was important to complete what he saw as the circle of life and death implied in the higher interpretation of the song. 'I was so happy because it made the video work on a different level,' said Johnson.

Johnson is ecstatic in his praise. 'Peter is a wonderful human being, he is a good soul. I have never seen him raise his voice at anyone in anger, all the people that worked around him, his janitor even, he treats with dignity, respect and human decency. It is a rare thing, there is no streak of "I am a big rock star". He is a sensitive, intelligent, humane person. He is not telling me to say this.'

The video cost £120,000, though not in the *Thriller* or *Bad* budget range, it was still a vast financial gamble for an artist who had not exactly stormed the singles charts in eighteen years of recording. But the investment clearly paid off, propelling the single to Number 4 in the UK in May 1986, and to Number 1 in the USA in July where it ironically dislodged Genesis' single 'Invisible Touch'. The album topped the charts on both sides of the Atlantic, going straight to Number 1 on release in the UK on 19 May. By the summer of 1987 the *So* album had sold 5 million copies worldwide, having gone double platinum in America with 2 million copies and double platinum in the UK with 600,000 copies.

Gabriel sent a copy of the new album to Alan Parker, then in Los Angeles working on the film *Angel Heart*. The day he received the album Parker was working with Mickey Rourke and Lisa Bonet, on what would become the film's most controversial scene, earning it an X-rating. 'The scene is two people making love,' said Parker. 'It is a nightmare sequence and the ceiling is leaking. The rain is coming through and this changes to blood. They drink the blood as they are making love. This caused me terrible problems and I had to trim ten seconds off the scene.

'The irony is that the first track on *So* is "Red Rain". I thought "Oh God", and I wrote Peter a little card immediately and said, "How astonishing that we are thousands of miles apart and I was about to do a scene that was a song you'd already done".'

The red rain Gabriel alludes to is blood. It is an emotive ballad based around a Brazilian rhythm. 'Years ago I had a recurring dream. I was swimming in a swirling sea of red and black. I remember a tremendous turmoil as the sea was parted by two white walls. A series of bottles, of human shape, were carrying the red water from one wall to another, then dropping down to smash into little pieces at the bottom of the second wall,' Gabriel explained. 'I used this for a scene in a story in which the red sea and red rain from which it was formed represented thoughts and feelings that were being denied.

'I believe that if feelings or pain do not get brought out, not only do they fester and grow stronger but they manifest themselves in the external world. For example, if a personal storm cannot be outwardly expressed it will appear in life in events with other people or in this case in a cloudburst.'

> red rain is pouring down
> pouring down all over me
> and I can't watch anymore
> no more denial
> it's so hard to lay down in all of this
>
> 'Red Rain'; Gabriel, 1986

'Don't Give Up' was a stylistic departure, in the main a country ballad, but also inspired by gospel, and with a lyric in the style of those traditions. Gabriel originally wanted a country singer to accompany him, but instead asked his friend and previous collaborator Kate Bush.

The twelve-string guitar, in the style of the Byrds, found its way back on to vinyl for 'That Voice Again', ten years after having been abandoned along with other Genesis musical associations. Like 'Red Rain', 'That Voice Again' was a reworking of songs written with the Mozo project in mind several years previously.

'In Your Eyes' is a gentle, soulful ballad which underwent a major-lyrical change during the recording. The song contains much of Gabriel's own personal realizations resulting from his separation from Jill. For the lyrics Gabriel transplanted ideas from another song, 'Sagrada'. 'It's a love song. There is a

tradition in Africa that intrigued me; that of writing love songs
so they can be heard as love of God or the love between men
and women. No one seems to do that in Western lyrics so I
thought I would try mixing images. The eyes are clearly a
focus point for the soul.' In the chorus the imagery is at its
most ambiguous.

> . . . in your eyes
> I see the doorway to a thousand churches
> in your eyes
> the resolution of all the fruitless searches
> in your eyes
> I see the light and the heat
> in your eyes
> oh, I want to be that complete

> 'In Your Eyes'; Gabriel, 1986

The most melancholic song on *So* is 'Mercy Street',
Gabriel's tribute to poet Anne Sexton. He dedicated three
pages in his 1986/7 tour programme to her, including printing
in full her poem 'In the Beach House'.

The tour programme explained: 'Peter Gabriel's song
"Mercy Street" is based upon the life and work of the
American poet Anne Sexton (1928–1974), with whom Peter
has long been fascinated. Anne married early, and following
the birth of her first child in 1953 she suffered her first
breakdown, one of many that she was to have during her
lifetime . . .' Sexton was encouraged to enrol in a poetry workshop by a psychiatrist after her first suicide attempt in 1956 and
published her first book in 1960. According to Sexton's friend
and colleague Maxine Kumin, 'No other American poet in
our time has cried aloud publicly so many private details.'

The poem 'In the Beach House', quoted in the programme, is rich in imagery, feelings and sounds, but it is

difficult to understand literally, like many Gabriel lyrics. Her poem '45 Mercy Street' was part of an unpublished collection she was still revising at the time of her death. Some of the poems were omitted by her daughter when the work was published, as she deemed them too personal and likely to cause pain to those still living. 'I don't reveal skeletons that would hurt anyone. They may hurt the dead, but the dead belong to me. Only once in a while do they talk back,' is a quote from Sexton used in Gabriel's tour programme. It mirrors his own reluctance to be obviously biographical or condemn in song anyone close to him. It is the spirit of Sexton, and Gabriel's empathy for solitary figures and those who have known suffering, that endears her to him.

Unlike 'The Family and the Fishing Net', Gabriel's homage to Dylan Thomas on the fourth album, Gabriel has not mimicked Sexton's style in Mercy Street. Instead he borrowed the title and the odd phrase while staying true to the mood and rhythmic flow of the poem. He takes up her theme examining the sham of her suburban existence collapsing under the strain of a mental breakdown. Sexton writes of her house, her 'green Ford' and her two kids. In Gabriel's lyric this is the 'dream' that never was. He borrows her phrase 'inside out', a reference to her husband not wishing to bring issues to the surface, and tweaks its meaing so that it refers to feelings that can no longer be hidden.

> *all of the buildings, all of those cars*
> *were once just a dream*
> *in somebody's head . . .*
>
> *dreaming of Mercy St*
> *wearing your inside out*
> *dreaming of mercy*
> *in your daddy's arms again . . .*
>
> Peter Gabriel; 'Mercy Street', 1986

'When I discovered her work by chance in a bookstore I was struck that, unlike most writers who are conscious of their peers or their audience, she was writing entirely for herself,' said Gabriel. '"Mercy Street" is filled with messages and imagery of dreams, and a constant search for a suitable father figure, whether it be a doctor, a priest, or God. That search kept her alive longer than many around her perhaps thought she could bear, gave her life a meaning, and now her work gives hope to others. That's a kind of magic, I think. Creation as therapy, both the fact and the gentle endorsement of that, is a thread in the material on *So*.'

During the recording of the album, the song's working title was 'Forro', based on a Brazilian rhythm Gabriel discovered while visiting the country. The 'Mercy Street' lyrics originally went with another tune, while the 'Forro' rhythm itself already had two previous sets of lyrics. Gabriel explained the derivation of Forro. 'While the English and Irish workers were building the railways in Brazil they used to throw wild parties to which the Brazilians were invited with the invitation "For All". The Brazilians assumed that the "For All", or "Forro" as it later became, was the name for the event and originated the rhythm on which this track is written.'

If 'Mercy Street' is melancholic, the mood is immediately altered with the next album track, 'Big Time'. It is a brash, funk number with bluesy organ based on a pattern derived from a Nigerian groove.

The press reviews for *So* were split as usual between the openly hostile and enthusiastic. 'Brilliant,' said the *Guardian*; 'Universal message that hope springs eternal,' ran *The Times* headline; 'The music is studied to death,' said *Sounds*; 'I love it,' said *Smash Hits*. 'The music which Peter Gabriel makes is terrifically uninteresting. It says nothing, being merely an ordering of sounds, mostly artificial,' said John McKenna in Eire's *Hot Press*. And Johnny Black in *The Beat*: 'Here, if you dare let it in, dare to listen closer, is music as exorcism, music to tear your fears out, music to drown inside and still come up feeling better for it.'

One unexpected outcome of this new stature was the request by Placido Domingo for Gabriel to perform on his album *España: The Passion of Goya*. Gabriel was asked to sing the tracks 'Picture It' and 'Viva España'. The record's composer Maury Yeston felt Gabriel was in tune with Goya's work, but Gabriel, although flattered, declined the chance to sing with the world's leading operatic star.

Gabriel interrupted his international promotion of 'Sledge-hammer' and *So* at the end of May 1986 to join the Conspiracy of Hope caravan tour across the United States for two weeks. He returned to the United States in November to start his first solo tour in the wake of *So*'s success. Half the band were stalwarts Tony Levin and David Rhodes, and joining them, Manu Katche, who had been on the Amnesty tour, and for the first time David Sancious on keyboards, a veteran of Bruce Springsteen's early E Street Band.

The tour was called 'This Way Up' though the title was rarely referred to. The first USA and Canadian leg of the eleven month on/off tour started on 7 November 1986 in Rochester, Illinois, and finished nearly six weeks later in Los Angeles. It was Gabriel's first solo show for just over three years. The success of the singles, albums and videos had broadened the audiences. The denim-clad, earnest intellectuals were now overtaken by fans of all social types and age groups, many unfamiliar with anything but *So* material.

Seven out of *So*'s eight tracks were performed at the first shows, not including 'This Is The Picture'. The rest of the set was made up of tracks from the previous four studio albums. The critics seemed to approve. 'There is — frequent press carping to the contrary — no art/rock pretence in Gabriel's ethno-treasure hunt . . . ,' wrote David Fricke for *Melody Maker* after seeing the Madison Square Garden show in New York. 'In embracing diversity Gabriel has in fact created a resonant pop sound beholden to no fad yet socially responsive and emotionally direct in its lyric address . . . Gabriel's rousing encore duet with Youssou N'Dour on "In Your Eyes" was an exhilarating demonstration of how easily two cultures can come together in a common inspirational sound. This, indeed, was the world calling – and 20,000 people answered with a hardy hello.'

Even the *NME*'s Los Angeles correspondent was complimentary. 'With his dramatic lyricism, good old-fashioned barn-stormers like "Sledgehammer" and the glorious "Solsbury Hill", and his oft-quoted commitment to Amnesty International, Peter Gabriel has achieved the perfect potpourri of poetry, pop and politics, a performance artist in the true sense,' wrote Jane Garcia.

On stage, Gabriel discarded the heavy style of make-up, as seen with his 'monkey' face on the previous 1982/3 tour, for the merest facial highlights. It was part of the same desire to open up his music and his personality that had been captured in the unadorned portrait on the *So* cover. He continued to rely on theatrical props, recycling hexagonal blocks used on the last tour for leaping on and off. Together with lighting engineer Jonathan Smeeton he devised the praying mantis mobile lighting cranes, which were at their most menacing when they ensnared him crouching foetus-like on the floor for 'Mercy Street'. Gabriel continued with his backwards leap into the crowd for 'Lay Your Hands On Me'. The largest crowds of the tour were on his return to the United States in July 1987 to play the Giants Stadium at Meadowlands, New Jersey, when there were 50,000 people for each of the two nights.

Rehearsals for the tour had taken place at Gabriel's new complex, christened 'Real World Studios', in the village of Box just outside Bath, five miles from Ashcombe House. It was still a building site in October 1986 when the band went in to clear a space where they could practise. Faced with little choice but to leave Ashcombe at the end of his lease, he decided to invest in a state-of-the-art studio.

Box Mill is on the site of an early nineteenth-century flour mill built in the distinctive stone of the region. The twelve-acre complex includes barns and outhouses converted into offices, accommodation for visiting artists, and the headquarters of WOMAD. Bordering one side on a high embankment is the main London Inter-City railway line where trains rattle past around every half-hour. An unusual sound and vibration obstacle for a site where undisturbed sound is the bedrock of business, this required special insulation and construction techniques. Here all on one site was Gabriel's love of water, trains, music and technology. Here Gabriel could realize his long-term plans. 'He's not going to be trying to play rock and roll for the next ten years,' said David Rhodes who was still in a job as Gabriel's guitarist over ten years after making this remark.

Real World Studios would not have been possible without the financial rewards that accrued after the success of *So*. By autumn 1987 some of his investment plans had to be curtailed as the budget got close to £2 million. Throughout 1988 the studio continued to eat up the bulk of his royalty cheques, eventually costing £5 million. As opposed to Ashcombe House, which was essentially his private facility occasionally leased out to other artists, Real World became a full-blown commercial enterprise which had the added function of subsidizing Gabriel's hunger for the latest hardware.

He hoped Real World would be so far ahead of anything comparable in studio design and technological features it would encourage artists to express themselves differently. 'I wanted to create another new way of recording and have a sort of cellular structure around some shared facilities and shared intelligence, so I have one large acoustic studio, then a lot of control ones around the outside. Instead of having a Fairlight, Synclaviers and all the rest in each studio, you can share some of the intelligence and access it by computer from any point on the site,' Sharing synthesizers made sense when they cost around £50,000 each, but within a few years they would become affordable for all. His idea to network the studio computers was once again foreseeing an innovation that was to become standard. Other idealistic notions, like installing five or six artists in their own rooms to create an artistic community, proved impractical. Likewise plans for a public café on the site remained a never to be realized dream.

Gabriel's new main studio building was erected surrounded by a moat with a stream running beneath it that was visible through the studio floor. The design of the main studio was innovative. Its control room was unusually big enough for performers to record their vocals inside. The thinking was to make everyone feel part of the creative process instead of feeling cut off behind a conventional glass partition. No detail was too small to consider. The air conduits in the main studio are ceramic instead of the standard metal. Gabriel believed metal ducts increased the level of negative ions within the studio and induced fatigue.

His plans for Real World included setting up a facility for technological research and development. With that in mind in February 1987 Gabriel went on a technology tour of the United States. He visited the Media Lab at the Massachusetts Institute of Technology guided by Stewart Brand, author of a book on the lab, who he knew through Peter Schwartz's un-realized space project. Gabriel then went to San Francisco for a tour of Silicon Valley, with Schwartz. It was an excuse to satisfy a hunger to explore the latest developments in computers and video, as well as seeing what could be put to use at Real World where he also planned to build an audio-visual studio.

Gabriel feasted on computer graphics, sound technology, and speech-recognition computers. He visited Sun Microsystems and Apple Computers. At Apple the engineers had digitized 'Red Rain' from the *So* album and played it to him. That spring Apple used 'Red Rain' as the theme music for the launch of their Macintosh II computer in Los Angeles.

Gabriel and Schwartz also visited Industrial Light and Magic, *Star Wars* film director George Lucas' studio in San Rafael, California, which would achieve huge success in the nineties with its computer animation and THX cinema digital-audio technology. There the technology tourists saw the Pixar, capable of creating 3D images. Gabriel wanted one, at a mere $70,000.

He wanted Real World to be a centre of video as well as audio excellence. With David Gardener, who edited the 'Games Without Frontiers' video in 1980, he planned to start a television post-production company specializing in digital effects. (Gardener had the distinction of turning down the edit of the 'Sledgehammer' video because he was too busy working on Channel 4's *Chart Show*). Gardener and Gabriel were enthused by the possibilities of the Inmos transputer, Britain's own semi-conductor chip, made nearby in Bristol. Their scheme evaporated with the demise of Inmos. Gabriel did get his TV post-production company however after agreeing to invest in Post Haste Television in partnership with two editors who had worked for Spafax, the post-production company that had previously occupied Box Mill. By the mid-nineties Gabriel rationalized his business interests and sold his share in Post Haste.

There was a brief music-video boom in the eighties. It soon waned in the face of consumer indifference, and with it any plans for future elaborately conceived and lavishly budgeted videos. Few artists went beyond stringing a few promos together or releasing concert performance videos with some backstage action. As an acknowledged video pioneer, Gabriel could not resist trying to break new ground. 'I would like to get Box set up to be ready for developing long-form video which I think will become a really exciting medium,' he said as Real World was still under construction.

He had intended making a video of every track on *So*. 'We worked out the budget. If I do all of the tracks, it will cost something like $1.5 million. And the possible income, even if it's very successful, will be something like $750,000. So I have either to trim my ideas or trim the number of tracks. I don't mind not making a profit on it, but I do mind losing money, because the studio itself is about three times as expensive as we were planning.'

Coming to his commercial senses, he abandoned the video album idea. The compromise video, cryptically entitled *CV*, was released in February 1988. It included five tracks from *So* and two earlier classics.

'Sledgehammer' was the video's premier track, the greatest video ever made according to *Rolling Stone*. Another video directed by Steve Johnson, 'Big Time', uses similar techniques though the overall effect is disjointed and less satisfying. The opening images of a cracked dry earth bubbling into a swamp and turning into lush fertile ground would regularly feature in Gabriel's later work. Grotesque plasticine monsters appear in the earth before being swamped by beautiful flowers as the video moves into its main cartoon animation sequences. It is a literal portrayal of the song's underlying theme, how the demons of avarice and ambition have to be unleashed if you want a share of success, money and materialism. The images move from real life to cartoon claymation. Gabriel has on a false smile, a loud jacket and bow tie. He goes past skyscrapers and mansions, strutting along in this contradictory paean to grabbing life for all it is worth and grabbing everything that is shallow and worthless.

In the normal commercial world, record companies commission videos to promote singles. Gabriel's attempt to defy this convention for his video album was self-indulgent. He hired Matt Mahurin to direct 'Mercy Street', a track on *So* never released as a single. Mahurin specialized in creating eerie images in his work as an illustrator and photographer. His style was well suited to the mood of 'Mercy Street', filmed in black and white. Using the dream references in the song, he constructed a sequence of random memory shots, moving from a woman in shadow with closed eyes to visions of a boat being pushed out, a child in the boat with a father rowing, and a hospital gown viewed by its wearer looking down. The images refer to Anne Sexton and her mental health problems, and her desire for her daddy's arms. Gabriel in a heavy overcoat, also to become a familiar image, is pictured pushing and rowing the boat.

Mahurin was hired again to direct 'Red Rain', another video high on atmosphere and low on action, filmed in a blue tint. A static Gabriel with his hand up and palm out looks like a prophet warning of an impending apocalypse. The cracked parched earth is there again. Around Gabriel is a dancer in flowing robes illustrating the spiritual, mental and emotional turmoil of the song. A red glow on the horizon is a foretaste of the impending, possibly nuclear, disaster. The state of innocence is expressed through a naked unprotected baby and doomsday by the earth catching fire. In shadow a liquid, the red rain of blood, runs down a wall. The disaster in the world around him is the outward manifestation of the consequences of denial in all its forms expressed in the song.

The most difficult song to realize on video was 'Don't Give Up'. Gabriel's first choice of director was Jim O'Brien, who had worked on the celebrated TV series *The Monocled Mutineer* and *The Jewel in the Crown*. Their collaboration was abruptly brought to a halt by Gabriel before production began. 'We had this dramatic script and I suddenly panicked at the eleventh hour and pulled out of it, which I found difficult as I have developed a lot of respect for Jim,' said Gabriel.

He then called in Kevin Godley and Lol Creme, among the leading video directors of the eighties, known for their award-winning video of their own song 'Cry' as well as their work with Duran Duran and Frankie Goes to Hollywood. They had an unshaven Gabriel trying to look like a Depression-era proletarian clasping Kate Bush to his breast. Gabriel and Bush slowly rotate on the spot while the giant flaming sun goes in and out of eclipse behind them. 'I wasn't that happy with the way it came out, but it was getting late and the single needed a video,' was Gabriel's judgement.

Third and last choice was American Jim Blashfield, who directed 'The Boy in the Bubble' for Paul Simon and 'And She Was' for Talking Heads. Because of other commitments, Gabriel was unable for the first time to oversee one of his video productions. What he got back was a sepia tinted, soft focus drama.

Taking his own lyrics literally, Gabriel refused to give up and asked Blashfield to try again, this time minimizing the use of actors. 'That song has to be one hundred per cent convincing, it's quite personal, and it can easily fall into sentimentality or kitsch,' said Gabriel. 'It was redone at extra cost, but it had all been a bit of a disaster.' The final edit is a dustbowl saga featuring a disconsolate, good-looking husband and his model-type harassed wife battling it out in between shots of a dole office, a huddle of unemployed workers and drives across country. Gabriel makes a brief appearance seen through a rain-splashed pane and Kate Bush is used even more minimally, a postage-stamp sized image slotted onto a scene. This alternative version is included on *CV* with the Godley and Creme video that won the contest to be used for promoting the single.

The rest of *CV* was filled with two videos from previous albums, 'Shock the Monkey' and 'I Don't Remember'. A project with friend and artist Graham Dean to co-direct a video of 'In Your Eyes' never materialized.

A tendency for grandiose schemes was a familiar Gabriel trait. For his 1986/7 'This Way Up' tour his original plan was to take on the road massive banks of video screens in varying sizes. He was dissuaded by Gail Colson, something he was later grateful for when he came to terms with how much of a drain on his finances it would have been. That did not stop him still harbouring similar video-based ambitions until beaten to it by U2 on their 1992–4 'Zoo TV' tour. He saw these shows on four or five occasions and realized he would be accused of copying them if he pursued the idea.

A song that did not make it on to the *So* album was 'Sagrada'. It was about how big and mysterious buildings are haunted by the spirits of their creators. The theme bore echoes of Gabriel's own fascination with unusual structures and forbidding landscapes. 'The song was named after the Church of the Sagrada Familia, which Gaudi, the visionary architect, began building in Barcelona in 1884 and was obsessed with until his death in 1926. The song was an interplay between his way of building and that of a lady named Sarah Winchester. She was the heir to the Winchester rifle fortune who, in San Jose, California, started building this enormous home because she believed she was haunted by the ghosts of all the people who had been killed by the rifle. By her death in 1922, she'd added 160 rooms,' said Gabriel.

For fifteen years Gabriel had spoken about his own grandiose scheme, a theme park. Events conspired in 1985 giving him a limited chance to make it a reality. Australian architect and academic Professor Neville Quarry brought to Gabriel's attention an invitation by the New South Wales Ministry of Works for submissions to develop Darling Harbour in Sydney. Quarry put Gabriel together with Will Alsop, a London architect with a reputation as a maverick. Alsop's unconventional approach included creating almost abstract sketchbook paintings instead of traditional drawings in the initial stages of architectural design. His talents were widely recognized in the nineties for his Hôtel du Department government buildings in Marseilles and the massive North Greenwich tube station serving the Millennium Dome in London.

By the time Gabriel formally commissioned Alsop to design a Real World 'park' for Darling Harbour in May 1986 there were just two and a half weeks left before the closing date for submissions. Gabriel's original vision had been for an underground park on a wilderness site, preferably close to the sea. The small two-acre Sydney site was by the sea, but in the middle of the city. Even so the opportunity seemed too good to pass up.

The concept for the theme park was already well developed in Gabriel's mind, and would not alter much over the years. 'I picture a lot of places in the future that are a combination of holiday camp, university and art gallery. It's the way things must go. With mass unemployment, it seems there are only three solutions to the prospect of massive riots – education, entertainment or warfare. And the first two are preferable to conscription,' he said at the time.

Gabriel wanted to extend the notion of transformation and make it a practical outcome of visiting the park. He talked with radical psychologist R. D. Laing about his idea for a Ride of Fears where you confront your own phobias and are awarded bravery tokens if you come through them without pressing the panic button. He wanted a Big Dipper simulator. He was interested in a device that was a precursor to the virtual reality headset, where miniature screens placed over the eyes created 3D effects. Here was a means of becoming immersed in mythical worlds where you could become part of the adventure. It was conceptually exciting, but technically had a way to go.

He was taken with a space flight simulator called the Magic Motion Machine capable of seating forty people in a theatre-like environment. He foresaw pressure-sensitive floors that could activate patterns on giant video screens and computer games played by groups of people. He talked to David Byrne about creating aural environments. Some of these ideas would become standard fare in amusement arcades in the coming years.

The Darling Harbour plan was based on a 250-metre-long crescented building that would include the world's longest swimming pool. It would be raised like a bridge, giving swimmers a view. The pool was to go the entire length of the building but would be only three metres wide, forcing people to keep moving. And, fittingly for Australia, the building would also house the world's longest bar, again the entire length of the building.

Alsop's task was to interpret Gabriel's frequently vague ideas. 'It seemed to me much more interesting to have something like that in the middle of a city,' said Alsop. 'To have something that is free to walk through and see what is going on and then pay to experience what you want. I was interested in the idea of mixing these experiences with prosaic parts of everyday life.' He wanted that to include supermarkets, launderettes and hairdressers, so the mundane could be enjoyed in a new context, as well as providing the opportunity to have a go at state-of-the-art 'rides'.

Gabriel and Alsop met up with Richard Branson who expressed an interest in investing the estimated £30 million required to make it a reality. It was probably fortunate for all that within a month the news came through that their bid had failed and a more traditional funfair project approved.

Gabriel was left out of pocket, having to pay Alsop's undisclosed fees. Though naturally, according to Alsop, it was money well spent. 'The return is that it actually gave a physical presence to some very vague ideas,' said Alsop. 'At least it shifted the Real World project, which was in Peter's head, to a description of just what it should be, therefore it is money well spent, and it gives you good grounds on which to continue with the conversation.'

The plans were resurrected a year later, in May 1987, after

Alsop was invited by the city of Cologne to submit designs for a media park on disused railway sidings near the city centre. More ambitious and diverse at a total cost of around £150 million, with the Real World element around £3 million, the Cologne project was intended to include some of the rides Gabriel had envisioned with Alsop's idea for a long and adaptable building. They had three months to prepare it this time, but again their scheme was rejected.

Alsop still had faith that Real World, what he once called Gabrieland, would become a reality, despite his reservations about the risks. 'The difficult task is that though we know what it could be, we have to be aware of the commercial reality, and if we let Peter go off on his own it could be a wonderful place, but a financial disaster.

'Involved in the business he is, and he is a lot more intelligent than a lot of people in that business, Peter knows it is not a very real world that he occupies. He needed to place his involvement with music in a broader cultural context and Real World is a way of grounding it. Real World gives him the opportunity to talk to people in different disciplines, and takes him away from music a little bit, but it can also feed back into the music in other ways.' Alsop's suggested course of action came to pass as did the benefits he predicted would accrue for Gabriel.

# CHAPTER FIFTEEN

IT WAS A FAMILIAR ENOUGH QUESTION WITH attitude from the cynical British press corps. Do rock stars get involved in events like Amnesty International's Human Rights Now! tour to get publicity for themselves?

There were gasps and titters from its intended targets. Bruce Springsteen, Tracy Chapman, Sting, Youssou N'Dour and Peter Gabriel were gathered at Wembley Stadium for the following day's inauguration of their world tour. Sting said, yeh, he really needed the publicity. It was Gabriel, having wrestled with his conscience after the success of his song 'Biko' and his involvement with Amnesty's Conspiracy of Hope tour of two years before, who now had an unequivocal answer. 'Let us suppose that everyone of us here is entirely out to get publicity. Does it really matter? If people are being rescued from torture, from execution, and if we push the cause of human rights, it doesn't matter a damn.'

Gabriel had never wanted to start the Human Rights Now! tour at Wembley. He knew how the hyper-critical Brits would seize on any weakness, and there were plenty. The shows were under-rehearsed, the staging and sound was creaky, the relationships between artists sometimes wary, and the overprotected Springsteen and the excruciatingly withdrawn Chapman were not used to the banter and baiting of press conferences. 'It started off that Bruce and Tracy were kind of grunting at the press conferences, and by the end they were being very articulate and answering spontaneous questions very well, and neither of them really wanted to do that at first,' said Gabriel. His experience with Conspiracy had shown that it takes time for 'a strong sense of community' to develop and for that to be transmitted on stage and through the media.

When Gabriel started working on the Human Rights Now! tour he and the organizers had enough experience of benefit shows to know that it would be more satisfying to have few acts doing longer sets than a wheel-them-on-wheel-them-off procession of names. The idea for the tour came in March 1987 from Jack Healey, flushed with the success of the Conspiracy tour, and Mary Daly, Amnesty's American PR adviser. They wanted to mark the impending fortieth anniversary of the Universal Declaration of Human Rights in 1988. They approached Gabriel and Sting, who were agreeable, and Lou Reed, who later had to drop out. Gabriel brought in Youssou N'Dour and Tracy Chapman but was warned by tour promoter Bill Graham that, though impressive, the line-up was deficient: 'We have a plateful of vegetables; we need the meat.'

Bruce Springsteen was just about the biggest rock star in the world in the late eighties. So stellar was he that a lesser star like Gabriel was unable to get a *direct* message through to him. Determined, Gabriel got to a Springsteen concert in San Francisco but failed to reach the Boss himself. He did, however, manage to talk to Jon Landau, Springsteen's manager, by hitching a lift in one of the band's vans. Gabriel delivered his 'best sales pitch' on the Universal Declaration and the value of the tour. Soon, Jack Healey was summoned to a Springsteen concert at Madison Square Garden, New York. After listening to Healey's case, Springsteen said, 'Whatever it takes, I'll be there.'

The English summer is capricious enough. When it turns September the risks of inclemency rise considerably. It was only the start of the month, Friday, 2 September, but there had been showers early on the day of the concert, and a chill wind was slapping around the twin landmark art-deco towers of Wembley Stadium.

For everyone except Springsteen it was their second appearance at a benefit show line-up at Wembley in under three months. In June they had been part of the concert celebrating Nelson Mandela's seventieth birthday and protesting at his continued imprisonment. It was then that Tracy Chapman became an instant star when she performed her gut-wrenching, self-penned folk songs.

A new expression came into currency after the public's heartstrings and wallets had been so successfully plucked by Band Aid and Live Aid – compassion fatigue. Gabriel was aware of another term for artists who too frequently turned up at this or that Aid during the boom in rock-charity shows that followed – 'benefit whores and worthy bores'. With his reputation for supporting human rights, Gabriel received endless requests for good causes. In 1988 he probably agreed to too many things; he risked diluting the effectiveness of his name. As well as the Mandela show, he graced the Prince's Trust Rock Gala at the Royal Albert Hall alongside Phil Collins, Elton John and Eric Clapton; he reaffirmed his right-on credentials by signing the Northern Ireland 'Time To Go' charter calling for the end of the British military presence; he lent his name to a campaign to reprieve a prisoner on death row in America; and appeared in support of GreenNet, Amnesty's new computer information network.

Fear of overexposure led Gabriel to turn down Amnesty International's request to appear at their Festival of Youth at the Milton Keynes Bowl just one week after the Mandela show. Other big names touted to appear, including Van Morrison and Simple Minds, had second thoughts leaving the concert with B-list headliners Aswad, Joe Strummer, Aztec Camera and The Stranglers. In the barren, grassy amphitheatre of brave new Milton Keynes the 10,000 audience on the first day, and 12,000 on the second, was not enough to conjure atmosphere or a profit for Amnesty as it tried to push its new youth wing.

The prognosis for Amnesty's Human Rights Now! show at Wembley Stadium, despite its A-list names, looked equally bleak. On the day, journalists reported seeing desperate touts trying to offload tickets at a loss. One asked £10 for two £22.50 tickets and still found no takers. He should have been more patient. It seems a big chunk made up their minds to attend at the last minute. Promoter Harvey Goldsmith reported a sell-out with a crowd of 72,000 at start of play at 4 p.m.

In the audience were veterans of previous Wembley benefits. Free Nelson Mandela T-shirts were plentiful, and there were even a few Live Aid shirts from three years before. The declared aim of the tour was not to raise money but awareness. 1.6 million passport-sized replicas of the UN Declaration of Human Rights were printed in over a dozen languages with the relevant version distributed to the audiences at every show.

The sun shone briefly and the rain stayed away, but the sense of occasion at Wembley was muted as Springsteen, Gabriel, Sting, N'Dour and Chapman ambled on stage holding hands and falteringly paid lip service to Bob Marley's 'Get Up, Stand Up'. Youssou N'Dour was left to start the show proper. After his set there was a half-hour wait before Peter Gabriel defied the star-system ranking to come on before Tracy Chapman.

Gabriel battled with technical defects and the wind to be heard. He previewed 'Of These, Hope' from his yet to be released soundtrack album, *Passion*, a number not designed to electrify crowds. Introducing songs with little human rights messages, for 'Games Without Frontiers' he deplored 'racism and nationalism and 40,000 needless casualties in Nicaragua'; for 'Biko': 'This song is about a country where there is daily abuse of human rights. It's about a great black leader who was found dead in his cell in South Africa. In recent weeks, a young union leader was also found dead in his cell with head wounds – the song is just as relevant today.' He tried to loosen up with 'Sledgehammer', but the overall verdict was that his performance was leaden.

Sting's jazzy rock was slick and his songs also relevant, but it was Springsteen who most had come to see. His usual three-to four-hour set was expertly spliced into one hour. Instead of pontificating he was true to type delivering a little homily recalling how when he was a kid he heard freedom encapsulated in the chords and words of classic, three-minute rock and roll records. 'Suddenly, the whole long day became an event, the crowd galvanized into a dancing, clapping, swaying sea of humanity, the chill of the night air forgotten,' wrote David Sinclair in *The Times*. For the finale the troupe traipsed on to join Springsteen on Dylan's 'Chimes of Freedom' and a reprise of 'Get Up, Stand Up'. The show ended triumphantly after six hours.

Views of the event were varied. The *NME* snidely detected 'a bad smell of herd-them-in-herd-them-out conveyor belt benefiteering. There must be a better way of raising cash and consciousness than this huge, empty-headed stadium business. I'm not so much a prisoner of conscience that I have to lap up this rubbish for a good cause.' The *Financial Times* trumpeted, 'The start of the most altruistic six weeks in the history of pop.'

The following day in Paris, Gabriel regained his performance poise. Edna Gundersen reported in *USA Today*, 'Though the first concert was uneven, the artists regained their footing in Paris and delivered powerful and absorbing sets. Springsteen was the muscle, Sting the mind, Peter Gabriel the heart, Tracy Chapman the conscience and Senegalese singer Youssou N'Dour the soul . . . Peter Gabriel's set was the most successful blending revelry and purpose.'

The world political map, though sadly not its record of atrocities, was about to change beyond the widest-eyed optimism that surely anyone could have entertained in 1988.

Within two years the Berlin Wall would come down and Nelson Mandela would be free and on the road to becoming president of an apartheid-free South Africa.

For the moment though, the Human Rights Now! tour was pleased to breach the Wall, reaching Budapest where the regime was still living on a legacy of repression bestowed by the Soviet troops who helped quell the Hungarian revolt of 1956. There the wife of Party Secretary Janos Bereoz egged her husband along to the gig resulting in Amnesty being allowed to set up an office in the country. In the Soviet Union, where the show was not allowed in, the official newspaper *Pravda* was starting to treat Amnesty with something like respect. The tour succeeded in shifting the perception of Amnesty International around the world. In the capitalist world it was seen as a communist front, and in the communist world a capitalist tool. But rock and roll, or more likely the sexual power of Bruce Springsteen, seemed to skip all barriers.

Amnesty had brokered separate deals with promoters in each country. A local act which had some connection to human rights issues was meant to be selected as the support; in some countries their main connection seemed to be a management deal with the local promoter. There were some shady financial deals where Amnesty got paid $50,000 for a show that Jon Landau reckoned should have netted $500,000. The tour was only made possible by the sponsorship of sportswear manufacturer Reebok International. They provided $2 million to get the tour rolling and underwrote it with a further $8 million. Some had predicted it could cost $12 million, so the final charge to Reebok of $8 million in comparison seemed reasonable.

Where they could, politicians, promoters and the media used Amnesty for their own purposes. In multiracial Zimbabwe, President for life Robert Mugabe labelled his impending visitors 'Amnesty Lies International'. He relented when the tour arrived and allowed government ministers to attend the show as a gesture of goodwill.

Gabriel, with his fondness for the power of technology, had hoped a TV crew could accompany the tour and relay weekly reports by satellite. Money was set aside for the project but it never materialized. The world's media were largely uninterested until a rich irony forced the tour on to the news bulletins. A week before they played Zimbabwe the performers were told the only available public address system would have to be imported from South Africa. They objected and another PA was found in neighbouring Lesotho, supposedly imported from America for a visit by the Pope. Press reports indicated this was simply a yarn and that the PA was still South African. In the end, when introducing the song 'Biko' on stage in Harare, Gabriel told the crowd, 'If this PA comes from South Africa, we will turn it up so loud that everyone there can hear what we're saying.' He need not have worried, they were closer than he thought. The crowd was 60 per cent white, and many of those, an estimated 30,000, were South Africans, some of them certainly soldiers. He was oblivious to their jeers as he introduced 'Biko'. 'Apparently there were some boos,' he said, 'but they didn't want to make too much noise because there were a lot of black Zimbabweans around and it wasn't their country.'

There were modest firsts. Gabriel's performance of 'Biko' could be heard on radio in South Africa via Capital Radio in the 'Tribal Homeland' of Transkei. The station's lawyers thought they could get away with broadcasting banned material because it was news coverage of a live event. In New Delhi, despite *The Times of India* attempting to make the show appear more a celebration of their birthday than a human rights event, it became the first major rock event to visit the country. In the Ivory Coast the 98 per cent black audience made a loud American audience seem restrained.

Along the way they met people involved in the human rights struggle, a moving experience for all. The tour reached Mendoza, Argentina, as close as it could get to the border of repressed Chile. Sting and Gabriel would not have received a warm reception from the all-powerful military had they crossed the Andes from Argentina into Chile: Gabriel had shown his sympathies publicly having met a Chilean woman on the Conspiracy of Hope tour who was a victim of torture and who within days of her meeting with Gabriel suffered the murder of her son; and Sting had embraced the Mothers of the Disappeared and written a song celebrating their plight, 'They Dance Alone (Cueca Solo)'.

At a press conference in Philadelphia before the show at the John F. Kennedy Stadium, Gabriel said, 'If we can help activate people all over the world through this tour, even if it's only one per cent of the audience we reach, then ten or fifteen years from now the effect could be enormous. And I am very hopeful a lot more of these documents will find their way, through the will of the people, into the legal systems of the countries we are visiting and of those we are not.' The tour achieved Gabriel's aim of bridging the First and the Third worlds, democracies and one-party states, reaching twenty-three cities on four continents.

Travelling together the performers inevitably got to know each other well. Though it was Gabriel who Jack Healey observed did not muck in. 'I watched you on the plane on our DC-10,' he told Gabriel when later interviewing him for *Spin* magazine. 'You sat in front of me and most of the time you worked. You were friendly with everybody, but you seemed basically a loner.'

There was tension between Sting and Springsteen because Sting was always 'mouthing off', according to Gabriel. 'He talks first and thinks later sometimes. But he slagged off Bruce at some time in the past, so there was a certain amount of apprehension there from both sides. I think both Jon Landau and Bruce thought who is this arrogant mop-haired English-man.' Sting was then sporting shoulder-length hair. 'Sting has a great sense of humour and that was I think what broke the ice and they got on like a house on fire.'

Springsteen took his duties seriously and spent a few hours briefing himself on the background and political history of each country he visited and learning a few words in the local language, as did Gabriel.

As the artists loosened up they would make more regular appearances during each other's sets. For the final show in Buenos Aires on 15 October, Gabriel and Sting devised a prank at Springsteen's expense. They raided his wardrobe, each stripping off their shirts and donning one of his waistcoats, slipping on his boots and joined him on stage for his final number as doppelgängers, both aping his routine of pouring water on his head and flicking his hair back, making out he was an overheated soul singer so tired he couldn't carry on. 'He had no idea that we were going to do this,' said Gabriel. 'I'm still not sure how it went down. It may be more of an English sense of humour. But the band loved it, that's for sure. He was smiling, but I'm not sure whether he thought we were taking the piss too much or not.'

Standing by the side of that stage in Buenos Aires was Gail Colson. She was in tears as Gabriel sang 'In Your Eyes', moved not by the song but the knowledge that she was witnessing Gabriel's last performance while still his manager. Gabriel and Colson had grown up together in the music business since meeting in 1969 when she worked for Tony Stratton Smith at Charisma Records. She had been his manager since he embarked on his solo career.

Gabriel had decided in the autumn of 1986 to end his management agreement with Colson. 'I really felt that my interest in world music, WOMAD, the experience park, and other more visually based projects were all things that were becoming increasingly important to me. And although Gail and Tony Smith were fantastic when I was in trouble such as in the WOMAD crisis and organized the Milton Keynes benefit to get me out of debt, I didn't feel they supported or had been interested in these new activities and were much more concerned in a traditional music career, reasonably enough.'

On the first working day of 1987 Gabriel had turned up unannounced at Colson's Knightsbridge office and asked if she would come to lunch at the local Italian restaurant. By the end of lunch they were both in tears. He told her he no longer wanted her to manage him, intending to handle the job himself. The timing seemed perverse. After years of struggle Gabriel's career was finally moving into the top league. The afterglow of success from the album *So* was still strong and he was in the middle of touring major venues across the globe.

Colson's and Gabriel's recollection of these events differ. For her the issue of money seemed to preoccupy him. She says he emphasized that she was due £1 million as her share of his earnings. She picked him up on the point. 'I said, "Peter, you never talk about money. Has this got to do with how much I'm going to make? You've told me a million pounds three times now. You've forgotten the ten years when there's been no money. And if I'm going to make a million, how much are you going to make? But has this got anything to do with money?"'

He answered, 'No, no, no.'

Colson said to him, 'You can't do this in the middle of a tour.'

He replied, 'But I just want you to know, this is what I want.'

Gabriel does not agree that money was the major issue. He was meeting to explain all his frustrations to try to reach a settlement. 'I felt that I had stayed in the camp for quite a while longer than I'd originally intended, and that was partly for reasons of loyalty. Which in a way was a repetition of what

I had done in Genesis when I had been asked to stay on a year extra to make sure people got a fair crack at some income. But I did want to cap what I owed Gail at a million pounds, so that certainly came up in conversation, but it was not the reason for leaving.

'I think they viewed a lot of my non-music activities as irrelevant. I think in their view, besides looking after their own interests, they also felt that they were protecting me from my artistic whims whereas I saw these activities as central to my future.'

Back at the office Colson informed her staff and closest business associates of Gabriel's decision, feeling they all had a right to know. They were Simon Draper at Virgin Records, Ed Rosenblatt at Geffen Records, Mike Farrell, his agent at the William Morris Agency in America, and his American lawyer John Franca. Then there was her business partner Tony Smith, Gabriel's original manager in Genesis, and Gabriel's British agent, Steve Hedges of The Station agency.

Colson's confidence was shattered by Gabriel's pending departure. With only the modest career of Peter Hammill on her books she needed new artists if she was to carry on as a manager. For the first time she doubted her abilities. Over the next two years she sought out Jesus Jones, then bright young things on the new British dance scene that was developing in the wake of the Acid House phenomenon, and was approached by a veteran of eighties miserablism, Morrissey, embarking on his solo career after the dissolution of The Smiths. Though Jesus Jones' success was brief and her relationship with Morrissey ended in acrimony, Colson has gone on to further success managing Chrissy Hynde and former Suede guitarist Bernard Butler.

Little outwardly changed in Gabriel and Colson's working relationship after he had stated his intentions. He seemed to be half-heartedly scouting around for a new manager and approached old hands like Ed Bicknell, manager of Dire Straits, and Bill Curbishly, manager of the Who. Gabriel would phone Colson and tell her who he was seeing and ask her advice. 'I said, "Peter, do you really think I'm going to advise you on what manager to go and get? That is asking too much of me." '

'I certainly was not trying to get Gail's professional advice on the merits of alternative managers, that would be like discussing with a wife the merits of other potential lovers,' says Gabriel. 'I just didn't want her to hear any back-door gossip on who I was meeting. I wanted her to hear it straight from me. She would inevitably offer opinions on the strengths or weaknesses of whoever it was I was talking to, which I was very happy to listen to.'

Colson carried on with her managerial duties. One or two more people were told about the situation. Finally rumours started to surface publicly, first in *Hits*, the American music-radio trade magazine, saying managers were lining up to take on Gabriel.

In a Parisian café in September 1988, on the second day of the Human Rights Now! tour, Colson sat down with Gabriel and told him she had had enough. It had been twenty-one months since he told her he wanted to leave, and if he would not set a termination date she would. She told him, 'There are too many rumours. This can't carry on. As of December 31st you're on your own.'

One rumour that was to come to Colson's ears was that his agent Steve Hedges was taking over as manager. 'So I called Hedges and I said, "Look, a little birdy tells me that you've been talking to Peter about management." And there was this silence and he said, "Absolutely no way. I've worked with you for ten years. I know he's unmanageable. There's no way I would do that to you Gail." And I said, "I knew, you know, I knew." I believed him, I believed him. And about three months later, Peter phoned me. We were still talking every day, and he said to me, "You spoke to Steve."

And I said, "Yeh. I'd heard this rumour and he said it was rubbish." And Peter said, "Well actually it's not, Gail. I have been talking to him." And I went cold. I thought, "I can't believe that. I cannot believe that Steve Hedges lied to me like that."'

Steve Hedges says, 'When she asked me that question I wasn't [his manager] because Peter had talked about the concept but we had no arrangement. With the benefit of perfect hindsight would I have said we have discussed this? Yes, I would have told her.' His reasoning was that he didn't want to ruin a business relationship with Colson over discussions with Gabriel that might come to nothing.

Gabriel concurs. 'When I was talking to Steve first he said he very much wanted to talk to Gail and Tony before I did as he felt he'd been in business with them a long time, as I had, and was concerned about losing his other gigs with Genesis and Phil Collins. I think he was also nervous about talking to them and concerned that I might change my mind and he would have jeopardized some of his other business.'

Steve Hedges had been a fan of Genesis since he first saw them perform in 1969 at Farx club in Southall, Middlesex. He had known Colson since her days at Charisma when he worked for the Bron Agency. When Gabriel went solo in the seventies Colson hired Hedges as agent, a connection that led to Hedges winning the business for Genesis, Phil Collins and Genesis offshoot Mike and the Mechanics and enabled him to set up business on his own.

Colson was drawn to Hedges because of his sense of humour, but neither she nor Tony Smith were amused by the confirmation he was taking over as Gabriel's manager. They felt betrayed at his duplicity. Colson's office is in the same building as Smith's. On hearing the news, and without informing or consulting her, Smith sent an immediate fax to Hedges terminating his arrangement with Genesis, Phil Collins and Mike and the Mechanics. Colson took away her remaining acts, Peter Hammill and Jesus Jones, though they soon returned to the Hedges fold.

The following day Colson received a call from Hedges. 'He just said to me, "I'm sorry." And I said, "Well it's a bit fucking late for that now, Steve, isn't it?"'

A tall, ponytailed, long-beaked man, Hedges' amiable, almost bumbling, hippy appearance hides as shrewd and ruthless a businessman as ever wore a pinstripe suit. His attitude and abilities become clear in this exchange between us.

Q: Do you have strong negotiating skills?
A: Some would say. Some that have been brought to tears at show settlements have probably said that in the past, yes.
Q: So you drive a hard bargain.
A: Yeh.
Q: Tough but fair.
A: Depends what the circumstances will bear and necessity requires.
Q: You have an abrasive character. Some would say that.
A: I know what I want and sometimes I can be slightly too clear pointing that out.
Q: Ruthless.
A: I wouldn't say that.
Q: Others might.
A: Others have.
Q: Why would they accuse you of that? Does it mean you drive too hard a bargain sometimes?
A: If people agree to a deal then they must agree to the conditions of the deal.
Q: Right, so no mercy.
A: Supply and demand. If they actually want something it would be foolish to not negotiate it to the point where one's client is rewarded as positively as possible.

Gabriel clearly wanted a tough, no-nonsense representative, but then Colson fitted that bill too. Hedges was more open to the emerging world of multimedia, and happy to take over duties covering responsibility for Gabriel's other commercial enterprises, which Colson was not. 'I felt Steve had been one of the best agents I'd ever worked with and he'd always seemed warm, friendly and enthusiastic,' says Gabriel. 'He was excited by new ideas. He seemed very interested in some of the extracurricular pursuits and was a believer in the impact of new technology on multimedia, world music etc. He seemed to share some of the vision. And also, I think the traditional school of rock management has tried and tested ways of doing things which doesn't have a lot of leeway for extracurricular activities. Because Steve had come from a different part of the business I thought we'd both be working on creating a new way of doing things.'

Gabriel's choice of date to break the news to Colson, at the start of a new year, gives a clue to how much he must have agonized over the decision, resolving to start the year afresh with this irrevocable decision. At the time he was still going through the emotional turmoil of divorce from Jill, dealing with his volatile relationship with Rosanna and attending regular therapy sessions. Gabriel would later say, 'I had two divorces that year, my wife and my manager.'

Ultimately, dispensing with Colson appears to have been an emotional rather than a business decision. Gabriel had gone through life with a series of strong women, his mother, his wife, Rosanna Arquette and Gail. He wanted to take control, dictate rather than be dictated to. Though his future career in multimedia or as an 'experience designer' was yet to be crystallized in his mind, he knew Colson was not suited, either temperamentally or creatively, to guide his new direction.

For Gabriel and Colson the split was 'incredibly painful on both sides', says Colson. 'I remember sitting in the office, both of us crying, and we said, "Right, we'll go out to dinner," because if you're having dinner, you can't cry. And we both ended up crying over dinner. And I said to him, "Peter, you know, I can't believe this. There are so many artists, managers that hate each other, don't trust each other, you know, we've got this relationship. I can't believe you're doing this."

'But now I understand why. I totally understand why. What released it was when he said, "Look, Gail, sometimes I'll ring you and it's my mother." He'll think he's ringing me and he'll have rung his mother. I realize even now when I talk to him, ten years on, it still is this kind of bossy mother–child relationship.'

The domination was not just one way. Gabriel was very controlling, and would bully Colson in his passive-aggressive way. There were plenty of times Colson would advise Gabriel to do one thing and he would do the opposite.

He told her, 'An artist only has one career. A manager can carry on and manage other artists and become more successful.'

'At that time,' says Colson, 'I was so emotionally down that I didn't believe him. But, of course, he was right.'

Colson has never believed in management contracts. She only has a verbal agreement with her clients and charges a standard fee of 20 per cent of net earnings.

At first negotiations to end Gabriel's business arrangement with Colson and her partner Tony Smith were informal. Gabriel realized it was time to get some professional advice and hired solicitor Michael Thomas of leading showbusiness lawyers Sheridans. Gabriel defends Thomas as a lawyer with a reputation for being fair and reasonable. They met on 20 March 1989, prior to a meeting later that day between Gabriel, Colson and Smith. 'I hadn't worked with Peter before and I think the reason Peter asked me to get involved was he wanted somebody completely fresh who hadn't been involved in the history. He spent eighteen years with advice from Gail and Tony. It's not unreasonable to get independent advice in trying to come to a resolution with them,' says Thomas.

Colson was very upset that Gabriel had resorted to seeking legal advice. All four met for the first time on 1 June. 'The meeting ended with Tony Smith losing his temper, and he only loses his temper once a year. Me crying. It was awful,' recalls Colson.

This differs from Gabriel and Thomas' recollections. 'I explained to them the advice I'd given to Peter on a formal basis, that given Peter's relationship with them over the years he wished to reach an amicable resolution,' says Thomas. 'Gail didn't cry in the meeting. She was very together. Tony did get quite cross and the nub of the issue really was would Peter pay them on work he did in the future, to which we said no. But what Peter was offering and how it was all resolved was based on payments on work done historically. Peter felt that was fair to recognize, that Gail had done a lot of work, perhaps hadn't had some of the gravy that would now be around, but didn't think it was reasonable to pay old management on records that weren't in existence yet.' A few days later Thomas sent his formal proposals to Colson and Smith and in return received a letter from Tony Russell, the solicitor who was to later handle George Michael's High Court battle to free himself from his contract with Sony Records. Affronted by the legal turn of events Colson had hired Russell, resolved to find 'the worst solicitors' she could, meaning the toughest.

'Peter phoned me at home the following night and he said, "You've gone and got this really heavy lawyer." And I said, "Well, what do you expect? You walk into a meeting with a lawyer. I'm not walking away after twelve years with nothing." And we settled it on the phone that night,' says Colson.

Again the Gabriel version is different. Russell's letter merely stating he was instructed to act on Colson's behalf and would come back to them. A month later, having heard nothing further, Gabriel resolved to phone Colson to settle it.

Both sides allege the other was aggressive. Colson and Smith were upset at what they perceived to be the implication that by combining the roles of manager and publisher they had not been working in Gabriel's best financial interests.

According to Colson, Gabriel had never questioned the financial arrangements before. 'He would send up a chequebook of signed cheques and I would be the counter-signatory, and I can account for every single penny that ever went through his accounts,' says Colson.

There was never a question of any financial impropriety, but Gabriel had been uneasy about having his management controlling his song publishing, a practice common enough when he entered the business but which has been increasingly regarded as a possible conflict of interest. 'Having a manager and publisher in-house was clearly something I knew about, accepted and understood, but I was not comfortable with it, which I had expressed to Gail,' says Gabriel.

The settlement that Gabriel and Colson agreed was for her to receive £1 million, paid over five years for reasons of cash flow. It is not unusual for former managers to secure a percentage of their erstwhile client's future earnings in perpetuity. Colson disagrees with such deals on principle. Despite the hiccup, Colson and Gabriel severed their business ties on a friendly basis.

On his return from the Human Rights Now! tour Gabriel continued work on the interrupted *Passion* album which had long since missed the deadline his record company had hoped for, to coincide with the release in August 1988 of the film *The Last Temptation of Christ*.

Gabriel had been commissioned back in 1983 by director Martin Scorsese to write the score for the movie. As with Alan Parker on *Birdy*, he was always open to working with great directors though his experience with Hollywood had confirmed his doubts that film music could be satisfying in itself. 'But if you think there is a great piece of work going to come out the other end of it, that would be exciting,' said Gabriel.

Scorsese had wanted to make *Last Temptation* since 1972 when he first read the novel *The Last Temptation of Christ* by Nikos Kazantzakis, author of *Zorba the Greek* and Greece's most celebrated and overbearingly intellectual writer of the twentieth century. Kazantzakis had portrayed a Christ with mortal doubts, reluctant to take on his role as Messiah. In 1983, Paramount had come up with the $12 million, but sensing the impending controversy they slashed the budget in half. A month before filming was due to start Paramount pulled out. Scorsese told Gabriel he hoped one day to rekindle the project.

In 1987 after Scorsese again proved his bankability with *The Color of Money*, MCA, owners of Universal Studios, agreed to back *Last Temptation* with a meagre budget of $6.5 million. The movie temporarily had the safer working title of *The Passion*.

Gabriel spent the first half of 1988 composing the soundtrack. In July he took his tapes to New York to start mixing with Scorsese just as the outrage and fundamentalist religious demonstrations over the film erupted. They worked on the sound in the Brill Building, where Carole King and Jerry Goffin, Barry Manilow and Paul Simon had all worked. 'Instead of having six weeks to finish off we ended up with three weeks to do it, so it was a rush because Universal were anxious to get it out,' said Gabriel. 'At that point it had all been pretty much recorded, so I don't think the character of it was changed. But there was definitely an energy, a sense of excitement that we were working with something that was explosive material.'

Scorsese, who as a teenager briefly trained for the priesthood, tried to prove the sincerity of his Catholic faith to his accusers during his media interviews, slotted between editing and final mixing with Gabriel. One of Scorsese's assistants left a Bible by the editing desk where it was continually consulted. 'Quite often Bible quotations were used against the film, so we would fight fire with fire,' said Gabriel. 'It sounds weirder than it was.' Priests would come into the editing room to have discussions with Scorsese. But there were ominous threats too.

The TV evangelist the Rev. Jerry Falwell of the Moral Majority promised that the release would spark a 'wave of anti-Semitism' targeted around Lew Wasserman, then head of Universal Pictures. The Jewish-dominated film industry was accused of paying for the image of Christ to be destroyed. Bill Bright, of the Campus Campaign for Christ, offered $10 million for the print so that he could destroy it.

In September 1988, *Billboard* magazine reported, 'Has the controversy surrounding the Martin Scorsese film *The Last Temptation of Christ* rubbed off on the film's soundtrack album? The score by Geffen Records artist Peter Gabriel has mysteriously dropped off the Geffen release schedule. The album, which Geffen had tentatively listed on its schedule with the title "The Passion" has been "bumped off the schedule or is on hold" according to a label spokeswoman.'

There was no mystery. Gabriel was going out on the Amnesty tour and had no time to finish the album which had been scheduled for release in spring 1989, the film's original projected release date.

The zealots had nothing to fear from *Last Temptation*. As Gabriel said, 'No one lost their faith watching the film.' Its poor reception from the critics and at the box office ensured that any influence the film might have had was muted. The *Hollywood Reporter* showed no mercy. Critic Duane Byrge called it 'aesthetically graceless and philosophically turgid'. It was a 'hopelessly bathetic and ultimately commonplace inter-pretation'. He continued, 'All too often Jesus comes across as sounding like someone who's been trapped for forty years in a Grateful Dead convoy; his numerous utterances on "love" seem as if they've been gleaned from packets advertising bath oil products rather than from on high. Throughout, Schrader's screenplay is a curious philosophical cross of physical and spiritual asceticism with the platitudes of the Woodstock Nation.'

Gabriel's score was trapped inside Paul Schrader's arid

screenplay and director Martin Scorsese's bleak vision. The story of Christ had been reduced to such a commonplace level that there was little scope to express the grandeur or intensity of Gabriel's music. Scorsese did not set out to denigrate Christ, his intention as a Catholic was devotional. Though Paul Schrader had his own powerful take on religion. Schrader, screenwriter of previous Scorsese classics *Taxi Driver* and *Raging Bull*, was brought up in a strict Dutch Reform community. As a child he fantasized about becoming a missionary and spreading the good news like St Paul, his namesake. Instead, as an adult he abandoned his beliefs for a hedonistic godless lifestyle.

'*The Last Temptation* is not a religious or transcendental film,' he told Kevin Jackson in *Schrader on Schrader and Other Writings*. 'It's really much more a psychological film about the inner torments of the spiritual life; it's not trying to create a holy feeling . . . it's a tortured human struggle about a common man possessed by God and fighting it. God is a demon in that way.' It was inevitable such an attitude would lead to conflict in America.

Schrader's own devout father successfully campaigned to have the film banned in his home town. Schrader admitted, 'The picture was a provocation and I enjoy debate and argument. It would be very hypocritical to say that you don't enjoy it when you incite it.' According to Schrader, apart from the redemptive theme in *Last Temptation*, Scorsese's films are 'all of the same cloth; they're about lonely, self-deluded, sexually inactive people'.

It was not just the doubting Christ the fundamentalists objected to. There was a scene of Jesus watching Mary Magdalene at work as a prostitute, and while on the cross, the last temptation from Satan sees Jesus fantasize about leading a contented family life, married to Mary and surrounded by cuddly children in suburban Judea, before finally accepting his fate as the Messiah and dying on the cross.

Scorsese's high ideals reflected his own struggles since his days in a Catholic seminary, and were echoed by the quote opening the prologue to Kazantzakis' novel shown as the film starts. 'The dual substance of Christ – the yearning so super-human, of man to attain God . . . has always been a deep inscrutable mystery to me. My principal anguish and source of all my joys and sorrows from my youth onward has been the incessant, merciless battle between the spirit and the flesh . . . and my soul is the arena where these two armies have clashed and met.' This is followed in the film by a disclaimer: 'This film is not based upon the Gospels but upon this fictional exploration of the eternal spiritual conflict.'

In their desire to strip Christ of his aura, Schrader and Scorsese left Gabriel with no alternative but to write music that matched the parched landscape, both physical and emotional. There is little warmth and some absurd lines in the film, like the Schrader–Scorsese in-joke, 'See, this is what happens when a man doesn't marry, the semen backs up into the brain,' that relates to Travis in *Taxi Driver* and Jake La Motta in *Raging Bull*.

The tortured Christ may have appealed to the tortured side of Gabriel but more relevantly here was an artistic opportunity to work with one of Hollywood's greatest directors. It gave Gabriel the chance to step off the rock and roll treadmill and become absorbed in the world music he was so keen to explore and champion. Scorsese's brief was for the music to give a sense of what it might have been like to live during the time of Christ. It was not necessary for the score to be historically or geographically accurate beyond having a Middle East fla-vour, it should feel both ancient and modern. Gabriel listened to hundreds of pieces from around the world, dug up for him by Lucy Duran at the National Sound Archive, part of the British Library. He would make cassettes of ten pieces and send them to Scorsese for his views on which piece would match what scene. Gabriel created a huge sound palette. In his studio he would have masses of cassettes and pieces of paper stuck around the room with names and illustrations to help him quickly match sounds or head off in new directions.

It could go from Armenia to Senegal to Egypt to Brazil as Gabriel explored rhythms and moods on his keyboard, bringing in members of his regular band, notably guitarist David Rhodes and drummer Manu Katche, and musicians like jazz drummer Bill Cobham who happened to be around one day. It was mostly planned, but Gabriel also wanted an improvisational element. One memorable session was with the Pakistani singer Nusrat Fateh Ali Khan and the Indian violinist Shankar. Khan had, in Gabriel's opinion, one of the greatest voices in the world. He sang in a devotional Sufi moslem style called qawwali – designed to promote a mystical union between the individual and God – on a passage for the scene of Christ carrying the cross to Golgotha. Gabriel mixed his panoply of digital hardware with instruments that were unknown in the West, like the arghul drone and the kementché. He drew on the sacred traditions of church music bringing in cor anglais and oboe and a choirboy.

His own religious beliefs similarly drew on different traditions. He could not escape the Christianity of his upbringing and the cloisters of Charterhouse School, but he also felt drawn to Buddhism. When it came to organized religion, despite his respect for holy men he had met, he preferred to take a sceptical view, siding with Bob Dylan's sentiments in his song 'With God On Our Side'.

In the film the music drives the drama only in a few scenes. In the beginning there is a dramatic guitar strum from David Rhodes for the introductory shot of Christ lying on the sand. This music does not appear on record. The tune 'Of These, Hope' adds intensity to Christ wiping Mary Magdalene's feet and a similar motif can be heard throughout the film. And on 'It Is Accomplished', the title taken from Christ's final cinematic words, the eternal salvation and hope represented by Christ's death and resurrection is reflected in Gabriel's soaring tune. Elsewhere the music tends to feel below the surface.

When it came to the *Passion* album Gabriel deconstructed and resurrected the film music in his own image. He abandoned the chronology of the film to allow the album to flow more effectively. Tunes with names of relevant scenes differ on film and record. On the album is a track called 'Stigmata' with strings, synthesizer, percussion and wailing vocals, in the film we hear only the wind and an impending storm when blood seeps from Christ's hands, a premonition of his crucifix wounds.

Gabriel spent seven further months working on *Passion*. 'I think it's some of my best work and I called it *Passion* rather than *Last Temptation of Christ* because I didn't want it to be regarded as just film music. I think that it's a piece of music that stands up in its own right,' he said. The musical setting of Christ's suffering during his last days, traditionally known as the Passion, had an august pedigree that included Bach's *St Matthew's Passion* and Beethoven's *Il Passionata*.

Gabriel achieved his aim of making *Passion* a work independent of the movie. It is homogeneous despite the diversity of its sources. Though he drew from museum archives, it is a breathing work and a departure from anything he had released before. Gabriel avoided the clichés of film scores with their epic sweeps, fanfares and melodrama. There are impressionistic layers of sound, a rhythmic heartbeat and moving melodies. He successfully steered clear of any resemblance to the shallow instrumental New Age style popular in the early eighties. 'With This Love', one of the Western sacred tunes on the album, is intense and beautiful. The whole work is sacred music in the purest sense, evoking a universal spirituality. Despite its inherent darkness, *Passion* has a cleansing meditative power.

It is not, however, easily accessible, more an album that

should be dipped into or used as an atmospheric backdrop. It must have baffled record executives who were used to artists only too ready to capitalize by sticking with the style that brought them success. The press release from Geffen Records, his North American record company, stated, 'This is not the follow-up to the multi-platinum *So* album.' Canadian magazine *Music Express* noted, 'As you read the release sheet from Geffen Records . . . you swear you can hear the sound of execs grinding teeth and ripping hair!' By so avowedly distancing themselves from *Passion*, Geffen were implying it was in some way inferior or a side project, whereas for Gabriel it was a natural development and a work of art to be proud of.

*Passion* was released in June 1989 with an accompanying album, *Passion Sources*, which had tracks from the artists who had helped Gabriel on the main album. For the *Passion* album cover gone were the accessible graphics of *So*, replaced by a bleakly monochrome silhouette of a Christ-like figure.

The critics' views were mostly favourable though often confused by the style of music. In *Q* magazine Robert Sandall wrote, '*Passion* is a potentially mould-shattering marvel. Atmospheric in all the ways that New Age or whatever it calls itself nowadays would like to be but far more *present*, this is the best movie you will never see . . . The album's best tracks are ambiguous, operating in the gap between anguish and serenity. They hold the private, worried world of Peter Gabriel in a delicate balance with the more cheerful, communal idioms of Third World folk music.' *Rolling Stone* opined, '*Passion* is that rare progressive-rock album that isn't so enamoured of its own cleverness that all it does is show off its own technical achievements . . . stirring, stunning stuff.'

For the *Los Angeles Times* there were 'lovely' moments, though 'for all its exotic textures it comes perilously close to being just another synthesizer-heavy "new age" album, suitable for accompanying the occasional wistful wishy-washiness of Scorsese's New Age Jesus'. *Melody Maker* kept up the fine tradition of vitriol and insult in the British weekly music inkies. 'Peter Gabriel is Mr Middlebrow. Everything he's done has been a coffee table version of the ideas of the moment,' wrote Simon Reynolds. After an obscure philosophical diatribe attacking the humanism of world music, the writer schizo-phrenically conceded, 'What sticks in the craw is that it is all rather listenable. Beats like Doric columns, a bass sound like the world turning, winding mists of muezzin prayer wails drifting across from distant dunes, a Cecil B. de Mille approach to the organization of sound . . . Manipulative but undeniably massive.'

*Passion* and *Passion Sources* were the first releases on the Real World label, set up under a finance deal negotiated by Gail Colson and Gabriel with Virgin Records, who wanted to capitalize on the general enthusiasm for world music and dared not let Gabriel secure a deal with a rival major label for fear it might tempt him to defect when his own contract was up. Also released on Real World the same day were Nusrat Fateh Ali Khan and artists from Cuba and Zaire. British journalists were flown out for the launch in Paris, a city with a rich African music tradition. 'Real World is not my label, really; I'm just part of the artist and repertoire team,' commented an over modest Gabriel. Like WOMAD, the label, also housed in Box, served a dual purpose, providing a handy resource for his own explorations and serving his idealistic desire to see world music flourish. He was enjoying the world coming to his armchair with a procession of musicians and dancers visiting his private studio.

No one seriously imagined the Real World label would be a money spinner. Budgets were extremely tight. Even for the late eighties, £10,000 to make an album, including recording, design and marketing, was modest when a new signing to a major label would have at least ten times that amount. With projected sales a mere 2,000 to 10,000 copies per album the budget had to be curtailed. Still, Gabriel was ambitious for his new label. The Real World logo on all albums includes a nine-colour band, each colour signifying a different region of the world. He wanted one day to see record stores carry racks for each region and see the end of the tag 'world', or in America 'world-beat', which he believed implied a certain condescension.

Once more he faced the accusations of cultural imperialism and his response became more forthright and erudite. 'The way I look at it is that you should steal ruthlessly from the things that excite you and turn you on. If you look at a painting like Picasso's *Demoiselles d'Avignon* you can see that he's taking his ideas directly from African masks. Out of that grew Cubism and the movement to modern art. It's equivalent to the distinction between vomit and shit. Vomit goes into the process and gets regurgitated without being digested. Whereas shit goes right through the person's process and is digested and is the healthy way of stealing.'

He expanded on this view to *Premiere* magazine. 'Some people say ethnic music shouldn't have anything to do with rock music and must stay in its own country. To me that's saying, "Stick it in a glass case in a museum." It'll end up maybe as some token tourist piece. To me, that is a far more colonial, imperialist, racist attitude. It's a kind of cultural apartheid. We're learning all the time that events in other countries, whether they're political or environmental or economic, are all interconnected. The days of pretending you can be an isolationist in the world are gone. To encourage people to listen to the world is really important now.'

The hoped for explosion in world music in the late eighties never materialized. TV and radio took a limited interest but audience figures were disappointing despite a modest expansion in the market. Real World was following other innovative British labels: Stern's, the London retailer, label and distributor who were selling a respectable 400,000 albums a year, Earthworks, and the now defunct Mango succeeded by Palm

Pictures. Big labels were on the lookout. Youssou N'Dour, who was signed to Virgin, and Salif Keta on Mango, part of Island Records, looked like they would be breakthrough acts. Despite some successes their following remained in the cult category.

The market in world music has matured showing a gradual and steady increase over the years. Real World Records struggled for the first few years but has since exceeded those early expectations. Nusrat Fateh Ali Khan's first album went on to sell a respectable 60,000 while his later albums topped 100,000. On average Real World albums sell between 20,000 and 50,000. The label's most successful album, the *Afro-Celt Sound System, Volume I*, reached close to 250,000. Though the company has not engendered profits for Gabriel, it is self-financing and has not needed an injection of his cash for several years. Unusually for a record label, most of its albums recoup the initial investment and go on to make, albeit sometimes modest, profits. Virgin Records has found that their indulging Gabriel has turned into a serious piece of business.

It was a younger, altogether hipper, outfit who really started educating a wide public to the appeal of ethnic sounds. M/A/R/R/S, a group of DJs and producers, had a Number 1 hit with 'Pump Up The Volume' in 1987, heralding the impending dance revolution. One of the vocal samples on 'Pump Up The Volume' was culled from an Israeli Yemenite singer, Ofra Haza. Her song, 'Im Nin'Alu', was itself a hit in 1988. Suddenly it was hip to include a bit of an ethnic sample, preferably a heart-rending wail, on a rap or dance record.

There was a major shift in British music culture in 1988 with the advent of the Acid House dance-music phenomenon. Fuelled by the drug Ecstasy, built on the frantic Balearic Beats and relying on the outdoor rave scene and burgeoning club culture, this was never going to be an art form Gabriel could make inroads on, and served to make *Passion* appear further out on the esoteric fringe. Though *Passion* could be heard, to Gabriel's delight, in 'chill-out' rooms at raves.

The difficult task of steering the promotion of *Passion* and the Real World label was one of Steve Hedges' first duties as manager. For Hedges it was a test of strength and *Passion* became a subject of intense argument between the Gabriel camp and Virgin Records. Without any obvious single on the album, Geffen in North America and Virgin throughout the rest of the world were unsure how to market *Passion*.

'They wanted to market it as a pop album, but to do that you have to have hit singles off it, and they're not on it,' says Jon Webster, former managing director at Virgin Records. 'It wasn't a Peter Gabriel album as the world expects a Peter Gabriel album to be. It might well be a Peter Gabriel album in as far as Peter thinks it is. People don't go out and buy it just because it says Peter Gabriel on it, unfortunately.' Gabriel did not want his name or the title of the album printed on the cover, instead he wanted it on a removable sticker so that the CD buyer could appreciate the artwork as art. Webster thought it nonsense, but Gabriel still got his way.

'I was testing out the idea that the visual image on a sleeve was more important as an expression of the contents than the title, that the visual work had a chance to speak more clearly without text all over it which branded it as a piece of merchandise. If I go through my own collection it's the pictures that I remember, the sleeves more than the titles,' says Gabriel.

Hedges was relentless, asking Webster why he wasn't pushing the album more. 'We succeeded in making people more aware of it from time to time,' says Hedges who got tracks included on compilations, but in record company parlance *Passion* 'underperformed', though it did make the UK Top 30. Virgin Records sold 90,000 throughout the world, bar North America. Geffen sold 50,000 in Canada. However in the United States sales were surprisingly respectable, in excess of 500,000, with the final worldwide tally topping a million.

For Jon Webster *Passion* fell into what he called the IAGO syndrome, meaning, ' "I've Already Got One". And when you've already got one, why do you want another one?' He believed the limited public open to such records might want one ethnic record in their collection, but one was enough. There was some comfort for Hedges and Gabriel when *Passion* received a Grammy Award in February 1990 for Best New Age Recording and a nomination for Best Original Score.

'When I first decided to take the project seriously I was being discouraged by the record company and management who told me at the time that the maximum sales I could expect from such a record would be in the region of 10,000. We went over a million a while back so I had quite a smile on my face when I got that news,' Gabriel recalls.

Hedges set about trying to make sense of the Gabriel empire. Real World Studios was up and running and offering itself as a unique recording venue: in what other studio would you see a stream and fish beneath your feet?

Mike Large was moving up the hierarchy, from running the studio to becoming Head of Operations of Real World Holdings. This was a new company created on the recommendation of a management consultancy brought in to suggest how Gabriel could rationalize his operation and stop money haemorrhaging. Steve Hedges came in believing rationalization and control of Gabriel's various companies was one of his prime functions. Unfortunately, so did Large and Maria Pedro, an old school friend of Jill's who Gabriel hired as his business manager after Colson's departure.

The first of Gabriel's companies to be axed was Syco Systems, formed by his cousin Stephen Paine to distribute the Fairlight, the first commercial sampler. After a period of high profitability in the mid-eighties, Syco was undercut by advancing technology as the price of samplers plummeted.

Syco had invested its extra cash in an innovative product called the Tablet (for those in the know the Tablet was a hard-disc-based digital-audio editor) that used the Inmos Transputer. According to Mike Large the Tablet was at least ten years ahead of its time. The product was built at Real World and twelve were sold to the BBC. Being home grown they were not, in the jargon, product engineered, and were highly unreliable. Gabriel, aware he could not fund the product to get it properly engineered, tried to sell the company. He declined an offer from Studer, the prestigious Swiss tape manufacturer, in favour of a British company, who subsequently went bust, by which time the Studer offer had disappeared. The Tablet operation, and with it Syco Systems, had to be closed. It was a compelling example of why Gabriel should step back from day to day business affairs.

Gabriel was also a partner in Box Products with designer Russell Bagley and his wife Hilary, who were recommended by Gabriel's friend, the artist Graham Dean. Box Products produced a limited range of home furniture and light fittings, not immediately the kind of business one would associate with Gabriel. However, their philosophy fitted in with his own concept of 'high-tech and hand made' that applied to everything emanating from Real World. There were chairs and chests of drawers made out of steel, copper and glass. Box Products also provided a design consultancy for shops and bars. The products were expensive and turnover limited. Gabriel was eventually persuaded to sell his share to the Bagleys.

Hedges focused on creating cash flow by using Gabriel's core business, his music. Aware that at Gabriel's usual work rate a new album was not going to be forthcoming for a couple of years he turned his attention to a leftover project, the live concert video of the *So* tour, which was filmed but never released. It had been a tortuous process since it was first planned.

Gabriel's search for a visionary director for the video had taken him to Nicaragua in May 1987 to see if he and Alex Cox could work together. Gabriel also pursued and met David Lynch, director of *The Elephant Man, Eraserhead* and *Blue Velvet*; Bernardo Bertolucci, director of *Last Tango in Paris, La Luna* and *1900*; and he talked to Volker Schlöndorff, director of *The Tin Drum*. All had other commitments.

It was not until the last European leg of the tour that his plans finally looked like they would be realized. Martin Scorsese came to the rescue. Though unable to direct he sent in his place his cinematographer Michael Chapman who had worked on *The Last Waltz*, the classic concert film of The Band's final performance, on *Taxi Driver, New York, New York* and *Raging Bull*, and on Michael Jackson's video *Bad*.

By the official final date of the *So* tour in Budapest, Hungary, on 15 September 1987, his first time behind the Iron Curtain, Gabriel had played to over one million people. For the purposes of the video two extra dates were fixed for Athens a month later. Michael Chapman, credited as concert director on the video, arranged the set, lighting and camera angles on Scorsese's instructions. Scorsese planned to edit the result, though in the event he was only credited as executive producer.

Prior to the final leg of the tour Gabriel, on Scorsese's recommendation, met the playwright Dennis Potter. Gabriel was enthused as they discussed the possibility of co-writing some fantasy sequences. It was an idea that never materialized, along with so many other grand schemes for the video. Gabriel explained what he was looking for. 'Live shows can be pretty boring by the time they get to film. I would like to try and somehow get to represent what it is like to be in my position. Normally you have the concert as seen from the audience, it would be nice to cut away and treat the music as raw material so if you want to stop in the middle of a number and cut away to silence you can do that rather than requiring the music to stay intact.' He wanted to satisfy the demand for performance footage while escaping the genre's predictability.

The resulting work, *P.O.V.*, is no conventional performance video. The show footage is considerably enhanced through careful editing with newsreel, family film and special effects. The keen-eyed will spot Rosanna Arquette by Gabriel's side for a second as he arrives in a tuxedo at a film gala in Cannes. Gabriel is holding a camcorder and filming his tormentors, the press photographers. This illustrates the opening track, 'This Is The Picture'. The show proceeds through twelve numbers. 'San Jacinto' has him projected on to rippling blue water, there is a Red Indian dressed in feathers performing a ritual dance and shots of chiefs. The camera catches the show from every angle, from crowd's-eye view to aerial overview. The waving arm shots are thankfully minimal and gleeful fan faces mercifully non-existent.

Piecing together the flashes of family archive film, the story of Gabriel's life unfolds, though Jill gets left out. We see a happy boy playing football and Cowboys and Indians ('Games Without Frontiers') cut with child soldiers and child concentration camp inmates and Jack Healey addressing a press conference on the Conspiracy of Hope tour. 'Mercy Street' has the line 'in your daddy's arms' and we see baby Gabriel on his father's knees and his own daughters as young children. In the backstage shots of 'Sledgehammer' there's a glimpse of then manager Gail Colson. As Gabriel takes his bow in the performance it switches to a Genesis-era Gabriel bowing.

The film successfully captures Gabriel's terror and courage in performing 'Lay Your Hands'. He builds the song as if going into a trance, willing himself to the inevitable climax, standing on the edge of the stage, back to the audience, his arms are held out crucifix-like. Aloft on the audience's arms you catch his face, his fear hidden as he feigns having fun. He vainly tries to hold on to his white jacket as the crowd rips it off. Carried back on stage his T-shirt is in tatters and he is visibly elated.

The finale, 'Biko', was always arresting throughout that tour. Youssou N'Dour was on stage to add to the impact; he and Gabriel in their matching many-coloured ethnic jackets. It is cut with film of coffins being lowered into the ground and Gabriel sings his forbidding lyrics, 'You can blow out a candle/ but you can't blow out a fire.' He finishes punching the air and uttering, 'For all those still in jail in South Africa. For all those still being tortured. For all prisoners of conscience. For Steven Biko.' It was a scene Gabriel and N'Dour would repeat in concerts for Nelson Mandela and the Human Rights Now! tour.

*P.O.V. – Point of View* – was joyfully received in *Q* magazine in December 1989. That Gabriel is 'one of the most irresistible rock performers of all time would seem to go against nature', wrote Phil Sutcliffe. 'But it's the truth and this video of his 1987 tour is there to prove it for posterity.' Unfortunately for Gabriel the review was drastically premature, the video had been sent out for review by mistake. He had hoped *P.O.V.* could be first shown in cinemas. It was another year before the video was released after it became clear there would be no cinema distribution. By then anyone enthused by the *Q* review, a magazine targeting Gabriel's key market, would not still be searching for it in the shops.

Steve Hedges had a more profitable project in mind for Gabriel, who had never issued a greatest hits album. Hedges knew if he was to get Gabriel's approval for such a release he had to present an artistic rather than a commercial case. Gabriel had long resisted the idea of a hits compilation. It was not making money that he found distasteful, he did not mind cashing in if he felt he had done something creatively to deserve it. What he found distasteful was the usual practice of marketing departments taking charge of hits packages, making a simple selection based on sales. That was far too straight-forward for Gabriel's taste, and anyway, there had been only five Top 30 singles up to this point in his career, enough to fill just half an album.

Gabriel put some fresh if modestly applied artistic blood into the compilation, *Shaking The Tree: 16 Golden Greats*. The title had a sly twist in it, a parody of old hit compilations with the same title. Golden Greats are not necessarily greatest hits. The selection was idiosyncratic, reflecting what he considered his greatest achievements. The title track was relatively obscure, co-written with Youssou N'Dour, it had appeared as a single the previous year and had only made it to Number 61. The song 'Zaar' from the *Passion* album was there, it was never a single. By including it he could draw attention to an album he considered cruelly overlooked. The most notable omission was 'In Your Eyes' from *So* in favour of the less accessible 'Mercy Street'. With five tracks from *So* he had to be careful not to over represent the album.

Most of the classics included from his career are the original versions. He removed the tinkly and dated early-eighties synth pop sound on 'I Have The Touch' and made it rhythmically stronger. The only dramatic transformation was 'Here Comes The Flood', newly recorded and sung solo to piano in a Randy Newman style, avoiding building into the anthemic chorus. It is muted and all the more effective for it.

The album was released all over the world in December 1990. Its chances of becoming the intended money spinner in the United States looked less likely when Gabriel insisted that the CD should not be packaged in the 'longbox' – a cardboard and plastic box the length of an LP and half the width which served no purpose other than to enable stores to display CDs in their old LP racks.

'It was the source of a tirade from David Geffen saying this was commercial suicide. Peter felt strongly, and I felt strongly, with regard to the stupidity of this. We weren't trying to change the world, but certainly if there's anything you can do to stop such stupidity with regard to waste I think one has some sort of responsibility,' said Steve Hedges.

With Canada having recently abandoned use of the long-box, America was left as the sole country using this wasteful packaging. One estimate reckoned that it used the equivalent of 200,000 trees to manufacture the cardboard CD longboxes sold in the United States in 1991.

Eddie Rosenblatt, president of Geffen, told the *Los Angeles Times* in November 1990, 'When Peter came to us a few weeks ago and said he wanted to put this out without a longbox, I told him of all the consequences. He knows this means he's going to lose a lot of sales, but he's willing to take the punishment. It's difficult to quantify, but judging from our discussions with our sales and distribution people, it could cost us 40 per cent of the records we'd normally ship to our accounts.' The newspaper estimated Geffen were shipping 100,000 less than its normal 250,000. Rosenblatt did not want to antagonize retailers, saying he believed they wanted to phase out the longbox 'in an orderly fashion'.

Retailers defended the longbox's size as a deterrent to shoplifters, complained about the cost of redesigning store fixtures and feared the theft of the more pocketable 'jewel box' – the standard plastic container which they said was too small to catch the eye of consumers. The major record companies were not keen to put pressure on retailers, particularly since some record companies had a financial interest in the longbox manufacturers. The only dissenting voices in the industry were small labels like Rykodisc and I.R.S. who banded together under the name Ban the Box to campaign for an end to the longbox.

The longbox was staunchly defended by Russ Solomon, president of Tower Records, who told the *Los Angeles Times* in April 1990 that phasing out the longbox was 'just not going to happen. We're adamantly opposed to it.' He believed the jewel box worked fine for Europe and Japan because of 'the small stores that they have over there'. Though many artists may well have not objected to the longbox, concerned not to alienate retailers and lose sales, none were vociferous in support of keeping the longbox in circulation.

Gabriel was the second major artist to insist on a jewel-box only release. The first, in September 1990, was Raffi, a popular children's performer, whose contract with MCA Records stipulated his album *Evergreen Everblue* was released in a jewel box. When *Shaking The Tree* was released in America on 4 December, 1990, some stores refused to stock it. So concerned were other retailers over jewel-box thefts they kept *Shaking The Tree* CDs stocked behind the counter, a hindrance to impulse buying. The Wherehouse Entertainment chain informed Geffen they would definitely have sold more of *Shaking The Tree* if it was in a longbox and raised the price on Gabriel's CD because of additional merchandising and handling costs.

The album entered the Billboard chart at Number 48 and slipped to 50 the following week. It was not as bad as it seemed. Geffen's fears of a 40 per cent loss of sales proved pessimistic, in the end they reckoned the loss was 'minuscule'. In the early nineties the CD market was still vying for format precedence, accounting for around 40 per cent of total recorded music sales. Geffen found Gabriel was selling 65 per cent of *Shaking The Tree* on CD, though his older and more affluent core audience were more likely to own CD players anyway. In the end, at sales of 2 million in the United States, *Shaking The Tree* has become his second bestselling album after *So*. It was a similar pattern in Britain where sales reached 600,000.

Gabriel's environmental campaigner colleague and friend Sting released his album *The Soul Cages* six weeks after *Shaking The Tree*. Sting did not take as proactive a stance as Gabriel, leaving his record company a freer marketing hand. His first 300,000 albums were released in the longbox and the rest in an alternative more recyclable version of the longbox. The retailers and record companies realized they had to bow to the mood of the consumer which was strongly for change. On 24 February 1992, the day before the Grammy Awards in New York, the heads of the major American record companies met and agreed to phase out the longbox by April 1993. It was a decision met with fury by Tower's Russ Solomon, saying it was 'the coward's way out'. The record companies said they would help towards the $100-million estimated cost of converting record-store racks across America. The CD longbox was finally consigned to the dustbin of consumerism where it had belonged from the start.

# CHAPTER SIXTEEN

FTER THE FINAL BUENOS AIRES DATE OF the Human Rights Now! tour, Gabriel jetted to Los Angeles to be with Rosanna Arquette. He had a date with her and Hollywood. Arquette was in mid-film, starring opposite Nick Nolte in 'Life Lessons', a fraught, emotional tale of a viciously jealous painter and a distraught girlfriend desperate to escape his clasp. It was directed by Martin Scorsese, Arquette and Gabriel's mutual friend, his part of a triptych called *New York Stories* whose other directors were Woody Allen and Francis Ford Coppola. Gabriel had a ten-second, walk-on part as a guest at a party. An uncharacteristically strident Gabriel is seen rudely interrupting Arquette who is trying to say hello to Steve Buscemi, who then ignores her to say, 'Peter!' Excusing his lateness and rudeness, Gabriel utters quite convincingly, 'I have a friend here. I'd like you to meet Hank.' According to Arquette it took him twenty takes to get it right. Gabriel treated it in the spirit it was offered, joking, 'I'm quite hopeful about my chances for an Oscar.'

The passionate affair between Arquette and Gabriel was worthy of its own Hollywood screenplay. From the start of their relationship in 1982 they had been torn and drawn; Gabriel between loyalty to Jill and the family, Rosanna with her marriage to James Newton Howard. Ever since their original split in 1984 Arquette and Gabriel had kept in touch and, according to Arquette, 'never really let each other go'.

In October 1987 they were back together. By now Rosanna had separated from Newton Howard, and Gabriel was attempting to separate from Jill, though as Christmas approached he returned to his family. 'And that was a very, very, very painful time in my life, when I told him I wanted no contact and didn't want to hear from him again,' said Arquette. From January to May 1988 they never talked. She was in Cannes promoting the film *The Big Blue* when, 'He called me there, he said he had moved out. I was silent on the phone. I don't know how he found me either, so it was really his decision. He loves me, but he made his decision without me around and I had no idea that this is what he had to do.'

Divorce proceedings were underway for the Gabriels. After living temporarily in his studio at Real World, Gabriel moved into a small terraced house in the village of Box for a while, not wanting anything bigger because he did not have the energy to deal with it. In 1988 he bought a mill cottage just up the river from the studio and enjoyed the fact that he could row to work.

'This is a very exciting time but it is a very personally painful time for all of us . . . Nobody wants to hurt anybody but this has been a lot of years and we have tried to go on with our lives and forget each other,' Arquette said at the time. 'He cares very deeply for and will forever be deeply connected to Jill.' She was gracious in her praise of Jill.

In trying therapy to sort out their problems the Gabriels had followed an un-English tradition. Arquette had, as a Californian, long been an enthusiast. When Gabriel abandoned the couples therapy with Jill he continued solo with Meg Sharpe, a colleague of Robin Skynner's. He was encouraged by Arquette who said, 'We are both growing spiritually and finding out who we are by going to therapy, and that is very important.'

Gabriel knew that by advocating therapy in Britain one is forced on the defensive, and supporting spiritual growth, however admirable or necessary, invites scorn. 'I wish people wouldn't see therapy as something that happens when you're sick, you could avoid a lot of sickness,' he told *NME* in June 1989. 'As soon as you go in there and see the people you're doing it with you don't feel in the presence of a company of nutters.'

He noted how he had progressed during his time in therapy. 'It was interesting when I first went to the group, I think I was seen more as a man or child, and when I left I was seen as man or parent. There were shifts in the way other people behaved towards me, and I got more comfortable being an adult.' The group was protective towards him at first. 'I came in bruised,' he says. 'In truth we're all composed of three elements, child, adult, parent. There are different balances for different people.'

As a glamorous couple Gabriel and Arquette were not going to avoid interest from the press. She told *Rolling Stone* in August 1988, 'We're together, and we don't want to talk about it. We want to keep it pure and not get it all disgusting in the press. That's from both of us.' It was a futile wish. They became regular tabloid fodder over the next couple of years.

After the Human Rights Now! tour Gabriel was to spend as much time as possible with Arquette. At the end of 1988 and in early 1989, while he was finishing off the *Passion* soundtrack at Real World, she came to stay. In February 1989, somewhat belatedly, the *Sunday Mirror* reported that the on-off affair of Peter Gabriel and Rosanna Arquette 'has been rekindled in the plush French resort of Val d'Isere'. We were informed that the couple, with Anna and Melanie, had been keeping a low profile in the ski resort. As guests of Richard Branson, 'They have been seen sampling Branson's champagne hospitality.' Whether they were seen on the piste with a bottle of Bollinger in hand is not clear.

The *Daily Star* reported the following April that the couple were to marry, six months ahead of the *Sun* who revealed

Gabriel had splashed out on a *fictitious* £10,000 emerald engagement ring and presented it to Arquette during a 'candle-lit dinner' at an Indian restaurant in Corsham, Wiltshire. They even made the pages of gushy *Hello!* magazine pictured, kids in tow again, at the premiere of *Back To The Future II*.

The difficulties and uncertainties ever present in their relationship surfaced in an interview given by Arquette to the *Daily Mail* in 1990. 'I love him,' she said. 'We are both in love and spend a lot of time together. In fact, I intend to come and live in Britain but who can tell whether Peter and I will remain together in the long term? I don't know.'

Whatever their personal frictions, the strain of bicontinental careers was always going to be difficult. It was Arquette who attempted the move to Wiltshire, rather than Gabriel to California, a move bound to affect her career. The inevitable consequence was a devaluation of her own worth by subjugating her personality and career to his. She later claimed she had turned down offers of major movies in order to be with him. When she appeared in romantic scenes in movies he admitted being jealous. She believed Gabriel was threatened by her celebrity, though he thought it a non-issue.

Increasingly she felt like one of his entourage. Early on in their rekindled relationship she had celebrated their mutual supportiveness. How he read her scripts and she listened to his music. She would later contradict this saying there was no respect for what she did and that it was all about taking care of him and making him look good. Gabriel remembers reading scripts until the end of their relationship and spending much more time discussing her career than his.

Over Easter 1990, just before the tribute concert celebrating Nelson Mandela's release, Arquette went shopping for clothes and other items for Gabriel's band. Backstage at Wembley Stadium he was frantic and asked her to relay a message, 'Tell them I can't talk right now.' As she was passing on, 'Peter can't talk right now,' she had a sense she had 'lost it' as an actress, that this was where she had ended up, doing roadie work for Peter Gabriel. She told him of her unhappiness in a characteristically blunt way, 'Do you know what?' she said. 'This is crap.' When Bonnie Raitt came up to her at the show and said how much she enjoyed her work Arquette was sure her instincts were right. 'I said, "I'm going to LA." I went the next day and I got three movies back to back within three days of being there.'

On the cold day of the Mandela concert the rain cleared as Gabriel joined a varied cast that included Daniel Lanois, Dave Stewart, Neil Young, Simple Minds, Natalie Cole, Lenny Henry and Denzel Washington, who acted the part of Steve Biko in *Cry Freedom*. A banner over the stage read, 'The Struggle Is My Life', the title of a book of Mandela's writings and speeches. Even then the end of apartheid seemed difficult to imagine as Mandela, just two months out of prison after twenty-seven years' incarceration, told the crowd, 'Reject any suggestion that the campaign to isolate the apartheid system should be wound down.' He predicted, 'It will not be long now before we see an end to the apartheid system. The dreams of millions of people to see our country free and at peace will be realized sooner rather than later.'

The relationship between Gabriel and Arquette had three more months before playing itself out. Near the end, in July 1990, the *Sunday Express* published an interview with Arquette in which she revealingly, if jokingly, said, 'You English are all the same – you're afraid of emotion! I live with an Englishman, I know.' In August she was interviewed by the *Today* newspaper at the Edinburgh Film Festival where she was promoting the movie *Black Rainbow* and talked of wanting marriage and children, though Gabriel no longer appeared to be indispensable in that set-up. To avoid having to talk about the true situation she maintained the deception that the relationship was still continuing. 'Peter and I talk about getting married but we have just been having so much fun living in sin,' she told

Lester Middlehurst. 'I think we are both on a journey of self-growth right now and marriage is a really big decision that we will come to sooner or later, with or without each other. The thought is there. We are very happy together and I would like it to happen – but marriage is such an important commitment that I want to be really sure that it is with the right person.'

That same August the *Daily Mirror* surmised that Arquette was terrified Gabriel would dump her when he found out she had appeared nude on the cover of the September issue of *Playboy* magazine and her frolics spread over eight pages inside. Gabriel has always dismissed the notion that this had any impact on the relationship. Arquette had not read the small print when she signed her contractual release for a swimsuit modelling session in Florida. The photographer was able to sell the pictures on without her permission. Technically, though not morally, the *Mirror* was correct in its assertion that, 'Top photographer Bert Stern insists she signed a contract allowing him to sell the sexy snaps for publication anywhere except Britain – where Gabriel lives.'

For Arquette's thirty-first birthday on 10 August Gabriel took her and his daughters to Disneyworld in Orlando, Florida. Arquette had marriage on her mind. Gabriel was in no mood to make a commitment. The result was a furious row and their relationship ended in the theme park. It was already over by the time Arquette had given her interview to *Today* and the *Mirror* had speculated on Gabriel's *Playboy* fury.

It took six weeks for word of the break-up to filter into the press. The papers turned into pseudo-fact the *Mirror*'s original supposition about Gabriel's attitude to the *Playboy* pictures and cited that as the cause. It compelled Gabriel to make a statement: 'Rosanna and I are no longer together. We are very fond of each other, and will continue to be friends. It is untrue that the *Playboy* pictures had any influence on our decision. I have never had any problem with nudity or with these photos, which I think look great, and do not belong to the traditionally exploitative school of photography.' He was angry not with Arquette, but with the photographer for ripping her off and *Playboy* for not paying her anything. 'They were taken for a smut-free travel magazine and the photographer agreed with Rosanna that they would under no circumstances be sold to *Playboy*.'

Within a few months Gabriel was again issuing a statement about a relationship, this time with Sinead O'Connor. The two had met at An Embrace Of Hope, an Amnesty International concert for human rights in Santiago in October 1990 to celebrate Chile's freedom from seventeen years of tyranny under the military dictatorship of General Augusto Pinochet. Just two years earlier the Human Rights Now! tour had been refused permission to enter the country, now six months after the detested Pinochet had finally relinquished power Gabriel was on stage in the country's national stadium duetting with O'Connor on 'Don't Give Up'.

More prosaic issues were concerning the *Sun* newspaper. Gabriel's spokesman told them, 'I've spoken to Peter and he says he has become very good friends with Sinead. That is all he wishes to say.' The paper had been alerted by a story in Q magazine quoting Sinead as saying, 'Peter's a weirdo but I think he's lovely. He's one of the most beautiful people I have ever met. He is incredibly unusual for a man. He goes out of his way to help people and be normal and friendly. He is absolutely bonkers too though – barking mad.'

Chile had become a safer place. Elsewhere the world was becoming far more unstable. In August 1990 Iraq unexpectedly invaded Kuwait and then refused to comply with UN resolutions demanding its withdrawal. In December 1990, at the annual Reebok Human Rights Awards in Boston, Gabriel made a speech attacking Saddam Hussein, and the West for not responding to the plight of the Kurds. 'We are all now aware that Saddam Hussein is a gross violator of human rights. Reports from Iraq and Kuwait are chilling. Yet when Hussein systematically attacked tens of thousands of Kurds in Northern Iraq with bombs and chemical weapons, killing over 10,000 men, women and children, where was the outrage, where were the governments, the champions of human rights?'

Gabriel introduced Akram Mayi, there to tell the assembled dignitaries and celebrities like Jackson Browne, Lou Reed, Joan Baez and Carly Simon the plight of his people who had been driven from their villages in Iraqi Kurdistan by the use of chemical weapons. Twenty-seven thousand Iraqi Kurds were forced to live in Turkish refugee camps where there were reports of mass poisonings, beatings and lack of medical supplies, water and electricity.

In January 1991 the American-led build-up of troops in the Persian Gulf reached its inevitable conclusion with the start of the Gulf War. Technology put on its ugly face introducing us to the concepts of so-called smart bombs and surgical strikes. A massive air attack on the capital Baghdad and other targets failed to budge President Saddam Hussein's forces. Then at the end of February the multinational forces began their ground attack on Iraqi troops in Kuwait, liberating the country within days. In the north of Iraq, on its borders with Turkey and Iran, the Kurdish minority, encouraged by the Western powers, had rebelled against Saddam. It had terrible consequences and the pictures of fleeing refugees starving and shivering in the mountains stirred the heart of Jeffrey Archer, then known chiefly as deputy Chairman of the Conservative Party and writer of popular fiction.

Archer enlisted the help of promoter Harvey Goldsmith, who had organized the Live Aid concert. The first artist to volunteer his services to what became known as Kurd Aid was Chris de Burgh, who donated his song 'The Simple Truth' to the cause. On 12 May 1991 The Simple Truth concert for Kurdish Refugees opened at Wembley Arena, attended by Prime Minister John Major and Princess Diana, and was linked via satellite to Manchester then to The Hague where Peter

Gabriel sang 'Games Without Frontiers' accompanied by Sting. They were followed, also in The Hague, by Sinead O'Connor who sang a new song, 'My Special Child'. The link-ups then continued around the world.

The concert was bedevilled by controversy. The day before the show, with fresh disasters in Bangladesh and Ethiopia subsequent to the Kurdish crisis, Sting, Gabriel and O'Connor called for the cash raised by the concert to be distributed more widely. 'I am not trying to cast a cloud over Kurd Aid and we are not threatening to withdraw,' said Sting. 'But because of new circumstances we feel that it would be inhuman to ignore other tragedies that have occurred since.'

The British Red Cross, the main beneficiary of Kurd Aid with the United Nations, said that as the appeal was set up specifically to help Kurdish refugees they were legally not allowed to spend it on other purposes. But by freeing funds they would otherwise have allocated to the Kurds they were able to spend it in other areas. Controversy clouded the concert's achievement of raising £57 million. Newspaper allegations that the money was not passed on to the relevant agencies proved unfounded.

Inspired by his involvement with the 1988 Human Rights Now! tour, Gabriel was fired to take a more activist role in the human rights movement. Reebok was keen to carry on its commitment to human rights which was to become an integral part of the company's ethos. In 1988, the annual Reebok Human Rights Awards was set up to honour and draw attention to non-violent human rights activists around the world below the age of thirty.

In recognition of his standing, Gabriel was invited to sit on the Board of Advisers by Paul Fireman, chairman and CEO of Reebok and the architect of Reebok's human rights activities. Gabriel joined President Jimmy Carter, R.E.M. singer Michael Stipe, the poet Rose Styron, Kerry Kennedy Cuomo, the founder of the Robert F. Kennedy Memorial Center for

Human Rights, and other worthies and human rights professionals.

They meet every year for one day of brainstorming at Reebok's headquarters in Stoughton, outside Boston, to choose the four winning recipients. 'It's extraordinarily emotional to read and to be inspired by their stories,' says Sharon Cohen, vice president of publicity for the Reebok Human Rights Foundation. The recipients donate their $25,000 award to their nominated human rights organization. There is always one recipient from the United States to counter charges of human rights imperialism.

Gabriel and his fellow advisers are on hand throughout the year to advise the Reebok Foundation on human rights issues and may be asked to intervene, for instance in the case of an imprisoned recipient. 'It's not a name board that goes on letterhead. Everybody works on it, everybody is really engaged and involved,' says Cohen, effusive in her praise of Gabriel.

Reebok is not alone in being a socially responsible company, Levi Strauss, Ben and Jerry's, The Body Shop all have their own programmes; ethical business has become a millennial catchphrase. Reebok unusually encroaches on the kind of dangerous territory where many such companies, concerned for their shareholders, may fear to put their cushioned trainers, and bans child labour from its factories, enforcing its own monitoring system. With a turnover of $3 billion and growing, Reebok has muscle and is yet to experience any detrimental effects on trade arising from its human rights stance. According to Sharon Cohen the company's ethical policy is a great source of pride to employees, which by stimulating loyalty is itself beneficial to trade, though she doubts it makes much difference to customers. 'If an employee feels good about where they work that's got to improve your market share ultimately. Does anybody walk into a store and say I'll take the Human Rights Award brand? No.'

It occurred to Gabriel while on the Human Rights Now!

tour that the immediacy and impact of video footage could be put to good use in the human rights movement. He had taken his camcorder with him to make a personal archive of events as they unfolded backstage, on stage, in the audience, at press conferences, on the plane and just about everywhere in between. It was here that the idea for the Witness Program germinated. He believed the media was more likely to pick up stories if footage was available. Footage could also be a source of hard evidence of human rights abuses and in the televisual age more likely to have an impact on public opinion than the written word.

He discussed his idea with Paul Fireman of Reebok who was enthusiastic and provided the finance to set up the project through the Reebok Foundation. Also keen was Michael Posner, executive director of the Lawyers Committee for Human Rights and a fellow member of the Human Rights Award board. The Lawyers Committee had been campaigning since 1978 to hold governments, including that of the United States, accountable to the standards of the International Bill of Human Rights, and Witness seemed a natural adjunct to their struggle. Posner gave Witness space in the committee's New York offices. At the Witness launch in March 1991 Posner announced, 'It's time for us, the human rights movement, to better use the communications revolution to expose abuses and galvanize public opinion to stop them.' Gabriel gave some tasty soundbites at the launch, including 'cameras are more powerful than guns', and 'technology transcends all borders. Information is power.'

Gabriel wrote of Witness, 'Very often things are reported in the press, but governments can deny what is going on, and do deny it frequently. It's very hard to say it didn't happen when you have a piece of video and it gets on the news. So, as with the Rodney King case in California, there are, I think, examples of video having an increasing impact in the campaigns for civil and human rights.' In March 1991 King was captured by an amateur cameraman in Los Angeles as he was being beaten up by four police officers. The acquittal of the policemen on assault charges in 1992 sparked off three days of rioting and arson in Los Angeles that left fifty-three people dead and caused $1 billion of damage.

Gabriel's vision appeared to be immediately vindicated. That initial year of operation the first cameras went to Haiti at the request of local human rights activists after the elected President Father Jean-Bertrand Aristide was deposed by the military. According to Gabriel, 'within a day they were being used to film people being beaten up on the street'. But when the footage was offered for sale to the news networks and the proceeds pocketed by the cameraman Witness realized a lot of the small print in their agreement with human rights groups had to be sorted out.

There were inevitably many unforeseen hurdles. It seemed a simple enough idea, marrying Gabriel's belief in the power of technology with human rights, yet simply getting cameras into the field could be tricky. Several Witness cameras have been either impounded or had prohibitive customs charges placed on them. Witness has smuggled cameras over borders, deemed necessary where recipients might be put at risk, and smuggled film out again.

It became apparent that not everyone was as conscientious as they might be about using the cameras. In 1992 the advisory committee donated fifty cameras to activists under the umbrella label Non-Government Organizations around the world, but returned footage was scarcer than expected. By 1995 only ten NGOs had been providing worthwhile footage. A mantra came to be adopted at Witness, 'a camera is a relationship'. There is now a careful vetting process, human rights groups have to sign a contract detailing their obligations to Witness in return for the equipment. Training is provided in the field, both technical and on how to create stories and set goals. These are skills many regimes would not like to see developed.

RIGHT: Gail Colson, Peter Gabriel's manager from 1978–1988, in a peaceful break from a stressful life touring, summer 1987.

BELOW: Bon viveur and raconteur Tony Stratton Smith holds forth. His belief in Genesis despite early failures was crucial in allowing their talent to develop and mature. (Barrie Wentzell)

ABOVE: Gabriel and Rhodes jump to it at the Tourhout Festival in Belgium on 1 July 1983 during the Playhouse '88 tour. Picture taken by Larry Fast from his synthesizer position during 'I Have the Touch'. (Larry Fast)

BELOW: The multi-award-winning 'Sledgehammer' took a hundred hours to shoot over eight days in Bristol, April 1986. (Armando Gallo/Retna Pictures Ltd)

ABOVE: At his Ashcombe House studio with the Fairlight CMI synthesizer in 1986. Gabriel predicted the synthesizer and sampler would become the most important instrument of that decade and, as it proved, the next.

BELOW: Gesture plays an important part in Gabriel's carefully choreographed stage movements. During the first leg of the This Way Up tour on 16 December 1986 at the Los Angeles Forum. (Margaret Maxwell)

ABOVE: The song 'Lay Your Hands On Me' was the cue for the most dramatic moment of Gabriel's stage show as he plunged into the audience. It frequently resulted in the loss of clothes and shoes, as here at the Los Angeles Forum on 16 December 1986. He has subsequently given up the practice. (Margaret Maxwell)

LEFT: Jill and Peter at the Ivor Novello songwriting awards in London, in April 1987, a year before they finally split. (Syndication International)

ABOVE: Peter Gabriel and President Daniel Ortega of Nicaragua, his ministers and officials during their ninety-minute meeting in May 1987 when Sandinista rule had reached its short-lived zenith. (Matt Mahurin)

BELOW: Gabriel and Sting were not sure Bruce Springsteen was amused when they surprised him by dressing up in his own clothes to impersonate him in 'Twist and Shout' at the final Human Rights Now! show in Buenos Aires on 15 October 1988. (Neal Preston)

LEFT: As glamorous film and rock stars Rosanna Arquette and Peter Gabriel put on their best showbiz grins for the paparazzi at the *Dick Tracy* movie premiere in London in June 1990. (Pat Lyttle)

BELOW: Having previously shied away from surrounding himself with a bevy of beauties, as is a rock star's birthright, Gabriel finally gave way on the 'Steam' video, as this break in filming shows, with girls somewhat less modestly clad than himself. (Stephen Lovell-Davis)

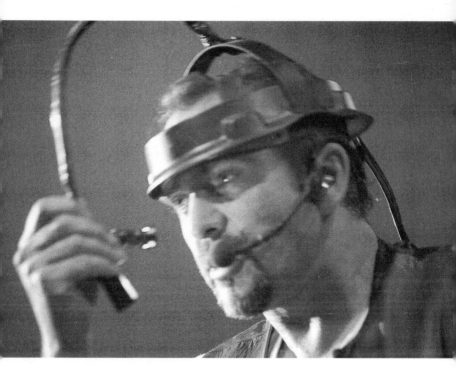

ABOVE: Performing 'Digging in the Dirt' on the Secret World tour in Modena, Italy, in November 1993. The micro-camera poised at the end of the antenna attached to Gabriel's cranium gave audiences a dentist's eye view of his features via a video display. (Stephen Lovell-Davis)

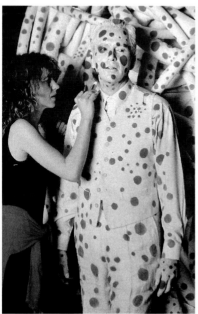

LEFT: Gabriel in a spot of bother as he is apparently uncomfortably made up on set for the video of 'Lovetown', where his inner decay is represented on the outside by a nasty skin and clothes rash. (Stephen Lovell-Davis)

CLOCKWISE:

The drama of this day, at the MTV Awards at the Universal Ampitheatre, Los Angeles, on 2 September 1993, was about to unfold with a suicide attempt by Sinead O'Connor whose wish to rekindle her affair with Gabriel was rejected. (Steve Granitz)

Gabriel checks out the theme-park competition at the celebrity opening of Space Mountain at Disneyland, Paris on 31 May 1995. Trying to not look too goofy he leaves an imprint of his hands cheered on by a spacesuited Mickey Mouse.

A portrait of the artist in 1992 staring meaningfully into the middle distance. Face to face Gabriel is an intense eyeballer. A man with a vision, he sees a future most of us are yet to even dream of. (Stephen Lovell-Davis)

When Sukenya Pillay, the programme director, organized a training workshop in Cairo in 1995 for Middle East human rights activists all cameras were confiscated at the airport despite prior government approval. The activists were followed throughout their stay in Egypt and their cameras returned only on their departure.

Such activists are aware that merely pointing a camera can be a dangerous act, as in some countries is mere possession of equipment. Government soldiers have ransacked NGO offices and destroyed Witness cameras and tapes in Liberia and in the Mobutu regime in the former Zaire, now the Democratic Republic of the Congo.

There have been basic difficulties in getting film out of troubled regions. It took four months for footage of refugee massacres to get out of the former Zaire, footage that was eventually transmitted on TV. Witness hopes the advent of digital cameras and the transferral of video over the internet will overcome such problems and is building an archive so that evidence is immediately on hand.

Witness cameras have provided irrefutable evidence of atrocities. Exhumed mass graves have been filmed in the former Yugoslavia and in Rwanda, and Witness hoped its film would be used as evidence in the International Criminal Tribunals investigating war crimes in those countries. They have filmed graves being exhumed in Haiti in the gathering of evidence against coup leaders. One of Witness' earliest triumphs was filming torture victims in Turkish Kurdistan.

As well as exposing past atrocities, they hope they can discourage future violations of human rights by compiling reports or being on the spot as trouble develops. Cameras have been used to gather information for the United Nations Human Rights Committee on the activities of the Bolivian Government. One group in Guatemala claims its camera has been helpful in actions they are bringing against the police for having tortured or beaten up street children.

In 1996 and 1997 Witness cameras used by the Committee on the Administration for Justice monitored the two week summer Marching Season in Northern Ireland. Witness was proud its footage of alleged Royal Ulster Constabulary abuses was used as evidence requested by the US Congressional Hearings on Northern Ireland, the Parades Commission, and RUC Chief Constable, Ronnie Flanagan.

Gabriel takes an active role in the strategic long-term planning for Witness, attending around four meetings a year in New York and maintaining constant contact with Posner and Li Li Brown, the Development Director. 'Peter has a zillion ideas,' says Brown. 'His heart is behind it, his head is behind it, he gets others involved in it and is a great spokesman for it.' Having appointed a new director, Gillian Caldwell, in July 1998, the organization was reorganized and planned to build its annual budget from $350,000 to $1 million. Gabriel continues to give his time and support. He performed on a bill with Lou Reed at a special Witness benefit concert at the Beacon Theater, New York City on 11 August 1994, just prior to his Woodstock appearance, and at a VH-1 concert at the Universal Ampitheater, Los Angeles on 28 April 1996. Reebok is no longer the major source of finance for Witness, which relies on private donations, fundraising events and promotions like the Witness T-shirt, sponsored by the Hard Rock Café, that raised in excess of $100,000.

Gabriel uses his contacts to raise funds or get gifts of equipment. One anonymous donor paid for fifty cameras given at cost by Sony. During the American leg of his Secret World tour in 1993 Gabriel asked for donations of equipment for Witness. His audience were well intentioned, but the technological flotsam, some broken, the rest in the American NSTC format, which was unsuitable for the rest of the world which uses the PAL system, was used for training purposes but was of little use in the field.

That the organization has saved lives seems likely, but as Brown said, 'Human rights groups have a hard time saying that. Usually it's multiple factors that contribute to the saving of lives and the stopping of human rights abuses. The mandate of the programme is to promote awareness of human rights and to hold perpetrators accountable, and so does that save lives, yes.'

It was natural in 1989, that year of global political convulsion, that the massacre of thousands of students demonstrating for democracy in Tiananmen Square, Beijing, should inspire someone with Gabriel's human rights commitment to start writing a song as he planned his next album. The tragedy of El Salvador, then still in the throes of a vicious civil war, was also the subject of a song. As he formulated ideas for what was to become the US album, Gabriel was not sure what direction he wanted it to go in. One idea was to record two albums, one of 'textural' moody songs and the other based around rhythm and dance. He had learned a lot from recording the Passion album and wanted to develop further his notion of breaking up conventional song structures. He had pushed the boundaries in that album and wanted to do the same again.

He was not the sort of writer who would have ready-made lyrics waiting for the rhythm and melody to be slotted in, nor a set of chords mapped out in a neat verse-chorus-bridge-verse-chorus-verse formula. He would get to those places, but not before a struggle. He wanted to incorporate the different rhythmic patterns, chordal structures and intricate scales that he had come across. He wanted to find a way of creating a spiritual sound, getting to the core of his being and expressing it.

It soon became apparent that Gabriel would have to aim for a more conventional album of songs as opposed to the more esoteric soundscape of Passion. As writing progressed he realized that songs about Tiananmen Square and El Salvador would have to wait for another album. He was being drawn to write an album about his personal journey.


Gabriel's inner sanctum is the loft studio at the Real World Studios, known as the Work Room, where he is seated behind his 'keyboard castle', his rigs of synthesizers. Ever since he had discovered the rhythm box in the late seventies, while record-ing the third album, he had been concerned to first find a rhythmic 'groove' that moved him as he started the composi-tion process. That evolved into ideas being thrown up by percussion loops and drum programmes as he improvised on the keyboards with chords and harmonics and sang in 'Gabriel-ese', making vowel sounds or making up words or lines as he etched out a vocal melody. It was a painstaking process done in sections that were gradually meshed together over days, weeks, months and even years. There might be part of a vocal recorded one year knitted together with another recorded maybe a year or year and a half later, and there might have been thirty takes in between with the song changing structure maybe three or four times.

'Peter's favourite phrase is "I know there's a way we can make this work." And he usually does,' his engineer Dave Bottrill told the Box, Gabriel's new fan magazine. 'Peter is very loathe to let anything go that he believes in. Sometimes at the eleventh hour when you think this is never going to work he will pull something out of the hat that makes the whole song hang together. Peter's very good at that − he knows there's a way, it's just a matter of finding it.'

When Gabriel had some basic song structures he was happy with, he would call in his studio band, the core of guitarist David Rhodes, bass player Tony Levin and drummer Manu Katche, to develop the songs further. When the band were together he liked to work with them quickly, aware that their energies could be quickly dissipated and this would reflect on the work. Along the way were a myriad of other musicians either called in specially or passing through and recording at the Real World complex. Magpie Gabriel might hear something he liked at a session and adapt it for his own use or invite visiting musicians to his sessions.

Gabriel had produced himself on *Passion* but he wanted Daniel Lanois, the producer of *So*, back for what was to become *US*. For Gabriel, who previously liked to move around producers, it was to be the first time he had worked with the same producer over three albums. Lanois was expecting the call. 'I assumed that our relationship would continue to evolve somehow or other. I thought we still had something left to say.'

Since *So* Lanois had become established as one of the world's most respected producers, with the hallowed Bob Dylan joining the illustrious list. As on *So*, which he worked on around the same time as *The Joshua Tree*, Lanois again was faced with simultaneous Gabriel and U2 projects. Gabriel was aware that Lanois had felt frustrated and imprisoned with the *So* sessions going on so long and the two came up with a solution. Lanois could produce U2 (for what became the *Achtung Baby!* album) while taking time off to spend from two to six weeks with Gabriel. 'In some ways that was good because he'd come back with fresh ears and a whole load of new reactions to works we'd done,' said Gabriel.

Lanois was happy with the arrangement, and so were U2. 'The guys really have a high regard for Peter as an innovator. They just saw it as, OK, Dan he's over there being educated at Peter's and he's going to come here and we're going to stick it all on our record. We'll send Peter a cheque.'

Gabriel and Lanois were more than professional partners. Their bond had become a deep one over the years. 'You can imagine having done the soundtrack for *Birdy* and then *So* that really puts you in somebody's trenches, you become part of their life, very much so. We got to be pretty close on a spiritual level and even to this day when I hook up with Peter, even though we're not currently working together, there's still something underneath. It's like an undercurrent communication that we have that we respect and regard.

'These things are felt rather than talked about. I just have a feeling that the underneath of it all there is the communication, and it is the underneath of it all that made its way on to those records, and it's the abstract part that is difficult to talk about. Once you get past the skills, approach and what people tangibly bring to a project, probably the most powerful ingredients are the ones you can't talk about, they're the ones that are just about lifetime experience, what you've got in your gut and how your instincts drive you through a day. So I think that's the work communication that I have with Peter, and its the social communication that I also have with him.'

It had started well with Lanois playing a more varied role, criticizing and praising the lyrics, being an active musician as well as producer. Gabriel was particularly taken with Lanois' soulful Dobro guitar playing. When Lanois was not around Gabriel would carry on alone with some of the slower, more detailed work, even finishing some of the final mixes without him.

The toing and froing worked well enough. That was not the problem. It was Real World itself that started to irritate Lanois. 'The So record was done in a relatively private way. It was at Peter's previous location, that was a sort of converted old cattle barn [Ashcombe House], and that place had something private and small about it. It was not a hive of activity, the only activity was about what we were doing. There'd be a kitchen and a phone and maybe one assistant.

'On the US record, Peter had acquired his other location and that became a mega project with all sorts of going ons, the record company, research projects. Even though I have a high regard for all of Peter's adventures and all that he's trying to do there, for Peter record making I think isolation is probably quite necessary. If you have a record company and invite people to become employees and to be interested in what you're doing they're going to be tugging at your sleeve, even if they're not physically, they're putting energy into the air.'

The unit of Lanois, Gabriel and David Rhodes had been the crucial nucleus around which *So*'s music and feeling of cohesion was built. 'We built everything on sketches. It felt like it was real and had a vibe about it that you could never stray too far from. I think there was less of that on the *US* record. The *US* record was more about the technology, the possibilities. Peter had five more computers by then.'

Gabriel and Lanois started to clash over their attitudes towards technology. Whereas Gabriel proselytized, Lanois was a sceptic. 'I'm of the opinion if somebody's gifted, talented and committed they can make art out of whatever tools are put in the sandbox. If you have too many tools at hand, and too many possibilities and options, I think that's probably the greatest enemy. It can drive you mad,' says Lanois.

'Let me clarify that. First of all I love technology. I'm interested in any tool that provides a result. But as tools go, you have to really be excited about a few tools and you master those tools and then you come up with something great.'

As a producer Lanois wanted everything at his command. He objected to technology that made the sound he was after too difficult to get at. 'It was that way with *US*. There would be mountains of information hidden away in memory banks. And you had to have somebody in the building to operate it. Ultimately you still end up with ten songs on a record and it's still forty minutes long. None of those parameters change at all, and people still want a record that feels good and speaks to them, so the ultimate form has not budged at all, but the technique for getting to that place has evolved in such a place, the candy store has become the size of a province. I would just like one candy can.'

There was no repeat incident at Real World of Lanois

locking Gabriel in a room to finish his work. 'There were too many doors in the building for me to bolt. You know something, we had our fun there. That's a great complex. I don't want to paint too dark a picture of it. Peter likes a bit of a distraction. We have to allow him that.'

But Lanois was getting exhausted. 'In all honesty, and Peter knows this, I've explained it to him, I was pretty burned out. I was definitely not fully there towards the end of the record. Just being in that one room for too long considering too many options.'

They would reach impasses, and Lanois was less repressed about expressing the way he felt. Lanois comes from a humble background, his father was a hairdresser fending for four children. Brought up in French speaking Quebec, the family moved to English speaking Ontario. 'Having come from a fairly expressive culture and then moving into more of an uptight culture, it was confusing to me. I suppose it's always going to be a tug of war. It's part of the make-up. It's part of what's underneath. It's probably the part of it all that should never really be entirely figured out.' Lanois and Gabriel represented that clash of cultures in microcosm.

'We're both obstinate bastards. So we can really come to loggerheads. He's this mixture, on the one part sort of rough-and-ready backwoods man and then on the other this sort of sensitive feminine poetic soul, and I think that struggle makes his work interesting. It's also partly what makes him work very well with other artists. He's very good at recognizing the magic and pushing the writing,' Gabriel told *Music Express* magazine.

Lanois used a technique he labelled 'spotting', as in spotting the special moments that musicians might cast off as not quite right. His skill was to turn those moments into something more substantial, a crucial ability with Gabriel's tendency to over record. One technological point Lanois and Gabriel did agree on was keeping the DAT player running whenever they were in the studio, from the first cup of coffee to the final locking of the door. 'It's a great system as long as you're being prolific, if you're only standing round telling jokes, then it's not. Keeping the DAT running, and for that matter having the multitrack ready to roll at any given moment, is really important to record production. It's the lesson that I learn over and over and over again. When you don't think you're doing it that's when you're doing it.' By the end of recording there were one thousand filled DAT tapes.

From his first pre-production meetings with Lanois in March 1990 through to the final album mixes in the early summer of 1992, Gabriel was forever wrestling with other distractions that slowed his tortuous progress. There was the Nelson Mandela Tribute concert, an anti-apartheid concert in Senegal, the Simple Truth concert, the formation of Witness and Gabriel's involvement with the Global Business Network with his old friend Peter Schwartz. He was having regular meetings on the experience park and for the first time a serious site presented itself in Barcelona. There was an honorary degree from Salford University and an honorary doctorate from the City of London University (followed a few years later by another honorary doctorate from the University of Bath). There was the release of *Shaking The Tree* and a successful battle to divert a public footpath away from Real World Studios so fans were not peering in. He was a large shareholder in a consortium bidding unsuccessfully under the name C3WW for the Wales and West of England ITV franchise. Thieves broke into WOMAD on the Real World site and stole £10,000 worth of equipment. In July and August 1991, the first of the annual Real World Recording Weeks took place. And he tried to catch up on precious time by speeding down the M4 motorway in his gas-guzzling Range Rover at 99.8 mph, escaping an automatic ban by 0.2 mph: his excuse was he was late for a recording session. In common with many an environmentally aware rock star, Gabriel is keen on his creature comforts, even if they might go against the austere impulses of the ecology lobby.

The idea for the Recording Week grew out of the difficulty Real World Records had in finding space for its musicians at Real World Studios. As a commercial studio, artists paying for time had to take precedence over label artists, who were often flown in at great cost and squeezed in when there was spare capacity. Taking advantage of the number of Real World artists appearing at WOMAD at the end of July, it was cheap and easy to transport them the forty odd miles from Reading once the festival had finished. A week was blocked off in the studio to achieve the apparently unfeasible aim of recording Real World artists' albums at the rate of one a day, plus a compilation of guest artists' sessions. To make it more of a party an assortment of musician friends and soulmates were invited along, most prominently Sinead O'Connor, already contributing to the *US* sessions, and Van Morrison, who lived nearby in Bath and now owner of one of Gabriel's old haunts, Wool Hall Studios.

The pastoral scene was captured by Johnny Black in *Q*. 'Sinead O'Connor, wearing just a pair of jeans and a lacy white bra, lounges in the mid-August sunshine outside Peter Gabriel's Real World Studios, nestling in a sylvan glade beneath the Wiltshire village of Box.

'Rabbits peep out from surrounding hedges. Moorhen chicks dart for cover on the burbling stream. Van Morrison lurches past, scowling, shadowed by a constant companion in a dark business suit. If O'Connor sees them, she gives no indication. She and Morrison are here at Peter Gabriel's invitation, to join in a week of music making with the cream of the world's roots, folk and ethnic players.'

For Gabriel it was the idyll he had always imagined, lots of cross-cultural fertilization 'where musicians and technologists could drop in and work together, without the barriers and hassles of the music business'. Gabriel got carried away lapsing into hippy parlance in the studio where he talked of 'laying down some great grooves' and declaring after a session it had been 'really happening'. It was a suitably eclectic selection of musicians – a Russian folk ensemble, a calypso king, a French Quebecois folk group, a Japanese percussionist, a Chinese classical flautist, mingling with Paul Simon's producer Phil Ramone, Karl Wallinger of World Party and Jah Wobble.

Gabriel and O'Connor were performing together and appeared close. Morrison was his usual enigmatic self, reckoning he could connect with the Holmes Brothers, an American rhythm and blues quartet, on Sam Cooke's 'That's Where It's At'. It was after midnight when Morrison took a break to go and check the lyrics by phone. 'By the time he returned,' reported the vigilant Black, 'liggers on the porch included Peter Gabriel, Sinead O'Connor, freshly woken from sleep . . . About ten takes later, Morrison declared himself happy with the track. "That's it. We can all go home now," he mumbled, to much relieved laughter.'

The result appears on the album *A Week Or Two In The Real World*, a selection of recordings from the 1991 and 1992 Recording Weeks. Morrison and the Holmes Brothers are delightful as pedal steel guitar and Hammond organ give the song a southern grace and gospel groove. The week was crowned by a concert for the people of the village of Box. O'Connor did not attend, she had apparently gone off crop-circling, Van Morrison had gone home, though Gabriel played. He told Black, 'Maybe it's just because I've been up so late every night, but I've been very tearful lots of times this week. I love the quality of some of the things we've recorded.'

Gabriel was fragile. His emotional turmoil was uppermost in his artistic mind and *US* became an outpouring of all those feelings: the trauma of his divorce, his relationship with Rosanna, his involvement with Sinead, and five years of twice weekly therapy sessions which would soon come to a close in Christmas 1991.

The process of simply putting words to music was difficult enough for Gabriel. He usually set about perfecting the lyric writing once he was happy a tune had achieved most of the intensity he was aiming for. For more conventional writers the lyrics either come first and the tune framed around them or lyrics stretched and squeezed round a well-defined tune. It was never that straightforward with Gabriel. He found lyrics could be a weight on notes, dragging down the power of the music. Then he would have to set about restructuring, meshing lyrics and music together and hopefully finding himself in a new, even stronger, place.

One of Gabriel's lifelong quests has been to rid himself of the emotional body armour riveted into place by his English middle-class background. For him music was an important vehicle for ideas, now it had a further function, as part of the therapeutic process. 'I find I can say a lot with the music that I maybe feel difficult to say with words. With the therapy and in my music I suppose I'm acknowledging the monsters that get strong and menacing when they're buried deep inside, and once you do that you begin to wonder why they ever haunted you in the first place,' he told Cliff Jones of *Rock on CD* magazine.

For the process to be of maximum benefit to him he knew he had to be as sincere and soul baring as possible. 'Therapy taught me that it's always essential to be open about one's feelings and emotions, in order to get a grip on them,' he said. But however honest he was trying to be, it was inevitable that art as therapy had limitations. Songs can be confessional and revelatory, but when someone has Gabriel's reputation for integrity, his spin on events is likely to become the authorized version: he can fool himself and the world, even if those close to him know better. 'In some ways it is safe for an artist to put all of these very personal things into their work, because they are the director, and the editor and the writer – they can play God with things that are actually outside of their work,' said Gabriel.

It had been a tough few years emotionally and before

exposing it to the world he checked with Jill and Rosanna, not wanting to betray them or their privacy. They were, he said, comfortable with him writing about it all. 'I was very much looking at my part in it,' he told the *Los Angeles Times*. 'Not so much laying the relationships bare as the way I functioned in them.' He was doing his best not to apportion blame. 'One thing I learned is you have to own your situation. You can't make anyone else responsible for it,' he told *USA Today*, the effects of therapy terms apparent.

The world is composed of us and thems. Soldiers cannot torture or kill unless they are them and we are us. Likewise in relationships, in our hearts people become us, if they fall from grace they are them. The title *US* was suitably cryptic, following in the tradition of *So* and the non-titles of the first four solo albums. 'The new record is called *US*. Us as in two people, a relationship, and us as in all of us,' he announced. 'I read somewhere that the measure of man's civilization is where he places the line between them and us. When you put people in the box marked them, you can kick them around a lot more easily than you can when they're in the box marked us. So I think it's useful to try and empty the box marked them and fill up the box marked us.'

The opening song on *US* is a plea to become one of us. 'Come Talk To Me' was prompted by the difficulties he had communicating with his then adolescent daughter Melanie during his divorce from Jill. Anna, the eldest, was more open with her father, showing her anger and thereby making it easier for him to cope because there was a line of communication. Melanie blocked everything out and in the song Gabriel pleads for her to show her feelings and make it, 'Just like it used to be.' Others he loved and had difficulty talking to were also addressed in the lyrics.

It is an emotional song with surreal dream images which speak of a disturbed landscape where the natural order is distorted.

*The earthly power sucks shadowed milk from sleepy tears undone*
*From nippled skin as smooth as silk the bugles blown as one.*

'Come Talk to Me'; Gabriel, 1992

The percussive 'groove' was taken from a session he and a drummer came up with in Senegal back in 1980. The atavistic wheeze of bagpipes opens the track, stoking up the emotion. Further into the song can be heard the bereft wail of the double reed doudouk. 'The Armenians say that it contains all the suffering that people have experienced and when it's played well, everybody cries,' said Gabriel. For extra power he brought in Sinead O'Connor's pure soprano to sing in unison on the chorus.

The need for emotional breakthrough and the breaking down of barriers continues on 'Love To Be Loved', where Gabriel sings of 'That fear of letting go.' He said the song developed from one line he had carried in his head, 'Like to be liked, need to be needed, want to be wanted and love to be loved.'

Duets on a Peter Gabriel album always came with the inevitable baggage of is he/isn't he doing it with the leading lady? He suffered it when he sang 'Don't Give Up' on *So* with Kate Bush. Then it was pure speculation, but with Sinead O'Connor on 'Blood Of Eden' the inevitable rumours, however speculative, proved correct. Their chemistry added to the intensity of this pained duet. 'Blood Of Eden' is a love drama encompassing the ecstasy of intertwining souls, the despair of separation and nostalgia for loss. Here is a slash horror Adam and Eve, bloodied and finally at war.

*Is that a dagger or a crucifix I see*
*You hold so tightly in your hand?*

'Blood Of Eden'; Gabriel, 1992

It is not specific to their relationship, more a general comment on all intense romances. The dagger is a paraphrase from

Shakespeare's *Macbeth*, 'Is this a dagger which I see before me . . .', where Macbeth debates with himself whether he has had a premonition of a bloody event or has simply seen a symbol of his troubled mind. Gabriel uses it as an illustration for the twists and turns of love, where what appears blissful can so often turn to misery.

'Initially, Dan wasn't keen on the song and it didn't sort of settle down,' said Gabriel. 'I couldn't get the groove to work and it went through probably four or five different feels, until less became more in terms of rhythm. There is also, in the central part of the song, musically and lyrically a point of union, of breakthrough. So emotionally I feel quite close to it.' Gabriel wanted 'two emotional, "needy" voices' and he got them.

It is instructive to see the interaction between Gabriel and O'Connor during rehearsals for the promotional video of 'Blood Of Eden', shown on the documentary-style video release *All About Us*. Neither are the most effusive of people in word or body language. We catch moments where she puts her hands on his shoulders and where they make funny expressions. There is clearly a frisson of intimacy on the set of 'Blood Of Eden' that makes it to the video itself. As 'Adam' lifts the veil of the blood red dress of 'Eve' he sings,

> *What a moment this is*
> *Oh for a moment of forgetting,*
> *a moment of bliss.*
>
> 'Blood Of Eden'; Gabriel, 1992

There is a mischievous look in her eyes. They hesitantly kiss with the universe exploding behind them. It's a shame it's only one of those boring closed-mouth stage pecks. As the video ends we see an agonized-looking lone Gabriel remembering the bliss of their relationship as he falls into a vortex. O'Connor rubs her head in despair at the loss.

The low-budget 'Blood Of Eden' video, directed by Mike Coulson (no relation to Gail Colson), creative director at Real World, and Nichola Bruce, draws on the work of Israeli sculptor Zadok Ben David, one of the artists commissioned to illustrate each of the ten album tracks for the CD booklet. Ben David's little silhouette cut-out figures – of real and imaginary figures in motion or balancing in impossible situations – are brought to life in the video. Far from the extravagance Gabriel is famed for, this video was very low rent, at one point using a garden hose in a plastic bowl for a fountain effect. Fish fall like rain into the desert, surreal objects rise from the sand, a real child in a judge's wig and another in a bishop's mitre are inside a tree made of logs. Cut-out animals, a dinosaur, a centaur, a unicorn – representing the 'million unheard souls' of the song – make their way across the desert. Gabriel falls against the background of an endless house. O'Connor dressed as a dervish circles like a weather vane. The objects in this desolate Eden turn to dust in a sandstorm. The video ends as cut-out little Peter Gabriels tumble to form an egg shape enclosing a reclining real Gabriel. The matching lyrics state 'We end as we began . . . the union of the woman, the woman and the man.' This is an optimistic message, not borne out by the story of the song, that the sexes can be reconciled and become as one. Maybe we will have to wait until we are reclining in our graves for that one.

From the agony of this subject matter and ballad, Gabriel chose to completely change the album's mood for the next track 'Steam', which he was fond of saying was 'hot, wet and wobbly'. It is steam as in the heat generated by desire and rivalry, by the sex act and by orgasm. It was a quicker than average song to write, driven along by its natural boisterousness. The lyric grew out of an idea dating back to the third album, while its most obvious musical and lyrical link was with 'Sledgehammer'. Like 'Sledgehammer' its core is the Stax and

Atlantic up-tempo funky rhythm and blues that inspired the pubescent Gabriel.

'Steam itself is hot and wet so I think there was an obvious sexual reference there. There is also a character situation in the song about a relationship between a man and a woman,' said Gabriel. He added, 'The woman in the song is very bright, sophisticated, cultured – she knows everything – and the man knows nothing about everything. What he does know is about her, and she doesn't really know a lot about herself.'

The sex act is implied throughout. There's a dog sniffing the sexual heat. There's 'Whenever heaven's doors are shut/ You get them open.' There's 'It's going to blow, it's going to break/This is more than I can take.'

The video, as with 'Sledgehammer', was directed by Stephen Johnson, this time using the latest computer animation where before it was claymation. Gabriel's vision was brash. He first appears in the video dressed as a pimp who is stripped naked with his woman companion as they become animated computer graphic symbols penetrating each other in time to the music as they thrust their way through a lush paradise with swaying plant life and bobbing phallic mushrooms.

The video's most memorable image is Gabriel with the body of a muscle-bound Chippendale dancer. A rubber suit was created for the purpose and painstakingly attached to Gabriel's body. This is really taking Gabriel's personality to its opposite extreme. Chippendale Gabriel dances on a podium as admiring women put dollar bills down his briefs. Then a woman detaches one of his arms, another a leg, another holds his decapitated singing head. His disembodied bulging briefs dance in mid-air. The sexiest part of the video is in a steam room with laughing beauties clutching towels to their nakedness sliding along a bench that tilts like a see-saw. They bounce into Gabriel at one end who is more modestly clad in a bathrobe. He was having a good time and getting paid for it.

The video is packed with little sex scenarios: the life-sized striptease pen that strips off a woman, then the trick is made politically correct and turned on Gabriel who is left in his impressively bulging briefs; the housewife whose jeans and T-shirt give way to corset and suspenders; the cliché of a thrusting phallic steam train with Gabriel's smiling face morphed on to the front end like an overexcited Thomas the Tank Engine.

The video's producer, Prudence Fenton, was keen to forestall charges of sexism. She assured us the video was a parody and that it played with the way men see women as well as the way women see men. Yes, there are beautiful models, but other examples of womanhood are in there too. 'We had this large discussion about the kind of women we would use in the casting, all kinds of women, all women are great, no matter what size and shape,' she said. It was another brilliant tour de force from Stephen Johnson who packed a stunning amount of densely layered images into the video to dazzling effect, and which helped the single 'Steam' become the album's biggest hit when it reached Number 10 in the British charts in January 1993. In America it was the only single off the album to reach the Top 40, peaking at 32.

Gabriel got a chance to wear the purple pimp suit and rubber muscle armour performing 'Steam' in front of live audiences at the Brit Awards at Alexandra Palace, London, in February 1993, and the following month at the Grammy Awards at the Shrine Auditorium, Los Angeles, where the names of the superstar guests whose bums would soon fill empty seats are captured in the *All About US* video. Mike Coulson, Gabriel's creative director said, 'Peter went pale when he realized that the likes of Little Richard, Michael Jackson, Eric Clapton and James Brown were going to be in the front row of the audience. He made an instant executive decision to axe the part where the girls ripped off his trousers to reveal a pair of red frilly panties.'

Where 'Steam' was all playfulness, 'Digging In The Dirt'

was grim and unrelenting, the video even more so. A snail moving around Gabriel's face represents the opening line, 'Something in me, dark and sticky.' Gabriel argues with a woman who throws a can of drink over him. His anger turns into him hacking away at the earth uncovering his own head lying underground. It becomes a skull with nasty slug-like objects crawling through eye sockets and grotesque creatures changing shape. This was the work of animator Joan Gratz who startlingly transformed the interpretation of the track in the CD booklet by Spanish artist Zush. The naïve style of Zush captures Gabriel's febrile mind. There is a giant vulva floating by a figure with an erect penis and a long slobbery tongue. Faces grimace malevolently.

Restored to normal Gabriel swats a wasp as the woman swerves out of the way. After the line, 'To open up the places I got hurt,' a wristwatch turns back time to a child whose sandcastles get kicked over by Gabriel as a sadistic father who then pours scalding tea over the boy as his mother laughs.

The video opens with grass growing in the shape of the word 'DIG'. After the child's trauma we see 'HELP' form from growing fungus. It closes as flowers bloom to map out 'HEAL' in the grass around a supine white-suited Gabriel.

The musical seeds of 'Digging In The Dirt' came from a groove that was inspired by a slow, sombre drum sound, first heard at the start of the track 'Zaar' on *Passion*. It was given a funky edge and the tune built around it. Gabriel came up with one line, 'Shut Your Mouth', which he kept repeating as he did test vocals for the song. In the music he was after something 'quite dark, sticky, steamy'. The guitar sounds are bluesy and funky and he was playing a distorted Hammond organ with its sixties feel. The lyrics sway between the aggression of 'Don't talk back/Just drive the car/Shut your mouth/I know what you are . . .' to the more familiar plea for awareness of 'Stay with me I need support/I'm digging in the dirt/To find the places I got hurt.'

The theme for 'Digging In The Dirt' came from research Gabriel had already undertaken as part of an artistic project he started with Ariel Dorfman, the celebrated Chilean dramatist and author of the play *Death and the Maiden*, which deals with a woman's revenge on a man she believes tortured her as a young woman in a country that is in transition from dictatorship to democracy. Gabriel was researching why people kill, and reading about prisoners on death row. That project was left dormant but it gave rise to the realization by Gabriel 'that maybe some of my own anger and murderous feelings were attracting me to the subject'. He concluded, 'I don't think we're as far away from murderers or those that we project all the evils of the world on to as we'd like to think.' He agreed it was a very angry, almost abusive song. 'In relationships I can be both passive and aggressive,' he told *Interview* magazine. 'And I started to recognize some abusive things in me that were hidden. So there are two threads interwoven in the song – the killer, and my own personal history.'

'By digging around in my past, I learned I'm not always conscious of how aggressive it is when I've rejected someone. I'm more in touch now. "Digging In The Dirt" is just an analogy of the therapeutic process. Negative stuff buried underground gets explored and exposed to the daylight, which neutralizes it,' he told *USA Today*. He said he had learned to accept what was there and come to terms with it. He wanted to show the world that the saintly image painted of him as a humanitarian caring-sharing bloke was a distortion of his true character. 'I'm sick of that. I don't think I'm Mr Nice Guy. There's an aggressive, mean bastard and a playful, humorous character in my make-up, and I don't get to show those faces so often. Perhaps I want to point out that I'm just as capable of doing nasty things as the next guy,' he told American *GQ*.

Director John Downer was hired for his experience on the BBC nature series *Life Sense* and *Super Sense* where he used sophisticated time-lapse filming, doing the same for 'Digging In The Dirt' where he layered the film with different images at varying speeds. Gabriel had been very excited when he first came across Downer's work which showed the real world from a fresh point of view, that of animals, insects, bedbugs and birds.

Gabriel suffered for his art in the video as the juicy snail crawled over his reclining head. Dr John Hutchinson, a zoologist, explained in *All About US* that the snails used 'have a very complex jaw, which is a bit like sandpaper. Sandpaper moving in a way like a chainsaw moves. And these little teeth will actually rip into flesh.'

Initially the snail was meant to just crawl over Gabriel's ear. Since he did not seem to mind the film-makers became more adventurous and the snail was allowed to crawl over his eye and then his mouth. The sequence, which opens the video, is vastly speeded up as we see the snail make uncharacteristic haste. 'It does hurt,' Gabriel told Andy Gill of the *Independent*. 'Most of the time they just sort of slime across you and try to stick on, but this one has these little teeth-like things, like forty little fork-ends, against which it sucks soft material and scrapes it. That's how they eat. Which is fine, except when it's your skin.'

The film is ambiguous in the scene where Gabriel swats the wasp. There is fear on the woman's face that she will get hit next. It seems it was not Gabriel being autobiographical. 'It's more of a look at the more aggressive parts inside of me, and should not be portrayed as violence towards women. It's more the innocent, unsuspecting wasp who gets most of it.'

Also worrying was the scalding-tea scene where you see the tea steaming off the boy's skin. The trick was simply to film it in a refrigerated room so that warm liquid steamed realistically. But John Downer had his fears. 'We deliberated over the scene where Peter appears at first to be attacking the woman – he isn't – in fact he's attacking a wasp. Peter initially wanted to approach that scene in an even more overt way. He was trying to illustrate the violent emotions that reside in all of us; it's what the song is all about. I had to draw back from that – I was very concerned that the film might be construed as condoning violence towards women.

'The scenes with the little boy were important because they concerned uncovering trauma from the past. The events of childhood shape our adult lives and we were trying to illustrate what can occur when these events become hidden or buried. Again, I would have liked it to have been softer but Peter felt it was important not to compromise the strong emotions he wanted to portray.

'We wanted the film to be provocative and to stand as a piece of work in its own right. Peter was continually pushing the boundaries but I wouldn't have gone along with the violence if I had felt that we were making it attractive in any way. We didn't want people to emulate it or even think that it was OK. But we did want the audience to think about it. In the end I felt comfortable knowing that it would make people feel uncomfortable.'

There were voices raised in objection. One psychologist was concerned about the effect the video might have on people with post-traumatic stress disorder, though there have been no reports of admissions to psychiatric units from disturbed viewers. The intensity and gruesomeness of the video imagery prompted many a video show and music station to hold back from airing it. The single only reached Number 24 in the British charts in September 1992 while in America it only reached Number 52. At least it scored at the 1993 Grammy Awards where 'Digging In The Dirt' won for best shortform music video.

Sitting alongside the brute reality of 'Digging In The Dirt' is the spirituality that runs through US; 'Only Us', 'Washing Of The Water' with its Biblical references, and 'Fourteen

Black Paintings' are reflective and uplifting. These three songs more than most show the stylistic influences of *Passion* on Gabriel's work.

The song 'Only Us' contains the central theme of the album.

> *I can find only us breathing*
> *Only us sleeping*
> *Only us dreaming.*

'Only Us'; Gabriel, 1992

It inevitably contains some self-reproach. 'Seduced by the noise and the bright things that glisten/I knew all the time I should shut up and listen.' But the angel Gabriel is still in there fighting. 'These battered wings still kick up dust.' One of the musicians playing with Gabriel was, unbeknown to him, a Sufi spiritual leader. Kudsi Erguner, who had worked with Gabriel before, played ney flute. Gabriel only discovered his other career when reading an article on world spiritual leaders in a Sunday supplement. Perhaps fittingly the song is about the battle for the soul. It was the album track that took the longest to make and it is the one whose sounds and textures Gabriel expressed greatest satisfaction with.

'Washing Of The Water' is a spiritual song in the gospel sense, both lyrically and musically. It expresses the desire to be spiritually cleansed. There is a river in there which has no name, though by the sounds of it it could be the Jordan way over yonder. Gabriel was worried the tune had a bit of a cheesy Holiday Inn cabaret feel, more pronounced is the feel of English hymns and church music, an influence not apparent in his work since Genesis days.

The cryptic solitary verse of 'Fourteen Black Paintings' is not so much a lyric as a declaration of Gabriel's 'Digging In The Dirt' creed.

*From the pain come the dream*
*From the dream come the vision*
*From the vision come the people*
*And from the people come the power*
*From this power come the change.*

'Fourteen Black Paintings'; Gabriel, 1992

It is chanted rather than sung, and for Gabriel, who admits that lyric writing is hard work for him, this is a way of expressing emotions without the weight of too many lyrics. 'Sometimes it feels like wordless singing is just free-flowing emotion and spirit; whereas words, when they work well, register in other parts of the brain, and the reverberations last longer. They're equally valuable, but they're doing different jobs,' he told *Details* magazine.

'Fourteen Black Paintings' had been on Gabriel's B-list of songs and looked unlikely to make the album. Asked by John Paul Jones, former Led Zeppelin bass player, to contribute a work to Barcelona's Art Futura Festival, of which Jones was musical director, Gabriel dusted the track down. Jones started mixing the track with Gabriel's engineer Richard Evans and Gabriel again got interested in it. He reorganized the song and finished it off for inclusion on the album.

The title 'Fourteen Black Paintings' was inspired by the murals of Mark Rothko in the Rothko Chapel in Houston, Texas. Rothko, who committed suicide in 1970, was a leading post-war abstract American artist and in the chapel, com-missioned in 1964, strove to express a range of emotions through the use of simple form and dark colours. David Rhodes had recommended the chapel to Gabriel. 'When he described it to me it really didn't sound like a place that I would have any interest in at all. But I went there – it was full of these fourteen black paintings and it was one of the most spiritual places I have ever been. It was a very powerful experience and the whole place, as I discovered, is dedicated to human rights, civil rights and has links with Martin Luther King and Ghandi. It's a multidenominational chapel, so it's very open from a religious standpoint. And so that's how the title got locked in, because it felt like a very spiritual track.'

Gabriel dedicated the album, 'To all those who have taught me about loving and being loved.' He specified his parents, his children, his therapy group, whose leader and participants he names. It is also, 'To Jill, for giving so much in all the time we were growing up together,' and, 'To Rosanna for all your love and support that I didn't properly acknowledge.'

The presence of Jill and Rosanna is strongest on the closing track, 'Secret World', which contains some of Gabriel's most beautiful lyrics.

> *I stood in this unsheltered place*
> *'Til I could see the face behind the face*
> *All that had gone before had left no trace*
> *Down by the railway siding*
> *In our secret world we were colliding*
> *All the places we were hiding love*
> *What was it we were thinking of?*
>
> 'Secret World'; Gabriel, 1992

He explained: '"Secret World" is about the private world that two people occupy, and the private worlds that they occupy as individuals within that space, and the overlap of their dreams and desires. It came out of a difficult period, many years of marriage and then a powerful relationship afterwards; there were some mixed references for me. I feel that by looking in the darkness and by plunging into it, diving into it, that there is some light at the other end, which otherwise if you bury gets suppressed. Having worked through some of the stuff, with the therapy and then with the songs I realize that it was a painful period, but I think I'm on the other side of it now.'

After the emotional zigzags of the album, here is a track that again explores the difficult terrain of relationships and again comes up with no answers, and yet there is finally a feeling of resolution. Having pondered in 'Secret World' the making up and the breaking up and the what went wrong the final words are 'Ssh listen . . .' The sentiment feels out of place with the rest of the lyrics, the tagged on words merely a device to allow the tune to close on an uplifting instrumental passage which he felt was important for the fading out of the album. He wanted there to be a feeling of hope, of uplift, of acceptance and of moving on.

There is one further track on the album, 'Kiss That Frog', which despite the risqué imagery at its core is not solely about sex. More fundamentally it is about the transformation that awaits those willing to search the murky depths for truth.

For the music Gabriel yet again raided his vaults, developing a Latin-influenced groove that began life when he was working on the *Birdy* soundtrack about seven years before. It grows into a sensuous, insistent dance rhythm that takes up the theme. For the story Gabriel uses as his guide the Brothers Grimm fairy tale 'The Frog Prince'. The frog brings the beautiful princess back the golden ball she has lost in the water. The ungracious princess fails to honour her word and tries to forget the frog. Despite her revulsion the amphibian insinuates its way into her life. Forced by her father the king to fulfil her obligations she has to let the frog eat from her plate and share her bed. At her moment of deepest frustration she at last confronts the situation rather than tries to run from it and throws the unfortunate clammy creature against the wall, at which point it becomes the handsome prince.

Gabriel stays fairly faithful to the story on both obvious and subconscious levels. The frog invites the princess to jump in the water (have sex), he wants to introduce his 'frogness' (penis), the frog is 'all puffed up' (erection), he wants her to 'kiss it better' (oral sex), he wants to 'eat right off your plate' (oral sex) and he wants her to 'get wet with me' (arousal).

'The lyrics are a bit on the edge, I wanted them to fall on the sort of sweatier side,' said Gabriel.

'On the deepest level frogs may symbolize our earliest existence, on a more acceptable level they represent our ability to move from a lower to a higher stage of living,' wrote the psychoanalyst Dr Bruno Bettelheim in *The Uses of Enchantment*, the book that inspired Gabriel to write the song.

'On another level the story tells that we cannot expect our first erotic contacts to be pleasant, for they are much too difficult and fraught with anxiety. But if we continue, despite temporary repugnance, to permit the other to become ever more intimate, then at some moment we will experience a happy shock of recognition when complete closeness reveals sexuality's true beauty.'

Bettelheim explored the value of fairy tales in a child's development, warning we should be careful before we look down on the way previous ages dealt with sex. Fairy tales helped children develop healthier attitudes to sex whereas modern sex education makes a mistake when it gives the facts before children have the emotional equipment to absorb them. 'The fairy tale, by agreeing with the child that the frog . . . is disgusting, gains the child's confidence and thus can create in him the firm belief that, as the fairy tale tells, in due time this disgusting frog will reveal itself as life's most charming companion.'

Bettelheim goes deeper in his exploration of 'The Frog Prince', tracing it back to the ancient myth of Cupid and Psyche. In that story sex is 'a huge serpent with a thousand coils'. Cupid fights to win the beautiful Psyche who having acquiesced betrays him and has to suffer great hardship before she wins him back. The names themselves, Cupid, or in its Greek form Eros, means sexuality, while Psyche means soul.

Bettelheim wrote, 'Not physical man, but spiritual man must be reborn to become ready for the marriage of sexuality with wisdom. This is represented by Psyche having to enter the underworld and return from it; wedding of the two aspects of man requires a rebirth.'

One of Gabriel's favourite poets, Anne Sexton, who inspired the song 'Mercy Street' on *So*, wrote a poem called 'The Frog Prince' touching on its darker oedipal connotations. 'Frog is my father's genitals,' she wrote in an irreverent version of the classic tale.

Leaving aside the sexual connotation of 'Kiss That Frog', the significance here for Gabriel is how the song represents a lack of control in his own life. Prey to his own desire he cannot resist a beautiful and powerful woman. He, the controller of so much in his professional life who can determine so many aspects of his artistic fate, is uncomfortably powerless when involved with one. The reality of relationships rarely matches our initial idealized projections. We are all both frog and princess. The child who has to take responsibility for its own actions and through independence discover maturity, as well as the frog with its sexual symbolism and qualities of transformation.

Gabriel tried to capture the themes of the album in the cover artwork. On the back is the *US* logo, the U in a square, the S in a circle, a motif that would later be developed for the Secret World tour. The square representing the male and the circle the female, with the square and circle overlapping. The symmetrical typeface contrasts with the background splash of blue paint against the red backdrop, with connotations of the conflict between raw emotion and the ordered world. For the cover Gabriel is pictured his arms outstretched attempting to capture a spinning, ethereal, naked female figure. It is a reminder of the Adam and Eve theme, his attempt to capture the union and the separation of man and woman in one frame.

The critical reception was mixed. From the doubters there

was incomprehension at lyrics that were deemed pretentious and worse, harking back to Genesis excess. *US* was generally agreed to be less commercial, an accurate prediction, and many commented on the similarity between 'Sledgehammer' and 'Steam'. Most prominent among the naysayers was Jim Farber of the *New York Daily News* who, though not wholly damning, accused Gabriel of being too predictable. 'The kind of thing we expect from an artist of Gabriel's lofty aspirations – a sense of edge and exploration – rarely breaks through.' Farber added, 'Joining Axl Rose and Bruce Springsteen on the couch, Gabriel seems anxious to display his new shrink-born sensitivity . . . Unfortunately, his images are so stripped and basic, they lack realistic dimension. Emotions to him are forces of nature; he crams his lyrics with images of deserts, lightning, earthquakes and redemptive rivers. The result is so overwhelmingly elemental that the nitty gritty specifics of human interaction get swept away.

'More problematic, however, is Gabriel's implication that such primal emotions become more convincing when backed by world beats, unconsciously suggesting that these other cultures are somehow more "primitive" and thus more honest.'

*Rolling Stone* writer Greg Kot felt queasy: 'In the end, the opaque melodies and exotic rhythms reward the patient listener, but not without a struggle.' And he concluded, 'With its wave upon wave of rhythmic innovation, *US* hints at catharsis. Instead, this extended meditation on the frailty of love settles for a sobering nobility that matches – but does not transcend – its subject.'

When Gabriel was praised though, there were virtually no limits. For the poet Michael Horovitz, reviewing *US* in the *Spectator*, 'The lines of pared thought and diction come through with plangent clarity, every syllable reinforced in settings of the most sympathetic interpersonal sophistication.' Horovitz knew Gabriel and had attended a Real World Recording Week. He wrote of Gabriel's 'determined stripping down of ploys and masks', how 'His soft, husky, yet forthright voice, modulating at appropriate points without strain into falsetto, has never felt more natural . . . He's singing from the gut, without self-pity or attitudinizing, about the most chastening period and secret scenes of his life . . . These are intelligent songs of and for real people, with a longer view than the mill-run of pop music's coming of age.'

In *Billboard*, Editor-in-Chief Timothy White wrote a full-page eulogizing piece entitled 'Eros & Enchantment: Gabriel's *US*' where he praised an album 'whose unsparing personal inquiry and post-world beat arranging feats find Gabriel at an instinctive new plateau'.

It was against these kind of reviews that the *NME* could be relied on to send a spanner sceptically into the works, here in the person of Stuart Maconie. After commenting on how non-prolific Gabriel was he wrote, 'The pluses are obvious; each record is seen as an event and is discussed in hushed tones by the discerning – i.e., grown-up – pundit. But, conversely, the more cynical among us begin to tire of all of this gravitas, all this sermon on the mount solemnity. Peter Gabriel is an incontrovertibly nice man, but after *So* . . . so what?' Maconie acknowledged the 'heartfelt symbolism' sometimes works, 'but when it doesn't you come to the inescapable conclusion that *US* is staggering, albeit elegantly, under the weight of its own earnestness.'

'The results can be enthralling,' thought Jon Pareles in the *New York Times*, though some lyrics 'verge on psychobabble'. He gave a depressing prognosis for Gabriel. 'There's no reassurance in Gabriel's love songs, no faith that the split can be repaired . . . Alone now rather than a loner, the singer faces not fantasies and visions, but the unending expanse of ordinary unhappiness.'

But ecstasy seemed to win the day. In *Time Out*, Nick Coleman wrote, 'Ten plays in, however (yes, it takes that long), it's only clear that this is a brilliant piece of work, a tender, fierce, passionate, rapt exposition of muddy, English soul.'

And awarding the album five stars in Q, Robert Sandall wrote, 'The effect is endlessly surprising and often quite stunning . . . You realize that this record simply sounds like no other. That it also makes the style of the old Peter Gabriel seem rather grandiose and padded by comparison is only a tribute to the vast menu of musical detail and texture that is in evidence here . . . US is, first and foremost, start to finish, a truly wonderful blast.'

# CHAPTER SEVENTEEN

GABRIEL KNEW INSTINCTIVELY THAT THIS album, because it was less accessible than *So*, would need a concerted promotional push. He was less precious than he used to be about making himself available, having come to terms with the issues in his own mind and shedding that rather English disdain for the world of commercialism. 'I have no wish to live at the minimum necessary to survive. And, to be honest, I don't want to compose any songs which are inaccessible to anyone in the world except myself. I consider that a kind of masturbation. You can see, then, that I'm not so free of compromise as people like to think. But at least I can offer the guarantee that I won't put out a title which I can't stand behind,' he told *Rock World* magazine. 'It is a very satisfying feeling to reach this point after a lot of toil and effort. Then just for a moment you can lean back and take a deep breath – and then apply yourself to the next opportunity. This permanent quest, and the overcoming of difficulties, is the single great purpose of my life.'

Steve Hedges set about putting the machinery in place to make sure *US* got maximum coverage in the media. In Britain he took responsibility for Gabriel's press away from Virgin Records and hired Laister Dixon PR, viewed as one of the most dynamic independent music-promotion companies. Hedges had a long acquaintance with one of the partners, Bernard Docherty, also press agent for the Rolling Stones and

Tina Turner and formerly for Paul McCartney. Docherty put the Gabriel account in the hands of Caroline Turner, who had a knack of making Gabriel do that bit more than he ever intended by way of interviews.

America needed a different strategy. Here there was friction between Hedges and Ed Rosenblatt, president of Geffen Records. Hedges had already undergone what he called 'a massive learning curve' moving from being an agent to a manager. Used to hard bargaining he wasn't so adept at the schmoozing that is necessary in some branches of the industry. 'I think Ed and I largely saw eye to eye and still do, but I probably want to know a lot more information than a lot of people do and that could cause some consternation,' said Hedges.

The pure logistics of running the different strands of Gabriel's organization in Britain were proving taxing enough, and Hedges decided he needed, however reluctantly, to devolve power. One person he knew he could trust not to try and usurp his position was Bruce Kirkland, a New Zealander who had worked in London at Stiff Records during its late seventies heyday.

In 1983 Kirkland had set up Second Vision, a Los Angeles based company representing foreign artists. He played a major role in the American success of Depeche Mode and Erasure. Kirkland had been one of Hedges' friends and associates whom he sought advice from before accepting the Gabriel management job. According to Kirkland he had 'bludgeoned' Hedges into taking it. Now the favour was being returned.

Kirkland understood the complexities of American radio with its narrowly targeted formats. For him market positioning was an art form, he talked of 'imaging devices' and trying 'to sell a perception'. He also had the advantage of being in the right time zone.

Spending all his time going into record companies and critiquing their marketing plans, Kirkland had a clear, if jargon heavy, vision of where he saw the campaign to promote

Gabriel and *US*. 'We needed to contemporize the record and put it in a contemporary concept, position it as cutting edge.' He banked on the loyalty of Gabriel's core classic audience dating back to Genesis. 'The key was to position Peter up against the new group of artists, Depeche Mode, U2, R.E.M., so that the product is received in the market place as new, fresh.' Though clearly not too radical.

Kirkland had numerous requests from adult oriented radio shows, 'We were gods in AOR.' He wanted to take Gabriel away from the traditional pop image associated with the likes of Phil Collins and play a riskier game. He booked Gabriel on *Modern Rock Live*, a one-hour alternative radio show syndicated to between fifty and sixty stations. 'It worked incredibly well and impressed Peter. It was a call-in show, taking calls from all over the country. Peter was sitting there and having some nineteen-year-old kid from say Witchita, Kansas, questioning the meaning of a lyric on some obscure Genesis album.' Gabriel was willing to play the game if it meant his new album would get played. 'A show like that means you can reinvent your audience, if the music is great the appetite is there. I think we were successful in repositioning him in alternative radio. I think we were Top 5 for twelve weeks in the alternative charts,' said Kirkland who even got Gabriel to acquiesce to possibly the industry's most derided and lowliest chore, the 'meet and greet', shaking hands with the people who actually sell, make or distribute your records.

During his promotional visit to North America in September and October 1992, Gabriel did extensive press and radio interviews. The power of good exposure was unquantifiable in terms of direct sales. When Gabriel was guest presenter at the MTV Video Music Awards, Bono of U2, who shared Daniel Lanois as a producer, told him how much he was looking forward to the release of *US*. The endorsement of perhaps the biggest band in the world was a big plus for Gabriel.

The saturation coverage and aggressive marketing from

Geffen seemed to be paying off. *US* debuted in the Billboard album charts at Number 2. *So* had only managed to enter the charts at Number 35 though it reached the Number 2 position. The first single, 'Digging In The Dirt', had been released two weeks before and the video was receiving respectable airplay on MTV and VH-1. It failed to reach the Top 40, peaking at Number 52. In Britain it managed to get to Number 24, still disappointing for one of the major tracks off the album, especially considering the effort put into the video. 'Steam' became the album's biggest hit when it reached Number 10 in the British charts in January 1993. In America it at least breached the Top 40, peaking at 32, though way short of mirroring the success of 'Sledgehammer', which had reached Number 1.

He was back on the rock and roll treadmill and committed to success. Yet there was still a sense that Gabriel was play-acting as a rock star rather than it defining him in the way it does younger or sadder colleagues. However vague the concept to the rest of us, Gabriel saw all his work as part of his bigger plan to become an 'experience designer'. He had never given up on his dream of creating the experience park, despite the disappointment of the failed Darling Harbour and subsequent Cologne projects.

In 1989, through contacts in Barcelona, where WOMAD was considering staging a festival, came what seemed a God-given invitation from the city authorities for Gabriel to construct his experience park to run as part of the Cultural Olympics, an arts festival planned to run around the time of the 1992 Summer Olympics. He was offered a site on Montjuic, an old stone quarry that bore the remains of a fifties funfair. At twenty-five acres, about the size of London Zoo, it was a manageable size. And had, as Gabriel had always dreamed, a view of the sea.

To steer the project, Gabriel hired as the park's artistic co-ordinator, Michael Morris, a former director of performing arts at London's Institute of Contemporary Arts. After leaving the ICA, Morris set up two companies – Art Angel which commissions artists to create works in unusual places, and Cultural Industry, a production company which presents experimental international theatre, dance and music in mainstream institutions. Morris had an established reputation as an innovator. He staged the British productions of dance company La La Human Steps and set up their artistic collaboration with David Bowie. Choreographer Eduard Locke devised Bowie's over theatrical and mockingly received 1987 Glass Spider tour. Another Morris ICA production was staged at the London Dominion, one of the capital's largest theatres. Here in 1983 Laurie Anderson mounted her epic eleven-hour United States show. Backstage Anderson introduced Morris to Peter Gabriel.

Morris cites his expertise as 'encouraging artists to do things they wouldn't normally do', a neat fit for the experience-park project. Gabriel had started meetings with sympathetic minds back when architect Will Alsop was planning the Sydney project. This was carried on by Morris and Rolf Engel who drew up agendas and presented minutes at the discussions. Engel was logistical co-ordinator for the park and later to become technical designer and co-ordinator for the Secret World tour. Engel is an audio-visual specialist. His company, Atelier Markgraph, based in Frankfurt, mounts arts events, exhibitions and trade fairs. Joining Gabriel as core members were Laurie Anderson and Brian Eno. Ideas were fed via soirées Gabriel labelled the Dinner Club. 'Film-makers, musicians, psychologists, painters, comics, architects and technologists were invited. Armed with food and several glasses of wine, the Dinner Club started to generate many wild and wonderful ideas,' he said. The evenings took place at Gabriel's London office in Conduit Place, Paddington, and at Real World.

Morris and Engel were hired to steer the Barcelona project.

They visited the site with Gabriel, Brian Eno and Mike Large and their imaginations ran loose as fanciful ideas abounded. Presenting their preliminary proposals in Barcelona, Gabriel & Co. found themselves facing the first of many impenetrable decisions buried in the arcane traditions of politicians and bureaucrats on the competing administrations of Barcelona, Catalonia and the Federal Government. For no apparent reason they were told the Montjuic site was not available and were offered a more urban site in Vall d'Hebron. Instead of the sea view, Vall d'Hebron was a strip of land bound by four motorways in the middle of a residential area of tall blocks of flats. Putting a positive spin on it some of the group, notably Brian Eno, thought the change of site presented them with a more satisfying challenge. Even when Montjuic was in their sights it was clear that there was no way they could build the experience park in time for the Olympics. As Vall d'Hebron was the site of the Olympic tennis tournament, clearly no work could begin until the competition was over in the late summer of 1992. And since this was no longer an Olympic project another department at the City Authority was assigned responsibility. Before Gabriel could go further he needed a financial commitment from the city to fund a concept design and business model. A frugal amount was forthcoming from the authority, presumably shrewdly surmising Gabriel might wish to dip into his own pocket for a project he so passionately believed in.

Seeking to familiarize himself with the latest technology Gabriel, accompanied by his friend Peter Schwartz, set off in 1991 on what they called their Virtual Reality tour around Silicon Valley and the San Francisco Bay Area. They spent time with maverick software designer Jaron Lanier, who coined the term 'virtual reality' and developed the VR helmet, the image most closely associated with this new medium. In the tradition of wayward Californian polymaths Lanier is a musician, a composer of modern classical music who has performed concerts with 'virtual instruments', a painter and computer scientist.

Lanier's vision was for people to be immersed inside a computer-generated landscape. To facilitate this you had to wear a helmet or HMD (head-mounted display). Gabriel was more inspired by what he saw at the NASA Ames Research Center under the direction of Scott Fisher who was developing the ideas of telepresence. 'Lanier's world was a virtual reality world which was a wonderful concept but very much restricted by looking like a bad computer game,' says Gabriel. 'Scott Fisher's project was that you had two stereo cameras in another place so you are actually looking at the real world. For instance I could put them on you and see myself in stereo from the position of your glasses if I mounted the telepresence cameras on your glasses. We wanted to do that in terms of the experience park on a micro world. You could mount two little cameras on the back of an insect and have it crawling through some strange terrain, or have robot cameras under-water or even going through the body. The great thing about when that happens is that you really perceive it as if you are inside it, a little like you do with 3D.' Like Lanier, NASA had also developed its own helmets for use in telepresence and its own virtual reality project. Though Lanier had coined the term 'virtual reality' there was a debate as to who had invented the first system. NASA developed telepresence so that people on earth could repair spaceships and feel like they were there carrying out the work. It is a technique increasingly used by doctors and surgeons who can work from home or with patients in remote areas.

The concept of virtual reality caught the imagination of the media in the early nineties, though as Gabriel noted, the hype was about ten years ahead of the technology. Lanier's attempt to make money out of his concepts, including the

HMD, foundered when the products failed to reach the mass market everyone was so convinced awaited them.

Even so, it was clear that information technology, and one day virtual reality, were pivotal in Gabriel's dream for the experience park. To him technology provided the means where the arts, communications, entertainment and education could converge. To him computers were the cutting edge of culture. What even he did not see was the imminent and rapid emergence of the internet and World Wide Web, terms that never featured in any of the discussions during the meetings of the Dinner Club between 1989 and 1992. They did not have the terminology, but they were aware of what it has made possible. Michael Morris recalls, 'What we were trying to get towards was the way this park would have a physical presence, but it would also have a virtual presence, so you would be able to access certain aspects of it whether you were in Barcelona or not.'

Brian Eno was another visionary who had long been travelling a parallel path to Gabriel. Since his days looking like a reject spaceman as keyboard player with Roxy Music he too had been searching for new forms of musical and artistic expression. Eno coined the term 'ambient music' in the seventies, a music that blossomed in the more reflective electronic sounds that emerged in the dance-music scenes of the late eighties and nineties. A sometime collaborator with Gabriel, most recently contributing to the US album, Eno was U2's producer before Daniel Lanois.

Eno, like Gabriel, saw the experience park breaking down barriers between passive watchers and active artists and between the way artists used the natural environment. Eno wanted to alter the way people viewed and used parks by making them at the same time more organized and more wild. To fulfil these visions it was necessary for the experience park to be in an urban as opposed to out of town site. 'It must be kept in relationship to making a park,' wrote Eno. 'We don't want to just build a crowd of buildings with lots of clever tricks inside them. What we really want to start here (but it is a secret) is a new system of education. We want to make something that people love to go to and during which they have real learning experiences, but we want them to think that they are having fun. That's all.'

The image of the park was not too distant from the ideas of Gabriel a decade before, outlined in fantasy form at the start of this book. Its central emblem would be a maze. The entrance would be framed by sixty-foot-high tornadoes, created by the park's own weather system. Laurie Anderson saw 'forests of talking trees', trees with concealed speakers. Screens mounted on totem poles would display virtual exhibitions, films and information. Water was to feature heavily. Behind the twelve waterfalls would be a doorway leading into the mysterious underworld of experiences, where you would find the original Ride of Fears and The River of Life.

A promotional video superimposed Gabriel, Eno and Anderson over abstract plans for the park. They spoke in turn but as one:

Gabriel: 'I've always pictured it would be great to be inside the work of other artists.'

Eno: 'Not just stand around and look at it from the outside but get in there together and engage in a dream together.'

Anderson: 'It should be a place for people to explore, to discover something about themselves that we didn't really ever know before . . . There are also streets of water that lead to a floating screen. The screen moves and is animated as the park transforms itself, especially at night when all the pure, pure water turns blood red.'

Visionary, certainly, but practical, possibly not. Despite the enthusiasm and commitment of Gabriel's team, they lacked one essential ingredient, experience in running a living, breathing theme park in the real, real world. Nick Winslow was a consultant for the firm of Harrison Price in the rarefied business of Leisure Analysis. Harrison Price had made its name in the fifties drawing up the feasibility study for Disneyland at Anaheim, California. Winslow was regarded as one of the best in the field.

His thick document with its cost-benefit analyses, statistics on the demographics, the number of visitors to Catalonia, where they came from, how much they were prepared to spend on entertainment, grounded the team. 'He'd say, that's fantastic, but you could only get five people in at once and it would take you twenty-five minutes to get them through here. He was the voice of reason. He was very good at working out formulae which told you how many people would be queuing and for how long,' says Michael Morris. Queues were the enemy and a way had to be found if not of eliminating them, then of making people unaware they were in line because they were distracted by something else.

The blunter edge of reality was provided by David Eno (no relation to Brian), then married to Gabriel's business manager, Maria Pedro. After fifteen years' experience as a merchant banker financing projects for large corporations, Eno had set up his own company to specialize in the arts and leisure industries and was hired as a financial consultant. A fluent Spanish speaker he was able to navigate through the tortuous Spanish bureaucracy. The development costs for the park were likely to be in the high tens, if not hundreds, of millions of pounds. Eno pursued Real World's contacts with high technology companies like Apple Computer and Sun Microsystems who were interested in principle, but without an infrastructure it was impossible to get firm commitments.

In April 1992 Gabriel and his project members made their presentation to the authorities in Barcelona. It was a slick display using videos, slides, music, Gabriel and his team speaking and answering questions. Gabriel himself struck up a warm relationship with Pasqual Maragall, the socialist mayor of Barcelona. 'That was what was so strange. We were all hyped up, it was the first time we'd put on the full dog and pony show, and the project did look really impressive. All of us who were working on it were up on stage with a sophisticated intelligent audience of people in that city authority looking at it and loving it, and then we just heard nothing,' says Mike Large. What happened was the Olympics, followed by the near bankruptcy of Barcelona, though as Gabriel told journalists throughout 1992 and 1993 he still believed the park was 'in serious danger of getting taken seriously'. Gabriel appeared at the WOMAD festival in Barcelona in May 1993 during his Secret World tour and contacted the mayor to get an update. He was given what Large describes as 'a rather woolly letter of intent'. There was silence again, no amount of contacting the authorities could clarify the issue and the project slid out of view.

It was not until early 1998 that Gabriel once more heard from the Barcelona authorities. They visited him in Box and said the original Montjuic site was once more available. He was invited to make a bid. It was clear that whatever its original cultural commitment the council now seemed more concerned with revenue. 'So we went back to them and said look it doesn't really work for us to tell you how much you're going to make out of it. It isn't really the way we've been working with you in the past. So it hasn't really progressed,' says Large.

Over a six to ten year period Gabriel has spent what Large estimates could be £400,000, though it might even be double that. 'He was pained that he'd spent a lot of money and it didn't come to fruition in 1992,' says Large. 'But he was pleased that some of that creative work could get used.' In particular in the Secret World tour and the CD-ROMs.

One of the more sceptical voices attending the Dinner

Club was Peter Schwartz, who says he was always doubtful the park would ever happen, though he was careful not to be discouraging. 'He might just be the guy who breaks through.' He thought Gabriel's vision was outrageous and wonderful, too much so for potential investors. 'He is further out than the people who make such things happen would be willing to buy into,' says Schwartz.

Schwartz had enlisted Gabriel, Brian Eno and Laurie Anderson for his own project, the Global Business Network. Essentially a high octane 'think-tank' composed of experts in science, technology, politics and the arts, GBN holds meetings and workshops to try to predict business and social trends. With one hundred corporate member firms paying an annual fee of $35,000 it is also a profitable business in its own right. Gabriel and friends are termed 'network members' who give their advice when called on and in return have GBN's information services and access to influential fellow members like Professor Richard Cooper, chair of the US National Intelligence Council; Professor Francis Fukuyama, author of *The End of History* and *Trust*; Esther Dyson, one of the world's leading experts on software technology and emerging markets; William Gibson, author of *Neuromancer*; Daniel Hillis, vice president of Disney; and Russell Schweickart, the Apollo 9 astronaut and an old acquaintance of Gabriel.

According to Schwartz all members share a 'ruthless curiosity' and are 'information junkies'. Gabriel has attended GBN meetings and workshops, including one with a typically far-reaching agenda: The Future of Capitalism. And when called on Gabriel will share his insights, as he did with Hewlett-Packard, the formidable American computer company which has a research laboratory in neighbouring Bristol, over discussions about new media technologies. 'We pay members in information because, the honest truth, we can't pay Peter enough cash. There's no amount of money that really buys his time because he doesn't sell his time. He sells his ideas and creativity,' says Schwartz. For Gabriel there was also an emotional element to this. When he attended a planning conference on the future of fibre optics held by the American AT&T telephone company he felt like his father's representative. Ralph Gabriel, as chief scientist for Rediffusion, had co-designed Dial-A-Programme, the first fibre-optic-based cable-television service some thirty years before. Like many British inventions it was totally underfunded, and new ideas of education and entertainment on demand and electronic democracy fell on deaf ears.

Gabriel used the services of GBN to organize a workshop for Witness in New York, in May 1997. Gabriel was one of the speakers with Schwartz seeking to help Witness focus on its future development, and relations with the media and other human rights organizations. The workshop carried out on a pro bono basis as a favour to Gabriel would have cost $100,000.

In his vision for the Real World Experience Park, Gabriel had years earlier been enthused by Magic Motion Machines. Based on the airline flight simulators used to train pilots, the machines did the same for space flight to an audience of forty. (Coincidentally, Redifon, based in Crawley, Sussex, were later to develop the Star Tours ride for Disney theme parks. This factory had been managed by Gabriel's father in the early days of flight-simulator technology.) The next generation of ride technology was the Mindblender Rock Motion Theater created by the Iwerks company of Burbank, California. Gabriel's involvement was engineered by Danny Socolof, a breed of 'rainmaker' who brought Iwerks, Pepsi and Gabriel together. 'Kiss That Frog' was always planned as a single, and therefore would have a video to go with it. Socolof's invitation had the benefit that someone was actually prepared to pay him to make his own video and cover the budget.

Enthused by the Mindblender technology, Gabriel put forward his own innovation, instead of static seats he wanted the seats to hydraulically move in time to the music, thus creating a literal as well as visual and aural ride. The project was sponsored by Crystal Pepsi (their short-lived clear cola). For Gabriel Mindblender was a useful promotional tool that would help publicity for his record and the Secret World tour. The launch was designated for his Madison Square Garden show in New York City on 24 June 1993, which left just two months to have the project completed.

Gabriel had admired the work of Brett Leonard, director of the successful 1992 film *The Lawnmower Man*, the first mainstream movie to tackle the subject of virtual reality. The movie features twenty-three minutes of computer graphics and, despite an unerotic representation of virtual sex, was also the first film to have a convincing computer graphic 'synthespian' who talked and acted. The setting is high-tech but the movie is a variation on the Frankenstein theme: village idiot lawnmowing man becomes brainbox through the power of technology and shows who's boss. Pierce Brosnan, a future James Bond, plays the deranged scientist working for a shady corporation, and utters the film's essential cautionary note: 'Man may be able to evolve a thousandfold through this technology, but the rush must be tempered with wisdom.' Moderately gripping as a drama it was a useful pointer towards the way technology could be harnessed in the cause of art, a theme close to Gabriel's heart.

With timing so crucial for the Mindblender, the agreeable Brett Leonard was told by producer Danny Socolof that a first-class ticket to London would be left in his name the following day at the Virgin Atlantic desk at LAX airport. On landing Leonard went straight to Box to meet Gabriel, which as a long-time fan was an added bonus.

Gabriel and Leonard adjourned to the studio and listened to the new mix for 'Kiss That Frog' as they discussed the video. 'I came up with this concept of the archetypal princess and frog story told through a kind of a mytho-sexual imagery that also had the feeling of an illustrated storybook,' said Leonard. 'One of the concerns Peter had was to not make the computer graphics look computer graphicy. Whereas *Lawnmower Man* was a celebration of the computer graphic aesthetic, and it was right to be that because it was about the virtual reality world, he wanted to do something more organic that did not indicate computer graphics but to use the technology to give you something that was very new.'

The solution was to have an artist do detailed coloured-pencil illustrations, and using a technique called 'texture mapping' turn 152 drawings into animated 3D-effect computer graphics. Instead of a soulless silicon airbrush the animation has a warmth and depth closer to the best drawn cartoons. According to Leonard this was the first time hand-drawn illustrations had been turned into animated computer graphics. It was also the first music video with 'wall to wall' computer graphics.

Leonard chose an acquaintance, fine artist A. E. Bunker, to be the illustrator. 'Kiss That Frog' provided Bunker, whose work was sexually charged and often surreal, with an orgy of opportunities from penis trees to vulva plants. 'If you look very closely, almost everything is either male or female genitalia. There's tremendous detail and we always did it so that it wouldn't be overt. The feeling was that this song was very deeply about sexual fear, sexual angst and then the rebirth, penis envy in relation to sex. There's a lot of that imagery buried inside there, in very subtle ways, in the texture. That's one of the things that I think makes it a very rich piece to watch again and again,' said Leonard. 'Peter is simultaneously a proper English country squire and a very primal man and that's what I found incredibly fun to work with. As I told him, I always thought it was a song about oral sex.'

Overlaid on the graphics were the filmed images of Gabriel and his princess, the actress Mara Duronslet. Gabriel flew into

Los Angeles for the arduous task of sifting through 400 actresses in a one-day casting session. Duronslet, according to Leonard, had the 'world global tribal look' they were looking for.

Like the fairy tale, in the video the princess represents innocence and perfection. The frog appears first as a tadpole, representing not only its most penis-like form but also the sperm swimming to the egg. It undergoes a rapid metamorphosis into the mature frog whereupon it spies the princess on a lotus leaf floating on the water. Delighted to meet him she sheds her outer garment to reveal a water costume hugging a figure of womanly perfection. She dives in to play with the frog underwater, believing it to be an innocent game, only to recoil when she sees his lascivious tongue or should that be penis. Then the frog pursues her as she flees for her life, only to suddenly waken as if from a dream, momentarily relieved, but then finding the nightmare is real with the frog on top of her making lurid squelching noises. She is thrust into underwater weeds, one of which has the face of the singing Gabriel. Entwined in the frog's tongue she is swallowed, descending into its stomach bearing the remains of flies and insects while the frog and Gabriel's slimy vocals reassure her, 'don't ever be afraid. You might like it if you lower your defence.' Released from the stomach and clasped by the frog's webbed foot, now in an Elizabethan bridal dress she is enthralled as she glides through an underwater vortex emerging into a beautiful colourful world bedecked with flowers. Here she delicately kisses the frog on the lips and sighs at the sensation. The frog morphs into Gabriel wearing Elizabethan courtier's garb, including ruffed collar, singing the obviously suggestive 'Jump in the water, c'mon baby get wet with me.' The couple dance. Gabriel somersaults and gracefully dives along while the enchanted princess smiles in wonder. Hand in hand they ride the rocky waves, they double somersault and become tucked into a womb-like formation which morphs into what appears to be a classical image of Eve. The image morphs again into the frog's eye as the frog makes one last appearance to the sound of the princess' sated sigh.

It was all too sexy for MTV, who asked for a special edit removing some of the more obvious double entendres, much to Leonard's astonishment. 'If you read the *Grimm's Fairy Tales*, all sorts of diabolical metaphors for sex and violence are intrinsic in them. I thought we handled that in a sensitive manner,' said Leonard. Though even MTV cannot have been aware of some of the more heavily disguised imagery. It does not seem to have affected the audiences of all ages able to view the large high-definition screens. The video was the first to be filmed in a new Sony High Definition format, so detailed it gave a 3D effect. It was stretching the limits of computer technology with forty graphics stations working twenty-four hours a day for two weeks to achieve the desired animation effects.

It was unprecedented for Gabriel to trust a director to carry out his vision for a video with such scant direct supervision, but he had no choice. He was in the middle of planning the Secret World tour and could spare only three days for the shooting. The rest he controlled by faxes and phone calls. 'The great thing about the collaboration is that we were in sync from the very first and we had to go with first thought, best thought. We had to go with our guts in a sense. That actually was a fairly new thing for Peter. I always felt like I was the guy pushing him to just go with it because he's a man who likes to rework everything,' says Leonard.

In the rush one crucial point had been forgotten. The animation was timed to go with the mix of the song given by Gabriel to Leonard. Gabriel then teamed up with hip producer William Orbit to remix the track, throwing out all Leonard's timing. Leonard told them, 'Guys, I'm doing frame by frame animation here.' To which Orbit replied, 'Well, Brett, it's rock 'n' roll man.' Leonard could only insist, 'Well man, it's frame by frame animation man.' Orbit and Gabriel, just days away from the start of his tour, had to fly to Los Angeles and over twenty-four hours remixed the track again to put everything back in sync.

Premiered at Madison Square Garden in June 1993 on the Secret World tour's arrival in New York City, two 75-foot Mindblender 'mobile simulation' trailers went on to tour sixty-three cities throughout the United States, visiting festivals and shopping malls and reaching an estimated 300,000 people at $5 a ride, or free to those who bought merchandise in whoever's selling space the Mindblender was parked. Audiences were strapped into their pulsating seats, there were three elevated rows of six seats each, and reported a sensation of going down the frog's throat. Gabriel stated in a Pepsi-Cola press release, 'It's very powerful because it's a completely new medium that convinces the audience they are inside the music-video experience. It's an entertainment dimension I've long been interested in exploring.'

For Gabriel the road to Madison Square Garden had been paved with bruised egos and near impossible deadlines as his creativity ran at full tilt. Mindblender and the 'Kiss That Frog' video had been a side project to the Secret World tour. Planning for the tour had begun in the summer of 1992, before the US album was mixed, though what Steve Hedges was meant to be planning for he was not quite sure until uncomfortably late in the process. At first he believed he was booking halls for a traditional proscenium-arch show and alerted agents and promoters around the world to start pencilling in venues.

Gabriel was certain of one thing, he wanted Robert Lepage to devise the show. He had been enthused about Lepage's work since seeing *Tectonic Plates* at the Royal National Theatre in London. An epic play it covered a range of big and small subjects including geography and the effects of continental drift, differences between the nineteenth and twentieth centuries, personal relationships and sexual politics. 'It was about drifting and colliding and people moving and fighting,' Lepage sort of explained.

Lepage was celebrating his thirty-third birthday on 12 December 1990 when Michael Morris brought Gabriel to meet him. Gabriel and Lepage attach importance to the symbolic power of numbers, and the date of their meeting appeared auspicious. Numbers often featured in Lepage's works, *The Seven Streams of the River Ota* and *The Dragon's Trilogy*. If it was not within the title then numbers would be represented in notions like duality. They only had that one meeting before Gabriel invited Lepage to work with him. They then met at a restaurant where Gabriel calculated on a paper napkin the number in numerology that corresponded to Lepage's name. It was the same as Gabriel's, seven.

Just before meeting Gabriel Lepage was working on *The Dragon's Trilogy*, improvising Tai Chi scenes to the *Birdy* soundtrack. In the book *Connecting Flights*, Lepage, in conversation with author Remy Charest, said, 'The music had a lot to do with how the show evolved, and so I told Gabriel that he had, without knowing it, been an inspiration for the *Trilogy*. He was pleased to hear this, but, more important, he explained that since *The Lamb Lies Down On Broadway*, he has developed all his shows according to the I Ching and the principles of Yin and Yang. And the I Ching was one of the principal work tools in the *Trilogy's* development.'

Lepage recounts how thinking about the way his works were creating such expectations from the public he wondered what the reaction would be to one of his shows presented under another name. Getting out a game of Scrabble he juggled the name Robert Lepage and came up with the anagram Peter Gabroel. 'The difference is a single letter, an "o" for an "i". You can go a long way with this kind of a crazy connection. You could say that because our anagrams are similar, because our number is the same, we were meant to work together, that in fact I'm Peter Gabriel's double, and so on. It's like the people who try to find hidden meanings in Shakespeare's name. I find this fascinating. It's not so much that I believe in it, but that it's a kind of poetry that helps me to create. Maybe the connections are only made because we decide to give meaning to the games of numbers and forms. But even if we don't understand why they exist, these connections are nevertheless there,' Lepage told Charest.

Lepage had made his name for his innovations in opera as well as theatre, from *A Midsummer Night's Dream* at the Royal National Theatre to Schoenberg's *Erwartung* for the Canadian Opera Company in Toronto. Though celebrated by the intelligentsia, Lepage professes his ignorance of opera before staging any productions. Rather it was the shows of Gabriel-era Genesis, and other progressive rock artists of the early seventies, Emerson, Lake and Palmer and Jethro Tull, that fuelled the imagination of the twelve-year-old boy when they visited his home town of Quebec.

Gabriel was drawn to Lepage's work unaware of his own role as one of Lepage's principal influences. 'I told him that he was a great influence, but of course I guess when you're a popular icon you probably expect people to say that to you to be polite, but it's sincere, he really changed my way of seeing art,' says Lepage who had originally wanted to be a musician, not realizing until he saw Genesis that to be satisfied he needed a more visual experience. 'I could see that it's more interesting to be a renaissance artist than a musician only or a painter only or a dancer only. I think that Peter is this kind of renaissance man where you don't really know when he's actually an engineer or a musician or a painter, a bit like Leonardo da Vinci. He's as much interested in how things work and what he can express with them. That is a great quality and that had a very, very profound impact on me. A lot of rock artists around were really interesting, I had a lot of idols, but they weren't as influential as Peter was.'

Gabriel invited Lepage to the experience park Dinner

Club, where he joined Terry Gilliam, director of *Time Bandits*, *Brazil*, and *Fear and Loathing in Las Vegas* and former Monty Python's Flying Circus animator, and Nicholas Negroponte, acknowledged guru of the digital age, professor of the MIT Media Lab and a long-standing acquaintance of Gabriel. Lepage's contribution was confined to a couple of these occasions. It was while finishing rehearsals for *A Midsummer Night's Dream* that Gabriel asked Lepage to work on the tour. With Lepage spending time in London he and Gabriel were able to establish their friendship. The invitation coincided with Lepage's reputation heading skywards and bookings two to three years ahead. So keen was he to take on the task that to accommodate Gabriel he had to postpone some of his engage- ments at the last minute.

Lepage went to the inner sanctum of Real World Studios to hear the final mixes of *US*. 'I had the privilege to be in on some of the material that nobody got to hear. That was very inspiring because a lot of things that never really made it on the record were really strong: songs around the same themes of Adam and Eve and a couple breaking apart.'

He began to see Gabriel as a *ludique*. 'It's difficult to translate in English. It means playful or playfulness, but in a more serious manner. That's one of the great qualities of Peter's genius, his playfulness, pun intended – play in the sense of theatre as a player, what he does comes out of playing [music] a lot, and the idea of playing. I think that's also why he got involved in this theme park thing, this idea that there's so much to be transmitted and communicated through playing. When he rehearses with the band you really have the impression that they are playing together in either sense of the word. So it was important that I got a chance to go to Real World and play with him and try things out and play around. So we invented a miniature playground for this show and I got to explore with him some of the ideas of the show really early on.'

One idea was to have a railway line run round the perimeter of the auditorium with the stage set up as a railway station. A camera rail was laid in a barn in Box with a camera dolly doing train duties. Lepage was in a phase of having objects and people fly around stages and had Gabriel harnessed up and flying round the barn. They experimented with new ways of incorporating visuals into the show using lighting, shadows and projections. Lepage draws a parallel between Gabriel's way of working in the studio and how Gabriel devises his shows. He likens it to an impressionist painter layering colours to build up an image. He was drawn into the same process and finds it hard to disentangle who had what idea. It was Gabriel's idea to build two stages, one square in the traditional proscenium position and a circle in the centre of the auditorium. Before building began Lepage visualized the set through drawings and architectural models. The square representing the male and circle the female led them to separate songs further for inclusion on each stage into urban and organic. Like the square and circle artwork on the album cover, it reflected the relationship themes of the songs on US. The angular square was both male and urban, the flowing curve of the circle was feminine and organic. For both of them transformation has been a constant theme. 'The square stage represents the male and the round domed stage the female, the walkway between them providing communication and the link between the sexes. The link also becomes a road or a river, a place of travel and transformation, from one stage literally to another,' he told Box magazine.

Lepage was keen to bring the show as close to the audience as possible. 'It was at a time where every rock band on earth was using video screens to do close-ups of the singer. We resisted that idea as much as we could,' he says. No one else had the 360-degree revolving screen that Lepage devised which could glide and spin above the stage. And where there were video-screen close-ups they were abstract, like the uncomfortable fish-eye close-ups of Gabriel's face on 'Digging In The Dirt' achieved by a miniature camera mounted on a helmet. 'I said to Peter, if we're going to sometimes give in and show your face on the screen up there it has to be for an artistic reason. It should not be because people are not seated well and they have to get their $25 worth.'

Gabriel's past successes on stage, though often dramatic, had veered throughout his career from pantomime to political rally. For Lepage, realizing the US album had to be on a different level to anything that had gone before, 'Peter wasn't just doing "Shock The Monkey" and dancing round. He was also trying to be very intimate and saying very profound dark things, and that was quite a challenge, to be intimate in a huge unintimate place.'

With his background in the highbrow arts, Lepage was aware that he had to avoid devising a show that went too far above his audiences' heads, in more than a literal sense. 'It really put me in contact with very basic things. What is entertainment? What do you want to say? If you want to attract huge crowds what is it that is universal and how do you approach it? Opera is very unpopular amongst the young. It's too bad, they should teach it in school because actually that's what rock shows or concerts in general are made of, people singing about fundamental things. People go to these big venues because they want to hear things that are very fundamental and mythical and universal. They don't go there to hear about politics.

'The average mental age of a stadium is rather low. No, it's true. It doesn't mean you have to treat them like animals. Peter's quality is that he knows that these people sitting way up there who don't see well, don't hear well, who drank two twelve packs of beer and are watching the show, he knows how to get to these guys, but not in a primal way, he does it in a very intelligent way. He believes in the intelligence of the audience, that's what I admire.'

Gabriel attempted to explain this to Robert Sandall in *The Sunday Times Magazine*: 'Sometimes the air of meaning is as important as the meaning itself. Musically and visually it's really about creating pictures.'

By January 1993 the basic format of the show was finalized and Steve Hedges had to inform his agents that this was to be an unusual show. With Gabriel's schedule of promotion, videos, the experience park and a new CD-ROM project, and Lepage's varied commitments, simply being in one place at the same time was proving difficult. They grabbed a few days here and there in Box, New York and Montreal. The tour was to start at the Globe, Stockholm, on 13 April 1993. Final three week rehearsals were booked for the village of Shepton Mallett, location of the 1982 WOMAD disaster, preceded by a two-week band rehearsal. The village was proving unlucky again. The large Bath and West Showground Hall was freezing and a nasty flu bug wreaked havoc among crew and band. Tension was high and morale low. New lighting equipment arrived at the last minute and the sheer complexity of the technical innovations was causing problems. The dome which was lowered over the circular stage had to have parts remanufactured. Prop designers used to working for the theatre and stage had to adapt to working in tougher materials that had to withstand life on the rocky road. The sixty-foot walkway linking the stages failed to work for the entire rehearsal period, preventing the band from finishing a clear run through the set.

One week before the tour started the band decamped to New York to test the music, devoid of the elaborate staging, in front of a modest crowd at the Academy. Gabriel told them, 'We're here to knock a little rust off before we do this on a bigger scale.' It proved worthwhile ironing out glitches like the whistling sound emitted by Gabriel's synthesizer which was clearly not part of the set. 'This is what's known as a dramatic pause,' he joked. 'And what's also known as a technical fuck-up.'

Steve Hedges was fighting to keep the show within budget, which proved impossible. 'It wasn't easy to quantify everything beforehand because one was breaking the rules,' he says. He and Gabriel were acutely conscious that they could be heading for financial disaster with development costs well over £1 million and a weekly bill of £100,000 just to keep it on the road. Hedges and Maria Pedro would try and impose budgetary ceilings. 'But there'll always be a good argument as to why you need to spend just that bit more', says Hedges. Pedro told *The Sunday Times*, 'Peter always puts his money where his mouth is. I have arguments with him about it and invariably I lose.' She predicted the tour, even if a sell-out, would do little better than 'wash its face'. With initial ticket sales in Europe appearing sluggish fears of financial meltdown loomed. As Gabriel wryly observed to Q magazine, 'You want a piece of wood to solve a particular problem and you think it'll cost £10, but by the time you've flown it round the world it's cost you £10,000.' To minimize costs Hedges had stipulated a rigorous schedule for the tour. The technical magazine *Sound on Sound* noted, 'It is incredibly adventurous for a touring show. A complex set that you would expect to leap-frog in duplicate on tour is in fact being rigged and de-rigged back-to-back (i.e. in and out of each venue in the space of less than eighteen hours) across Europe. And nor is the tour playing a comfortable two city/four show weekly schedule; five nights in five different cities has often been the task facing Gabriel's crew, and that's very hard work.' Or as Q put it in its jocular style, 'This is by some distance the most ambitious, and possibly most lunatic, tour of one-night stands in the history of indoor rockular entertainment.'

Initially fired by his admiration for Gabriel's artistry, Hedges was no longer enjoying his job. He found the pressure and frustrations intense and his role usurped. He had always lacked one essential power when he took over as manager, control of Gabriel's finances. When Gail Colson quit they had been placed in the hands of Maria Pedro. 'Peter was saying I want my money to be managed by somebody I'm employing. And I think that was probably the turning point, because at the point where the money is managed in-house all the management has to be done in-house,' says Mike Large. 'Steve might say well, we're going to do this, but if Maria wouldn't sign the cheque or didn't feel it was right financially it would make it very difficult to move forward, so there was conflict there definitely.'

Then there was the way Gabriel wanted to be kept informed on the smallest detail. 'He likes to be involved in making a lot of micro decisions and there are a lot of them so it is not surprising he ends up being logjammed a lot of the time. And I must say if I was in his position I probably would want to be involved in those decisions, particularly as he has such strong artistic and moral views on most of the things he is doing. I can only liken it to trying to put Stephen Hawking on a Thomsons Holiday,' says Hedges.

The whole notion that Gabriel needed a manager was flawed from the start. 'I think anybody who tries to manage him is going to be in trouble because Peter isn't somebody who wants to be managed, he wants to be part of a team of people taking a very creative approach to managing all his businesses, including his career,' says Mike Large. 'He doesn't want somebody to tell him what to do. And Peter is always willing to listen to other people. Peter is very good at taking on board loads of opinions. Something that people in any of his management positions find very frustrating is that he will listen to everybody's views, not necessarily just over his man-agement, and, yeh, the structure that had been created with Maria, myself and then Dave T and Steve, I think, was completely untenable for Steve because the three of us were full-time employees for Peter, we worked directly for Peter on salaries. Steve had his own business and took commission on some measure of success of Peter's career and it was bound to end in conflict.'

At the start of the tour Dave Taraskevics, known as Dave T, who had helped produce Gabriel's previous live shows, was switched from running Real World Studios to managing the tour. Dave T hired Dave Parry as tour manager. Hedges was a manager looking for a role. His experience as an agent naturally inclined him to take an interest in the smallest details that go into touring, and it was Dave Parry in particular who came into most conflict with him. 'I think Steve knows the nuts and bolts of how it should all work and therefore wants to make sure the people carting the nuts and bolts are doing it the way he thinks they should be. Certainly there were people out on the road who thought they could be doing Steve's job better than him, and that not only should he not get involved in what they are doing but they weren't very pleased with his strategic planning.'

Mike Large had several meetings listening to various grievances and tried to steer Hedges into a more strategic role, to get him to plan where the tour should go next rather than day to day issues. 'But eventually things came to a head and at that point it was something Peter had to deal with.'

Bruce Kirkland, Hedges' ally in America, was hearing the varying stories. 'Steve is a very uncompromising, demanding, super-intelligent guy who doesn't truck idiots easily. He is very brusque and started to rub people the wrong way. Peter was starting to get feedback, there was a bit of a mutiny from his camp. It was very difficult for Peter. He agonized over it for a long time. He definitely had a great liking for Steve.'

Hedges was at a disadvantage working from his office in Islington, North London. Gabriel might walk across the courtyard and give instructions to staff in Box, but this would not always filter through to Hedges. 'The machine was running by that point largely from there, and me trying to move battleships on the great war chart from up here was more difficult because I couldn't always have all of the information,' says Hedges. Hedges felt the irony of being treated as an outsider by the Real World operation at a time when Gabriel was talking about us and them. 'The definition of US relative to the album is you are one of us or you are one of them. I was geographically one of them. Certainly spiritually from my point of view I was one of us,' says Hedges.

Eleven days into the Secret World tour Hedges was with Gabriel in a car in Rotterdam when they agreed to part company. It was never called a sacking, though for Hedges it was not unexpected. Rumours had been circulating in the business for some time. For any manager to leave an artist mid-tour, when round the clock business and negotiating skills are called on, is a sign of how far the relationship has broken down. Ten days later a press release explained as non-specifically as possible that as increasing aspects of Gabriel's career were being looked after by Real World Studios it was decided that full, in-house management was a logical step forward.

Hedges watched the show that night and the following day returned to England. 'It kind of left a void. It was like getting off a fast-moving train,' he says. Over the next few months they worked out their financial settlement and severed all business ties.

The first leg of the European tour trundled on, nine trucks hauling 60 feet of conveyor belt, two stages, an 8-foot tree, a red British telephone box, giant heads, 58 crew and a band party of 12, performing 36 shows in 32 different cities in 49 days.

Lepage's view was that all his stage productions were works in progress as much after the first night as before. He had no choice either way as the Secret World tour hit the road. One song, 'Lovetown', was dropped from the album at the last minute because it was too downbeat, but Lepage had kept it in the show designing an elaborate set of an outsize hotel room and TV sets rising on to the stage with Gabriel singing in bed. 'It was a wonderful moment of theatre, it's just that the song wasn't upbeat enough to survive this huge enterprise, so after the Stockholm and Oslo shows it was out of there,' says Lepage. At least the conveyor belt worked for the first time after its failure in dress rehearsals as Gabriel came out of the telephone box clutching a telephone with its cord extending 60 feet. The other effects: geysers of steam shooting up for 'Steam'; the video screen displaying thrusting and tugging train axles; Gabriel standing with a pole as if punting along, courtesy of the conveyor belt, for 'Across The River'; the tree rising on cue for 'Shaking The Tree' ready for its appearance on 'Blood Of Eden'; the screen swivelling for 'San Jacinto'; for 'Digging In The Dirt' the micro-camera poised on the end of an antenna attached to a helmet on Gabriel's cranium giving us uncomfortably graphic shots of his facial anatomy and craggy dental work; the giant suitcase gliding on the conveyor belt for the finale of 'Secret World' as the band disappear into it and the dome lowers to cover Gabriel; and then the encore as the dome rises for 'Don't Give Up'.

Catching the show at the start of its British leg at Sheffield Arena, the thirtieth date of the tour and with most of the kinks ironed out, David Sinclair of *The Times* declared: 'An original, highly complex and superbly judged production even by his scrupulously high standards, the Secret World show is Gabriel's most ambitiously theatrical work since his days with Genesis . . . For an arena production such as this, there is an unusually high quota of slow songs, but the ingenuity of the staging is enough to compensate for a slight feeling of sag which creeps in near the middle of the show.'

Writing later in *Rolling Stone*, Sinclair was more fulsome. 'As the dust settles at the end of his European tour, it's clear that Peter Gabriel has snatched an astounding triumph from the jaws of potential disaster. Media and audience responses to his Secret World show have been ecstatic.' There were dissenting voices, like Gavin Martin in the *NME*, who wrote, 'It's a big production that feels empty, underwhelms, fails to ignite the emotions.' An Italian critic got closest saying, 'The music has modern nerves, an ancient skin and sudden openings on the future.'

Gabriel felt triumphantly vindicated. He told *The Sunday Times*, 'I was always optimistic about this tour. There were always pessimists among us, doubts whether everything would work. But I, ah, did not share them. I did have the, ah, riot act read to me from time to time. But when you've got something set up in your head, it's very hard to cut it down.'

He told me at the time, 'In some countries in Europe ticket sales started off very badly and I thought, uh, uh, here comes the slide. Then I started getting philosophical about that. I've always said that failure can teach you more than success, so I may actually have to taste it myself, and fortunately, or unfortunately, depending on what way you look at it, we started playing and word of mouth started moving tickets and now it's got stronger. In America I think it's stronger than it ever has been.'

For the final British shows at Earls Court, Gabriel brought in Sinead O'Connor to guest with him on 'Come Talk To Me' and 'Blood Of Eden'. On tour Gabriel duetted on these songs with Joy Askew, his new keyboard player. O'Connor's appearance highlighted the drawback of having Askew singing from behind her keyboards, where being virtually static she was limited in her ability to tap the drama of these songs and be an emotional and dramatic foil to Gabriel. He had been generous in his praise of Askew in the tour programme notes. 'It's great having a woman's energy in the band.' This turned out to be a premature sentiment. Her presence as the first female member of a Gabriel band in fact caused friction, another case of us and them. Despite the expected liberal credentials of a Gabriel band, machismo insidiously won through. 'The band were very unhappy with the presence of a female musician amongst them,' says Lepage. 'I don't think Peter had that problem, I think he really tried to make things work and to be a good father in all of this, but I think the rest of the band were very resistant.' Askew was replaced by a new talent, Paula Cole, whose stunning looks and stage charisma complemented Gabriel's energy. A couple of years later Cole emerged as a major star in her own right in North America.

Gabriel had one extra date wedged in before Earls Court. He had agreed to appear at the Peace Together concert in Belfast. When the announcement of his involvement was made in March 1993 he thought he would be just one of several mainly Irish stars. In the event he became the only major act.

The concert, due on 29 May in front of a crowd of 35,000 at the Boucher Road Playing Fields, was billed as Northern Ireland's biggest ever pop concert, one of three simultaneous shows in Belfast, London and Dublin. Gabriel had not played in Ulster since his Genesis days. That rock and roll could be harnessed in the cause of healing the tortured politics of the province was the noble, if quixotic, aim of the non-sectarian, non-political organizers, the rock musicians Robert Hamilton of the Fat Lady Sings, who was born in Dublin, and Ali McMordie of Stiff Little Fingers, from Belfast. All money was to benefit youth organizations throughout Northern Ireland.

By mid-May, instead of simultaneous concerts, the shows were to be held over a more manageable three consecutive weekends while the Belfast concert was scaled down, transferring to the 7,000 capacity King's Hall. The line-up was confirmed as Gabriel, Maria McKee, Saw Doctors, The Orb, The Levellers and Del Amitri – only one of these main acts was Irish and none from Ulster. It was clear ticket sales were desperate and, despite their denials this was not a marketing ploy, the organizers offered a free T-shirt to everyone who attended the show in the hope of luring wavering punters.

An IRA bomb at the proposed concert hotel, though unrelated to the event, did not help confidence. Convinced the promoters had pulled out Gabriel jumped rather than face a débâcle. He did not need the aggravation on top of the stress of his own tour.

Gabriel explained his decision in a statement: 'I am a great supporter of the spirit behind Peace Together and, when originally approached by the organizers to lend support to a benefit concert, which would feature predominantly Irish musicians, I was delighted to take part.

'My original intent was to contribute rather than to be the driving force behind what I believed would be an Irish-led festival. Unfortunately, the eventual line-up, ticket sales and the reluctance of other peace movements to support the show, seem to indicate that this is neither the right time nor the right way to stage such an event.

'I am extremely concerned that there may be a feeling of resentment amongst the people of Belfast, who live daily with the problems of conflict and who were faced with an English artist headlining a show to highlight the issues of peace in Ireland.

'If it can be postponed and restructured along the lines originally proposed, then I would be more than happy to be involved, if at all possible.' That was never to be.

The promoters contested Gabriel's claim that they had withdrawn their support, though they did suggest the organizers cancel or postpone the concert. When Hamilton and McMordie raised an extra £50,000, to cover costs in case not enough people bought tickets on the day, the concert was back on. By then it was too late. With Gabriel announcing his departure they could not risk going ahead.

Apathy if not downright scepticism towards peace organizations, supposed opposition from rival promoters and the organizers' own lack of experience all contributed to the concert's failure. The following week's Peace Together concert at The Point in Dublin did go ahead with New Order and Liam O'Maonlai of Hothouse Flowers, but Sinead O'Connor pulled out. She was in a nervous depression, though she had appeared just four days earlier with Gabriel at Earls Court. The Dublin concert was attended by 3,000 people, less than half capacity. Gabriel did appear on a single, 'Be Still', the Hothouse Flowers song, with Feargal Sharkey, O'Connor, Liam O'Maonlai and Nanci Griffith. Though this too sold poorly.

The Gabriel promotional machine was a slicker creature in North America where Bruce Kirkland applied his marketing nous. Kirkland knew that it was important to concentrate on selling tickets as soon as they went on sale rather than wait in hope for the show to hit town. He came up with the concept of the area closest to the catwalk being designated Peter Gabriel's Secret World. Through radio promotions competition winners were awarded these privileged tickets. 'It was a first for a radio promotion of that type in America and a lot of bands took up the idea after us,' says Kirkland. 'The winners were made to feel like they were in Peter's inner sanctum. Radio stations jumped all over it.' Combined with good word of mouth and critical reviews, Gabriel was able to buck the initially poor showing in Europe and the American tour mostly sold out quickly. Far from being able to just 'wash his face', Gabriel achieved the near impossible and made a profit from the tour, which returned to Europe having finally played in all five continents and to an audience of over one million.

In early May 1993, during a day's break from touring France, Gabriel had flown to Paris to meet Rosanna Arquette, on her way to promote a film in Cannes. It was their first proper meeting since their break-up. Arquette was in a fragile state. She had just split with her boyfriend Paul Buchanan and was mourning the death of Lulu, her beloved lhasa apso, killed by a coyote outside her home in the Hollywood Hills. Reconciliation was in the air. Just a few weeks before this I found myself, unexpectedly, in the last salvo of crossfire from Rosanna towards Peter.

I had requested an interview with Gabriel on behalf of the *Daily Mail* some months before and was not sure he would agree since he did not normally give interviews to tabloids. Subsequently I also requested an interview with Rosanna on behalf of the *Mail on Sunday*'s *You* magazine and her agreement came through first. I flew to Los Angeles and interviewed Rosanna in a musty suite in the Mondrian Hotel, then a faded sixties slice of modernism on Sunset Boulevard. Rosanna came with Lulu and we had an entertaining time trying to make a decent English cup of tea. Rosanna was plugging an awful new film, *Nowhere To Run*, in which she starred with Belgian bone-cruncher Jean-Claude Van Damme.

Aware I was probing about her relationship with Peter when I questioned her about coming over embittered and hurt she said, 'Oh come on, come out with it, Spencer. What do you really want to ask me?' I told her about the coincidence of me interviewing Gabriel in the coming weeks. The emotional floodgates did not need much prising open.

She wanted to demolish every accepted opinion of him: He was 'a real fake. I think he rips off people; He's one of the most ambitious men that I've ever met in my life; his nice guy act is a front and he is manipulative doing it in the guise of, "I'm so humble and [she imitates his soft voice] um, um, I just, um," that kind of thing. That's what he does and that's what he's master at, and it's crap.'

This was her first opportunity to respond after having their affair dissected on *US*. 'What I don't like is he constantly brought up our relationship in the process of selling his album. I'm not with this man any more. I have no desire to be with him ever again. I admire that he is able to have people worship the way he is.' As she has long planned her own film about the affair she may be able to get her own back. The movie,

*Access All Areas*, has love obsession as its theme and is being co-produced by Arquette and her friends, the actress Meg Ryan and leading Hollywood producer Linda Obst.

Fundamentally, Rosanna believed that her love for Gabriel was flawed because it owed more to romantic delusions than a grip on reality. 'I was so young when I met him, and impressionable, and it was all fantasy. What I did learn was it wasn't love, and I had to learn that the real hard way. I bought this myth of love, what I thought was love, and it really, really, really was nowhere near what love is. It was fantasy, it was a fairy tale.'

Therapy helped her realize why she was drawn into such relationships and stayed with them. 'You're buying the myth of these little moments of happiness when the whole picture is incredibly bleak. And that is the lesson, that a lot of women buy moments, just little moments and think that they can base their whole life on twenty-four hours of happiness. Well it's a hard lesson to learn.'

In the contest of wills he came out the stronger, resulting in her feeling her life blood was being sucked from her, something she believes also happened to Jill. 'There is a similar thing that we both have and that's obviously what he was attracted to, but that was ultimately what he tried to destroy in both of us, which was our independence and fire. He tried to take from us what he himself didn't have. And, ultimately, if you give somebody all that you're left with nothing.'

In Rosanna and Peter's case they each had to contend with high-profile careers which, instead of being complementary, caused friction. Each a star in their own right found it hard to deal with their partner's celebrity. Rosanna, against her nature, became submissive to please her man. 'I never in my life will get myself into any kind of situation like that where I would lose myself. I truly got nothing out of the relationship at all, nothing. I just gave and really got taken.' And furthermore, 'I walked away from this with a real sense of self. If I had stayed I probably would have died in this relationship. [Meaning the death of her spirit.] I think losing myself is a death on its own.'

Rosanna has an excitable way of talking that is little girlish despite the venom and seriousness of the subject. In our interview she was aware of what she was revealing while convincing herself it was all right to be so indiscreet. As if answering a disapproving parent or friend she says, 'I just don't care. I really don't care. I'm going to tell the truth.' She could contradict herself in the same sentence, worried she would come over embittered even though she admitted that she was. 'The guy is such a narcissist that if he thinks in his soul that I was hurt or bitter he would just love that.'

She resented what she thought was the public's perception, that she was the tart who stole him from his wife, saying the reality was the opposite, that he pursued her for years. She greatly admires Jill and says the biggest mistake Gabriel ever made was to leave Jill. 'I know ultimately in that whole break-up I was just one thing, and that was the catalyst to get him out of his marriage, which is what he really needed.' For Gabriel, recently out of a long marriage, there was an unwillingness to slip into another one when he had never really been a single man. This was borne out by the retinue of beautiful, often high-profile, women he was seen with during these years.

Most men admit to difficulties controlling their hormonal imperatives. Rosanna put it down to the effect of dominating mothers and the consequent fear of symbolic castration. 'Men are really afraid to commit. It's their mothers. They're afraid they're going to have their dicks cut off. Excuse me. It's true, I'm sorry. They feel suffocated and swallowed up as soon as they feel they have to commit. What is it?' The disintegration of Arquette's relationship with Paul Buchanan ended a line of distinguished musician boyfriends. Within a year her long expressed desire for a child would be fulfilled when she became pregnant with her daughter Zoe and married Jon Sidell, an executive at Interscope Records.

Having delivered my article to meet the six-week print deadline of *You* magazine, I went to Nimes in southern France to interview Gabriel who was appearing at the town's open-air Roman amphitheatre. I was informed by Gabriel that he and Rosanna had met up the day before. She had forewarned him about having vented her spleen.

I wrote at the time, 'As we sit in the ground-floor boardroom of the Hotel Imperator Concorde a few fans knock on the window. Peter, ever polite, waves and works up a smile. He'd escaped a crowd of over 200 waiting outside the Roman arena where he'd performed that evening. The fans waited by the tour bus as the band piled in. They should have looked more closely at two figures on bicycles making their way through the crowds. One of them was Peter having some after show exercise.

'He can be the nice guy and he can be the crafty deceiver. He's more the latter according to Rosanna Arquette. "I know there's a lot of bitterness there. One of the characteristics of the two of us was that she would always say more than she felt and I would say less than I felt. When a relationship breaks down you tend to think the other person's a bastard, particularly if they've been the one who's ostensibly destroyed things. She's a very emotional person." Gabriel and Arquette subsequently resolved their differences. "I'm very fond of her, so I don't mind if she's unloaded this stuff."'

I read him a list of Rosanna's main accusations. 'She's a very emotional girl. Sounds like she was feeling quite hurt . . . It's certainly not the way she behaves towards me and I think . . . Well it upsets me, obviously [Lots of pauses]. Well it doesn't add up with how she was talking through a lot of stuff yesterday.

'I'm not getting into a tit for tat. What really matters much more than gets in the newspapers is how we deal with the stuff ourselves. There's been a lot of shitty feeling and also I think that's cleared up very largely now. We had a heart to heart last night. I think if you were to catch her in an interview now I don't think she would come out with the same stuff.

'I would say I'm very hurt that she felt it necessary to say those things, but I actually feel in a very good place with her right now. The fact that she's out of this other relationship [with Paul Buchanan] has allowed a certain amount of space for us to look at stuff that was not really cleaned up. With Jill I had really good joint therapy, and I should have given that to Rosanna because I didn't do that at the end of that relationship.' He refuted the suggestion that it was a bit idealistic to expect lovers who have had a massive fallout to go together to therapy. 'No, I don't think so. If there was a love there in the first place, there should be an openness to sorting things out. And if you take the view not that the other person is trying to pull you back in, but that you're trying to actually learn about yourself and the other person, how you worked in that relationship, then it will reduce the chances of that happening a second time.'

Answering some of Rosanna's specific points he said, 'I don't know about being ambitious, hard, dark, having that part of my personality. I don't want to be this amiable teddy bear because I've never felt that's all of me anyway. I don't think her characterization of me is particularly fair either. I'm a human being made up of good and bad.

'I actually still think I treat people pretty well; there's a compassionate element in me that is naturally sympathetic, that's in my nature. But with people that get very close to me, when it starts getting threatening to me, or when it starts pressing my buttons, then I can be cold and cruel I think. I wasn't conscious of that for a long time because it's a shut-down mechanism. I think the only people that I've hurt a lot are those that I've loved.'

It brings to mind the quote from Kenneth Tynan that he incorporated, with the permission of Tynan's estate, into the song 'Lovetown'. 'We seek the teeth to match the wounds.'

'It's a great line, I think it is true. If I've got some emotionally disturbed elements they're going to be drawn to emotionally disturbed elements in other people. So the best chance you have is if you and they: one, both know that; two, are prepared to work on it, and three, are prepared to work on that together. That I think is a realistic way of looking at relationships rather than assuming everyone else is shitty or you've got to wait for the prince or princess to come along.'

Despite his advocacy of therapy, he was aware of its limitations. Some things you simply inherit from your parents whether they are good or bad. 'From my mother I got a love of music, a passionate and compassionate nature, energetic enthusiasm and her need to organize, perhaps to over organize. From my father I got a love of invention, new ideas and the more withdrawn, reflective and meditative side.

'I think there's a certain amount of inherited behaviour that you pick up from generation to generation. I look upon it that you get dealt a hand of cards and of those twelve cards maybe you can change two or three in your lifetime but the rest you hand down to your kids. It's a matter of trying to work on that and doing the best you can. As an adult you can end up blaming everybody, even your forebears. You have to take responsibility for your own actions.'

So we are trapped and free at the same time, and if Gabriel is playing a clever act then it's no more than many of us attempt. And as for Rosanna's snipe at their sex life and his need to catch up on the lost freedoms of his youth: 'I think I probably was backward in coming forward. I used to have insecurities about love making and all the rest, which I don't any more. I mean if I get a malfunction it can bring out some fears, but basically I feel, eh, um, much more comfortable in my own skin than I was before.'

On my return home I found the following messages on my answer machine from a sombre Rosanna: 'Hi, Spencer, this is Rosanna Arquette calling. I'm actually in Paris 331 . . . And I wanted to talk to you about our article, I don't know if it is too late, but anyway. I realize I was pretty awful about Peter and I feel awful about it. A lot of things have happened, one of which is Lulu my dog got killed by a coyote, it did something really amazing to my life. A lot of my bitterness and anger, I guess it was coming off that way, was protecting my relationship with Paul, who has found it very humiliating to constantly have to read about my past relation-ship and the glory of what people think it was, and it was incredibly hard for him. But Lulu died and [tragi laughter] my relationship with Paul has broken up, although we are still friends, and I realize that in this article I've just done this whole number.

'There were some things . . . Peter didn't want to be in the relationship because he needed his freedom and all that stuff. I think that was really, really extra tough and I feel bad about it. I don't know if there is anything you can do about that. If there is I would appreciate it. You've got my number here in Paris . . . [Cuts off. Rings back little while later.]

'Hi, Spencer, it's Rosanna again, Arquette. I'm calling from Paris. I left you a message earlier today and you haven't gotten back to me [Sounds tearful]. I'm very upset with my behaviour and anger and resentment, obviously at Peter, that came out at you. All that I can say is that there was a tremendous amount of love there and a lot of it never got to be healed up. I just wanted to say that I really need to take full responsibility for this whatever the consequences are in terms of my responsi-bility and the things that I said.'

Rosanna continued the conversation, saying she took responsibility for what she had said but wanted it known that she was now recanting, and explained: 'I was in a difficult position and felt really a lot of unresolved anger that was never able to really be resolved until recently, and it's a really good thing.'

She continued, 'If it's going to be that I come off looking like a total lunatic jerk then that's OK with me because I don't want to just slag Peter off as a terrible person. We had a very intense, intense relationship and it was very painful to break up for me, and I never really got to fully express the hurt. It was painful that, ultimately, he needed to be free and I think it's hard for any man to deal with the fact that I have a career that takes me away and puts me in the arms of other men on screen. I don't know if that was a real threat to Peter, but I just know that that's something I'm dealing with in life and that's my dilemma in life.

'I'm alone right now [close to tears] without my dog, without a boyfriend, without a relationship and I am really [cheers up] OK. I am standing on my own two feet . . .' She scolded herself for being a 'blabber mouth', and said, 'It just came out in an emotional gush and I was angry and it obviously was a way to protect Paul and to hurt Peter.'

She concluded that Gabriel was 'very aware of his dark side, and everybody has a dark side, and it's great that he's coming to terms with his and it doesn't mean that he's a bad guy or a terrible guy and I feel really, really clear and healed with him and it is actually really an amazing, wonderful feeling to have that in my life, and I need . . . is it recording? . . . OK . . . Bye.' When I got the message I did try to ring Rosanna in Paris, but she had already left. The magazine article had already gone to press and was due to be published the following week, there was no way of stopping it.

Rosanna was not the only beautiful woman associated with Gabriel to be the subject of column inches. There had been a relationship with Marie Helvin and speculation about flings with supermodels, and in August 1993 a picture appeared of Gabriel on a boat off the Spanish island of Majorca with a topless Claudia Schiffer. It wasn't as exciting as it sounded when you realized her mother and sister were present too. Schiffer threatened to sue Italian, French and German magazines who published the picture on the grounds it jeopardized her contract with her model agency which forbad naked photographs. She was legitimately pictured clothed for *Hello!* magazine celebrating her twenty-third birthday at a Paris restaurant with Gabriel singing 'Here Comes The Flood' in German to her, apparently it was her favourite Gabriel song. It was a charming scene, and their brief affair was surely an undemanding relationship, a welcome contrast to his other involvements.

The emotional flood was coming however in the person of Sinead O'Connor. She had been experiencing a drawn out mental breakdown. The catalyst had been her bold if self-destructive actions in America in the autumn of 1992 when, in a protest against music censorship, she refused to play a gig if it was preceded by the American national anthem, and tore up a picture of the Pope on the *Saturday Night Live* TV show as her way of blaming the Roman Catholic church for her abused childhood. She subsequently sold her home in Los Feliz, California, and moved back to Dublin. Preying on her mind was her abusive mother, who died in 1985, and the breakdown in her relationship with her father and brother angered about her speaking out on the issue. She saw in Gabriel someone who could heal her and attempted to rekindle their brief liaison. In September 1993, as a mark of her affection she dedicated her album of covers, *Am I Not Your Girl?*, to 'the angel Peter Gabriel'.

O'Connor told Phil Sutcliffe in Q magazine the following year that Gabriel was the person she had felt closest to. 'I needed him as a father, not as a lover. He didn't want to have anything to do with me because I was such an emotional rollercoaster and this hurt me so much, because I was in a bad way. It was all awful.'

Gabriel found it hard to deal with the unstable O'Connor,

who despite publicly expressing a desire for a father figure made a convincing show to Gabriel that she wanted a fully-fledged relationship. Gabriel says, 'There had been various emotional outbursts on tour. There was a set of events where she'd made clear her feelings. I certainly had been clear that I didn't want to get into a committed relationship. I was really fond of her but I should have pulled out a lot earlier given that I wasn't going to commit.'

Gabriel and O'Connor attended the MTV Video Music Awards at the Universal Amphitheatre in Los Angeles on 2 September 1993 where 'Steam' won the best editing and best special effects categories. Off stage Gabriel was having a drama with O'Connor. 'I'd seen some old girlfriend in LA, that triggered a little bit of bad stuff, so I knew she was very unhappy with me,' he says.

Sinead put a different spin on the story to Q, 'He went off with all these glamorous women because all these glamorous women are always queuing up to shag him and then there was going to be a three-day period when I was going to be by myself because there was no gig and I couldn't face it so I wanted to go to sleep, but I said to God in my mind, whatever God is, I said, I don't care if I die.'

Gabriel had a long-standing engagement to meet up with his daughter Melanie. Though O'Connor had never expressed a desire to commit suicide, and Gabriel had never suspected it was on her mind, he was sufficiently concerned about her behaviour to get the hotel manager to let him into her room. They found her in bed, apparently asleep.

'We could wake her but she looked like someone who had woken up with a hangover or the morning after taking sleeping pills. Heavily asleep rather than an attempted suicide. Both I and the hotel manager, who was totally independent of any of this drama, hadn't felt that she was in danger. Had either he or I really felt there was danger at that point we would not have left her.'

Unknown to Gabriel and the hotel manager, O'Connor had passed out having taken a pile of sleeping pills washed down by vodka. 'All I could hear suddenly was, Is there a pulse? And I'm inside myself saying, Fucking hell, there is! I'm here! Peter took one look at me and said, I'm not having any part in this, which I can understand because he thought I'd done it because he wouldn't go out with me.'

Gabriel was annoyed. 'I wasn't sure how much of what I was seeing was real and how much was to get a reaction. I thought that the situation was being exaggerated and that there was some sense of competition between the time I'd organized with my daughter and the time she wanted to have with me.'

Removing the remaining sleeping pills, Gabriel left her to sleep it off. 'What I did after that, of course, was ring the hotel doctor, get another bottle of sleeping tablets and pass out till Saturday morning,' said O'Connor.

In a previous interview, where she first revealed the suicide attempt, O'Connor scolded Gabriel for his reaction. 'I feel very strongly about this attitude about people who try to kill themselves, that they're just looking for attention. This is something I came up against with Peter Gabriel. I would take it very, very seriously if anyone said that they were going to kill themselves. I would not even leave a stranger alone like that.'

Gabriel issued a statement at the time saying, 'Looking at it in hindsight, it is clear that we misread the situation . . . I am very fond of Sinead, she's a wonderful woman, and I have always tried to be a friend. Obviously this time she felt that I let her down.' He was contrite having learned the gravity of Sinead's state of mind, though the incident highlights an insensitive and intransigent side of Gabriel that usually remains hidden. All concerned were fortunate that Sinead's *cri de coeur* did not slip into something altogether more tragic.

Gabriel was angry, though not enough to bounce her off the WOMAD tour of America which she had requested to join. To make sure she got on her way, and he could avoid dealing with her, he sent his tour manager to help her pack. They flew on the same plane on their way to Saratoga, upstate New York, but he refused to talk to her. 'He had this very punishing attitude towards me where he was really angry and wouldn't sit near me. He assumed I was trying to get attention.' He was not aware that O'Connor was already a changed woman, claiming a conversion to a positive attitude when she awoke from her pills and vodka fog. 'I was suddenly so grateful for my life in a way that I never had been before,' she told Q.

This was to be WOMAD's first tentative steps in the United States where the multicultural formula that had worked relatively successfully in fourteen other countries needed fine tuning if it was to adapt to the rigid genre and racial demarcations peculiar to the American music market. A previous attempt at a modest tour in 1990, with Ry Cooder as the headline act, was abandoned, no doubt wisely, when WOMAD realized it lacked the financial and organizational muscle to ensure success. And just three weeks before the start of this tour two opening Canadian dates were cancelled because of feared losses.

In the wake of recent financial disaster, WOMAD was particularly wary about incurring losses in America. In December 1992, ten years after its first financial crisis, six of the organization's eight companies were forced into voluntary liquidation with debts of over £300,000. It had been stung by poor attendances at the previous summer's World in the Park celebrations in Bath, and overstretched itself that year of economic recession celebrating the tenth anniversary of its first festival with seventeen festivals around the world.

Though sharing the Real World complex in Box, the WOMAD companies were separate financial entities to Gabriel's organization. As in 1982 when Genesis and Tony Smith came to WOMAD's rescue with the Genesis reunion at Milton Keynes, Gabriel was again helping out though this time trying to make sure the financial management could not get WOMAD into trouble again. 'I didn't want to control WOMAD, but I did want to make sure that everyone was not put in jeopardy as I had been the first time round. I found it very scary to be the fat cat sued by creditors; there were death threats at the time. It was very unpleasant,' says Gabriel.

Real World Studios was one of WOMAD's major creditors. The studio itself was going through a lean period, business and studio rates had nosedived. 'We were living courtesy of a bank manager,' says Mike Large. 'Based on our business plans and cash flow and management accounts they could see that it was a business whose best chance was digging itself out of the recession rather than just collapsing.'

In January 1993, World in the Park, part of Gabriel's Real World group, paid the receiver around £30,000 for WOMAD's name, trade and assets. Some of the twenty staff made redundant were rehired and the machine carried on smoothly with founder and artistic director Thomas Brooman still at the helm. Gabriel's total investment in WOMAD rose to over £100,000 before the business was secure. He performed at the next WOMAD festival, WOMADelaide in Australia, in February 1993. Now Gabriel had an interest in protecting his investment as well as a commitment to world music. It also marked the first public performances of material from the forthcoming US album.

To stand a chance of success in America, WOMAD had to make compromises. Instead of the usual weekend festival it became a one-day event, and toured to maximize resources. The musical format also had to be altered, reversing the 60/40 ratio favouring world music over Western pop-rock in a country where world music had a minimal audience. They had to bank on Gabriel's star attraction. He was appearing without the special effects of the Secret World tour which would resume in Central and South America in the autumn. Crowded House, P. M. Dawn and Stereo MC's, plus Lenny Kravitz and

Ziggy Marley at a couple of dates, were among the pop-rock acts joining eight Real World artists such as the Drummers of Burundi and Sheila Chandra. At a press conference in Saratoga, Gabriel was candid about needing to 'get the market in', though he was uneasy with the compromise. His ambition, he told reporters, was to take WOMAD to Central Park, New York, and said he would appreciate any pressure the press could put on the authorities.

At Saratoga and a couple of other venues, much of the festival was inside an arena sized 'shed', thus restricting the enjoyment of an event whose habitat is naturally outdoors, where food stalls, craft markets, classes and kids' activities are essential WOMAD features. There was confusion in the crowd about the strange sounding name of the festival. Artists were repeatedly asked, 'What is a WOMAD?' The question was unintentionally pertinent. Artists had their own variation on the name – WOE-MAD.

The main charm of WOMAD is wandering relaxed between stages to catch different musical cultures. The weighting towards pop-rock on the main stage left the Saratoga crowd unsure where to find the best fun. David Herndon from *Rolling Stone* wrote, 'The imbalance was a pity, because the festival vibe was much more in effect at the smaller stage. In the main pavilion, many of the orchestra seats had been reserved by people who skipped the festival and came late to see Gabriel.' He noted, 'Grins were in short supply at this strangely sober festival,' and it took Gabriel, 'to gather the loose ends and make the crowd of strangers into an audience'. It wasn't a good omen when, before his own set, Gabriel came on stage to introduce Sinead O'Connor who was booed by a hostile section remembering her outbursts. What the baying rabble didn't know was how fragile she was after her suicide attempt of just a few days before. Not that they would have cared.

The lack of a festival atmosphere was similar in Chicago,

until the forces of nature stepped in. 'Artists, audience and venue observed each other a trifle warily until a massive electrical storm transformed the evening into something magical,' wrote Mark Cooper in Q. The storm forced James to abandon their show and move to the main stage for a brief well-received impromptu acoustic set, building the atmosphere, which Gabriel capped. Cooper wondered why promoters had not alerted the kind of crowd that went to see Grateful Dead or Neil Young shows. 'Most of the 10,000-plus crowd were MTV regulars in their early twenties and many of them only turned up in time for Gabriel,' he wrote. The poorest turnout had been 7,200 in Pittsburgh on the second night, but as the festival made its way westwards interest grew, and for the final date at the Polo Fields in Golden Gate Park, San Francisco, the anticipation was unprecedented. The gates had to be closed in order not to endanger the crowd estimated at over 110,000. At last WOMAD felt like it was achieving the critical mass Gabriel and Brooman so passionately believed was its due. The irony was that here at its peak it was ill-prepared for its own success. While the critical response was positive, as it had largely been throughout the tour, the high turnout left some of the crowd fearing for their safety. Amy Marks, writing to the San Jose Mercury News summed up a common complaint, 'We risked our lives (and feet and hands) to hear music and get walked on for four hours,' adding it was too dangerous to leave her spot to explore the rest of the festival. Still, the show achieved a status hitherto undreamed of for WOMAD. It was reported to be the largest paid concert in the world for 1993.

In WOMAD America, Gabriel saw the opportunity to gain first-hand experience of how crowds react to the emerging interactive media technologies of the kind he wanted to see in the experience park. The idea he conceived with Brett Leonard was the Future Zone. Leonard described the concept impenetrably as a 'swarm-cam blendo station'.

'Future Zone was conceived as a place where people could

explore and experiment with new ideas in technology. Brett was one of the people we contacted to come up with some ideas and he suggested sending out a group of guerrilla cameramen: giving a lot of people video cameras, which could then come back and get blended into a vast bank of images,' says Gabriel.

The zone was funded by Apple Computer and proved enormously popular. People waited in line for hours to have a go. Leonard continued to develop virtual reality and interactive media 'entertainment experiences' through his company L² Entertainment for powerful clients like Creative Artists' Agency and IMAX, and planned to collaborate again with Gabriel in this field.

The 1993 WOMAD USA tour was enough of a success for them to try again the following summer. There were similar problems, West Coast dates had to be cancelled and the show in Jones Beach, New York State, had to be downgraded to a smaller venue. Thomas Brooman called the tours 'a semi-disastrous march around the Enormo-Domes of America'. Gabriel told the *New York Times*, 'This is not the easiest country to sell the idea of a willingness to listen to other cultures and other traditions.' It was not until July and August 1998 that WOMAD USA was established as a three-day annual festival on the model of everywhere else in the world when it found a home in Redmond, east of Seattle, Washington State. Welcoming that event Gabriel acknowledged, 'Over the years, we have discovered that a different sort of spirit evolves in a weekend event than a single event.'

According to some reports at the end of 1993, Gabriel was one of the largest paid performers in the world for 1992. Sadly for Gabriel this was simply a slip of a decimal point. Instead of the £16 million he paid himself according to the *Guardian* it was in fact £1.485 million. The article appeared with a Kipper Williams cartoon of a goofy, ponytailed, sunglasses-wearing rock fan checking out a record store CD rack displaying the categories Rich, Very Rich, Loaded and Rolling In It. The newspaper corrected the mistake two days later. The report was based on figures supplied by *Labour Research* magazine. It was still a sizeable amount of course (though way behind Phil Collins' £12.6 million), particularly since it was before the profits from *US* and the Secret World tour would have rolled in. As he had done with the success of *So* which financed the setting up of Real World Studios, Gabriel liked to reinvest his money in apparently high-risk enterprises often against the wishes of his advisers. His increasing wealth enabled him to finance his further ambitions with his new company Real World Multimedia which was producing his first CD-ROM.

# CHAPTER EIGHTEEN

I T WAS A BOLD SPECULATIVE MOVE. TAKE ONE of your favourite artists. Stick some of his videos, music, lyrics and graphic style all on a computer disc, and try and sell his work back to him as the next stage in artistic and technological evolution.

Chance and chutzpah conspired to give Steve Nelson the connections he needed to approach Peter Gabriel with the idea that became *Xplora 1*, to date the most successful music CD-ROM ever produced.

Steve Nelson was a risk taker in the American tradition, heading west to seek his fortune. First to Hollywood where he worked as a director and writer for news magazine shows and marketing videos. At college, where he had studied architecture and design, psychology and linguistics, he taught himself to programme. This multi-disciplinary education was ideal for the emerging world of multimedia.

Nelson's marketing videos were commissioned by computer companies, and through them came a connection with Apple Computer and their offshoot software company, Claris, where he devised an authoring tool that allowed people with no programming experience to write their own programmes which ran ten times faster than conventional programmes. His programming and media skills seemed ideally suited to the work of the Apple Advanced Technology Group, who hired him to work on a portable CD-ROM player and devise a news magazine programme for CNN.

With the profit from a programming licence he sold to Apple, Nelson set up his own company, Brilliant Media. Nelson's first commission was setting up an intranet for Warner Brothers where executives could, among many more mundane tasks, look up from their desktop PCs any actor in Hollywood and see how much money they had made, the work they had done, and view video clips of Warner films. This was a system way in advance of any other company. Like Gabriel, Nelson shared an interest in, as the marketing men say, being ahead of the curve.

Compact Disc Read Only Memory, a clunky name for such a slick and shiny five-inch diameter slice of plastic polymer, was a natural development of the digital-audio CD discs invented by the giant Sony and Phillips corporations and first marketed in the early eighties. Capable of storing hundreds of thousands of pages of text, the CD-ROM was seen at first as a useful tool to catalogue what in the not too distant past had been stored in an office full of filing cabinets. It was not too big a leap of the imagination to see its possibilities as a multi-entertainment media by adding video text and graphics to audio.

As Gordon Moore, co-founder of Intel Corporation, had predicted in 1965, chip speed would double every eighteen to twenty-four months. This rate of exponential growth in processing power has continued and been matched by parallel advances in all forms of computer hardware.

In late 1991, when Nelson founded Brilliant Media, personal computers were just at the point where they could process all the information needed to make CD-ROMs run smoothly, and there were enough CD-ROMs in people's homes to make investing in the medium commercially viable, if somewhat risky.

Nelson knew that if there was to be a market anywhere for CD-ROMs it had to be among music consumers. Despite being a fan of Gabriel's, Nelson says setting him in his sights was a hard-headed calculation. 'This was definitely a decision based on demographics in the market places as much as anything else,' he insists.

One of Nelson's consultancy jobs was at the American Film Institute in Los Angeles. It was there he met Mark Geiger, co-founder of Def American records, one of the most influential labels in the eighties rap scene. Nelson showed him his mock-up CD-ROM based on the *So* album, using Gabriel's videos with screens showing lyrics and graphics. Geiger, a business acquaintance of Steve Hedges when he was an agent at Primary Talent, effected an introduction.

Nelson and Hedges met in Los Angeles in the summer of 1992. Hedges was intrigued enough to get a copy to Gabriel. Soon Nelson was visiting Real World to work on the planning of what became *Xplora*.

Gabriel had long been familiar with the technology and years earlier had taken part in an experiment in interactive TV with Professor Diana Gagnon at the MIT Media Lab, an experience that had inspired him to explore the artistic opportunities presented by the new technology. Gabriel was interested in Nelson's CD-ROM ideas, although the aesthetic of the original demo was too sci-fi for his taste. Nelson's timing was perfect, fitting in with Gabriel's plans to move into multimedia. Before any money was invested, Gabriel's first business concern was to secure his own rights to copyright and publish his own work in multimedia formats. Hedges set about the task.

As when Gabriel had foreseen the coming of video promos and negotiated the rights for himself, so it was with CD-ROM. 'We were negotiating earlier than we were putting the CD-ROM together the position where we had the rights to put whatever we wanted into a multimedia form, which caused some confusion to the labels because they at the time weren't aware what multimedia was,' says Hedges.

In effect Virgin and Geffen were allowing Gabriel the right

to release, through his own company, work to which they owned the licence. Hedges says it was a bone of contention between him and Ed Rosenblatt, president of Geffen, annoyed that Hedges was bringing up an issue he could see no future in, feeling the then yet to be released *US* album was a far more pressing issue.

With his rights ensured, Gabriel set up Real World Multimedia to embrace the experience park and CD-ROM. Already on board as a consultant was David Eno, who with the experience park in abeyance transferred to the development of *Xplora*. Nelson financed his own software development while Eno's job was to get investment from potential distributors, supervise the drawing up of contracts and marketing. Here was another source of conflict that had made Hedges' position untenable. Having introduced Steve Nelson to Gabriel, Hedges wanted to manage the CD-ROM project. He was opposed by David Eno and Maria Pedro who, according to Mike Large, argued the project should be brought in-house at Real World with Eno in charge. Eno says he found the political manoeuvring distasteful and tried to stay aloof from it.

Convergence, synergy, symbiosis seemed to be flying around the eighties vocabulary. These words reflected Gabriel's belief in the inevitability of art and technology coming together. With the dawn of the nineties, multimedia and the information superhighway became buzzwords. Multimedia's time had come as personal computers cranked up their processing speed capable, with the help of the fast-growing number of CD-ROM units, of showing video and audio.

The experience park had provided Gabriel with a forum in which to explore the possibilities of emerging media. His success, particularly in the wake of *So*, provided a passport with which to meet the foremost prophets and exponents in the arts and sciences. Gabriel's computer of choice was the Apple Macintosh, which Apple likes to trumpet as the dominant machine favoured by the creative community for its smarter graphical interface and superior graphics software. Gabriel took fifty Macintoshes with him on the Secret World tour where the machines performed sundry crew functions from controlling the lighting to handling the accounts.

Gabriel had been an Apple fan since the release of the first Macintosh in 1984 and, like so many, saw in the machine's user friendliness and Apple's emphasis on innovation and quality a continuation, however misplaced in the brutal world of corporatism, of sixties idealism. It was assumed Apple Mac users were also more likely to be Gabriel fans than the Microsoft fraternity. The plan was to develop *Xplora* initially for the Macintosh. As that was where Nelson's programming skills lay they had little choice, though not developing a simultaneous Microsoft Windows version was an oversight that would heavily hinder potential sales.

Nelson went to Box to use Gabriel's archives and create a prototype to attract investors. He met with John Sculley, then Apple CEO, who was so impressed his company used the test CD-ROM to demonstrate the capabilities of multimedia, though Apple declined an investment role. After nine months, with funding still not in place, Gabriel took the plunge and invested his own money in the hope backers would turn up. In spring 1993, as the Secret World tour started, Nelson and a team of production artists began work full-time on the final product. There had been some classical music CD-ROMs, taking a scholarly approach where a music score was shown progressing in time to the music. Gabriel and Nelson agreed *Xplora* had to be innovative, high quality and 'non computery'. They didn't want buttons or many words, their interface had to be intuitive and based almost entirely on imagery.

Key to the final look of *Xplora* were Mike Coulson and Nichola Bruce who were appointed Gabriel's visual co-ordinators for *US* and commissioned all the artwork. Coulson and Bruce were partners in a company called Muscle Films whose work was admired by Gabriel. With the experience they gained working for Gabriel they were able to bring a coherent vision to *Xplora*. 'Though Peter has a very strong visual sense, he isn't a visual artist. He can't draw for instance. So what they did very well was act as interpreters between Peter saying, "I really want something that looks and feels like this," and producing a set of sketches or sitting down with a designer to create a look that Peter wanted,' says Mike Large.

Gabriel and his team at Real World came up with the look they wanted to see on *Xplora*, using archaeology, geology and the elements to evoke a natural interface as a means of progressing through the disc. It was stylistically in keeping with Gabriel's videos and other work and the album covers for Real World which were based on natural textures and natural photographs.

Nelson and Gabriel spent many hours discussing the *US* album on which *Xplora* was to be based. 'A lot of *US* was about getting into your psyche and uncovering things you don't necessarily want to look at. So the whole interface is subtly about digging deeper into things,' says Nelson.

Nelson found himself having to readjust to the Gabriel way of working, taking his place in the Gabriel circus, catching up with him on tour where necessary to show him his latest work or hold discussions. It was a professional relationship rather than a friendship. Nelson found Gabriel remote in that English way he has. 'I understand why someone in his position probably needs to be very guarded who they open up to,' he says diplomatically, while full of praise for his creativity. 'For me the greatest bonus of working on this was getting to spend time with him, seeing how he works.'

Gabriel's vision was to allow the audience to get inside his work, an extension of the ideas of the experience park. Some of the development work was surprisingly low tech. Artists' sketches were brought to Gabriel to show him the design of each screen. Nelson had a programme that could help sort out ideas and find ways of connecting them, though he also used

Post-It notes stuck on a big board and moved around. Story-boards were created for planning the action in the same way they are used in movies and promo videos.

For the final six months of *Xplora*'s nine-month development, David Eno moved to San Francisco, basing himself at GBN's offices in Emeryville. 'It was the only way that it was going to get done. It was very difficult to control the developers from the other side of the Atlantic,' says Eno. That's not the way Nelson saw it: 'I didn't find him particularly helpful. He took some very aggressive stances with us.' Eno had tough negotiations with Nelson's lawyers that infuriated both sides. 'I think people found Steve Nelson frustrating,' says Eno.

The antipathy was mutual and even more vitriolic from Nelson's side. He found Eno, 'very difficult and petulant to deal with', adding, 'he was obviously very much out to be the star'. At one point Nelson and his lawyers pulled out of the project because they could not work with Eno. The situation was resolved by Gabriel's effective co-managers, Mike Large and solicitor Michael Thomas.

Eno felt his input was crucial. 'I thought it was a great opportunity for Gabriel, and I wanted to make it happen, so I made it happen. It wouldn't have happened if I hadn't dedicated a lot of time and effort to make it happen.'

Large disagrees. 'You could just as easily argue that it would have happened quicker. When I reached a settlement with Steve about his royalties I had to discount all of David Eno's costs out of the project because Steve didn't feel those should be attributed to the project. That is an indication of how things had broken down.'

As egos were being bruised and Gabriel distracted on tour, it was a wonder that the project came to be realized. The combination of Gabriel, Real World and Nelson's joint vision, design and programming skills resulted in a product unlike anything that had come before. The key was a belief that the medium had to be humanized. 'It's much less about the graphics than it is about creating a good experience for people and understanding how people think and creating a virtual language on screen so that they can navigate through that information or that experience,' says Nelson. 'Interactive design shouldn't be about the technology, more about the human face of the technology, trying to create an experience for people.' Computer buttons on the interface were ruled out.

The images are rich with 3D effects, the use of photocompositing to give a glossy slickness and subtle design touches. Gabriel's design aesthetic had become more homogenized, and Nelson's team conformed to the style established by Malcolm Garrett who had designed the *So* and *US* covers and Real World albums. The four elements, earth, air (in the form of electricity), fire and water are used as a backdrop for all the action. Screens are littered with natural imagery, cunningly or sensitively used to reflect the mood of the adventure. When clicked, the earth viewed from space leads us into a section of world music. Consuming flames and scorched earth surround the gruesome film of tortures and executions on the Witness section.

In the same way Gabriel used the *US* album to dig beneath the layers of relationships, so the CD-ROM is designed to go from outer space, through the clouds, through the sea, past waterfalls and calm lotus-flowered lakes, on to landscapes either lush or barren or frozen, through moist soil and beneath the ground as your adventure proceeds.

'One of the things we're trying to do with this *Xplora* is get under the skin. In a sense there are things that you can deconstruct and reconstruct, one of which will be my face, which is actually the vehicle which allows you to travel round other parts of the disc,' said Gabriel in an electronic press kit, a video introducing the medium. Clicking on his mouth takes you to the *US* album and videos, the nose to a look round

Real World Studios and rehearsals, the ears to WOMAD and Real World, and the eyes to Witness, Amnesty, information on Gabriel's solo albums and a family picture album.

Despite his attempt to literally give the technology a human face, for the techno-naïve it is a daunting experience, one where the initial feeling is of panic when confronted with a screen that has the options to Explore, Resume, Watch or Quit. Clicking Quit by mistake I'm surprised when a postage-stamp-sized video of Gabriel pops up in the top left-hand corner and says, 'Congratulations. You did it. You're a genius.' (I later find many irrational moments where the programme responds in an inappropriate way.) This innovation, building intelligence into the way the programme reacts to your actions, or lack of them, is known as a 'smart agent', which Nelson claims as a first.

Those not willing to be interactive can click Watch and ride at random through the CD-ROM as if they are on automatic channel scan. It is unsatisfying and defeats the object of the technology. Nelson calls it Eyeball Mode and claims it as another innovation. There are two other levels of usage. The Interactive Mode where you watch what videos you want, listen to the music of your choice and check out the human rights and career information in Peter Gabriel's world. Woven into Interactive Mode is the puzzle solving Game Mode.

Solving a simple puzzle – putting Gabriel's face back together in a police identikit picture, matching the right nose, eye and mouth – allows you to get on your way with *Xplora*. Once inside the most satisfying section is based around the *US* album. Here you see beautiful graphics of a lawn with daisies mapping out the word *US*. On the lawn is the first puzzle object, a solitary daisy which when clicked opens up a little suitcase, like the one Gabriel used on the Secret World tour, where the daisy is placed inside. There are twelve such objects dotted throughout the CD-ROM, which as they fill the suitcase give access to special visual treats.

The different sections in the CD-ROM are like different TV channels. Click on one and you can see Peter Gabriel videos, watch how they were made, see the director or producer or artist explain their work. Click another channel and you see artists playing instruments from around the world, like the kalimba and the valiha, and watch them briefly explain the instrument, while you can click a picture of the instrument and make your own crude sound. You can visit WOMAD and have a virtual festival experience, from people buying tickets to wandering into different activities and viewing artists on stage. Click another channel and you are in the Real World Studios complex, feeling like you are holding a shaky video camera and hearing the gravel crunch under your feet. As you go up to one studio an engineer greets you and takes you inside where you see Peter Gabriel rehearsing with Daniel Lanois and David Rhodes. In another studio you are greeted by Brian Eno and see a host of musicians rehearsing, you click on their faces for different combinations of sounds and video snippets. In another studio you wander round with a dog's-eye view thanks to a camera strapped on a dog named Spider. You can find a not very convincing looking mixing desk, and mix and save a previously unheard version of 'Digging In The Dirt', fading vocals or instruments in and out. Within the limits of the technology Gabriel argues this was a major innovation. 'It was the very first time that you could get inside a mix and change the relationships between any of the elements of the drums, guitars, keyboards and voice, albeit in a very crude way.' Click another channel and you see distressing footage of victims of brutality and can read short passages about Amnesty International and the Witness Program. You can find a family album with pictures of young Gabriel, clicking on the picture animates it into a brief film.

Boredom or bloody-mindedness makes one want to subvert the system. By not clicking for a while you activate the 'smart agents'. A little video of Gabriel appears saying, 'Try clicking on the colour bars, down there.' When you don't do as you are told a rather frustrated Gabriel pops up and tells you, 'Just try anything.' There are many variations of these little Gabriels, urging you to 'click your small furry thing' or some other jocular instruction. There is even a stern schoolmasterly Gabriel urging you to 'Get on with it. Come on, we haven't got all day.' While playing the musical instruments, doing nothing for a while brings on Gabriel instructing, 'Just try playing this with your pointer.' He then corpses, as if realizing the nuance of what he has said.

The puzzles act as motivators. Even if you are bored with what you are seeing you want to find another item to click into the suitcase to open up secret parts of the CD-ROM. The disc's greatest charm is the unexpected – Gabriel's messages, or the animations that appear when you freeze a video in the US section, prompting a mini-video of a trudging dinosaur or chuffing train. Clicking these you see extra videos, of a snail expert with a giant snail on his arm praising their slimy charms or a psychiatrist dissecting the phenomenon of trainspotting.

One of the toughest puzzles to crack is the Love Bomb. A little Gabriel pops up from time to time urging, 'Have you found the Love Bomb?' Steve Nelson was peeved at Gabriel's insistence on including the Love Bomb. It consists of flashing psychedelic colours and snaps of tasteful bosoms and backsides, outtakes from videos shot for the US cover. It was not the raciness that bothered Nelson, but the fact it was 'goofy'. It is not up to the high design standards of the rest of the CD-ROM, but otherwise it is harmless enough light relief. It was certainly an antidote to the most sombre part of the disc in the human rights section. Because of the footage of executions and mob violence there was a discussion that Xplora might need a ratings sticker warning of adult content, though the concerns were never acted on.

*Xplora* was successful because it brought some real innovation to the music CD-ROM market. It did not reach the peaks of sales of games like *Myst* and *Civilization*, which have sold in their millions, because it was not a fully-fledged puzzle solving CD-ROM. Whereas puzzle CD-ROMs are almost infinite in their variety, *Xplora*, despite its boast of 100 minutes' worth of video, 30 minutes of audio, over 100 still images and more than a book's worth of text, feels very finite. However, *Xplora*'s appeal was broad enough as one of the first and most advanced music CD-ROMs on the market to sell to an audience of not necessarily Peter Gabriel fans.

Gabriel, Nelson and their design team were limited by the confines of the technology at the time, where you could only get video on to CD-ROM at a quality inferior to VHS, and only viewable in a quarter of the screen. *Xplora* overcame such handicaps through visual tricks and the quality of design.

There were some real software advances. Nelson was proud he was the first person to devise a programme that pre-dates Apple's own Quicktime VR programme, allowing you to view a panoramic realistic landscape at will. He filmed the scenes wandering through the studio complex himself, handing over the camera to make a Hitchcock-like cameo appearance barring entry to one studio where he says the CD-ROM team are trying to sleep.

Nelson's sense of achievement was tempered by a realization, as the project progressed, that though breaking new technological ground, in essence what they were really doing was providing a new tool for the promotion of Peter Gabriel and his great works, and anything that did not fit that picture fell on the new technology's equivalent of the cutting-room floor. Gabriel was careful not to shoot himself in the commercial foot because of any possible overlaps between the

CD-ROM, albums and videos. The only complete *US* tracks on *Xplora* are the four that include videos, the rest are only snippets. The poor quality of the videos would make fans prefer to buy *All About Us* which contains a broader and visually sharper range of Gabriel's more recent work.

'Peter is very, very interested in, and savvy about, self-promotion to the exclusion of other things,' says Nelson. 'I had a say in defining what was in there too, I'm not going to blame Peter and say it was all him wanting to promote himself. I think we all thought about it and agreed this is what we want given the limitations of time and budget. Had we not had some of those constraints I think all of us, Peter included, would have liked to have had more interesting interactivity, more depth to this experience. It was important to get it out there in the time frame we did. It was important to keep it within a reasonable budget because Peter was funding it himself.'

*Xplora* is inevitably self-serving, as Gabriel's first foray into the medium of CD-ROM. It embodies the conflict he always grapples with, the need to expose his private persona in the pursuance of art, shedding enough light on Peter Gabriel the individual to satisfy our curiosity, while maintaining an aura of celebrity and enhancing his reputation as an artistic adventurer. Any successful star relies on the cult of personality to sustain their egos which so often become bloated as they achieve success.

Gabriel takes exception to the notion that his work on *Xplora* is an example of him being overly self-centred. 'The implication is that I find myself more interesting than anything else, and although on one level everyone is interested in themselves, when it comes down to content I find the non-Gabriel stuff more interesting to work with than rehashing or redoing anything that I've done before. I was always trying to push non-Gabriel material and it was Steve amongst others who was trying to get maximum Gabriel material because he thought it would be more commercial.'

Nelson says he has nothing but the highest regard for Gabriel's creative talents but he does not listen to his music any more. He explains this is because he overdosed when making *Xplora*. His experience with Real World soured because he believed he was not being provided with full accounting details and accurate sales figures and hired successive legal teams to deal with the situation. In 1996 Mike Large visited Nelson in San Francisco and believed he had resolved the issue by paying him an additional advance even though Real World claimed the project still had not recouped. Nelson however was still left with a feeling that the issue was unresolved and as late as 1998 was still considering legal action, though at a subsequent friendly lunch with Gabriel and Large at Real World the issue was not even discussed.

Nelson claims to have had the foresight in 1993, just as the world was waking up to the significance of the internet, to see how the on-line world and multimedia would feed each other. He says he built programme hooks into *Xplora* that would allow it to be upgraded, using a PC's hard disc, by downloads from the internet. If Nelson did show such foresight he did not share it with Real World who were sceptical of his claims. They did hold discussions with Nelson about producing a new *Xplora* disc that was capable of running on either the Mac or PC, and a version for a never-to-be-realized computer games platform called the Pippin being developed by Apple and Bandai, but market research indicated neither would be viable. Nelson didn't believe CD-ROM as a medium would last long. At the time he said, 'It will turn into interactive television and other distribution mechanisms.'

Gabriel, however, was positively evangelical. 'This is in no way a peripheral activity for me. I think that this type of media is going to be at the very centre of what I do in the future,' he told Martha Ladly in the *Box* in 1994. He saw this new art form as creating a fundamental revolution in the way people communicate with each other. 'I think that it's going to change the way people interact, the way that we live and even the way that we think.' He saw CD-ROM as being with us for ten to fifteen years until the on-line revolution took over. Despite its imminent arrival, even Gabriel could not foresee the impact of the World Wide Web.

For Gabriel the CD-ROM was a fundamental tool helping us on our way from being mouse potatoes to seekers of interactivity. It was but the first generation of a new technology we could only dream of, allowing us to make our own versions of artists' works. He saw within five years satellite communications allowing any village no matter how remote to join the information revolution using solar-powered, low-cost personal computers. 'As a result, pockets of the Third World, and eventually whole economies will be able to shift straight into information technology without having to pass through an industrial stage. I find that idea very exciting.' Though technically feasible a revolution in education was still a prerequisite for such a vision.

In a round of press interviews for the launch of *Xplora* in December 1993, journalists noted his evangelism with remarks like, 'To me, it seems like being alive at the time of the birth of cinema, or the birth of television; it's the birth of a new media. And in the same way that the first films showed trains going from one side of the screen to the other, we may be doing things very primitively at the moment, but when people look back in twenty years' time, it's great to feel you've been on virgin ground.' He thought that also within five years very few CDs would be released without some visual accompaniment. The reality was a few per cent.

Steve Nelson was also infected with Gabriel's optimism. Prior to release, he told *Keyboard* magazine, 'Just as musicians caught on to music videos and made it a big part of what they do, I think a lot of musicians are going to catch on to this and become multimedia artists.'

Suddenly multimedia was a buzzword throughout the record industry, and stars who deemed themselves cutting-edge, including Prince, U2 and Sting, thought they had better take part. Todd Rundgren, an electronic musical innovator in the seventies, rather pretentiously renamed himself TD-I, as in Todd Rundgren Interactive. His CD-ROM, *No World Order*, beat Gabriel's on to the streets of America in September 1993. Centred on a virtual mixing disc, it allowed you to shift the mood of the mix, say, from happy to sad. Deemed by one critic as more radical and interactive than *Xplora* though not necessarily more enjoyable, it was said to have a less innovative computer-style interface, responding to commands slowly. David Bowie's CD-ROM, *Jump They Say*, provided the ability to re-edit a video, and little more. The cult band The Residents had a highly praised product. Yet music CD-ROM sales were generally modest.

*Xplora* was praised wildly. '*Xplora 1*'s user interface has a beauty, simplicity and grace that invites exploration and experimentation. The visual layouts are masterfully executed – sometimes soothing, at other times challenging the eye,' said *CD-ROM Today*. It was 'mesmerizing' according to the *San Francisco Chronicle*, and 'quite simply the bee's knees . . . This is about as hip as it currently gets,' according to *Time Out*. But there were other views.

The cruellest one came from Jason Fine of the *San Francisco Bay Guardian*. '*Xplora 1* is, at heart, little more than a glorified video game . . . No matter how many choices are offered, how many tricks and surprises rise along the way, computer programmers still have the final word. In many ways, *Xplora 1* is not so much a "secret journey" as it is a brilliant advertise-ment campaign for one of pop music's most self-important stars . . . you learn a great deal about Peter Gabriel's products, but next to nothing about the man. And with a $50 to $60 retail price tag, the most notably "interactive" element of *Xplora 1* may be the act of the passive consumer being actively duped.'

Gabriel's timing proved immaculate, riding the wave of multimedia hype. His conservative estimates for sales hovered just over the 100,000 mark, the minimum needed to recoup costs. In the end it topped 200,000. While nowhere near the two million plus of *Myst*, it far outsold any other music CD-ROM. The only marketing hiccup was the delay in releasing the Windows version eighteen months after the Macintosh, leaving the impression among Windows users they were being sold an out of date product.

Nelson charged under $350,000 for his services. Gabriel's costs were a further $250–300,000. The elaborate *Xplora* booklet alone which came with the CD-ROM package cost $50,000, enough to make any book publisher weep. Gabriel secured a distribution deal in America, but in the rest of the world Real World arranged the manufacturing and distribution. Adding marketing and manufacturing costs Gabriel had to spend $1 million out of his own pocket before seeing any real return, a true act of faith in an as yet unproven market.

Whatever nervousness he might have felt soon evaporated as distribution deals fell into place around the world. 'We knew we had massive media interest in the project,' says Mike Large. 'It was a gamble. But taken in the light of a world in which we were operating where everybody was saying multimedia was going to be the next big thing, this is the death of the record industry, which is not something we ever said, we always said no it isn't. But we felt it was a big thing. We hit it at the right time and it was an enormously successful product.' As well as successful sales, *Xplora* also won more than fifteen awards, including product of the year from America's Digital Academy Awards.

With *Xplora* successfully launched, David Eno returned from San Francisco to see if any life could be breathed into the experience park. He had been having a fraught time, not just working with Steve Nelson and his lawyers, but dealing with the Real World camp itself, and new recruits like Megan Taylor. Nelson had introduced Gabriel to Taylor, a deal doer in the fine brash American tradition, and Gabriel hired her as a consultant to market *Xplora*. She counted among her friends Nancy Berry, who with her husband Ken headed up the Virgin organization in America, Jill Collins, wife of Phil, Steve Hedges and his wife, and Rosanna Arquette, though this did not appear to count against her. Gabriel saw Taylor's value in helping him form business relationships in North America. This brought her into direct conflict with David Eno, both competing for control of Gabriel's media development. Taylor also had differences with Peter Schwartz. 'I think she saw me as something of a barrier. Peter would talk to me and get advice that she didn't always agree with,' says Schwartz.

Feeling his strenuous efforts were not being appreciated, David Eno's relationship with Gabriel deteriorated fast. Claiming he was not a political animal he says, 'My loyalty was one hundred per cent to him, and if in my judgement people were trying to use him or had their own agendas I would try and point them out to him.' His relations with Nelson and Taylor were strained enough. Then in March 1994 came the appointment of David Stephen in the newly created role of Chief Executive Officer in control of the entire Real World operation. Stephen was to arouse the ire of several people. Gabriel seemed to be keen on hiring representatives with a Rottweiler approach to human relations, as in bite first, talk later. Was Gabriel overcompensating for his own mild manner? 'I refused to have anything to do with him. Gabriel was pulling the strings for Stephen and my grouse was with Gabriel. So Gabriel and I had some differences of opinion,' says Eno. Having known Gabriel since 1979 Eno could express his feelings more freely than most resulting on one occasion in a screaming match.

Pressure was mounting on Gabriel to do something about Eno. 'Steve Nelson and various other people we have business relationships with were all complaining about this guy,' says Large. 'He'd rubbed a lot of people up the wrong way. The problem from Peter's position is that people will always complain about the people who work for him because most of the time they are not giving people what they want, because what everyone wants is Peter, and at the same time.' Eno was sacked, and returned to the West Coast where his *Xplora* experience helped him secure the post of executive producer on *Voodoo Lounge*, the Rolling Stones first and to date last CD-ROM.

After Steve Hedges' departure in 1993, Gabriel was unsure whether he wanted another rock and roll manager. He again sought the services of the management consultancy who had helped him restructure Real World on Gail Colson's departure. He was persuaded he needed someone working out of Real World in sole control of all his business interests including his career as a musician. Following a recommendation by Michael Porter, a friend at Harvard Business School, Gabriel interviewed David Stephen. Stephen, a graduate of Oxford University and Harvard, was working for Sega UK. Gabriel interviewed him twelve times before taking him on. Stephen's brief was to make Gabriel's group of six companies more profitable. Though an expert on multimedia and trained in business jargon and practice, he had to learn as he went along in Real World: familiarizing himself with running a recording studio, WOMAD (he was a fan of world music) and a rock star's career.

In appointing Stephen, Gabriel was inadvertently shifting the focus of his career as an artist to a much broader range of interests. The mere fact that Stephen's expertise was in multimedia and not music meant he did not have the experience necessary to guide Gabriel with as steady a hand as a seasoned music industry operator.

'I had been very drawn to David's very wide range of interests and abilities from making documentary films on biology to Oxford and Harvard,' says Gabriel. 'He seemed to be very intelligent, imaginative, motivated, and with a good sense of humour. I felt he might be able to move Real World further down the path, to add a bit of dynamism to a much broader range of interests. I didn't have any misgivings about his lack of music business experience. I felt we had, with Michael Thomas advising us, and all the rest, good reservoirs of experience, and we would pull that in as and when necessary for live work and videos etc.'

Stephen's arrival coincided with a general excitement about multimedia becoming a major industry. 'As Peter realized and pointed out,' says Large, '*Xplora* had generated as much if not more press for him than *US* the album, so there was a lot of buzz around that, and David came from that background, so the excitement was about that business. In discussing David's role with him Peter focused on that and not on his own career.'

A new Peter Gabriel album was somewhere in the distant future. It gave Stephen time to hone his skills in the music industry, allowing him to concentrate on what concerned him most, expanding Gabriel's multimedia interests. 'The end result of that was to have somebody managing who wasn't focused on Peter Gabriel the artist, as indeed I think Peter wasn't at that time.'

Large continued. 'I don't think Peter downgraded his career as a musician. I think what it showed was in Peter's mind there was much more to his career than being a musician.' Citing multimedia, the Witness project and theme parks, Large said Gabriel saw a bigger picture. 'I think it was the start of Peter wanting to move, I guess from being a creator of music, to being a creator of experiences of which music is one.'

Stephen set about devising a business plan for each operation. In an interview with American technology and business magazine the *Red Herring* he said, diplomatically, that the state of the Real World businesses was 'unclear. Certain parts of the company were well run, while other parts were not so well run.'

Stephen came into immediate conflict with Maria Pedro. Not only was he responsible for firing her husband, but he had the power to overrule her on all business decisions. When Pedro took over Gabriel's financial affairs in 1988 she formed a company with him called Real World Associates to handle all his personal business matters. She would spend two or three days a week in Box and the rest in Conduit Place. She had been trying to rationalize Gabriel's business for years, but her brief, more liberal than Stephen's, was to manage his money 'in its broadest sense'. In the January edition of *BusinessAge* magazine she said, 'I find dealing with that kind of brief difficult sometimes – I occasionally forget and I try and make things more efficient and profitable and that causes creative tension.' Stephen was to be given a freer and more ruthless hand.

Stephen believed Gabriel's financial management should all be in-house rather than having it contracted out, even though Gabriel had the majority shareholding (51–49 per cent) in that company. Pedro was not prepared to compromise her independence. Gabriel was not her only client, she also managed sports stars. As the months wore on she became increasingly frustrated, growing furious at her treatment. Gabriel was caught between loyalty to a friend and a desire to support his new chief executive who was unhappy about the way the finances had been managed.

As part of his rationalizing of Gabriel's business, Stephen also wanted to dispose of Conduit Place. More egos were to be bruised as Gabriel's publishing company was moved to Box and Stephen sought to renegotiate the lease with Mark Borkowski, who ran a successful arts-based public relations company from the building. Discussions started off on friendly terms but ended in acrimony with lawyers. Borkowski accuses Stephen of being a 'power freak' and using 'heavy, threatening tactics' and blames him for ruining what had been a happy atmosphere. Stephen wanted Borkowski to take over the entire building. When they could not agree terms Borkowski vacated and Stephen disposed of it. Stephen did at least have an ally in Megan Taylor at Real World Multimedia. 'David Stephen was fine, he was trying to introduce a little order into the situation,' she says.

Stephen took up his duties as Gabriel carried on into the final stretch of the Secret World tour in Australia, New Zealand, Japan and Hong Kong in the spring of 1994. Gabriel took a break mid-tour in May to stay at his beach house in Dakar. He had been visiting Senegal since the late eighties to see Youssou N'Dour and bought the house in 1991. He did his best to get to the house three times a year to play, record and paint. 'One of the pleasures of arriving at Dakar airport is watching people walking around without hunched shoulders and that slightly fearful gait that you see in England,' he told *The Sunday Times Magazine*.

Any such lingering pleasure evaporated quickly when he was dismayed to find himself doorstepped by a reporter from the *News of the World*. By now used to tabloid interest in his love life, he was nonetheless ill-prepared for the interest of Britain's biggest-selling newspaper. What had excited them was the presence of Belle McLaren, who the reader was informed was a half-Chinese and half-Thai beauty. In fact she is an Australian of Filipino descent. Gabriel was quoted in a breathless style that seemed unfamiliar to those who know him, 'She's absolutely beautiful and I'm extremely attracted to her in a physical sense.' One quote did have the ring of authenticity. 'The *News of the World*? I don't believe it. I'm in Africa, for God's sake. How did you find me?' Belle was equally surprised it seems. 'Oh God, no, what am I going to do?' she is reported to have said. Her swimsuit clad picture graced the article.

It was a tale, tawdrily spun, implying Belle's husband, supposedly an old friend of Gabriel's, knew about his wife's holiday. In fact she was already separated from her husband, who she's now divorced from. Gabriel, who was also with a male friend, was quoted as saying Belle was 'tired and depressed and needed to get away from everything'. Unnamed 'friends' of Gabriel's insisted there was a romance. Gabriel was obviously disturbed by the intrusion and sought, possibly unwisely, to clarify the issue by phoning the journalist at his hotel. The report continued, 'Sounding tired and depressed, he said: "Look, who wouldn't want a sexual relationship with this woman? – although I'm not saying that's what it is."' Those that know Gabriel would realize that this sounds highly unlike his normal way of speaking.

Gabriel said he learned that tabloids could make up almost anything and get away with it. He very much wanted to take action for libel but was strongly advised against it. Gabriel says, 'In that story grains of truth had been embellished in such a way to make it much more salacious and a hotter story that would sell more papers. A lot of the quotes were invented. We were having an affair and I'd met her husband on two occasions previously. He's not an old friend. The story was fabricated around morsels of truth.'

He faced weightier issues returning to the tour to fulfil WOMAD dates in the Middle East. Gabriel had agreed to play at a Peace Concert in Jerusalem if the promoter could also arrange a concert in an Arab country. A date was secured in Cairo only to be cancelled because the authorities were worried it was a security risk. The Egyptians offered the alternative location of Taba, a resort on the Egyptian side of the border neighbouring on the Israeli Red Sea resort of Eilat. It was just over a year since the Oslo Peace Accord and there was still hope an Arab–Israeli settlement could be reached. For

Gabriel, wishing to show his support and encourage the us and thems to come together, Taba was the ideal place, close also to the borders of Jordan and Saudi Arabia and the location for peace negotiations between Israelis and Egyptians.

Gabriel had been sensitive about visiting the region in the past, feeling an appearance in Israel would be seen as support for the regime's policies. He thought now was the time to do his bit. 'It's very important for me personally and for us to try to support the peace process in any way we can,' Gabriel said. Bearing the slogan 'peace and culture without boundaries' the Red Sea Peace Concert billed for 18 June was to include Lou Reed and Sinead O'Connor and acts from South Africa, Morocco and Egypt. They believed they could expect to draw up to 14,000 fans from Israel, Egypt, Jordan and Saudi Arabia, though it was more likely the Israelis would heavily outweigh everyone else.

The night before the concert was due it was cancelled because the authorities feared they did not have fire, police and medical facilities close enough if there were any riots. Gabriel did not believe it was a political decision. The show was instead shifted to Eilat and special passes issued to Egyptians to make it easier for them to enter Israel without visas. There was speculation that the Taba concert was too fraternal a prospect to bear for the governor of South Sinai, fearing reprisals. It was a propaganda gift for the Israeli Foreign Ministry whose spokesman observed, 'People sometimes get stuck at the roadblocks of the past.' The danger to collaborators was real enough: one of the Arab artists, Adel Saloumi, had received death threats after he agreed to appear.

Gabriel also performed in Tel Aviv and tried unsuccessfully to devise a way of playing in Jericho within the jurisdiction of the designated Palestinian Authority. In the end all he was left with was the gesture of touring the Anata Palestinian refugee camp near Jerusalem.

The following week Gabriel was back on home turf, down

the road from Box in the fields of Pilton Farm, Somerset, singing to a crowd of 80,000 attending the annual Glastonbury Festival. The invitation to appear at Glastonbury was irresistible despite the fact it was impossible to perform anything like his full Secret World extravaganza. It was flattering to be regarded as one of the select set of older artists with enough credibility to make a largely young and critically demanding British audience want to watch and listen. For Gabriel, rooted in the area for twenty years, there was a special affection for Glastonbury and its Tor, which like Solsbury Hill and the Avebury stone circles were potent local symbols of an ancient spiritual and mystical heritage.

It was then on to WOMAD America before the final date of his seventeen-month tour, in front of 300,000 people at Woodstock '94. Gabriel was the headline act on the third and final day, coming on stage just before midnight on Sunday, 14 August at the mud-swamped site in Saugerties, New York State. Rain disrupted the event just as it did during those original days of peace and love at Yasgur's Farm in 1969. This time at least the stage didn't sink, but it rained more consistently resulting in tents sliding away and the crowd looking like extras from a lost civilization movie. The festival failed to recapture the revolutionary spirit of its forerunner, there were no Merry Pranksters or Hog Farmers, nor a crowd of nearly a million strong. But according to Jeffrey Jolson-Colburn of the *Hollywood Reporter*, it was not totally devoid of idealism. 'They braved the rain, the knee-deep mud, the cynicism, the spotty food service and half-mile lines for the toilets – and somehow found a voice for Generation X. "Mud people" who made it back to New York City were high-fiving each other on the streets.'

Gabriel wanted Woodstock '94 to be not just an exercise in nostalgia for a halcyon era, but relevant to present-day human rights issues. News had only recently filtered out about the horrors of the genocide in Rwanda that spring when an estimated 800,000 Tutsis were butchered by majority Hutu extremists. Gabriel asked the crowd to light a candle in memory of the victims. 'This powerful emotional gesture compensated satisfactorily for the absence of fireworks in his own show but, needless to say, he smouldered effectively,' wrote Adrian Deevoy in Q. Other reviewers were kinder, agreeing his set was the festival highlight.

Before the finale of 'Biko', Gabriel told the crowd, 'Twenty-five years ago people believed that you could change the world, if you fought for justice, if you fought for what you believed in, if you fought for your dreams. This is your Woodstock, these are your dreams.' Somehow in the mud-caked Hollywood Reporter writer's mind this became, 'This is your festival. This is your mud.'

Gabriel's stature had never been higher. US and the Secret World tour had consolidated his reputation as an estimable elder statesman of rock. He was no retro-act milking past glories, nor desperate to be frantically hip. He was certainly worthy, maybe stolid, but regarded as good value. Before setting out on the WOMAD America tour he had been interviewed by Jon Pareles of the New York Times. It was clear he was weary and was looking forward to coming off the road. Woodstock seemed an appropriate place to stop. 'And then, I'm going to take a serious break and give myself some time for normal life. I've been travelling so much I've lost touch. You know, evenings off, weekends, dinner parties. It may kill me, but I want to give it a try.' He said the gloom of recent years had lifted and for the past year or so he had felt much lighter.

It was not quite the end of the cycle. Peter Gabriel: Secret World Live was simultaneously released as a 100 minute double CD and video, capturing the feel of two concerts in Modena inserted into the schedule in November 1993. Gabriel had a special affection for Italy where he warmed to the uninhibited reaction of audiences. This was his first live album since Plays

*Live* in 1983. On the recommendation of Robert Lepage he brought in yet another French Canadian, Francois Girard, to direct the video of the concert. Girard was celebrated for *32 Short Films About Glenn Gould*, his documentary on Canadian pianist Glenn Gould.

It should have been just one show at the Palasport Nuovo in Modena. Gabriel was upset when he learned that an extra date had been added and tickets already sold. His fears proved right when neither concert was a sell-out, thus diluting the tension and excitement within the hall. 'It was a really tough environment to actually shoot this film,' recalls Lepage. 'Peter was very depressed. His voice also was not at its best. He was coming out of this flu and he had toured and sung a lot.' Gabriel was not above a little 'post-production' as it is usually credited on live albums, a euphemism for re-recording the bits he was not happy with. He was honest enough to spell out his tampering as 'additional recording and production' on the album sleeve.

Inevitably there were criticisms that the recording felt incomplete because he was such a visual artist. There is no way round that. There is an extra ingredient that is not found on his studio albums, a rawness that usually gets smoothed out in the painstaking production process. The live album scores by being imperfect, even if the after-effects of flu are evident.

Live albums polarize listeners more than their studio equivalents. If you have no affection for the artist then listening to them with annoying clapping, whistling and shouting fans makes it an even more arduous experience. In the critical response to *Secret World Live* there was an Atlantic split with leaden cynicism inevitably weighing in heavily on the British side and gushing praise on the American.

In Q, Mat Snow was unrelenting in his damnation saying it was, 'Like an orgy next door, full enjoyment of proceedings is dulled when prophylactically protected from even a glimpse of the fun. The theatricality of the show is to the detriment of the music in as much as the drilled production allows little room for spontaneous flight, though drummer Manu Katche energizes stretches which would otherwise plod in Gabriel's usual dawn-over-Kathmandu global anthem style . . . A 100-minute set . . . not only stretches Gabriel's repertoire but his voice too: though not exactly pony, it's certainly a little hoarse.' In *Vox* magazine the words dreadful, hopeless indulgences, and hammy sum up the reviewer's feelings. Not so for Susan Richardson of *Rolling Stone* for whom it was exuberant, majestic and prayerful. 'It's a rare moment when an artist takes his established, even iconic work and makes it still stronger,' she wrote. '*Secret World Live* is just such a moment.' She concluded, 'More than the studio originals, these versions elaborate on the dramatic potential inherent in them – the heat and magnitude of rhythm, the human/animal ambiguity of an otherworldly cry. *Secret World* enters an inner realm that is knowable only through the range of emotion it gives rise to, joining ecstasy and agony into music that avoids being larger than life and instead is as large as life itself.'

After the difficulties with *Point of View*, Gabriel wanted a straightforward concert film, without backstage shots, narratives or interviews. Girard achieved his aim of capturing a sense of intimacy from such a grand production, using twelve cameras to get every conceivable view, capturing the sophistication of Lepage's set, the not too embarrassing choreography, in particular the stately presence of Paula Cole, and Gabriel's dramatic ebbs and flows. Gabriel must have felt a warm glow of achievement when the video won the Silver Rose of Montreux, it qualified as a TV programme having been broadcast on ITV, and won Best Music Video Longform in the 1996 Grammys.

For Gabriel there was a certain irony in the success of the *Secret World Live* video. Though it was about a highly innovative show, the video itself was a retreat to a more conventional performance format, and yet it was still regarded, by the awards committee at least, as innovative. He could look back with satisfaction and gratitude at the dividends from his creative and financial investment in promo videos since his first forays in the early eighties. The success of 'Sledgehammer' and to a lesser extent 'Steam' had become major factors in establishing him as a groundbreaking multifaceted artist. In a field where marketing men and accountants hold sway, Gabriel had the independence and control to take video in whatever direction he chose. However artistic, the purpose of his videos is to market his records, but as with all his artwork, they are reflections of his own highly developed visual sense.

However ambivalent he might have felt about the validity of awards ceremonies, without such honours not only his ego but his creative reputation and bank balance would be adversely affected. He must have felt a certain amount of deflation with his mixed success at the 1993 MTV Video Music Awards. He was nominated for a highly respectable five awards yet won just two for 'Steam', while the stunning 'Digging In The Dirt', which had been up for Best Video, failed to garner any gongs. Neither song had managed to reach the American Top 30, a possible factor in the no show of 'Digging In The Dirt' in an industry more geared to backslapping than risk taking.

The effect of 'Sledgehammer' could be seen for years to come in TV commercials using similar claymation effects. In the intervening seven years between 'Sledgehammer' and 'Steam' the MTV generation and its successors were more blasé about special effects. They were influenced not just by videos, but by computer games systems where stunning 3D effects are commonplace. 'Steam', 'Digging In The Dirt' and 'Kiss That Frog', for all their innovations, were competing in a crowded market place.

'Lovetown', the track that failed to make it on to the *US* album and made a brief appearance on the Secret World tour, was used on the soundtrack to the movie *Philadelphia* and was released as a single in June 1994. *Philadelphia*, directed by Jonathan Demme and starring Tom Hanks and Denzel Washington, brought the AIDS tragedy to a mass audience not otherwise drawn to a tale about a gay couple. Gabriel's song was only relevant in so much as its message is about coming to terms with who we are. He at last got to use the Kenneth Tynan line 'We seek the teeth to match the wounds,' because it was about confronting the pain of the past so that we can move forward.

Gabriel made a video for the single based on the work of Japanese artist Yayoi Kusama, whose work derives from the hallucinations she has experienced since childhood. Hers is a disturbing vision she calls 'psychosomatic art', images of virus-like replications on skin, what appear to be maggots in frames or in the shape of a heart, a suitcase with scales. It was apparently a perfect match for the emotions Gabriel wished to express.

The video is verging on the abstract. The setting of the video is a trailer park as replicas of Gabriel in Homburg and overcoat holding a suitcase wander Magritte-like across a lawn. A supposedly normal family does its housework. Kusama's vision is brought to life in all its spotted and diseased horror, as if we are going beneath the surface of the skin to see people's rotten cores.

Though it did not storm the charts the single earned the praise of David Sinclair in *The Times*, calling it a better track than Bruce Springsteen's 'Streets of Philadelphia'. 'Slipping from a parched tenor to pleading falsetto, Gabriel's anguished performance lends an edge of quiet desperation to the sad, elegiac refrain while, underpinned by Tony Levin's sinister stick-bass line, "Lovetown" gently meanders into the wells of darkness that haunt the human soul.'

1994 was a year of collaborations: Gabriel's soulful version of 'Summertime' appeared on Larry Adler's *The Glory of Gershwin* album; and Gabriel recorded 'Taboo' with Nusrat

Fateh Ali Khan for the soundtrack to Oliver Stone's super-controversial movie *Natural Born Killers*. Nusrat's voice is chilling as he wails over a plangent soundscape created by Gabriel on instrumental duties. The song is built over the rhythm of what feels like the sound of a pumping heart recorded inside the body, and as it nears its end we hear the sound of gunfire and burning. It is Gabriel and Nusrat at their most desolate.


Paul Allen was always a rock and roll fan. He liked to play his guitar and worshipped rock's premier guitarist, Jimi Hendrix, a fellow native of rainy Seattle. As a rock fan he was interested in Peter Gabriel's music, and went to see him play in Seattle in 1983. It was a tumultuous year for Allen who, after being diagnosed with Hodgkin's Disease and then going into remission, resigned from Microsoft, the company he co-founded with his old school friend Bill Gates. Having helped design the disc operating system for the new breed of IBM personal computers, Allen wanted to branch out and invest in new technologies. He wisely maintained his shareholding in Microsoft, which turned him into a multi-billionaire.

There was a meeting of minds when he met Gabriel in Seattle, and over the years they became friends, travelling together and sharing their love of music and visions for the world of technology. In 1993 Allen founded Starwave Corporation to exploit multimedia and the internet. The company's early projects included CD-ROMs for Clint Eastwood and the Muppets. In September 1993 Starwave developers met with Gabriel in Oakland, across the Bay from San Francisco, where he had returned to fulfil a previously cancelled date from the Secret World tour. They showed him some of their ideas.

Gabriel and Allen's friendship helped, but he was an obvious person for Starwave to target for their venture into the CD-ROM market. Their hunch soon proved right with the release of *Xplora* which established Gabriel as the leading musician in the new field.

Megan Taylor, in her capacity as fixer for Gabriel, helped ignite Starwave's interest and secure the deal, and struck up her own friendship with Paul Allen (later to end in acrimony, and in its wake relinquishing her relationship with Gabriel). Mike Large was sent to Starwave's headquarters in Seattle to further investigate Starwave's programming abilities. He was particularly impressed with their ability to provide a visual 'toy' that could be moved about at will on screen creating and recording music. The Starwave offer was attractive for Gabriel. Unlike with *Xplora*, in which he invested heavily, they would bear all the development costs and would have the rights to distribute and market what was to become *Eve* in North America.

Mike Large and Gabriel's creative director Michael Coulson were put in charge of developing *Eve* for Real World Multimedia. What was meant to be six months of brainstorming turned into a year, and still there was no solid direction. There were certain elements all were agreed on: that *Eve* had to be an experience only possible using a computer rather than mimicing, in the way *Xplora* had done, a fancy magazine; there had to be a strong puzzle element enticing you to go further into the experience. As with *Xplora*, Gabriel wanted to avoid computer graphics and aim for a vibrant naturalistic feel best achieved using photographs meticulously pieced together (and the joins made invisible).

The promise of Starwave's considerable financial, technical and programming resources loosened Gabriel and his team's imaginations, often going well beyond what was practical. One idea was to have a 3D maze in a landscape full of hills and trees, a graphical representation of what they had hoped to build at the Barcelona experience park. Though technically feasible, the home computers that most people had at home, and were likely to have for the next few years, would make the experience too painstaking. That did not stop Starwave's developers attempt to square the silicon circle. 'Starwave at that stage felt a little too reluctant to say you can't do that. They almost took it as a challenge that they could do it. After a year we realized that this was mad, it would never get built,' says Mike Large.

Early in 1995, after consulting Gabriel, Large and Coulson had a serious brainstorming session. They locked themselves in Large's office for a week. They went from flow chart to script to storyboard. There would be more than one hundred screens; they devised the sort of puzzles that had to be solved, the journey that had to be undertaken and the environments that were to be experienced. They realized too that there had to be a clear division of labour, all artistic images should be created in Box, and then sent to Seattle for the boffins to turn the virtual into reality. They hoped the CD-ROM would be released by the end of 1995.

The studio mixing desk in *Xplora* that helped you change four sounds was starting to look crude by comparison. Star-wave's software allowed them to take a far more sophisticated visual and aural approach. Instead of dials and sliders there were animated segments. Clicking on Gabriel or Sinead O'Connor's heads made them fly across the screen and sing. Uncovering birds and bugs released movement and noise. All were added to a surreal representation of a recording studio. When pieced together the images made up one of four Gabriel songs which you could arrange to your own taste and record, or use to make a surreal video. The music was culled from session material that never made it on to Gabriel's records. The theory went that creating your own unique work of art would make for a more satisfying experience. This was the journey from passive consumer to active participator that Gabriel aimed for.

As with *Xplora*, Gabriel had wanted to include an area devoted to Witness and Amnesty. It soon became clear that one of the new rules of interactivity had to be adhered to. That if you were going on a journey you had to do so for a reason. In the jargon there had to be a 'back story'. There was no point in clicking on something just to get information, this was no database or encyclopedia. Human rights were concerns of Gabriel but covering this issue would interfere with the storytelling.

Human relationships were the core of the journey Gabriel came to embrace on *Eve* as the CD-ROM journey evolved. The plot that Coulson and Large worked out came back to a familiar Gabriel theme, the story of Adam and Eve. The video opens with a sperm that you need to guide to fertilize the egg. This takes you to a varied wild landscape. When you enter a mausoleum type building you find floating objects out of which falls that favourite Gabriel item, an old suitcase. This opens to release a Pandora's box of escaping objects including gnomes, Japanese stone lanterns and Gabriel's head on wings. Then a naked Adam and Eve extricate their entwined bodies and wander off apart. Our job is to take Gabriel/Adam on his journey through different environments to find Eve. *Eve* was an acronym for the convoluted Evolutionary Virtual Environment.

After trudging through primeval sludge the first building we come to houses the Human Relations Room. Inside what feels like a Delphic temple are chambers in the wall which when clicked reveal anonymous people giving candid video soundbites about their romantic lives. Gabriel felt compelled to join them in this exercise in soul-searching, though his observations are more circumspect than most.

We have to come back to the Human Relations Room and listen to more accounts as we reach different levels of the journey. As this is a voyage of (self) discovery, we have to go through a variety of landscapes that are metaphors for life's peaks and troughs: the mud you get stuck in, the lush pastures, the sweet flowers, the industrial desolation, claustrophobic gloom, wide horizons and calm streams. Photographers were dispatched throughout Britain and to France to collect the 22,000 photographs used in creating *Eve*'s images, from Avebury to a derelict house on a London film set.

In the different landscapes there are objects that when clicked perform different functions, they range from flapping fish to crumbling statues – they might change form and give a sound effect or lead you somewhere else, to a garden or rocky terrain. Everything you do is cumulative, providing the keys to new often dazzling screens. Cows and sheep grazing on pastures start glowing radioactively as you click them; ghosts float in a graveyard as tombs are clicked.

The Theme Rooms are dotted throughout the experience. Here human behaviour and relationships are discussed by eminent people. Among them are Gabriel's old family therapist Dr Robin Skynner, and the geneticist Dr Steve Jones, famous for his belief that we are all descended from one 'Eve'. The late Kathy Acker is there expounding on male–female differences, and the terrifying French artist Orlan who has her body surgically altered as an artistic statement. We hear her voice emanate from a statue saying, 'I fight God and DNA.'

Another building houses the IMX (Interactive Musical Xperiences). It is a vast improvement on the crude mixing desk of *Xplora*. Flying through the air are bugs, birds and other objects, which when clicked emit song snippets. This can be recorded and kept as your own mix of four Gabriel songs – 'Come Talk To Me', 'Shaking The Tree', 'In Your Eyes' and the music of *Passion*. There is a similar area where you can collect often surreal images and record your own video.

One of the central landscapes is a grassy panorama where Homburg and overcoat clad Gabriel mows a lawn. You click him or a variety of objects revealing special effects, or click on the buildings to enter into different worlds. There are four worlds in *Eve* which you continually travel between – Mud, The Garden, Profit and Paradise. As well as its unique landscape each contains its own art gallery featuring the works of four contemporary artists. Gabriel wanted to create a forum with the CD-ROM where visual art could be explored and appreciated by most of us who probably do not give it enough thought or enjoy its stimulations.

We have to uncover the artists' works and visit their galleries so we can progress. We get the chance to alter their art and create sounds with it. They are the kind of artists Mr and Mrs Angry Esq., from Tunbridge Wells would write letters to the papers about: Yayoi Kusama and her disturbing visions that represent the rotten core of our minds; Helen Chadwick whose often erotically shaped sculptures were made from organic materials like chocolate and flowers; Cathy de Monchaux with her strangely threatening and erotic combinations of hard and soft materials, metals, woods, fabrics, glass; and Nils-Udo who uses what he finds in nature to make a statement about the relationship between man and nature. He used the water and countryside around Real World to build eerie drifting objects to represent our shared humanity. His image of a naked boy floating in rushes is calming and optimistic as paradise is reached.

All the artists owned up to their own disturbed inner life, which was partly why they fitted so well with Gabriel's vision. 'It's not just an illustrator, but someone who's struggled in their own path with these issues, so it resonates much deeper,' Gabriel said. It is only Chadwick whose sense of play and humour seems unique. At one point we see Gabriel and Chadwick sitting in Duchamp's giant chocolate filled urinal tossing a bubble at each other.

The bubbling chocolate that you first see when you click on *Eve* is Helen Chadwick's *Chocolate Fountain*, which was exhibited at London's Serpentine Gallery where Gabriel saw her work and met her for the first time. Chadwick died of a heart attack in March 1997 as *Eve* was being completed. Her most controversial work, *Piss Flowers*, where she urinated in the snow and made casts out of the shapes, a joke that she was surprised to find had its own beauty, forms one of the alterable art pieces in *Eve*. 'She and Peter got quite friendly, mainly because she put so much energy and enthusiasm into *Eve* and had such a fantastic sense of humour that you couldn't fail to like her and be inspired by her,' recalls Mike Large.

In May 1995 *Billboard* reported that *Eve* was due to be premiered later that month at a multimedia festival in San Francisco. It was wildly optimistic. That July, Paul Allen visited Gabriel at Real World, not to discuss *Eve*, but to take part in Recording Week. It was becoming a celebrity event, the actor Johnny Depp and his supermodel girlfriend, Kate Moss, were also there. They could just look pretty, Allen had a more serious intent. An apparently accomplished guitarist, he even had his own rock band at Starwave. He joined in recordings with Gabriel, Karl Wallinger and Real World artist Geoffrey Oryema, though the results are yet to be released.

As sixty designers and technical staff soldiered on, another release date was pencilled in for spring 1996. That too passed. We were on Gabriel deadline time. *Eve* was finally showcased to the trade in the summer of 1996, ready for release for Christmas 1996. In its two years of development the CD-ROM market had radically altered. As Gabriel acknowledged, it had 'died a death'. Most theories on why the market should have crashed, despite exponentially increased CD-ROM-drive ownership, centred around the fact the medium was over-hyped in the first place and most products never lived up to expectations. The internet had rapidly taken over as the medium of the future. You could barely open a newspaper or magazine without reading about the information superhigh-way. If geeks were the main consumers of CD-ROMs they were too busy surfing the World Wide Web, and making the rest of us feel like myopic Luddites.

Starwave CD-ROMs suffered disastrous sales. Believing

there was no chance *Eve* could recoup costs of over $2 million the company honourably completed its obligations, but at the end of 1996 announced it was pulling out of CD-ROM development and in the future would concentrate on developing its internet-based operations. Paul Allen got out of the business, selling Starwave to Walt Disney, though his name still appears with Gabriel's as joint executive producer.

It was bad timing for Real World marking the start of unfavourable conditions which hampered *Eve*'s success in the United States, the world's most important market. They moved distributors to Graphix Zone who mounted a glitzy launch at New York's Chelsea Piers, but went bust soon after. *Eve* ended up being distributed by Valley Records, a specialist in selling records, not CD-ROMs.

The various delays had put back *Eve*'s full launch in America by nine months where it sold a disappointing 25,000 copies. Worldwide sales were 100,000, half those of *Xplora*, and not enough to recoup costs. Putting a positive spin on it, Mike Large says, 'In numbers it didn't sell as well as *Xplora*, but in 1997 100,000 was probably a hell of a lot harder to do than 200,000 in 1994.' They are hoping for further sales with a planned DVD version. DVD-ROMs, technologically superior to CD-ROMs, can hold about eight times the information and much higher quality video and audio.

Part of *Eve*'s problem was conveying to consumers the experience they were being offered. It sounded simple enough on the CD-ROM cover which termed it 'Eve: The Music and Art Adventure'. What exactly that meant was impossible to know without trying it. That meant not just sticking it in your drive for an hour, but spending days before you were likely to get the hang of it and wished to see more. Gabriel tried to entice people in. 'It's a spiritual and mythological collage,' he told *Salon* magazine, an electronic publication owned by Microsoft available only on the internet. 'We were trying to ask, if we were going on some journey, what would we like to encounter? What detours would we find interesting?'

Reviewers of *Eve* were often perplexed, sometimes openly hostile. The *Washington Post* had a nice phrase, calling the often frustrating experience the 'humdrum world of recalcitrant software'. *Newsweek* concurred, 'Unfortunately, *Eve* clunks along as a game: solving the puzzles becomes a tiresome obstacle to seeing more of the disc's content, which begins to feel arbitrarily hidden from view. That's too bad, because artwork this lovely shouldn't be such a chore to enjoy.' *Wired*, the bible of technophiles, complained, '*Eve* has countless rules that no one explains and that change with unsettling frequency.' While the *Los Angeles Times* cheered, 'Gabriel gives the stale CD-ROM genre a breath of aesthetic life with *Eve*.'

For sheer venom, once again a British publication delivered the bile. Adam Sweeting in the *Guardian* wrote, 'Getting to know *Eve* is as enthralling as watching paint dry – or mud actually, since you will spend ages trying to escape from expanses of dried mud, wet mud and bubbling mud. Advancing through *Eve*'s levels and landscapes is exasperatingly dull, literally one step forward and six steps back. The bits of music are usually bits of old Gabrielana remixed or recycled, and the gallery of people discussing their intimate relationships is so twee you want to put a boot through your monitor.'

Gabriel was best advised to use these publications for wrapping his fish and chips while framing the admittedly little-known magazine *Computer Arts* which gave *Eve* five stars and enthused, 'The artwork and sounds seamlessly combine to take you from the ambient, to the fraught. And the journey itself? From the moment you begin, your curiosity is piqued and sustained – exactly what a CD-ROM should do . . . *Eve* is the next step in the evolution of multimedia.' More important to Real World than these reviews however was the judgement of their peers. *Eve* won several awards including the industry's top prize the Milia d'Or presented at the Cannes Multimedia and Computer Entertainments Festival in February 1997.

Real World Multimedia had wanted to be at the forefront of the multimedia revolution under the guidance of David Stephen. He built up the division with confidence and optimism as *Xplora* revenues of around £1 million rolled in, capitalizing on the advantage of Starwave footing the *Eve* bill. The aim was to build a multimedia entertainment company that within five years would account for 50 per cent of Real World revenues, making it a viable concern independent of the vagaries of Gabriel's music career.

The accepted belief propounded by technoguru Nicholas Negroponte was that the lines between all entertainment providers – whether film studios, TV stations, record companies, or internet and multimedia designers – would blur when internet technology delivered instantaneous high quality video, TV or music. The rewards for the companies that knew how to exploit and deliver the new media would be immense.

Stephen was planning six new CD-ROM products during 1995. He took on extra staff, signed a deal to develop CD-ROMs based on the trilogy of illustrated *Griffin & Sabine* books by Nick Bantock, which had sold 3 million copies. There was a CD-ROM on world music and planning put in motion for the Real World web site.

Stephen continued with his other duties. He struck up a friendly relationship with Virgin Records bosses Paul Conroy and Jon Webster who saw him as 'very nice and very bright'. They appreciated Stephen not giving them a hard time, unlike his predecessor. 'He would listen to us and he would say he would take it back to Peter and he did,' says Conroy. Being liked of course is not necessarily the same as being effective. And Stephen's lack of experience was obvious to Mike Large. 'I think he had difficulty saying he didn't understand the business,' says Large. 'And a lot of the record business is all about history and how things are done and who you know. Where you can push things and where you can't is a bit of a minefield. David could have done himself a lot of favours by holding his hands up and saying I don't know how to do this, let me watch someone who does, but that wasn't in his nature.'

Gabriel had taken an extended break after the Secret World tour. He fulfilled promotional duties and helped on *Eve*, but took his eye off day to day developments at Real World. It was understandable that after three years of intense work he should wish to lighten up during 1995. At the end of the year however he looked up and realized his company was changing and much of it was happening without his knowledge or approval. When he had gone off at the start of the Secret World tour in the spring of 1993 there were twenty people working at Real World, now there were around seventy or eighty, and the wages were coming out of his pocket.

'He basically sat down with David and said what the hell is going on, everything has changed, you haven't spoken to me about it. David said well why do I need to? It's going fantastic,' says Mike Large. 'Peter felt he should have been actively involved in all the decisions as to where money was spent. And David's feeling was that this money was his to spend as he thought wisest.

'He and Peter had a very different view of things. David Stephen's view was that he had been employed to run these businesses and that Peter was, if you like, the shareholders at a distance. He should do whatever he felt was right to produce the best return for his shareholders, which was just Peter, but that he should be left to get on with the business, much like the shareholders of ICI don't really tell the board what to do. Peter felt that he should be running the businesses to do what Peter wanted, or that Peter should be an active participant in the running of the businesses and that was a fundamental problem.'

Stephen found himself confronting the core contradiction

in Gabriel's attitude towards business and management. Gabriel offered the freedom to act on his behalf, but his desire to be consulted and part of a team would always act as a brake to anyone who wanted the final say. Maybe he was unmanageable. Stephen departed at the end of 1995 after twenty-one months with the company. With Stephen's departure no new manager or CEO was sought. Instead duties were shared between Mike Large, taking the title Director of Operations, and Gabriel's solicitor Michael Thomas who are referred to as the management team. Both are even tempered men. Gabriel for the moment seems to have got over his fixation with the brusque. The multimedia operation was scaled down. The first *Griffin & Sabine* CD-ROM was a critical success and the world music CD-ROM was completed though a distributor was still to be found at the time of writing.

For Peter Gabriel, Nusrat Fateh Ali Khan is up there with Otis Redding as the most influential singer in his life. 'The supreme examples of how far and deep a voice can go in finding, touching and moving the soul.' Khan also became a beloved friend.

It was WOMAD that initially brought Khan to Gabriel's attention, first from his records and then witnessing his first performance in England at the 1985 WOMAD Festival at Mersea Island in the Thames Estuary. Thomas Brooman recalled the event. 'Nusrat came to the stage shortly before 2 a.m., awaited by a packed and expectant crowd already feeling the chill of the Thames riverside night within the large festival marquee in which he was to play. Almost four hours later, with dawn already breaking, the party left the stage and a profoundly moved and inspired festival audience. Grown men were seen to cry; the applause was unstoppable and truly reverent. The memory of this first concert by Nusrat at WOMAD remains for us as organizers one of our proudest and most moving musical memories.' It was not uncommon for a qawwali to last four or five hours, beginning late at night and lasting till dawn.

Khan was the leading exponent of a qawwali tradition that had evolved over six hundred years. His father introduced the innovation of taking a music that had been traditionally sung in holy places out into the world. Khan took it many steps further, collaborating with Bjork, Eddie Vedder of Pearl Jam on the *Dead Man Walking* soundtrack; his music had been mixed by Massive Attack and leading British Asian artists including Asian Dub Foundation. Before his death at the age of forty-nine on 16 August 1997 he was due to perform with Luciano Pavarotti.

He was a devout man, who despite the worldliness around him never compromised his music or beliefs. Sufism is some-times regarded as the liberal wing of Islam, others regard it as a non-specific faith. Khan paid homage to prophets from other religions as well as his Prophet. Religion never became an issue. 'Unlike many artists working with devotional music, Nusrat was very open, very generous and willing to try almost anything with anyone who was enthusiastic,' said Gabriel.

To Western ears qawwali takes some acclimatization. With the growing popularity of ethnic sounds and particularly their infiltration into dance music, Khan's music came more into focus. Around complex rhythms his voice would soar as he would go into a trance of wails using his voice like a percussive instrument.

Gabriel worked with him on *Passion*. 'It was, I think, probably the most magical feeling of that whole recording. There is a scene in the film with Christ carrying the cross, it is deeply spiritual music for me, and I think Scorsese too was delighted with that performance, and it's really Nusrat's voice that builds it and lifts it.'

Khan was signed to Real World Records who released eight of his albums. In tribute, Amanda Jones, label manager of Real World Records, wrote, 'Touched by genius, Nusrat Fateh Ali Khan was undoubtedly, spiritually and technically, one of the greatest voices of the day.' This was backed up by David Toop in *The Times*. 'As an improviser, he ranks along-side jazz greats such as John Coltrane, but his chameleon-like ability to blend into all environments places him at the fore-front of music making.'

Gabriel had personal experience of these qualities. 'He was an extraordinary improviser. He was capable of coming up with great melodies spontaneously. There's only two or three other musicians that I've ever met who can do that. But I think what he had perhaps better than them was a sense of overall structure as he was going into an improvisation it seemed as if he had the sense of timing, the build, the peaks, the valleys and the climaxes all in his head.'

In 1996, during a visit to California, Khan was advised to have an immediate kidney transplant. It is not known why he did not take this advice. 'We'd been aware that Nusrat was not well for some time with his dialysis, the diabetic problem and the weight problem,' said Gabriel. 'We were trying to encourage things forward with the kidney transplant which had been on the cards for about eighteen months prior to his death. It's very tragic that he was coming to London to stabilize his condition in preparation for the kidney transplant when he died. It's a terrible loss.' Having just renewed his contract with Real World Records for a further two albums he was due to use the same visit to discuss who he wanted as his collaborators for his next, never to be realized album.

Gabriel and Khan appeared together at the VH-1 Honors concert in aid of Witness at the Universal Amphitheatre, Los Angeles, on 28 April 1996. Rock and movie royalty turned out for the event with Michael Stipe, Gloria Estefan, Don Henley and Bryan Adams among the performers, Tim Robbins and Susan Sarandon presenting, and Oliver Stone and Sean Penn among the celebrity guests. It was a new departure for

VH-1 whose previous awards shows featured a host of stars with nothing to link them except the glitz. It was good publicity for Witness, and raised them $350,000.

At the show Gabriel and Khan performed 'Signal To Noise', a song destined for Gabriel's next album. It is an intense, muscular soul-rock number about how people or lovers transmit the wrong messages to each other. In the performance Gabriel appears delighted with the way Khan makes it lift off with his vocal improvisations, and joins him as the song closes. 'We had perhaps two rehearsals prior to this filming in front of a large TV audience and each time he was coming up with very different improvisations and they were stunning. I am very pleased that we'd had quite a few years working together prior to that and there was a relationship and trust because I think that would have been a little difficult otherwise. I think we both tried to make space for each other to do what we could. Me more on the arrangement side and him in terms of the verse, but it is a performance that I'll remember always and I think blew away a lot of the Holly-wood audience.'

The first available recorded glimpse of what the next album was to sound like appeared on the record racks in the spring of 1998 when Gabriel's song 'I Grieve' was included on the soundtrack to the movie *City of Angels* (starring Meg Ryan and Nicolas Cage). Though his song was billed as the centrepiece track on the album, which went to Number 1 on the Billboard chart and sold over one million in three weeks, Gabriel cannot take all the credit. The album also boasted Alanis Morrissette's first new track, 'Uninvited', since her stunning success with the album *Jagged Little Pill*.

Though sombre and intense in mood, as you would expect from a Gabriel ballad, there is also a feeling of uplift and transition. Whereas the *US* album was an examination of what had been going wrong in his life, this feels like he is acknowl-edging loss, freeing his spirit and becoming more at ease with himself. The title of the new album, *Up*, fits a mood that is an antidote to the downbeat tone of *US*, while retaining his penchant for minimalist album titles.

As snippets were eked out to salivating fans, we were informed on Gabriel's Radio Real World web site that the biggest surprise on the album was going to be Gabriel playing guitar and using it as his principal writing instrument, though this was to prove an exaggeration. However, using guitar marks a significant change in approach and style, enabling melody to take precedence after his long love affair using rhythms to start off songs. He was still experimenting with different rhythms but he was after a more pared down sound. It's an amusing thought, Gabriel coming out as a repressed axeman, though powerchords are unlikely to be his thing. Daniel Lanois had an unwitting influence. After the *US* sessions he had left behind his Telecaster guitar which Gabriel picked up and inspired some new songs. 'I still can't play guitar, but I love using it as a noise maker,' says Gabriel. He saw the album more as a natural development than a radical departure. 'It's still a group of songs. Some of the approaches sound different to me but probably to other people they sound like the same old stuff.'

The gap between albums was ever widening, and record company hopes that they might see an album five or even six years after *US* proved optimistic. By July 1996 Gabriel reported, 'I have lots of ideas at the moment, about seventy on the go.' He had spent three months working in Senegal, using some of Youssou N'Dour's band, and was starting to write lyrics, usually a sign that the process was nearing completion. Even he suggested it might be ready by the end of 1996.

In October and November of that year he was at Real World Studios with the old team of Manu Katche, Tony Levin and David Rhodes. The sessions were fast and productive, with what was surely an unprecedented nearly one track a day getting laid down.

By mutual agreement, Daniel Lanois and Gabriel's partnership was over. 'Nothing was ever said, although I saw Peter in New York [in July 1998] and I talked to him about it. And I said, "Listen, on *Birdy* you really had me, on *So* I had no social life, I was living in that studio, and you really had me again on *US*, I was very tired and disappeared, fading a bit at the end." I thought we said what we had to say and he knows I have a very high regard for him. I knew that he would probably get on with this new work in a different fashion. I don't think Real World should be the location for another Peter record. Strange as it may seem, as wonderful as the place is, I'm going back to the three months in the desert philosophy.'

Gabriel's thinking was on the same lines. Senegal was isolated, but nowhere could be more isolated than the Amazon. In the summer of 1997, Gabriel and his engineers Dickie Chappell and Meabh Flynn spent time on a friend's boat travelling up the Amazon, sailing from the borders of Bolivia and Brazil to Manaus in central Brazil. The boat, extraordinarily, had a fully working professional recording studio on board. Flynn was his new, low-profile girlfriend who he has happily been with since 1995.

It was not just the isolation of the Amazon that Gabriel was after. Ever since his childhood days building dams in the River Bourne, he had a fascination with rivers. The new album explores that theme. He had pared his seventy ideas down to thirty songs and was contemplating releasing two albums in quick succession (for him), one before the tour cycle and one at the end of it, which on past form could be a gap of two years. Though the intervention of the Millennium Dome project could set back his plans to tour by a year. His themes were varied, from a song about his father, the first time he had tackled a song openly about a family member, to one about a grotesque Jerry Springer style presenter of confessional TV shows.

He was forced to prematurely announce its title, *Up*, when

he got wind that R.E.M. were using the same title for their album released in October 1998. After a short deliberation he decided to carry on and use the same title. It was best to announce it beforehand to avoid charges of plagiarism. At the time he said, 'It's been called *Up* for about the last four years. I did think about changing it when I first heard about it, but it's in some of the lyrics already and I've recorded some songs, and I did a cover which was *Up* related. I've had this habit of doing two letter titles and changing the one letter at a time. There's a lot less flexibility if I keep to my dumb rules than there is for another artist.'

There were plenty of comic possibilities for the new album title, played up in the first press release announcing an album Virgin and Geffen were still biting their nails waiting to hear. The press release headline ran, 'Peter Gabriel Keeps It "Up"'. He went one further than R.E.M. informing us that he was also using the *Up* title for related projects including 'Up The Amazon', 'Up The Nile' and 'Up The Ganges'. It was a jokey nod and wink in the direction of the smutty slapstick British *Carry On* films with their penchant to *Carry On Up the Khyber* and other such places.

In his statement Gabriel said, 'When I first found out about the R.E.M. album title, I thought that my "Up" project, which had always been related to rivers, was now going "Up shit creek." However, after some reflection and consultation with R.E.M. I have decided to keep the name of my album intact. I have been living in the "Up" world for four years now and have no wish to come down.'

It was an opportunity for some mutual backslapping. Of R.E.M. Gabriel said, 'I have always loved R.E.M.'s music and respected their commitment to social change, as well as really appreciating the support of the Witness human rights programme. To find myself sharing a title with them is therefore not a problem.'

Michael Stipe was equally fraternal. 'We love Peter Gabriel

and we are honoured to have this association – great minds think alike.' But it was guitarist Peter Buck who rose up to the occasion. 'We first considered calling our album "Peter Gabriel's Up", but decided that just "Up" was the way to go. We hope in the future that all other bands will also adopt this title in a showing of solidarity.'

Prior to his Amazon visit, Gabriel was in a deep forest of another kind. In 1996 he collaborated with Deep Forest, the French ethnic-ambient duo known for their lush reworkings of world music themes. They invited Gabriel to sing over a track they had recorded called 'While The Earth Sleeps' for the movie *Strange Days*. Ever vigilant when samples are used, as Real World often had to defend the rights of its own artists, Gabriel and his lawyer Michael Thomas received assurances that all samples had been cleared. Gabriel was mortified to later learn that what he was told was a traditional Bulgarian folk song was in fact a composition by a retired Macedonian kindergarten teacher, Risto Pulevski, who said his song 'Dali Znaes Mila Majko (Do You Know Dear Mother)' had been used without his permission.

Unfortunately for Gabriel he was the person the composer gunned for. According to Reuters, Pulevski said, 'I felt insulted when I heard that Peter Gabriel's hit was described as an adaptation of a Bulgarian folk song. It is neither Bulgarian nor a folk song. I composed it and wrote it in 1960.' When Gabriel learned the truth he strongly took the composer's side and made sure the matter was resolved.

Gabriel was more at home collaborating with Joseph Arthur, his protégé signed to Real World Records. Arthur, from Atlanta, Georgia, is a literate folkie singer-songwriter with a nice line in bleakness. Which is why his song 'In The Sun', about a young friend who died, was apt when Gabriel was asked by Richard Branson to contribute to an album in commemoration of Diana, Princess of Wales. 'I did have the song "Grief" which was used on the *City of Angels* soundtrack, which I considered for the album, but I thought that the lyric on Joe Arthur's "In The Sun" was much more appropriate,' says Gabriel. He says it was a musical decision rather than an attempt to distance himself from post-Diana hysteria. It also served the purpose of giving Arthur some useful exposure. With its chorus of, 'May God's love be with you, always,' it was a sincere enough sentiment, while the elegy was too austere to be accused of sentimentality. In common with other artists, all Arthur and Gabriel's proceeds from the double CD, *Diana, Princess of Wales – Tribute*, went to her memorial fund.

Gabriel maintained his dignity even if appearing on the album was not going to win any credibility points. Richard Branson, who paid for recording costs, did not help when he said, 'This will be the most touching album ever made. It will reflect Princess Diana's life and how the country feels about her.' The *NME* reacted with predictable venom. 'The money may go to charity but the major beneficiaries of this and other similar projects are those creatively bankrupt members of a fading pop aristocracy who, in their dotage, have resorted to the toothless safety of sentimentality,' wrote editor Steve Sutherland awarding the record an almost unprecedented zero points.

As a solo artist Gabriel could always rely on his credibility. Not so his former colleagues in Genesis, who ever since punk arrived in the seventies were senior representatives of the dodo tendency, only fit to be stamped on and stamped out. Progressive rock was not just the most unfashionable of genres, to music know-alls it was akin to a mortal sin, inviting eternal damnation on its adherents. The common complaint about progressive rock was that it was pretentious, overblown and pompous. These charges are true. But that's not the whole story. For within their ranks, progressive rock musicians produced work as worthy as any other era in the great tradition of

British rock and roll. Progressive was never a homogeneous genre, it encompassed the Moog synthesizer experiments of Keith Emerson and the medieval folk resonances of Gryphon.

Gabriel was not the only artist whose work deserved serious reappraisal. Peter Hammill's lyrics and the musical territory he marked out with Van Der Graaf Generator should have earned him recognition as a major force. One of his fans was John Lydon who as Johnny Rotten was ironically one of the chief architects of progressive rock's decline. Robert Fripp's work with King Crimson and their pivotal progressive album, *In the Court of the Crimson King*, is another overlooked musical innovator.

In Genesis-era Peter Gabriel, the student in his digs or aspiring intellectual in his garret, for it was usually a he, could try and fathom unfathomable fantasies in the belief he was finding the holy grail. This image, the over indulgence of artists too fond of solos, the distorted view that progressive was middle class and therefore bad, all conspired in the genre's demise.

Time, distance and a new breed of successful Brit rock bands who did not use the name but, knowingly or not, plundered the ideas of progressive rock, all conspired to a renaissance of sorts. The Verve, Radiohead, The Divine Comedy, would not like the comparisons, but their orchestrations and complex arrangements all hark back to an era where such augmentations were a positive trait rather than a tendency that dare not speak its name. The highly credible, late Jeff Buckley had covered 'Back In NYC' from *The Lamb Lies Down On Broadway* on a recording released posthumously in 1998.

Thus the timing for the four-CD boxed set *Genesis Archive 1967–75*, released in June 1998, was unwittingly apposite. To promote the event a strange gathering of the band was arranged at the Heathrow Business Centre. Where else would be so convenient but an international airport for these (mostly) multi-millionaires welded to jet travel. It was Collins, based in

Geneva, who was proving most difficult to pin down, hence the suite of rooms wedged in the Queen's Building between Terminals 1 and 2. It was a jovial old boys reunion with much hugging and jolly banter. Gabriel, who looked a few pounds heavier than was usual, was there, his shaved head looking as round-domed as Phil Collins. Steve Hackett had his seventies hairstyle nearly intact. Anthony Phillips turned up, as did the two remaining original members Tony Banks and Mike Rutherford. The least recognizable presence to the outside world was John Silver, drummer for a year from 1968 to 69, who had become a businessman. The two drummers who preceded him, John Mayhew and Chris Stewart, did not make it. Silver explained he had left the group to take up a university place in America and was promised he would get the call to return should they secure a spot on *The Old Grey Whistle Test*. The call never came.

Unlike other ancient rock reunions where so often there is a desperate attempt to cover up old enmities or a sad desire to relive past glories, all with an eye to regenerating once healthy revenues, here Genesis past and present were simply enjoying the novelty of different incarnations gathering in one place. Whatever their personnel changes, Genesis were never a band who had lasting fall-outs between members.

The boxed set is made up in large part of live recordings: two CDs for *The Lamb*, another for their greatest moments including 'Supper's Ready' at the Rainbow, and the fourth early rarities, from defunct BBC radio shows and demos. There is a thread to all this. The songwriting is consistently strong, tunes like 'Lilywhite Lilith', 'Supper's Ready', 'Dancing With The Moonlit Knight', even back to 1968's 'Where The Sour Turns To Sweet'. It was not just Gabriel, it was a writing co-operative. And by the time they reached the *Lamb* tour and Gabriel had already handed in his resignation, the mastery which would take the rest of the group to sales of around one hundred million albums can be clearly discerned, just as Gabriel's experimental lyrics and more urban themes sign-posted his imminent solo career.

Some cheating had to be indulged in to make part of the resurrected material listenable, at least to Gabriel's perfectionist ears. Wearing a fox's head, old man masks or the Slipperman suit on *The Lamb*, where he could never get the microphone near his mouth because of his bulbous costume, meant his muffled voice rendered live segments unlistenable. Gabriel's later period rasp can be heard on about half of the new *Lamb*, including 'Back in NYC' and 'Carpet Crawlers', while the final song from the work, 'It', had to be lifted from the original album version because the tape ran out during the featured recording at the Shrine Auditorium, Los Angeles. All the band got together for a new version of 'Carpet Crawlers' but it was not included in the *Archive*. With the group back in the studio in 1996 to work on the material there were rumours of an improbable reunion. Surprisingly, it is not something Tony Banks ruled out. 'There's no reason why we shouldn't – there might be a point when it might be a good idea,' he told *Uncut* magazine.

Gabriel's theory on why the music is still valid is that it had a lot of heart in it. He can look back on it with affection. 'The time that I was in Genesis was really my late teens and early twenties, and so that's a time when you are testing out a lot of things, exploring things. It's awkward, difficult sometimes, you're trying to find out who you are, what place you have in the world, whether you can earn any money by doing any-thing, and all these things came up during that period with Genesis. But it was an era where we had a lot of great adventures, and I learned to experiment with a lot of things. We were one of the first groups to play with putting visuals with music in different ways. The phrase I usually say when people ask me about it is that it was just a healthy part of growing up.'

The landscape inhabited by Rael, hero of *The Lamb*, is not so dissimilar from the surreal landscapes later to be found on Gabriel's CD-ROMs or in his ideas for the experience park. Rael, as Gabriel narrated in an introduction to 'Back In NYC', was underground in a soft carpeted corridor, cuddling his prickly porcupine, and having to join thousands of little people kneeling and crawling 'towards a heavy, wooden door through which a spiral staircase would lead them into a chamber with thirty-two other doors, only one of which could get any of them out'. There was a plan not followed through to include a CD-ROM with the *Archive*, with straightforward video footage and photographs.

Though the former colleagues remain friends, coming together for the *Archive* brought into sharp relief how far apart they had drifted in their artistic endeavours. Phil Collins was pursuing a declining solo career based on his solid pop-rock personality, more grumpy than cheeky chappy these days, and indulging in big band fantasies. Tony Banks and Mike Rutherford reverted to an older Genesis formula of longer meandering songs with new young singer Ray Wilson, whose style owes more to Gabriel than Collins, and suffered a drastic decline in album and ticket sales in 1998.

Researching his own material for the *Archive*, Gabriel, who had been keeper of the tapes when in the band, failed to find some early recordings he thought he had stored away. He dusted down the script for *The Lamb Lies Down On Broadway* that he had developed with Alejandro Jodorowsky, and had had recent requests to consider turning it into a film. Admitting it needs some reworking, he is not averse to the idea. Like his more recent colleague Robert Lepage, his works are always in progress.

Gabriel and Lepage were collaborating again on another work in progress, the experience park. Or at least using ideas derived from it, revived under the unlikely patronage of Her Majesty's Government. Gabriel was commissioned to mount a performance work for the Millennium Dome in Greenwich. According to Mike Large the plans for the Dome bore some 'alarming similarities' to the Gabriel-Eno-Anderson dream showcased in 1992 to the mandarins of Barcelona, as Gabriel and Large found when they went for a meeting at the offices of the New Millennium Experience Company. 'It's an odd one,' says Large. 'I don't think there was any plagiarism, I just think a lot of those ideas that we had in 1991–92 have seeped out. Whether they have come from us and seeped into popular culture or whether it's just synchronicity I don't know.'

Perhaps multimedia is creating its own language form, for the literature put out by the New Millennium Experience Company is remarkably redolent of the Barcelona plans. 'Visitors join the Parallax Ride which takes them upwards on a moving pavement. As they do so huge multimedia displays rise towards the roof of the Dome. Coherent images form from colours and shapes: 3D objects float within the displays, activated by other visitors as they move past the displays,' and so on.

Gabriel was invited to join the project by architect Mark Fisher, known for designing the impressive U2 'Popmart' show, and shows for the Rolling Stones, Pink Floyd, Phil Collins and Jean-Michel Jarre. Gabriel was initially sceptical of the Dome project, believing the £758 million allocated to it should have been spent on architect Sir Norman Foster's giant Millennium Tower to house a new kind of health centre designed to shift medicine from being curative to preventative. Gabriel explains, 'In the old Chinese system you paid your doctor for keeping you well and you stopped paying him when you got sick. So the incentive was for the doctor to keep you well. The way we have it the incentive is for the pharmaceuticals industry to build their business through sickness. So it's in their interests to prolong, sustain and feed sickness. Now I don't know if that's what they do, but I think as individuals we tend to give responsibility to the medical profession and to drugs when we could take a lot of responsibility ourselves.'

He aired his doubts to Fisher. 'He called me up saying will you help me create this thing. I said if it's just music I'm not interested, but if he wanted a partner to try and build something exciting for the middle of it this could be a real buzz. I'm trying to shift my work from just music to a designer of experiences and here was a whopping experience, an opportunity to do something on a huge scale.'

He rejected any cynical assertions that this was a handy opportunity for him to have a chunk of the 12 million hoped for visitors to the Dome see some of his work. 'It's great to do something around the millennium, even if it is a fictitious idea. In a sense the world around us is all created from our thoughts, so if you can change the way people think and the way they think about themselves you can have deep impact.'

Having agreed to take part Gabriel spoke with Peter Mandelson, then Trade and Industry Secretary and Dome supremo. As well as his ideas for the show Gabriel used the opportunity to express his own vision for the Dome founded on trying to devise his own experience park. 'I thought the focus for the Dome should be about empowerment. People who go in there should have access to information that should make them feel better about themselves, anything they are interested in whether a work related hobby or general interest.' He thought this could be conveyed through what he called a 'huge information node' that could be accessed throughout the Dome.

Gabriel and Fisher spent the first year devising the story and designing the show with Gabriel then going off to write the musical score and Fisher in charge of creating the production. Gabriel plans to release his score as a Dome album that would include the work of other musicians and artists he hoped to bring into the project.

The Millennium Show created by Gabriel and Fisher is the centrepiece attraction of the Dome, a twenty-minute show performed in the central 12,500 seater auditorium four to six times a day. The show tells the story of the three ages of man, the natural age, the industrial/technological age, and the post-industrial age. Each age is represented by the three members of a family. There's a big theme – the need for nature and technology to work together. And a human-scale theme – seen through a family conflict of ideas and generations. Gabriel has drawn inspiration from the mystic vision of William Blake's *Songs of Innocence and Experience*, and the contemporary warning against the dangers of developments in biotechnology found in the book *The Biotech Century: Harnessing the Gene and Remaking the World* by Jeremy Rifkin.

Its budget of £25 million makes it the most expensive show ever mounted in Britain and replaces the production originally planned by West End impresario Cameron Mackintosh, holder of the previous most expensive show, the £4 million musical *Martin Guerre*.

Gabriel and Fisher hired their mutual friend and colleague Patrick Woodroffe who has designed the lights for Gabriel's and other leading rock shows. Fisher hired Micha Bergese, dance tutor to Mick Jagger and Tina Turner, co-founder of London Contemporary Dance and founder of Circus Space the circus training school based in East London. Bergese was charged with hiring the Dome Ensemble Company, a cast of 200 that includes acrobats capable of performing at heights of up to 120 feet. While Gabriel brought in Robert Lepage to consult and introduce a little of his magic.

The Millennium Dome and the show may seem overblown to a disbelieving world, but there is something entirely logical and consistent in Gabriel's involvement as it embodies so many of the ideas he has been pursuing throughout his career. Even the fact that the Tube station at North Greenwich has been designed by Will Alsop, the first person Gabriel hired back in the eighties to realize his experience park dreams, has some symmetry about it. However thwarted some of Gabriel's schemes might have been, however long in gestation, he was always trying to be ahead of the curve, thinking what had not been thought of before. That has always led him into areas that sound surreal, even batty. He outlined this kind of thinking in an interview for *The Future Show* for Italian television. 'I have friends at Interval Research in California who are designing clothes that will contain cameras and microphones. I think it likely that people will use them often to record "peak experiences" which can be stored like a video diary or shared with anyone appropriate around the world. Maybe we will even have physical responses recorded as well. I think we will gradually want to get to the centre, to the core of the way we function, the way our brain and nervous system works and share that.'

It is not a prospect all of us would share with glee. According to Gabriel we are at the threshold of an exciting new world where multimedia will inform the way we communicate and think. He is a cautious believer in the new age of enlightenment, if we can make sure the process of technologization, to coin a phrase, remains democratic. As an artist and high-tech visionary he is achieving his ambition: to describe him as a rock star would only tell part of the story. Experience designer it will have to be, even if it has a clumsy ring to it. Gabriel's shamanistic visions may be fevered and surreal, but he at least inspires curiosity, and at best is curiously inspirational.

The British music scene, and to a lesser extent the North American, had changed fundamentally since the release of *US* in 1992. It was not a revolutionary change of style like that brought on by acid house. This change was more subtle and more dangerous to an artist of Gabriel's era. The Britpop explosion of 1995 to 96 had done more than mark a renaissance in British rock music, it had opened up the ears of an older audience to a younger sound. Fortysomethings were not just posing when they said they liked Oasis, Blur and The Verve. They actually understood what such bands were getting at when they harked back so strongly to the likes of the Kinks, the Beatles and the Rolling Stones.

What was a gain to younger bands appeared to be an equal and opposite loss to established acts whose demise had long been predicted but never realized. There were unexpected casualties. The Cure had consistently seen successive high album sales, only to find their 1996 album, *Wild Mood Swings*, bomb. Phil Collins and Genesis were not the only ones suffering. Hitherto impregnable artists like Tina Turner and even R.E.M. experienced major downturns.

*US* had not matched the sales of *So*, and *Up* faces a similar uphill task. In Gabriel's favour is his reputation as an innovator able to cross the generational divide more easily than his peers. As an insider at Virgin Records stated of the wait for *Up*, 'This is procrastination on an epic scale.' Other artists have fought shy of putting out records in a hostile market, notably Annie Lennox and Kate Bush. By stating that he was aiming for a new guitar-based sound that was more stripped down, Gabriel was again trying to pre-empt what was expected of him and forestall a sales meltdown.

As he approached his half century in 2000, Gabriel was never tempted to follow the path of older contemporaries like Mick Jagger who seemed to want the rock and roll show to go on forever. Gabriel may not want to carry on in quite as choreographed and epic a way as he did on the Secret World tour, but advances in technology are likely to help him maintain a less strenuous yet still eye-catching stage presence.

It is tempting for those who surround Gabriel to elevate him to the status of an untouchable seer. His sensitivity, gentlemanly behaviour, ethical stance and general concern for the well-being of humanity is admirable, and it encourages intense loyalty and protectiveness. He has been concerned himself to point out his own failings, notably in his private life, though he does it with self-consciously studied grace. He is open about his flaws, refreshingly more so than many a celebrity. But those flaws do not detract from his essential dignity and integrity.

He has worked on his persona, releasing himself from his emotional straitjackets more than most public figures would care to contemplate. It was the appreciation of a different way of being that attracted him to Senegal. 'They have a very free and fluid movement and some of it brushes off on this tight-arsed Englishman,' he said. Reluctantly, he had to sell his Dakar home in late 1997 after some friends staying there were robbed at gunpoint. 'Peter realized a sad truth,' says Mike Large, 'that as a rich white guy, if you wanted to live there you had to turn your house into a fortress and have armed guards, or deal with the consequences, and he decided he didn't want to live in a fortress, so he sold it.'

In a career of over a third of a century long Gabriel has had to grow up in public as a person and an artist. He has played a major role in encouraging a greater acceptance of all the musics of the world. His standards in video, the visual arts and multimedia are among the highest of any artist, rock or otherwise. He has written some straightforwardly tuneful and heartfelt songs that have been life enhancing, thought provoking, stirring, plain fun and provided succour for those moved by the emotion. Unusually for a musician of his experience in the rock field, we can look back and appreciate Peter Gabriel's fine body of work, and know that there is a good chance there is more to come.

# DISCOGRAPHY
1967–1999


## ALBUMS

GENESIS:

### From Genesis to Revelation (March 1969)
'Where the Sour Turns to Sweet'; 'In the Beginning'; 'Fireside Song'; 'The Serpent'; 'Am I Very Wrong?'; 'In the Wilderness'; 'The Conqueror'; 'In Hiding'; 'One Day'; 'Window'; 'In Limbo'; 'Silent Sun'; 'A Place to Call My Own'.
*Decca SKL 4990. Reissued 1993 on Music Club MCCD 133*

### Trespass (October 1970)
'Looking for Someone'; 'White Mountain'; 'Visions of Angels'; 'Stagnation'; 'Dusk'; 'The Knife'.
*Charisma CAS 1020*

### Nursery Cryme (November 1971)
'The Musical Box'; 'For Absent Friends'; 'The Return of the Giant Hogweed'; 'Seven Stones'; 'Harold the Barrel'; 'Harlequin'; 'The Fountain of Salmacis'.
*Charisma CAS 1052*

### Foxtrot (October 1972)
'Watcher of the Skies'; 'Time Table'; 'Get 'Em Out By Friday'; 'Can-Utility and the Coastliners'; 'Horizons'; 'Supper's Ready'; 'i. Lover's Leap, ii. The Guaranteed Eternal Sanctuary

Man, iii. Ikhnaton and Itsacon and their Band of Merry Men, iv. How Dare I Be So Beautiful?, v. Willow Farm, vi. Apocalypse in 9/8 (Co-Starring the Delicious Talents of Gabble Ratchet), vii. As Sure As Eggs Is Eggs (Aching Men's Feet)'.
*Charisma CAS 1058*

**Genesis Live** (August 1973)
'Watcher of the Skies'; 'Get 'Em Out By Friday'; 'The Return of the Giant Hogweed'; 'The Musical Box'; 'The Knife'.
*Charisma CLASS 1*

**Selling England by the Pound** (September 1973)
'Dancing With the Moonlit Knight'; 'I Know What I Like (In Your Wardrobe)'; 'Firth of Fifth'; 'More Fool Me'; 'The Battle of Epping Forest'; 'After the Ordeal'; 'The Cinema Show'; 'Aisle of Plenty'.
*Charisma CAS 1074*

**The Lamb Lies Down on Broadway** (November 1974)
'The Lamb Lies Down On Broadway'; 'Fly On A Windshield'; 'Broadway Melody of 1974'; 'Cuckoo Cocoon'; 'In The Cage'; 'The Grand Parade of Lifeless Packaging'; 'Back in N.Y.C.'; 'Hairless Heart'; 'Counting Out Time'; 'The Carpet Crawlers'; 'The Chamber of 32 Doors'; 'Lilywhite Lilith'; 'The Waiting Room'; 'Anyway'; 'Here Comes the Supernatural Anaesthetist'; 'The Lamia'; 'Silent Sorrow In Empty Boats'; 'The Colony of Slippermen' (The Arrival. A Visit to the Doktor. The Raven); 'Ravine'; 'The Light Dies Down On Broadway'; 'Riding the Scree'; 'In the Rapids'; 'It'.
*Charisma CGS 101*

**Genesis Archive 1967–1975** (June 1998)
CD 1: *The Lamb Lies Down on Broadway* (live). Recorded 24 January 1975 at The Shrine Auditorium, Los Angeles. 'The

Lamb Lies Down On Broadway'; 'Fly On A Windshield'; 'Broadway Melody of 1974'; 'Cuckoo Cocoon'; 'In The Cage'; 'The Grand Parade of Lifeless Packaging'; 'Back in N.Y.C.'; 'Hairless Heart'; 'Counting Out Time'; 'The Carpet Crawlers'; 'The Chamber of 32 Doors'.

CD 2: *The Lamb Lies Down on Broadway* (live). 'Lilywhite Lilith'; 'The Waiting Room'; 'Anyway'; 'Here Comes the Supernatural Anaesthetist'; 'The Lamia'; 'Silent Sorrow In Empty Boats'; 'The Colony of Slippermen' (The Arrival. A Visit to the Doktor. The Raven); 'Ravine'; 'The Light Dies Down On Broadway'; 'Riding the Scree'; 'In the Rapids'; 'It.'

CD 3: 'Dancing with the Moonlit Knight' (live recording at Rainbow 1973). 'Firth of Fifth' (live recording at Rainbow 1973); 'More Fool Me' (live recording at Rainbow 1973); 'Supper's Ready' (live recording at Rainbow 1973); 'I Know What I Like' (live recording at Rainbow 1973); 'Stagnation' (BBC live recording 1971); 'Twilight Alehouse' (single B side, 3 August 1973); 'Happy the Man' (single A side, 10 May 1972); 'Watcher of the Skies' (remix of 1972 single)'.

CD 4: 'In the Wilderness' (rough mix without strings 1968). 'Shepherd' (BBC Nightride 1970); 'Pacidy' (BBC Nightride 1970); 'Let Us Now Make Love' (BBC Nightride 1970); 'Going Out To Get You' (demo 1969); 'Dusk' (demo 1969); 'Build Me a Mountain' (rough mix 1968); 'Image Blown Out' (rough mix 1968); 'One Day' (rough mix 1968); 'Where the Sour Turns to Sweet' (demo 1968); 'In the Beginning' (demo 1968); 'The Magic of Time' (demo 1968); 'Hey!' (demo 1968); 'Hidden in the World of Dawn' (demo 1968); 'Sea Bee' (demo 1968); 'The Mystery of the Flannan Isle Lighthouse' (demo 1968); 'Hair on the Arms and Legs' (demo 1968); 'She is Beautiful' (demo 1967, later 'The Serpent'); 'Try a Little Sadness' (demo 1967); 'Patricia' (demo 1967, later 'In Hiding').

*Virgin CDBox 6–7243 8 42221 2 3*

SOLO:

**Peter Gabriel 1 [Car]** (February 1977)
'Moribund The Burgermeister'; 'Solsbury Hill'; 'Modern Love'; 'Excuse Me'; 'Humdrum'; 'Slowburn'; 'Waiting For The Big One'; 'Down The Dolce Vita'; 'Here Comes The Flood'.
*Charisma CDS4006 (LP), Charisma 7208612 (MC), Virgin PGCD1 (CD), Atco/EastWest 19181*

**Peter Gabriel 2 [Scratch]** (June 1978)
'On The Air'; 'D.I.Y.'; 'Mother of Violence'; 'A Wonderful Day in a One Way World'; 'White Shadow'; 'Indigo'; 'Animal Magic'; 'Exposure'; 'Flotsam and Jetsam'; 'Perspective'; 'Home Sweet Home'.
*Charisma CDS4013 (LP), Charisma 7208621 (MC), Virgin PGCD2 (CD), Atco/EastWest 36147*

**Peter Gabriel 3 [Melt]** (May 1980)
'Intruder'; 'No Self Control'; 'Start'; 'I Don't Remember'; 'Family Snapshot'; 'And Through The Wire'; 'Games Without Frontiers'; 'Not One Of Us'; 'Lead A Normal Life'; 'Biko'.
*Charisma CDS 4019 (LP), Charisma 7150 015 (MC), Virgin PGCD3 (CD), Geffen GEF 2035 (CD)*

**Peter Gabriel 4** (September 1982)
(Released as *Security* in the USA)
'The Rhythm of the Heat'; 'San Jacinto'; 'I Have The Touch'; 'The Family and the Fishing Net'; 'Shock the Monkey'; 'Lay Your Hands On Me'; 'Wallflower'; 'Kiss of Life'.
*Charisma PG4 (LP), Charisma PGMC4 (MC), Virgin PGCD 4, Geffen 2011–2 (CD)*

**Peter Gabriel Plays Live** (June 1983)

'The Rhythm of the Heat'; 'I Have The Touch'; 'Not One Of Us'; 'Family Snapshot'; 'D.I.Y.'; 'The Family and the Fishing Net'; 'Intruder'; 'I Go Swimming'; 'San Jacinto'; 'Solsbury Hill'; 'No Self Control'; 'I Don't Remember'; 'Shock the Monkey'; 'Humdrum'; 'On The Air'; 'Biko'.
*Charisma PGDL1 (LP), Charisma PGDMC1 (MC), Virgin PGDLCD1 (CD), Geffen GEF 4012 (CD)*

**Birdy – music from the film, by Peter Gabriel** (March 1985)

'At Night'; 'Floating Dogs'; 'Quiet and Alone'; 'Close Up' (from 'Family Snapshot'); 'Slow Water'; 'Dressing the Wound'; 'Birdy's Flight' (from 'Not One Of Us'); 'Slow Marimbas'; 'The Heat' (from 'Rhythm of the Heat'); 'Sketchpad with Trumpet and Voice'; 'Under Lock and Key' (from 'Wallflower'); 'Powerhouse at the Foot of the Mountain' (from 'San Jacinto').
*Charisma/Virgin CAS 1167 (LP), Charisma/Virgin CASMC 1167 (MC), Charisma/Virgin CASCD 1167, Geffen GEF 24070 (CD)*

**So** (May 1986)

'Red Rain'; 'Sledgehammer'; 'Don't Give Up'; 'That Voice Again'; 'In Your Eyes'; 'Mercy Street'; 'Big Time'; 'We Do What We're Told (Milgram's 37)'; 'This Is The Picture (Excellent Birds)'– (MC/CD only).
*Charisma/Virgin PG5 (LP), Charisma/Virgin PGMC5 (MC), Charisma/Virgin PGCD5 (CD), Virgin PGCDP5 (Picture CD), Geffen GHS 2408 (CD)*

**Passion** (June 1989)

'The Feeling Begins'; 'Gethsemane'; 'Of These, Hope'; 'Lazarus Raised'; 'Of These, Hope – Reprise'; 'In Doubt'; 'A Different Drum'; 'Zaar'; 'Troubled'; 'Open'; 'Before Night

Falls'; 'With This Love'; 'Sandstorm'; 'Stigmata'; 'Passion'; 'With This Love – choir'; 'Wall of Breath'; 'The Promise of Shadows'; 'Disturbed'; 'It is Accomplished'; 'Bread and Wine'.
*Real World Records/Virgin RWCD1 (CD), Real World Records/ Virgin RWLP1 (LP), Real World Records/Virgin RWMC1 (MC), Geffen GEF 24206 (CD)*

**Shaking the Tree (16 Golden Greats)** (December 1990)
'Solsbury Hill'; 'I Don't Remember'; 'Sledgehammer'; 'Family Snapshot'; 'Mercy Street'; 'Shaking the Tree (Remix)'; 'Don't Give Up'; 'San Jacinto'; 'Here Comes the Flood (new record-ing)'; 'Red Rain'; 'Games Without Frontiers'; 'Shock the Monkey';'I Have The Touch'; 'Big Time'; 'Zaar'; 'Biko'.
*PG TVD6 (CD), Geffen GEF 24326 (CD)*

**US** (September 1992)
'Come Talk To Me'; 'Love To Be Loved'; 'Blood Of Eden'; 'Steam'; 'Only Us'; 'Washing of the Water'; 'Digging in the Dirt'; 'Fourteen Black Paintings'; 'Kiss That Frog'; 'Secret World'.
*RWR/Virgin PGCD7 (CD), RWR/Virgin PGLP7 (LP), RWR/ Virgin PGMC7 (MC), Geffen GEFD 24473 (CD)*

**Secret World Live** (30 August 1994 USA and Canada, 13 September 1994)
'Come Talk to Me'; 'Steam'; 'Across the River'; 'Slow Marim-bas'; 'Shaking the Tree'; 'Red Rain'; 'Blood Of Eden'; 'Kiss That Frog'; 'Washing of the Water'; 'Solsbury Hill'; 'Digging in the Dirt'; 'Sledgehammer'; 'Secret World'; 'Don't Give Up'; 'In Your Eyes'.
*Real World Records/Virgin PGCD8 (CD), Real World Records/ Virgin PGMC8 (MC), Geffen GEFC2/D2 24722 (CD)*

## MISCELLANEOUS

**Genesis Collection Volume One and Volume Two** (April 1975)
Boxed set one includes *Trespass* and *Nursery Cryme* and poster;
Boxed set two includes *Foxtrot* and *Selling England by the Pound*
and poster.
*(CGS 102/CGS 103)*

**Genesis R-O-C-K Roots** (May 1976)
Reissue of *From Genesis to Revelation* plus early singles 'Silent
Sun'/'That's Me' and 'A Winter's Tale'/'One Eyed Hound'.
*Decca ROOTS 1*

SOLO ALBUMS:

**Ein Deutsches Album** (June 1980)
'Eindringling'; 'Keine Selbstkontrolle'; 'Frag Mich Nicht
Immer'; 'Schnappschuss (Ein Familienfoto)'; 'Und Durch Den
Draht'; 'Spiel Ohne Grenzen'; 'Du Bist Nicht Wie Wir'; 'Ein
Normales Leben'; 'Biko'.
*Charisma CB360 (LP), Virgin XCDS CD4019 (CD) – Germany*
German language version of third album.

**Peter Gabriel – Deutsches Album** (November 1982)
'Der Rhythmus Der Hitze'; 'Das Fischernetz'; 'Kon-takt'; 'San
Jacinto'; 'Shock Den Affen'; 'Handauflegen'; 'Nicht Die Erde
Hat Dich Verschluckt'; 'Mundzumundbeatmung'.
*Charisma 6302 221 (LP), Virgin XPG CD4 (CD) – Germany*
German language version of fourth album.

**Peter Gabriel – Compact Collection** (1990)
Peter Gabriel CDs 1–3
Boxed set.
TPAK9

## SINGLES

GENESIS:

'The Silent Sun'/'That's Me'
*Decca F12735. February 1968*

'A Winter's Tale'/'One Eyed Hound'
*Decca F12775. May 1969*

'Where the Sour Turns to Sweet'/'In Hiding'
*Decca F12949. June 1969*

'Looking for Someone'/'Visions of Angels'
*Charisma GS1. 1970*
Promotional single for DJs.

'The Knife' (Part I) 'The Knife' (Part II)
*Charisma CB152. May 1971*

'Happy the Man'/'Seven Stones'
*Charisma CB181. October 1972*

'Twilight Alehouse'
(October 1973)
One-sided flexidisc issued free with *Zig Zag* magazine.

'I Know What I Like'/'Twilight Alehouse'
*Charisma CB224. February 1974*

'Counting Out Time'/'Riding the Scree'
*Charisma CB238. November 1974*

'The Carpet Crawlers'/'Evil Jam' (live version of 'The Waiting Room' recorded at Los Angeles Forum)
*Charisma CB251. April 1975*

SOLO:

'Solsbury Hill'/'Moribund the Burgermeister'
*Charisma CB301 7" single. February 1977*
A live recording of 'Solsbury Hill' from The Bottom Line, New York City, on 4 October 1978, was released as a flexidisc and given away at the Hammersmith Odeon concerts in London between 20 and 24 December 1978.

'Modern Love'/'Slowburn'
*Charisma CB302 7" single June 1977*
Label a nude picture of Gabriel with strategically placed record hole.

'D.I.Y.'/'Perspective'
*Charisma CB311 7" single. May 1978*

'D.I.Y.'/'Mother of Violence'; 'Me and My Teddy Bear'
*Charisma CB319 7" single. September 1978*
Gabriel rearranged the Coots/Winters children's song.

'Games Without Frontiers'/'Start'; 'I Don't Remember'
*Charisma CB354 7" single. February 1980*

'No Self Control'/'Lead A Normal Life'
*Charisma CB360 7" single. May 1980*

'Spiel Ohne Grenzen'/'Jetzt Kommt Die Flut'
*Charisma 6000 449 7" single, Germany. June 1980*

'Games Without Frontiers'/'Lead A Normal Life'
*Mercury 76063 7" single, USA. February 1980*

'I Don't Remember'/'Shosholoza'
*Mercury 76068 7" single, USA.*

'I Don't Remember'/'Shosholoza'; 'Biko'; 'Jetzt Kommt Die Flut'
*Charisma CEP 303 12" single, Canada. 1980*

'Biko'/'Shosholoza'; 'Jetzt Kommt die Flut'
*Charisma CB370 7" single★. August 1980*
★33 rpm 7" with full-length version of 'Biko'.

'Biko'/'Shosholoza'
*Charisma CBD137012. 12" single, August 1980*
Edited version of 'Biko'.

'Shock the Monkey'/'Soft Dog'
*Charisma Shock 1 7" single. Charisma Shock 122 7" picture disc.*
*September 1982*

'Shock The Monkey'/'Shock The Monkey' (instrumental)
*Charisma Shock 12 12" single. September 1982*

'Shock Den Affen'/'Soft Dog' (instrumental)
*Charisma 6000 876, Germany*

'I Don't Remember'/'No Self Control'
*Charisma 6000 661, Holland. October 1982*

'I Have The Touch'/'Across the River'
*Charisma CB405 7" single. December 1982*

'Games Without Frontiers'/'Schnappschuss (Ein Familienfoto)'
*Charisma GAB 122 7" single. July 1983*

'I Don't Remember'/'Solsbury Hill'; 'Humdrum'; 'On The Air'
*Charisma RAD 10. May 1983*
Special DJ selection from *Peter Gabriel Plays Live* for club and radio DJs.

'I Don't Remember'/'Solsbury Hill' (live)
*Charisma GAB1 7" single. July 1983*

'I Don't Remember'/'Solsbury Hill'; 'Kiss of Life'
*Charisma GAB12 12" single. July 1983*

'Solsbury Hill'/'Games Without Frontiers'
*Old Gold Series 9265 7" single. July 1983*

'Solsbury Hill' live/'I Go Swimming'
*Geffen 7–29542, USA. June 1983*

'Solsbury Hill' (live)/'Kiss of Life' (live)
*Charisma 814 0047, Holland. 1983*

'Walk Through the Fire'/'The Race' (by Larry Carlton)
*Virgin VS 689 7" single. Virgin VST 68912 12" single. May 1984*

'Walk Through the Fire'/'The Race'; 'I Have The Touch'
*Virgin VS68912. May 1984*

'Out Out'/'Gizmo'
*Geffen A12–4953. December 1984*

'Sledgehammer'/'Don't Break This Rhythm'
*Virgin PGS 1 7" single. April 1986*

'Sledgehammer'/'Don't Break this Rhythm'; 'I Have The Touch'
*Virgin PGS 112 12" single. CDT 4–85 Remix CD. April 1986*

'Sledgehammer' (dance mix/ 'Don't Break this Rhythm'; 'Biko' (12" extended version); 'I Have The Touch'
*Virgin PGS 113 12" single. April 1986*

'Sledgehammer' (dance mix)/'Don't Break this Rhythm'; 'Sledgehammer' (album version); 'Biko' (album version)
*Virgin PGT112 cassette single. April 1986*
Also released in limited edition of 2,000 flip-top cigarette-style silver boxes.

'Don't Give Up'/'In your Eyes' (special mix)
*Virgin PGS2 7" single. October 1986*

'Don't Give Up'/'In your Eyes' (special mix); 'This is the Picture'
*PGS212 12" single. October 1986*

'In Your Eyes'/'In Your Eyes' (special mix)
Geffen 7–28622 7" single, USA. October 1986

'In Your Eyes'/'In Your Eyes' (special mix); 'Biko'
*Geffen 20535–0 A 12" single, USA. October 1986*

'Don't Give Up' (edit)/'Don't Give Up' (album version)
*Geffen PRO CD 2680. CD single, USA. March 1987*
Promo single for American radio.

'Big Time'/'Curtains'
*Virgin PGS3 7" single, PGS312 12" single. March 1987*


'Big Time' (extended version)/'Curtains'; 'No Self Control' (live); 'Across the River'
*Virgin PGTB12 12" cassette single. March 1987*
Also released in limited edition gold box.


'Big Time' (extended version)/'Curtains'; 'No Self Control'; 'Across the River'; 'Big Time' (7" version)
*Virgin GAIL 312 CD single. March 1987*


'Red Rain'/'Ga-Ga'
*Virgin PGS4 7" single. June 1987*
'Ga-Ga' is an instrumental version of 'I Go Swimming'.


'Red Rain'/'Ga-Ga'/'Walk through the Fire'
*PGS4 12 12" single. PGSC4 12 cassette single. June 1987*


'Biko'/'No More Apartheid'
*Virgin PGS6 7" single. PGS612 12" single. PGSC612 cassette single. November 1987*
Live version of Biko recorded at Blossom Music Center, Cleveland, Ohio on 27 July 1987. Single used to promote *Cry Freedom* film.


'Biko'/'No More Apartheid'; 'I Have The Touch' ('85 remix)
*Virgin CDPGS612 – CD single. November 1987*


'Solsbury Hill'/'Moribund the Burgermeister'; 'Solsbury Hill' (live)
*Virgin CDT 33–3" CD single in pochette. December 1988*

'Shaking The Tree' (12″ remix N'Dour/Gabriel) 'Old Tuc-
son'★; 'Sweeping the Leaves'★
*Virgin VS 1167 7″ single. Virgin VST 1167 12″ single. Virgin
VSCD 1167 CD single. May 1989*
★from Youssou N'Dour album *The Lion*


'Solsbury Hill' (album version)/'Shaking The Tree' (1990
edit); 'Games Without Frontiers' (live)
*Virgin VS 1322 7″ single. Virgin VST 1322 12″ single. Virgin
VSCDT 1322 CD single reissue. Virgin VSC 1322 cassette single.
December 1990*


'Digging in the Dirt' (album version)/'Digging in the Dirt'
(instrumental); 'Quiet Steam'; 'Bashi-Bazouk'
*Virgin/Real World PGSDX 7 CD single. September 1992*
Limited edition brown or blue linen box.


'Digging in the Dirt'/'Quiet Steam'
*Virgin/Real World PGS7 7″ single. Virgin/Real World PGSC7
cassette single. September 1992*


'Digging in the Dirt'/'Digging in the Dirt' (instrumental);
'Quiet Steam'
*Virgin/Real World PGSDG7 CD single. September 1992*


'Steam'/'Games Without Frontiers'
*Virgin/Real World PGS8 7″ single. Virgin/Real World PGSC8
12″ single. January 1993*


'Steam' (album version)/'Games Without Frontiers' (Massive/
Dave Bottrill mix); 'Steam' (Oh Oh Let Off Steam mix 12″);
'Steam' (Oh Oh Let Off Steam mix dub)
*Virgin/Real World PGSDG 8 CD single. January 1993*

'Steam' (album version)/'Games Without Frontiers' (Massive/ Dave Bottrill mix); 'Steam' (Oh Oh Let Off Steam mix 12″); 'Games Without Frontiers' (live)
*Virgin/Real World PGDSX 8. January 1993*
Limited edition CD in black 'Cathedral' box.


'Blood Of Eden'/'Mercy Street' (William Orbit remix); 'Blood Of Eden'★
*Virgin/Real World PGSDG 9 CD single. March 1993*
★Special mix for Wim Wenders' film *Until the End of the World*.


'Blood Of Eden' (album version)/'Mercy Street' (William Orbit remix); 'Sledgehammer'
*Virgin/Real World PGSDX 9. March 1993*
Limited edition CD in trifold digipack.


'Blood Of Eden'/'Mercy Street'
*Virgin/Real World PGS 9 7″ single. Virgin/Real World PGSC 9 cassette single. March 1993*


'Kiss That Frog' (edit of album version)/'Kiss That Frog' (Mindblender mix)
*Virgin PGS 10 7″ single*


'Kiss That Frog'/'Digging in the Dirt' (Rich E mix); 'Kiss That Frog' (Mindblender mix)
*Virgin/Real World PGSDG 10 CD single. September 1993*
Digipak.


'Kiss That Frog'/'Across The River'; 'Kiss That Frog' (Mind- blender mix); 'Shaking The Tree' (Bottrill remix)
*Virgin/Real World PGSDX 10 CD single. September 1993*
Limited edition digipak with cut-out 'picture frame' cover.

'Lovetown'/'Love To Be Loved'
*Epic 660480 7 7" single. May 1994*

'Lovetown'/'Love To Be Loved'; 'A Different Drum'
*Epic 660480 2 CD single. June 1994*


## COMPILATION ALBUMS

**All This And World War II** (1977)
'Strawberry Fields Forever'
A soundtrack of World War II footage linked to Beatles songs
performed by various artists.
*Riva RVLP2*

**An Hour of Pop Hits – Reels on Wheels** (1979)
'Solsbury Hill'
*Mercury Reel 002*

**An Hour of Rock Vol. 2 – Reels on Wheels** (1979)
'Modern Love'
*Mercury Reel 004*

**Repeat Performance** (1980)
'Solsbury Hill'
*Charisma BG1*

**Hot Wax** (1980)
'No Self Control'
*K-Tel NE 1082*

**The Bristol Recorder. Volume 2** (January 1981)
'Not One Of Us' (live at De Montfort Hall Leicester, 24
February 1980); 'Humdrum' (live at Diplomat Hotel, New

York, 12 July 1980); 'Ain't That Peculiar' (live at Uptown Theater, Chicago 11 March 1977).
*Bristol Recorder BR002*


**Live in the European Theatre** (1981)
'I Don't Remember'
*WEA K58412*


**Music & Rhythm** (July 1982)
'Across the River'
The WOMAD benefit album.
*WEA K68045*


**Let the Children Play** (April 1984)
'Exposure'
A charity double album in aid of the British Peace Camps, the most prominent being the women of Greenham Common.
*Panic Peace 1*


**Raindrops Pattering on Banana Leaves** (June 1984)
'Lead A Normal Life'
Live version recorded in Normal, Illinois, 3 December 1982, for this WOMAD benefit album.
*WOMAD 001*


**Sometimes a Great Notion** (November 1984)
'I Have The Touch'
Charity album for the British Deaf Association.
*EMI Topcat 1*


**Greenpeace** (April 1985)
'Shock the Monkey'
*Towerbell EMI Fund 1*

**Sun City – Artists United Against Apartheid** (November 1985)
'No More Apartheid'
As well as his brief vocal appearance in the 'Sun City' theme song, Gabriel's voice was used more extensively on 'No More Apartheid'.
*EMI Manhattan MTL 1001*
'Sun City' (November 1985)
*EMI Manhattan MT7 7" single*

**Conspiracy of Hope** (November 1986)
'Biko'
Commemorating the worldwide Conspiracy of Hope campaign.
*Mercury Merh 99 LP. Merh 99 MC. 830 588–2 CD*

**Now 7** (August 1986)
'Sledgehammer'
*Now 7 LP. TC Now 7 MC*

**Now 8** (November 1986)
'Don't Give Up'
*Now 8 LP. TC Now 8 MC. CD Now 8 CD*

**Now 86** (November 1986)
'Sledgehammer'
*CD Now 86 CD*

**Seasons – Synthophonic 1986** (September 1986)
'Don't Give Up'
*CBS 450 1491. LP CBS 450 1494 MC*

**The Secret Policeman's Third Ball – The Music** (September 1987)

Live recording of Amnesty benefit with Gabriel performing 'Biko' at London Palladium, 29 May 1987. Line-up includes Lou Reed and Youssou N'Dour.
*Virgin V2458*

**Greenpeace Rainbow Warriors** (March 1989)
'Red Rain'
*Geffen GHS 24236*

**One World, One Voice** (May 1990)
Gabriel contributed to a 'chain tape', a musical version of a chain letter, that was overdubbed as it progressed over twenty days from studio to studio around the world involving 292 musicians. The project to promote environmental awareness was conceived by Kevin Godley. The *One World, One Voice* programme broadcast to an estimated worldwide audience of 200 million.
*Virgin CDV 2632 CD*

**Peace Together** (July 1993)
'Be Still'
Benefit album for Northern Ireland youth organizations. Gabriel sings on this Hothouse Flowers composition with Sinead O'Connor, Feargal Sharkey, Liam O'Maonlai and Nanci Griffith. 'Be Still' also issued as a single.
*Island Records*

**Woodstock 94** (1994)
'Biko'
*A & M 31454–0289–2 IN02 (2CD)*

**The Glory of Gershwin** (September 1994)
'Summertime'

Tribute album to celebrate Larry Adler's eightieth birthday, produced by George Martin.
*Mercury 522 727–2*


**Tower of Song: Songs of Leonard Cohen** (October 1995)
'Suzanne'
Tribute album celebrating work of Cohen.
*A & M 314540259*


**Huckleberry House 30th Anniversary Jam** (1997)
'Love To Be Loved'
Proceeds to benefit Huckleberry Youth Programme's 24-hour crisis services for Bay Area youth at risk.
*HYP-1967*


**Diana, Princess of Wales – Tribute** (November 1997)
'In The Sun'
Gabriel sings composition by Real World artist Joseph Arthur.
*V2 VVr10011052*


## FILM SOUNDTRACKS

**Against All Odds** (April 1984)
'Walk through the Fire'
*Virgin V2313*


**Gremlins** (October 1984)
'Out Out'
*Geffen GED 24044*


**Say Anything** (April 1989)
'In Your Eyes'
*WTG Records PK 45140*

**Until the End of the World** (1992)
'Blood Of Eden'
Wim Wenders' film.
*Warner Bros 7599267072*


**Philadelphia** (May 1994)
'Lovetown'
*Epic 474998 2*


**Natural Born Killers** (August 1994)
'Taboo'
Gabriel with Nusrat Fateh Ali Khan.
*Nothing/Interscope Records 6544–92460–2*


**Virtuosity** (August 1995)
'Party Man'
Written by Gabriel, Tori Amos & The World Beaters, per-
formed by Gabriel & The World Beaters.
*Radioactive RARD 11295*


**Strange Days** (October 1995)
'While the Earth Sleeps'
Gabriel with Deep Forest.
*Epic EK 67226*


**Angel Baby** (1995)
'We Do What We're Told'
*Icon 1*


**Phenomenon** (June 1996)
'I Have The Touch'
Robbie Robertson and Gabriel remix.
*Reprise Records 9362 46360–2*

**Jungle 2 Jungle** (March 1997)
'Shaking The Tree' (Jungle version)
Gabriel with Youssou N'Dour and Shaggy.
*Walt Disney Records 60847–7*

**City of Angels** (September 1998)
'I Grieve'
*Warner Sunset/Reprise 9–46867–2*

**Babe: Pig in the City** (November 1998)
'That'll Do'
Gabriel sings this Randy Newman song, which received a
nomination as Best Song in the 1998 Academy Awards,
performing it live at the Oscar awards ceremony in Los Angeles
on 21 March 1999.
*Geffen GEFD-25310*

## GUEST APPEARANCES AND COMPOSITIONS

*Cat Stevens*
**Mona Bone Jakon** (LP), released 1970.
Gabriel plays flute.
*Island ILPS 9118*

*Colin Scot*
**Colin Scot** (LP), released 1971.
Credits with thinly disguised names for contractual reasons
include 'P. Angel Gabriel', 'P. C. Genesis' (Phil Collins) and
'Van Der Hammill' (Peter Hammill). Album produced by John
Anthony; three songs were written by Martin Hall, later to
collaborate with Gabriel; other musicians included Jon Ander-
son and Robert Fripp.

*Charlie Drake*
**You Never Know** (7"), released November 1975.
Written by Martin Hall and Peter Gabriel, produced by
Gabriel, credited on the label as 'Gabriel Ear Wax'.
*Charisma CB270*


*Alan Ross*
**Are You Free On Saturday** (LP), released in October 1977.
Martin Hall and Peter Gabriel wrote 'Get the Guns', released
as a single in June 1977.
*Good Earth GD14*


*Tom Robinson Band*
**TRB Two** (LP), released January 1979.
'Bully For You' was co-written by Gabriel and Robinson.
*EMC 3296*
'Bully For You'
*EMI 2916 7"*


*Robert Fripp*
**Exposure** (LP), released April 1979.
Gabriel sings and plays on 'Exposure'. The album includes
what Gabriel calls the 'quiet version' of 'Here Comes the
Flood'. This track was digitally remixed for *Network*, a Fripp
compilation album released in 1985.
*Editions EG LP41*


*Johnny Warman*
**Walking Into Mirrors** (LP), released June 1979.
Warman was a friend of Jerry Marotta. Gabriel contributes
accompanying vocals, chants, screaming and effects on
'Screaming Jets'.
*TRAIN 17*

*Jimmy Pursey*
**Animals Have More Fun/Sus** (7″), released June 1981.
Both tracks credited Gabriel/Ellis/Pursey. Produced by Peter
Gabriel.
*Epic EPC-A1336*


*Tom Robinson*
**North By Northwest** (LP), released August 1982.
Gabriel and Robinson co-wrote 'Merrily Up On High' and
'Atmospherics (Listen to the Radio)'.
*TRTX4 Castaway/RCA*


*Laurie Anderson*
**Mister Heartbreak** (LP), released February 1984.
'Excellent Birds' written by Gabriel and Anderson. He plays
Synclavier Linn drum, vocals and co-produces with Anderson.
Also backing vocals on 'Langue D'Amour' and 'Gravity's
Angel'.
*WEA 9250771 (LP), Atlantic 9250772 (CD)*


*Phil Collins*
**No Jacket Required** (LP), released February 1985.
Backing vocals on 'Take Me Home', also released as 7″ and
12″.
*Virgin V2345 (LP), Virgin CDV2345 (CD)*


*The Call*
**Reconciled** (LP), released May 1986.
Backing vocals on 'Everywhere I Go', also released as a
remixed single.
*Elektra 960 440–1 LP*


*Nona Hendryx*
**Female Trouble** (LP), released June 1987.

Backing vocals and keyboards on 'Winds of Change (Mandela to Mandela)'.
*EMI America AML 3120*


*Robbie Robertson*
**Robbie Robertson** (CD), October 1987.
The former guitarist with The Band, co-produced by Daniel Lanois. Gabriel's backing vocals on 'Fallen Angel', also released as a single in November 1987. Song includes the line, 'Come down Gabriel, blow your horn.' Also vocals on 'Broken Arrow'.
*Geffen GEF24160 (LP), Geffen GFLD19294 (CD)*


*Joni Mitchell*
**Chalk Marks in a Rainstorm** (CD), released February 1988.
Vocals on 'My Secret Place', recorded at Ashcombe House, autumn 1986.
*Geffen GEF24172 (LP), GFLD 19199 (CD)*


*Sean Ono Lennon*
**Give Peace A Chance** (CD single), released 1991.
American promo CD single protesting at the Gulf War with Gabriel contributing brief vocals.
*Virgin PRCD PEACE*


*Manu Katche*
**It's About Time** (CD), released 1992.
Vocals on 'Warm Doorway' and 'Silence'.
*Sacre/BMG 262617*


*Geoffrey Oryema*
**Exile** (CD), released 1993.
Backing vocals on 'Land of Anaka'.
*RW14*

*Milton Nascimento*
**Angelus** (CD), released 1994.
Backing vocals on 'Qualquer coisa a haver come o Parariso'.
*WEA 9362454992*


*Manu Dibango*
**Wakafrika** (CD), released 1994.
Gabriel, Sinead O'Connor and Youssou N'Dour vocals on cover of 'Biko'.
*Blue Music BLM001CD/MC*


*Joy Askew*
**Tender City** (CD), released 1996.
Vocals on 'I'm Still Looking For a Home'.
*Private 01005821352*


*Paula Cole*
**This Fire** (CD), released 1996.
Vocals on 'Hush, Hush, Hush'.
*Imago Warner Bros 946424—2*


*Maryam Mursal*
**The Journey** (CD), released 1997.
Vocals on 'Kufilaw'.
*RW70*


*Hector Zazou*
**Lights in the Dark** (CD), released November 1997.
'Caoineadh Na Dtri Muire' [Keening of the Three Marys].
*Erato Disques France 3984—21662—9*


*Toni Childs*
**The Woman's Boat** (CD), released February 1998.

Backing vocals on 'I Met a Man'. Also contributions from David Rhodes, Nusrat Fateh Ali Khan and Robert Fripp.
*Geffen GED 24618*

*Sister Soleil*
**Soularium** (CD), released 1998.
Vocal improvisation on 'Blind'.
*Universal 53134*

**Brimstone**
Released 1998.
Forty seconds of music written by Gabriel as the opening theme for this American Fox TV series.

Peter Gabriel also wrote the music for 'Dans Le Creux De Ta Nuit' on the album *Soleil Dans L'Ombre* by Catherine Ribeiro.


SPOKEN WORD:

**Die Nixe – The Mermaid** (CD), released 1992.
The English version of this fairy tale is told by Gabriel and Annie Lennox. His vocals on 'Fisherman's Song'.
*EMI Germany 0777 781073 2 3*

**Snowflake** (2 CD), released 1993.
Readings of Paul Gallico's story. Words and music by Akira Inoue, David Rhodes and Sumiko Yagawa. Narration in English by Gabriel.
*JAP Toshiba-EMI TOCT–6917–8*

# VIDEOS

**CV** (1987)
'Big Time'; 'Don't Give Up 2'; 'Shock the Monkey'; 'Mercy Street'; 'Sledgehammer'; 'I Don't Remember'; 'Red Rain'; 'Don't Give Up 1'.
*Virgin VVD 241*

**P.O.V.** (1990)
'This Is The Picture'; 'San Jacinto'; 'Shock the Monkey'; 'Games Without Frontiers'; 'No Self Control'; 'Mercy Street'; 'Sledgehammer'; 'Solsbury Hill'; 'Lay Your Hands On Me'; 'Don't Give Up'; 'In Your Eyes'; 'Biko'.
Filmed live in Athens, Greece, 1987.
*Virgin VVD 626*

**All About US** (1993)
'Digging in the Dirt'; 'Steam'; 'Blood Of Eden'; 'Solsbury Hill'; 'Zaar'; 'Come Talk To Me'; 'Kiss That Frog'.
*RealWorld/PMI MVN 4912 813*

**Secret World Live** (September 1994)
'Come Talk To Me'; 'Steam'; 'Across the River'; 'Slow Marimbas'; 'Shaking the Tree'; 'Blood Of Eden'; 'San Jacinto'; 'Kiss That Frog'; 'Washing of the Water'; 'Solsbury Hill'; 'Digging in the Dirt'; 'Sledgehammer'; 'Secret World'; 'Don't Give Up'; 'In Your Eyes'.
Live video of Secret World tour filmed at Palasport, Modena, Italy, November 16 and 17, 1993.
*RealWorld/PMI MVN 4912 813*

VIDEO APPEARANCES:

**The Secret Policeman's Third Ball** (September 1987)
'Biko'
*Virgin VVD 802*

**Hurricane Irene Japan Aid Concert For Peace** (1988)
'Sledgehammer'; 'In Your Eyes'; 'No Self Control'; 'Biko' and
'Red Rain'.
*Virgin 3–50126*

**One World, One Voice** (1990)
Video of the various artists 'chain tape' project.
*BMG Video 74321–10054–3 BM510*

**Earthrise: The Rainforest Video** (1992)
'Don't Give Up'
A video to raise awareness of the disappearing rainforests.
*Weinerworld WRN 2027*

## CD-ROMS

**Xplora 1**, released December 1993.
Macintosh, Windows and Philips CDi versions.

**EVE**, released September 1996.
Macintosh and Windows versions.

**EVE**, Japanese Deluxe Edition, released August 1998.
Windows CD-ROM, illustrated book in Japanese, extra game
manual in Japanese.

# INDEX